Thomas Carlyle, Alexander Carlyle

Historical Sketches of Notable Persons and Events in the Reigns of

James I and Charles I

Third Edition

Thomas Carlyle, Alexander Carlyle

Historical Sketches of Notable Persons and Events in the Reigns of James I and Charles I
Third Edition

ISBN/EAN: 9783337094539

Printed in Europe, USA, Canada, Australia, Japan

Cover: Foto ©ninafisch / pixelio.de

More available books at **www.hansebooks.com**

HISTORICAL SKETCHES

OF NOTABLE PERSONS AND
EVENTS IN THE REIGNS OF

JAMES I. AND CHARLES I.

BY

THOMAS CARLYLE

EDITED BY
ALEXANDER CARLYLE
B.A.

THIRD EDITION

LONDON
CHAPMAN AND HALL
LIMITED
1899

[All rights reserved]

PREFACE

To write a Book on the Civil Wars and the Commonwealth of England, was one of Carlyle's earliest literary aspirations. His 'First Note-book,' beginning on the 22nd of March 1822, opens with comments and observations on Clarendon's *History of the Rebellion*, which he had then just begun to read. There follow many pages of criticisms on that Work and quotations from it, showing how deeply Carlyle was interested in the subject. Before a month had gone by he had read the most of Clarendon, the whole of Ludlow's *Memoirs*, a great part of Milton's Prose Writings, and other Works which throw light upon that period. Under date 15th April of the same year, there is this entry in the Note-book : 'Must *it*,' his contemplated Book, 'be sketches of 'English character generally, during the Commonwealth ; con-'taining portraits of Milton, Cromwell, Fox, Hyde, etc., in the 'manner of De Staël's *Allemagne*? The spirit is willing—but ah ! 'the flesh—!' In a few days more he had come nearer to a decision : 'Within the last month,' he writes on the 27th of April, to his brother Alexander, 'I have well-nigh fixed upon a 'topic. My purpose ... is to come out with a kind of Essay on 'the Civil Wars and the Commonwealth of England—not to write 'a History of them—but to exhibit, if I can, some features of 'the national character as it was then displayed, supporting my 'remarks by mental portraits drawn with my best ability, of 'Cromwell, Laud, George Fox, Milton, Hyde, etc., the most 'distinguished of the actors in that great scene.'

The scheme thus described had to be relinquished for a time; other engagements of a more promising or practical nature, intervened, which need not be recounted here. It is enough to say that it was not till about 1842 or '43, that he found himself free and in a position to attempt the realisation of his long-projected scheme. During these twenty years he had read extensively, as his Note-books show, on the subject of the Civil Wars and the Commonwealth; and one result of his studies was that he had been gradually led to form a very high opinion of the character of Oliver Cromwell, and to discern clearly that, whatever form his contemplated Book on the Civil Wars should take, Cromwell must be the hero of it.

In October 1843, after certain earlier attempts had proved abortive, a practical commencement was made. He chose the period of James I. as the starting-point, judging that the seeds of the Civil Wars were sown in this king's reign. He proceeded with the work for some months, evidently following the plan he had sketched in 1822. But as the writing went on, his esteem for Cromwell rose ever higher and higher, till by the time he had reached the Long Parliament, Oliver had become the one object of highest interest to him, the most noteworthy and noblest of all the actors in the great drama. Carlyle had, however, almost from the commencement of the writing, entertained doubts as to whether he had taken the best plan for representing Cromwell in his true character, or at least, for convincing the public that his high estimate of Cromwell was undoubtedly the correct one. He foresaw, for one thing, that his view of Oliver, so startlingly at variance with that hitherto almost universally entertained, would require, for its general acceptance, to be accompanied and supported by unquestionable evidence. The evidence wanted lay chiefly in Cromwell's own Letters and Speeches. Carlyle, therefore, changed his plan, early in 1844, laid aside what he had already written, and began to collect and edit with the necessary 'elucidations' these Letters and Speeches.

It is from the Manuscript, written and laid aside under the circumstances explained, that the materials have been selected for this little Book, which, for want of a better name, I have called *Historical Sketches*.

PREFACE

Carlyle in his Will (1873) refers to these Papers as 'a set of 'fragments about James I., which were loyally fished out for me 'from much other Cromwellian rubbish, and doubtless carefully 'copied more than twenty years ago, by the late John Chorley 'who was always so good to me.' Mr. Chorley, on returning the Manuscript and his transcript of a large part of it, wrote, March 1851: 'I believe that I have sifted out all that is sufficiently 'written-out to take its place at once in a series of chapters. . . . 'As it is, the collection is fit, I venture to say, with *very* little 'care from your hand (*viz.*, rounding off, introducing, and here 'and there crossing out what is given elsewhere) to make a most 'inviting little volume. . . . That you will not allow so much of 'what is good, the fruit of so much labour, to moulder in a box, 'I most earnestly beg. In copying my part, I have found only 'new reasons to desire this, for the profit of all who would fain 'come nearer to the *Life* of English History,—as well as for my 'own comfort and pleasure.'

Carlyle, however, never had the time or inclination to give the Work his finishing touches. Fourteen years after the copy had been made and the Papers returned to him, he wrapped the whole thing up into a packet and put it most carefully away, under the following docketing: 'About James I. and Charles I. 'The Chorley Transcript, with the *Original*, probably about 1849; '—have not looked at it since; nor will. T. C., 18 Feby. 1865.'

The original Manuscript is, for most part, a rough first-draft, without any division into chapters, or indication of the order in which the various matters were intended to appear when printed.

Mr. Chorley, in the part transcribed by him,—almost all of the section on James and different parts of that on Charles,—has given headings (many of which I have retained) to the various subjects; but he has not arranged the material into chapters, or in chronological or other order. He has occasionally given material for a footnote, or indicated the source from which one might be drawn.

I have taken the copy used by my printers direct from the Original wherever that was accessible, and have followed it as closely as possible under the circumstances. Blanks, left for dates and names forgotten at the moment of writing, have been filled up wherever I could do so with certainty; obvious slips of the pen, misdatings, and statements historically incorrect and marked doubtful by Carlyle himself, I have corrected by referring to acknowledged authorities, ancient and modern. In two or three instances, I have collected from different parts of the Manuscript all that was written on a particular subject, and placed it under one heading. This occasionally causes a little repetition or redundancy,—a fault which I could have avoided only by omitting matter of interest and importance.

Nearly the whole of the Manuscript which treats of James's Reign has been printed here; in the portion dealing with that of Charles, however, much has been omitted, especially matter referring specifically to Cromwell, and matter that has been superseded by fuller treatment in Carlyle's elucidations of the *Letters and Speeches*.

The chapters follow each other in chronological order as nearly as practicable. The references to authorities, Stow's *Chronicle*, Rushworth's *Historical Collections*, for example, are in the Manuscript often merely indicated in a general way by naming the Book or Author. These I have in every case verified, and where necessary, completed by giving volume and page; and in not a few instances I have added other references to well-known Historical Works, new and old. To the few footnotes by Carlyle, I have appended his initials. And for the convenience of readers who may not be familiar with the history of the Reigns of James and Charles, I have ventured to supply brief notes of my own, where explanation, corroboration or slight qualification of statements in the text seemed desirable.

A. CARLYLE.

26th October 1898.

CONTENTS

	PAGE
PREFACE	V
INTRODUCTORY—OF THE STUARTS GENERALLY . . .	1

PART I

IN THE REIGN OF JAMES I

CHAP.
I. JAMES AT HINCHINBROOK	9
II. ELIZABETH'S FUNERAL—SHAKSPEARE . . .	19
III. HAMPTON COURT CONFERENCE — PURITANISM AND ANTI-PURITANISM	23
IV. JAMES I.	43
V. BOG OF LINDSEY	58
VI. GUY FAUX AND THE GUNPOWDER PLOT . . .	66
VII. KNIGHTING OF PRINCE HENRY	72
VIII. MATERIAL PROGRESS IN ENGLAND — IN LONDON ESPECIALLY	78
IX. SPIRITUAL PROGRESS	85
X. PAUL'S AISLE: PAUL'S CROSS	92
XI. DEATH OF PRINCE HENRY: MARRIAGE OF PRINCESS ELIZABETH TO THE PALSGRAVE	94
XII. DUEL—SACKVILLE AND BRUCE	99

CHAP.		PAGE
XIII.	Shakspeare's Death—Cervantes—Kepler	103
XIV.	Effects of Court Doings on the Minds of Impartial Englishmen	108
XV.	The Overbury Murder	112
XVI.	King James's Discourse in the Star-Chamber	125
XVII.	Burning of the New Play-house in Drury Lane—A Puritan Riot	127
XVIII.	Bacon	130
XIX.	The King's Journey to Scotland	134
XX.	The Book of Sports	138
XXI.	Execution of Raleigh	140
XXII.	Court Precincts—Tournaments, etc.	141
XXIII.	John Gibb	145
XXIV.	The Spanish Match	147
XXV.	James's Parliaments	153
XXVI.	Glimpses of Notable Figures in James's Parliament of 1620-1—Acts of the same—Bacon—Monopolists	166

PART II

IN THE REIGN OF CHARLES I

I.	Charles and his Queen	181
II.	Charles and his Parliaments	185
III.	Church Provocations—Montague—Manwaring	191

CONTENTS

CHAP.		PAGE
IV.	Buckingham and the Isle of Rhé and other Discomfitures	195
V.	Charles's Third Parliament—First Session .	197
VI.	Popular Discontent on the Prorogation of Third Parliament — Buckingham — Felton — Rochelle, etc.	213
VII.	Charles's Third Parliament—Second Session .	221
VIII.	Religious Aristocracy in the Seventeenth Century	232
IX.	Nicholas Ferrar — The Nunnery of Little Gidding	234
X.	Dr. Leighton	242
XI.	Attorney General Noy	248
XII.	A Scotch Coronation	252
XIII.	English Men and Women in the Time of Puritanism	268
XIV.	Bastwick, Burton, and Prynne . . .	271
XV.	Laud's Life by Heylin	274
XVI.	Laud's Reformation	281
XVII.	The Colchester Prophets	288
XVIII.	Loom of Time	296
XIX.	Patience and Hope	298
XX.	'Jenny Geddes'	299
XXI.	Discovery of the Thurloe Papers—Tradition .	310
XXII.	Hampden and Laud—Realities and Phantasms .	317
XXIII.	Wentworth (Strafford)	321

CHAP.		PAGE
XXIV.	The Scots at Dunse Law—Pacification of Berwick, or the First 'Bishops' War' . . .	324
XXV.	Public Burning of the Scotch Declaration .	327
XXVI.	Meeting of Oliver St. John and Edward Hyde	329
XXVII.	A Scotch Army enters England—The Second 'Bishops' War'	334
XXVIII.	The Long Parliament	336

INTRODUCTORY

OF THE STUARTS GENERALLY

WHENCE came this Stuart, this unfortunate Dynasty of Stuarts; by what caprice of Destiny were they sent hither on an errand which they could not do; appointed to be Chief Heroes of England, and able only to be Chief Chimeras of England, and do solecisms? They came—it were long to tell where they came from! They came, like the rest of us, from the old Æons and Eternities; they were produced by the 'hereditary principle.' Time and chance, choice and necessity, foresight and blindness,—all the Past Ages, with their small radiances of earnest wisdom, struggling to illuminate their huge masses of indolent stupidity, had given to that present living Age James Stuart to be, under penalties, Chief Hero over it. This was what the Past Ages, hitherto, on that side of their affairs, had been able to do.

After all, there is something in the hereditary principle; in old times there used to be much in it, and in the newest times there will always be something. Of these very Stuarts it may be said generally, that they were a distinguished race; not common men. Indeed, all the old King genealogies, if we will look into them, had sprung from intrinsically superior or supreme persons, and were heroic more or less. The Nassaus of Orange, the Capets of France, the Hohenstauffens, Hohenzollerns, Vasas, Plantagenets,—people could not, in those old unfurnished times, clutch up the first comer, clap the King's cloak on him, and say: 'There!' By no manner of means. Nations needed to be governed; to have a Hero-captain go before them, and articulate for them what the dim purpose of their existence was. Their dim purpose,—very dim often, yet struggling always to become clearer, and utter itself in act and word,—was, and ever is, no other than this: To conform themselves to the Eternal Laws,—Laws of Necessity, revealed Laws of God, or whatever good or worse, or better or best name they give it: this ever is, and must be, the purpose of the sons of men. For which, very pressingly indeed, they do need a king to go before them; and must find one, if they have none!

I say, moreover, there is much in blood, in descent; and the hereditary principle is by no means nothing. Strong races will last you many centuries; will carry some lineaments of their Founder across the confusions of a long tract of Time. Do we not see, in these very days, a kind of Nassauism visible in this or the other Prince of Orange; a Bourbon physiognomy and eupeptic toughness of fibre in this or the other king of the French? Great King Races, before they die out, give many signs of greatness; and especially while they are dying out, give tragic signs. The last Vasa of Sweden,—it was melancholy to see how he had the long solemn visage of a Charles Twelfth, or of a Gustavus Adolphus, Lion of the North; something of the stateliness, the veracity, the lofty obstinacy, proud sense of honour, which had marked his hero-fathers: only the faculty, the insight and energy had been forgotten. Tragical enough. The outer physiognomy, the *case* of a true king and Vasa still there; but no king or Vasa within it:—wherefore the poor *case* had to be sent on its travels, as we know!

In Breadalbane Castle there is, or was, and in many Granger Print-books there still is, the Portraiture of a Stuart worth looking at. It is the Fourth James; he who rushed upon his death at Flodden. A brave enough, kingly face, beautiful and stern; his long black hair flowing down in rough floods; carelessly dashed on his head, the Highland cap with its feather: a really royal-looking man. You will note too, in his aspect, that singular dash of tragic, of Gypsy black, still visible in his distant Grandson, Charles Second, and lower. In the English Solomon,[1] in the Royal Martyr, in the Royal Pretender, you find the same bodeful and dark physiognomic element, now more, now less developed. They were all of one blood and bone; the same tragic element in their character and destiny, as well as in their faces. They descended all from Elizabeth Muir of Rowallan, and were a royal kind of men,—but, at their best, not royal enough.

The Poet King, the First of the Scotch Jameses; in him, still visibly to all of us, the world had assurance of a man. Of his melodious written Poems I say nothing; for a certain eternal rhythm and melody looked through the whole being of the man; struggling to unfold itself as an Acted Poem, much properer for a king. I find him a right brave man, the born enemy of all unveracities and dissonances; to whom oppressors, thieves, quacks, and every sort of scoundrels, were an abomination. He made enemies; infallibly enough, extensively enough. A hungry sanguinary pack of Earls, and such like, broke in upon him in Perth Monastery, and fiercely tore him down;[2]—as vicious dogs do, when their collars and leashes are not strong enough; when, alas, perhaps they have long been in the habit of '*eating* leather,' which, says the proverb, dogs should never be taught to 'eat.'

There is another James,[3] he that did *Christ's Kirk* and the *Gaberlunzie* Song, in whom, had he never done more, some pulse of a royal heart were traceable to me. This man too, had rhythmic virtue in him; an eye to see 'through the

---

[1] James I. of England and VI. of Scotland.

[2] The King was, perhaps too harshly, trying to curb the turbulent Nobles, when a conspiracy to murder him was formed by his kinsmen, the Earl of Athole, Sir Robert Stewart and Sir Robert Graham. On the 20th February 1437 the conspirators, led by Sir R. Graham, broke into the Dominican Monastery at Perth, where the Court was then residing, and after a desperate resistance the King was slain. The murderers were all taken and tortured to death. The authorship of the *Kingis Quair*, *Peblis to the Play*, and a *Ballad of Good Counsel* is generally ascribed to this James I.

[3] James V., the 'Commons' King.'

'clothes of things'; a genial heart, broad, manful, sympathetic; a laugh like an earthquake! And beautiful Mary,[1] surely she, too, was a high kind of woman; with haughty energies, most flashing, fitful discernments, generosities; too fitful all, though most gracefully elaborated : the born daughter of heroes,—but sore involved in Papistries, French coquetries, poor woman : and had the dash of Gypsy tragic in her, I doubt not; and was seductive enough to several, instead of being divinely beautiful to all. Considering her grand rude task in this world, and her beautiful, totally inadequate faculty for doing it, and stern destiny for not doing it,—even Dryasdust[2] has felt that there was seldom anything more tragical; and has expressed and still expresses the same in his peculiar way.

So many inadequate heroes; not heroic enough! It is no child's play, governing Nations. Nations are sometimes rather tragical to govern. When your Nation is at a new epoch of development, and struggling to unfold itself from Papistry to Protestantism, from Image-worship to God-worship, from torpid, slumberous Hearsay to wakeful terrorstruck and terrible Sincerity; and your Royal Race, perhaps, is on the downward hand, nearly bankrupt of heroism, verging towards extinction, and knows nothing of wakeful Nations and their meaning,—yes, then there will arise very tragic complexities; and Dryasdust will again have work cut out for him.

These poor Royal Stuarts who came of Elizabeth Muir, and, by the hereditary principle, without forethought of *theirs*, were sent to be Chief Governors here : may we not

---

[1] See also what Carlyle has said of Mary 'Queen of Scots,' in his 'Portraits of John Knox,' p. 144 (Peoples' Ed., 1875).

[2] An expressive compound word used to denote any dreary, longwinded writer who fills his pages with trifling details 'telling us nothing in many words.' It occurs in Sir W. Scott's Novels, and is not of Carlyle's coinage. It may be added that 'my erudite friend,' sometimes referred to in the following pages, is simply a variety of the genus Dryasdust, differing from the common type only in being more profoundly 'learned.'

call them 'fateful'? The Fates said to them: Be Kings, of talent, but not of talent enough. Kings of a deep, inarticulate People, in whose heart is kindled fire of Heaven, which shall be unintelligible and incredible to you. Take these heroic qualities, this dash of Gypsy black. Let there run in your quick blood a pruriency of appetite, a proud impatience,—alas, an unveracity, a heat and a darkness; and therewith try to govern England in the Age of Puritanism. That, we have computed, will be tragedy enough, for England and you.

PART I
IN THE REIGN OF JAMES I

CHAPTER I

JAMES AT HINCHINBROOK

[1603]

At Hinchinbrook Manor-house in Huntingdonshire, on the 27th and 28th of April 1603, as the eye through dim old Chronicles can still discern, there were really great doings; the ancient Borough of Huntingdon, ancient village of Godmanchester, and the whole Fen Country far and wide, all thrown into almost preternatural emotion. A new Scotch Majesty, James the Sixth as he was at Edinburgh, is progressing by slow stages towards London; to become James the First, and King of both countries;—Elizabeth the Queen being dead. He has got thus far on his journey: here, at Hinchinbrook, 'on the Wednesday afternoon,' he emerges from the northern twilight; he in person, with a mighty retinue, indistinctly glittering to us, in silk, silver and plumes; here a Knight, Sir Oliver Cromwell of Hinchinbrook, son of Sir Henry Cromwell, the 'Golden Knight,' is doing the impossible to entertain his Majesty. Here for unexpected reasons, History will glance fixedly on him for an instant or two.

His Majesty, we understand, has already been above three weeks on the road; ambling along in large cavalcade, at full leisure, in the bright Spring weather; a phenomenon notable to human nature;—chasing game, making Knights, eating dinners, chiefly hunting all the way; feasted everywhere, by sumptuous noblemen, by loyal civic corporations, regardless of expense; multitudes of human creatures crowding from all sides of the horizon to a sight of him: for it is not every day one sees a Majesty; and indeed, Kings, as the old Chronicle[1] says, are now grown doubly wonderful, so long have we, fifty years or more, been under Queens. Phenomenon once notable to human nature; now forgettable. Truly, of his Majesty's progress onward to Hinchinbrook, it is only Parish History and the Peerage Books that can say much at present. How he 'fired off a cannon on the walls 'of Berwick, showing skill in great artillery'; how he lodged 'at the Sign of the Bear and Sunne in Doncaster,' no noble mansion being near, and what the landlord's joy and terror were; how not far from Worksop Manor, His Majesty ate his luncheon on a green bank, pleasantly under the opening buds and birches, and anon in Worksop Park was accosted by kneeling huntsmen in Lincoln coats, who offered to show him some game thereabouts, a very welcome offer: all this, and more of the like, shall concern us extremely little. At York, and again afterwards, I read His Majesty's Proclamation, That such crowds shall not gather round our Royal Person: Heavens, we are but a man, though clothed and quilted in this extraordinary manner! At Newark, with still more interest, I witnessed the seizure of 'a cutpurse,' and instant warrant with Sign-manual to the Recorder of the town to have him hanged; which was straightway done, without judge or jury: a 'well-dressed cutpurse,' who had attended us with profit for a tract of days;[2]—probably a London artist; the oldest member of the swell mob taken notice of by History. He swings in Newark there, on the sudden, being seized *flagrante delicto*; a warning to men.

These things we note, though with little interest. His Majesty's progress, once glorious and divinely interesting as the very zodiac, has now ceased to interest any mortal; and claims principally to be, by all mortals who recognise the

---

[1] Stow's *Chronicle of England* (London, 1631); begun by Stow and continued by Howe.

[2] He confessed 'that hee hadde from Berwicke to that place played the cutpurse in the Courte.' Stow, p. 821.

phenomena of this world, forgotten,—left to Dryasdust and the Peerage Books.—But here, at Hinchinbrook, we say, human nature has still, for a reason little dreamt of by his Majesty, vocation to take notice of him. The reader shall know it by and by; his Majesty will never know it.[1] At Hinchinbrook and elsewhere there is always more going on than any of us dreams of. Among the huge flaring sun-flowers, illustrious hollyhocks, not to say grass rag-weeds, poisonous hemlocks, that cover the surface of feracious Time, who knows what everlasting Oak Tree may have germinated from its acorn, and be peering through the soil,—all irrecognisable among the hollyhock and hemlock crops!

But be that as it may, the fact, worthy of great notice or of little, is indisputable: Hinchinbrook, on Thursday the 28th of April 1603, *was* all in gala. Through the gulph of dead centuries we can still behold it, after a sort; look on it as with eyes. Hinchinbrook, while it was a Nunnery, never saw such doings. Hinchinbrook has been a Manor-house for half a century and more; it may become a Nunnery, an Iron-foundry, before it see the like again. The gates of Hinchinbrook are thrown open; the dignified courts of Hinchinbrook are filled with multitudes of nobility, gentry, respectable commonalty; and far and wide hovers and simmers, through Huntingdon streets and all heights and open spaces of ground, an extensive fluctuating crowd of human creatures, come from far and near to see this reed shaken by the wind. These are facts of the past tense: indubitable as the newest of the

---

[1] 'It is for the sake of little Oliver, roving about in the hand of his Nursemaid, unnoticed in these crowds; for his sake, and for his alone, that the human soul, may it please your Majesty, has come to pay its respects to your Majesty this day! No other errand had any soul; hardly Dryasdust, who has no soul. O Dryasdust, hadst thou noted down for me that little boy Oliver Cromwell, what *he* did, said, any foolishest word he uttered, what kind of look he had, cap or jacket he wore, how gladly had I given all the rest for that! The rest without that is dead as African guano, as the sweepings of Monmouth Street. Foolish Dryasdust, he has not so much as named this little Oliver; it is only by chronology and moral certainty that we see him there at all!'—T. C. (*In another unpublished paper of this series*).

present. Thitherward we also, for reasons of our own, will hasten to have a look.

Coming westward from the London side, if you pause on the heights of Godmanchester, where Drunken Barnabee's big Oak stood,[1] a pleasant prospect opens. Lazy, fat, or dropsical country, the very bogs of which looked green enough, has spread around you for many a mile; with fat, lazy-looking willow-trees, alder-trees; interspersed with church-belfries, with red brick dwellings of men. And now you are at the hill-top over Godmanchester, where Barnabee's big tree then was and now is not; and see the flat country broken thenceforth into undulations;—see the River Ouse, with large curvature, come sweeping by; on this side of it the low, long street of Godmanchester, an undistinguished stream or lake of simple houses with one high steeple; on the other side, leant up as in comfortable rest, the long Shire-town of Huntingdon, with Church-towers, spires, and the living smoke of hearths. 'The smoke-cloud sent up by 'busy housewives cooking their husbands' victuals,' as my German friend says:[2] it hangs there these many centuries under the serene of heaven. Mr. Robert Cromwell's chimneys from the west end of the place contribute their quota. David the Scotch King had a Castle here; but there rose quarrels respecting it, and Henry Plantagenet, Henry II., in his spleen, tore it down.[3] Portholme, a green meadow, spreads itself behind Godmanchester, on this side the River, pleasantly, for bleaching of webs, for running of horse-races, for cheerful promenading of men and women. An ancient Bridge, we can observe, connects the village and the town;—the Ouse takes such a sweep as indicates that he is in no haste about his journey: in fact this poor River has a sad fate to look for; fifty miles of Fen between him and the German

---

[1] See *Oliver Cromwell's Letters and Speeches*, i. 25 (Liby. Edition).
[2] Teufelsdröckh, in *Sartor Resartus*, book II. cap. ix.
[3] Camden's *Britannia*, i. 502.

Ocean, and such a bewildered race to run as few rivers have. Now branched into various arms; now stagnating in marshes, meres, black reedy plashes; now high in air, held up by main force in Bedford Levels and embankments; if you left him alone, he would drown whole districts, and leave nothing but the 'isles,' Isle of Ely and others: this is the fate of the river. Ouse; which here flows by unconscious, and of a common drab colour.

Huntingdon itself, we see, leans up against the edge of the Hill, secure from swamp and mud; and other knolls and faint ridges, ever bluer, ever dimmer, die away towards Kimbolton, St. Neot's and the Infinitude, in a pleasant manner. Kimbolton old Town and Castle, where the sad Queen Catherine, now divorced by questionable sentence, sat down to die; St. Neot's old Town and Church, where worthy Neot, the brother of our great Alfred, mingled with his mother Earth, and with the devout memories of men: these lie in the blue-grey haze of the horizon: in the horizon and beyond it lie so many things.

But leftwards to the south of Huntingdon, not half a mile of distance, where the green heights spread gently along shaded with sprinklings of wood,—thither, it is, to Hinchinbrook, O reader, that thou and I are bound on this occasion: let us quit the Oak of Barnabee, and hasten down. Hinchinbrook is not now a Nunnery; no, it only was one. Not a nun there these fifty years and odd. Henry the Eighth, big burly man, having divorced Catherine, dissolved all Nunneries; made this a Manor, gave it to Richard Cromwell, a man useful in these operations; 'affectionate nephew,' as he writes himself, of the famed Thomas Cromwell, Earl of Essex, who destroyed all Monasteries, and lost his own head in the business. But Richard did not lose his head; Richard became opulent, and the big King said to him, 'Thou shalt 'not be my Dick, thou shalt be my Darling.' Hereby is Richard's grandson now a man of opulence; son of a Golden Knight, and himself deserving to be called Golden. And here at Hinchinbrook, there is not worship of Saint Neot or of any Saint or Hero going on; but worship of a far different sort,—which, in Heaven's name, let us hasten down to look at for one moment if no more.

These thousands of abolished mortals, bone of our bone, flesh of our flesh, who do indubitably circulate here, with eager-gazing eyes, with multitudinous hum of English speech; so palpable that day, so vanished this; are they without interest to thee? To me they are as good as preternatural: there *were* they; where *are* they?—But who shall describe the inner solemnities; the gifts of jewelled goblets, the stately passages and ceremonials; the ambrosial sumptuosities of feasts,—seneschals and sewers with their white wands, and dishes of silver and gold, great they as generals on the day of battle; and far down in the interior, fat cooks puffing and perspiring, greasy scullions, sooty turnspits all in a broil; death-doing energy on every brow, the feeling that now they must cook or die! None can describe such things; nor need. The outer fountains of Hinchinbrook run mere wine; from the outer courts of Hinchinbrook no meanest rascal shall, this day, go away unfed. What your soul longs for, of victual or of liquor, is here to be had freely. One of the heavenly bodies is passing here: Hinchinbrook has become one of the houses of the Zodiac.

The Mayor of Huntingdon presented, as was proper, the keys and sword to his Majesty: the Mayor and Commoncouncil men have done and are doing, this day, their duty. And the Cambridge Heads of Houses have come along, with high-flown Latin compliment, in scarlet or other cloaks; and got such audience, such comfits and temporal and spiritual entertainments as were needful; and gone their ways again. These come and go: our Progress is like that of the Moon, escorted everywhere by the ocean-tides and land-clouds, full sea where our presence is. It was but the other day there came the 'Millenary Petition'—Petition purporting to be signed by a thousand, or near a thousand, clergymen of

Parishes, faintly, most humbly intimating that a point or two in our glorious Reformed Church was, or might by the human mind be conceived to be, short of perfection.[1] Which audacious though faint intimation Oxford University, all in cloaks of some sort, shortly after did earnestly denounce; apprising his Majesty that they had a right to do it, being such a body of men for Learning and real acumen of insight as his Majesty might vainly seek the like of in this world. Whereat old Archbishop Whitgift felt some comfort; having shuddered at such an audacious Millenary Petition; having lived this long while, as he said, 'in terror of a 'Scotch mist' coming down on him with this new Majesty from the land of Knox, or Nox, Chaos and Company.

All these things concern us little. Of the Cambridge Heads of Houses, of the Oxford Doctors unparalleled for real acumen of insight; of ancient Whitgift trembling for his Scotch mist; who, of gods or men, does take account of it at this hour? Even the 'Earl of Southampton, bearing 'the Sword of State before his Majesty,' has become almost indifferent to us. Of these thirty thousand or so, all bustling, jostling here, with eager eyes, in and about the Manor House of Hinchinbrook and Borough of Huntingdon, there are not ten persons known to me by face; not three whom I could wish any of my friends to know. Each of them truly *has* a face; face, for that matter, traced with cares, hopes, character, complete series of life-adventures: but they are strangers to me and History; they belong to brown Oblivion and others than me! Solely, or almost solely, among that fluctuating multitude which floods all Hinchinbrook in such deray and gala, we will note one little Boy of four years old gone Tuesday last;[2] led by his Nursemaid, as is like; and bustling to and fro, with due convenience, to all suitablest points of view, for seeing this solemnity: it is a Nephew of Sir Oliver the Landlord; his

---

[1] Neal's *History of the Puritans*, ii. 5 (edition of 1794).
[2] Oliver Cromwell was born on 25th April, 1599.

own name is little Oliver, or Noll,—poor little fellow! Mr. Robert Cromwell from his mansion in the west end of Huntingdon; Mr. Robert Cromwell, next Brother to the Knight of Hinchinbrook, and Father to this Boy; he and Dame Cromwell, who is a Steward from the Stuntney Stewards, and so of kin to this Scotch Majesty, are in the feast itself, I fancy; and Sir Thomas Steward the Knight of Stuntney, and much other kindred, though unseen to me, are there: but this our little Oliver strolls about, I think, in a state of glad excitation, in the hand of his Nurse-maid the while. Look at him, reader; him thou shalt look at. A broad-headed, bony-faced little fellow, with clear grey eyes; stout-made for his years; extremely full of wonder at present; —in what headdress of leather or cloth cap, in what body-dress and breeches, doubtless his best cap and breeches, is entirely unknown to this Editor. O Nollykin, my little man, how this unexpected sunburst of the new Scotch Majesty has transported thy poor little incipient spiritual faculty, and thou art all one wide-eyed wonderment: was the like ever seen or dreamt of? Huntingdon Fair, with its bellowing cattle, with its mystic showbooths, luxurious gingerbread bazaars, leathercoated drovers and bedizened men and women, was but a type of it. On the *tabula rasa* of thy poor young brain, the Destinies are pleased to write with such pigments. Destiny paints and writes daily, for every one of us, such 'Dissolving Views,' electric, miraculous enough; miracle after miracle; and the poor tablet retains what it may of them, and comes out a very miraculous tablet!—

Doubtless this 'Dissolving View' speedily enough dissolved out of the head of Nollykin, or retreated into the obscure depths of him, as all such do, one swiftly extruded by the other. Who can calculate what influences are thrown incessantly into the young soul of a broad-headed, grey-eyed, intelligent boy in this world? Of such electric pictures and dissolving views as we see here, there is great quantity day after day; and then—but there is no end of it; Heavens, only think what this means: They are teaching him the English Language! The English—not the French, German, or Mandingo; this they are daily speaking to the Boy Oliver; speaking, nay singing it with the Huntingdon tune or accent, as they term it: let a reader try to compute the probable effect of this alone. And then Pope Gregory, St. Austin, John Calvin, Martin Luther; onwards to Moses the Midianitish shepherd, and earlier! Shadows from all lands and ages; Shadows and lightgleams from the remotest continents of Space, from the uttermost shores of Time, fall and flicker confusedly over this young mind in the Town of Huntingdon here; are making his mind's tablet mysterious enough. For instance, these young eyes did not see the Gilt Temple at Upsala, with gold festoon-chains and seventy horses' heads in a state of forwardness; no, they saw Ely Cathedral dominating the Fen Country, with surplices, rubrics, and the long line of Archbishops not yet grown ghastly. A man is citizen of his age; yes—and a strange age he will always find it, if he look.

And so, at all events, whenever henceforth the Boy Oliver Cromwell hears mention of a king, *this* shambling, thick-speaking, big-headed, goggle-eyed, extraordinary Scottish individual in gilt velvet with fringing, will be the thing meant for him. Progressing in a very chaos of pomp, gilding and splendour; not unlike the heavenly Moon on her zodiac; drawing up mankind round him, and their choicest liquors, gold goblets, Barbary horses, and household effects and heartworship; a most gorgeous individual. 'O nursemaid mine, I think his 'Majesty's tongue is a thought too big for him? See how 'he drinks, eating his liquor from the cup, and at the corners 'of his mouth leaks somewhat!'[1]—'Hush, thou naughty 'Nollykin; hush!'

Now, however, on Friday morning, breakfast being fairly over, it is time his Majesty were under way. Sir Oliver, now

[1] Weldon, in *Secret History of the Court of James I.*, Edinburgh, 1811, ii. 2.

Sir and a knight, must escort his Majesty to the gate: and the little Oliver, from some street window or other place of vantage, may look his last at this Pageant. The new Majesty is gone,—may a blessing go with him!

In Godmanchester the people stood all drawn out in holiday clothes, with their yoked ploughs on the street; 'seventy fair new ploughs' with their sleek teams, all fluttering in ribbons and bedizenment,[1]—their style of ploughing, crop rotation, and general mode of Fen-agriculture, remaining somewhat obscure to us! His Majesty inquires, Why they have all these ploughs drawn out? The Bailiff, or other public spokesman, makes answer: May it please your Majesty, the ploughs are yours. We are your Majesty's poor socmen, and hold our land by that tenure, of offering you our ploughs and work-gear, every time you pass this way. —Say you so? Well, I am glad to find I have so many good husbandmen in one town. Keep your ploughs, my men; and rend the tough glebe to good purpose with them.— God save your Majesty! Universal shouts attend the king; and now, under Barnabee's Oak-tree, we will leave him on his way to Royston.

To Royston, to Brockesbourne or elsewhither, and gradually to Theobald's and to London;—which latter enormous city, half a million in population, and equal to Tyre or Sidon in trade, he enters on the 7th of May; 'riding thro' the 'meadows,' says old Stow,[2] 'to avoid the extremity of dust'; so many myriads of human creatures, mounted or on foot, thicker now than ever, thronging out to see him; the Peerages and Baronages, the officialities, mayoralties, the very Inns of Court, all waiting, 'ranked on Stamford Hill' or elsewhere. Thus has his Majesty traversed the length of England; mankind, with their choicest household effects and hearts'-reverences, escorting him, in a magnificent manner; as the Ocean-tides and land-clouds escort their celestial Moon. Here, at the top of the highest Spring-tide, let the

[1] Stow, 822.   [2] *Chronicle*, 823.

last glimmer of the Hinchinbrook solemnity die out; girdled by oblivion or imagination, by twilight sufficiently luminous.

We add only, that Sir Oliver who was not himself called the Golden Knight (so says Dryasdust), but was the *Son* of the Golden Knight,—of Sir Henry, namely, who built the new Hinchinbrook, and otherwise unfolded himself in a golden way,—did full certainly by this business become what we may call a Silver Knight; dwindling to a Silver-gilt, and at last almost to a copper one! In plain words, his light wasting itself ever more burnt dimmer and dimmer from this day; in some twenty-three years more, he had to retire to Ramsey Mere, deeper into the Fens; and sell Hinchinbrook to the Montagues, in whose hands it still remains.[1]

CHAPTER II

ELIZABETH'S FUNERAL—SHAKSPEARE

[1603]

In these same hours, so festive at Hinchinbrook, the Funeral of Queen Elizabeth is going on at London, as Stow's Chronicle apprises me; and this too is worth a glance from all of us. She died at Richmond, near five weeks ago, our noble Queen; but her body was privately carried to Whitehall; and this day, Thursday, the 28th of April, her Obsequies shall be. 'The city of Westminster is surcharged 'this day,' says Stow,[2] 'with multitudes of all sorts of people 'on the streets, in their houses, on the leads, and gutters, 'who have come to see the obsequy,'—no wonder. And now, in a chariot or hearse, drawn by eight black horses, and 'trapped' sufficiently in black velvet and the like, with Peers, State-officers, Dignitaries, 'to the number of 1500 persons 'that bore mourning,' she is borne to her long home. See,

---

[1] The date of the Deed of Sale of Hinchinbrook to the Montagues is 20th June 1627.   [2] *Chronicle,* 815.

slowly emerging from Whitehall Gate, and slowly wending by King Street and Old Palace Yard, to the Abbey Church of Westminster, the sable hearse with its eight black horses, and stream of 1500 mourners comes to view: on the coffin-lid lies her effigies 'counterfeited to the life,' gold crown on its head, in its hand the sceptre and ball; and quire-men of her chapel, in clear mournful tenor, are 'singing,' as they go, sad requiem into all hearts. It is the last we shall see, on this Earth, of our brave Queen Bess. On the coffin-lid lies her effigies counterfeited to the life; and *in* the coffin —! And now the quire, in clear mournful tenor, sing requiem as they go.

At sight and sound whereof, the 'universal multitude,' this is the thing my readers are surprised at, 'burst forth 'into sheer wail and weeping'; lifted up their universal voice and wept. Yes, there is her effigy painted to the life, the ball and sceptre in its waxen hand: her effigy; but her brave self, where is that? Gone, and never through the circling ages returns to us more. *Finis*; it is the end. She had 'gained the people's love,' says Stow, 'and continued growing 'in it to the last.' And now this day 'there is such a weep-'ing as the like hath not been seen or known in the memory 'of man; neither doth any history mention any people made 'such lamentation for the death of their sovereign';—her requiem singing itself, in most authentic mournful melody, through all hearts. So fares the noble Queen Elizabeth to her still home, in these hours; bemoaned with true tears. She was the last sovereign, if we will think of it, whom English hearts did truly love: the unfortunate English hearts ever since have been reduced, in great part and even in whole, to love the sovereign's effigy counterfeited to the life, no sovereign's self being properly there;—and to manage that sorrowful problem in such sort as they could!

'She was tall of stature; strong in every limb and joint; 'her fingers small and long; her voice loud and shrill: she 'was of an admirable ready wit and memory; very skilful in 'all kinds of needlework,' says poor old Stow ;—in fact, exceedingly skilful every way. She had a brave heart, a veracious clear intelligence; on the whole, a great and genuinely royal soul. She cast herself upon her people's affection,—not like a truckler either, but like a ruler, severe and stern withal. With a noble divination, beautiful in a woman, but in a brave and great-souled woman very natural, she apprehended what the heart of her English People meant; and she bent herself to lead in the doing of that,—to *be* their king, to go before them veritably as a heaven-sent Captain and guiding Pillar of Fire. It is the task of a king. If he can do it, joy to him and to us. Right loyally, devoutly will the People recognise him as the Sent of Heaven, their miraculous Pillar-of-Fire; at sight of whom all hearts burn, and Spanish Armadas, and Nightmare Chimeras in Rome or elsewhere, are swept swiftly to the Father of them : the king wills it,—the king of England, seconded by the King of the Universe. If your hapless king cannot do this task, if in his own heart there is not nobleness to divine it, to attempt it, and know it as the one thing needful,—alas, what *can* he do ? Retire from the trade, I should say ; that would be better for him ! Here where he is he can do nothing but fatuities and incoherences ; which sooner or later are very certain to *be* rejected, and not accepted ; inexorably and even indignantly rejected of Earth and of Heaven. I have known men lose their heads in such a business !—

William Shakspeare, the beautifullest soul in all England, that day, when the Cambridge Dignitaries came to his Majesty and Hinchinbrook, and the innumerable Fen populations were gathered, and the plumed silk-and-silver retinue were fugling and gesticulating, and the conduits running wine, and the little Boy Oliver looking at it without notice : William Shakspeare, I rejoice also to see, by chronology and moral certainty, was breathing in this world ;—a hale man of nine-

and-thirty; thinking of many things. Busy in Southwark, in the interior of the Globe Theatre on the Bankside, in a private way? Or gone out, he also with his human sympathies, with heart capable of real reverence, to take his last look at Elizabeth, borne in dirge-music to her long home, the last of our English kings? Thou beautiful Shakspeare, thou wert alive that day; and makest the dark Past and the ignorant Present and the uncertain Future brighter for us. At thy writing-desk in Southwark; thrifty among the stage-properties of the Globe Theatre, or out seeing Queen Elizabeth buried, thou shalt be very beautiful to us. How many sublime Majesties, sublime Pontiffs, Arch-overseers so-called, have faded away into the ghastly state, and claim from us passionately one thing, Christian burial and oblivion; and in thy bright eyes we still lovingly shadow ourselves, thou right royal, archiepiscopal one! Shakspeare, beyond the smallest doubt, was alive that day; a hale man of nine-and-thirty, with genius and Heaven's own light looking through the eyes of him: it is a fact forever notable.[1] And again, this Earl of Southampton who bears the sword before his Majesty: he has been in the Tower for Essex's sake; but has now got

[1] Elsewhere in this MS. Carlyle writes: 'In Dryasdust's huge stacks of print and manuscript, the lumber-room of Nature, you cannot get one leaf with intelligible jotting about William Shakspeare on it. A quarter of a leaf, half-intelligible, will hold it all. William Shakspeare, the beautifullest English soul this England confesses to have ever made, the pink and flower of remembered Englishmen; the greatest thing, it appears, that we have yet done, and managed to produce in this world: of him English History says—nothing! What *is* English History? The record of things memorable? I have known better recording by mere old ballads, by stone heaps and Peruvian quipo-thrums! But the average of human History is only a shade better than English. "I am always thankful," says Smelfungus, "that they did not forget to jot down the Four Gospels themselves, and dismiss the whole business as an insignificant case of Police!" . . . Yes, it is all ordered by the Heavens: Dryasdust, like Sin, if not caused, is permitted; and we must have patience.'—Steevens, one of the most acute of Shakspearian commentators, wrote: 'All that is known with any degree of certainty concerning Shakspeare, is—that he was born at Stratford-on-Avon;—married and had children there; went to London, where he commenced actor, and wrote poems and plays; returned to Stratford, made his will, died and was buried.'

out, under the new Majesty, and bears sword of state and such like; a most far-shining, noticeable man and Earl: does no reader know him? We all know him for the kindness he did to an astonishing Play-actor of genius,—the above-said Play-actor of the Globe Theatre, then alive in this world beside him! This world is all a Theatre; and so many poor Players act their parts; some in bright dresses, some in dim; some to great purpose, some to almost none. All a theatre; —but a very emblematic one: the coulisses of *it*, on this hand and on that, being Eternities; the purport and upshot of it being, as is rightly said, Life everlasting, Death everlasting!—

CHAPTER III

HAMPTON COURT CONFERENCE—PURITANISM AND ANTI-PURITANISM

[1603-4]

The Age of King James, after infinite reading, remains, as it were, inane to us; little better than no Age at all. Dim, dreary, without form or meaning; a sea of leaden-coloured vapour, with certain unmelodious ghosts confusedly shrieking and swimming in it! No soul of genius has yet resuscitated King James's Age for us,—or is in the least likely to do so. The Heavens have not created, nor I think intend to create, any soul that *loves* it: how can any soul teach us to love it, to body it forth again, and look on it? Fatal Dryasdust, who is still publishing new volumes on the matter, does not love it; he only loves his own dreary jottings and lucubrations on it;—and so it grows ever drearier, ever emptier: a sea of leaden vapour; sinking towards Chaos and the Bog of Lindsey,[1] I imagine!

One of the few things we could wish to save from such vapour-sea, and look fixedly upon, were that Conference at

[1] See *post*, p. 58.

Hampton Court in the middle of January 1604.[1] It is the first authentic appearance of Puritanism on the stage of official life. Puritanism, as Martin Marprelate in surreptitious Pamphlets, and otherwise, has long had a gaseous kind of existence; painful[2] ministers, suffering under surplices and scruples, have had High-Commission Courts, Oaths Ex-Officio contrived for them, and been ejected and imprisoned and sharply dealt with, in great detail: but here Puritanism comes forward as a unity, solidified, tangible. Millenary Petition, and various petitions and discussions which arose out of that, having somewhat unsettled the Public mind, his Majesty by Proclamation declares that he will settle it again;—summons four leading Puritans to meet his Bishops and him, and try whether they cannot settle it. Who but would wish, at this distance of time, to glance into such a meeting, if he could be spiritually present there?

Alas, it is not possible; we cannot spiritually *see* this thing by looking on it; this thing too is grown very spectral. Reynolds, Sparks, Chadderton and Knewstubs; Whitgift and Bancroft, Bilson and Rudd:[3] who can know them? They speak in the English language; but the meaning of them is all foreign to us; glances off from us with an irritating futility, oft repeated, with a kind of unearthly pricking of the skin. What *is* it that they want? They did want much; they do want, as it were, nothing. Defunct! The ghosts of the defunct are pale, dim; the living soul refuses to admit them; mind and memory contemplate them with a

---

[1] '1603, by the style then in use there; the English year beginning on the 25th of March; the Scotch and all other years beginning, as ours now do, with the 1st of January. Innumerable mistakes in modern Books have sprung from this circumstance.' T. C.'s Note.—The 25th of March continued to be called New-Year's Day, in official documents, until 1752.

[2] Painstaking.

[3] John Reynolds, Thomas Sparks, from Oxford; John Knewstubs, Lawrence Chadderton, from Cambridge, world-famous Doctors, were the spokesmen on the Puritan side. John Whitgift, Archbishop of Canterbury; Richard Bancroft, Bishop of London; Thomas Bilson, Bishop of Winchester; Anthony Rudd, Bishop of St. David's, were the chosen champions of Conformity in the Church.

natural shudder, and are in haste to be gone. Our sketches of Puritanism, still more of Anti-Puritanism, ought to be above all things brief!—

'Every revolution,' says Smelfungus, 'has its articulate
'respectable "Moderate Party," and then also its inarticulate
'or less articulate "Extreme Party," each with a several sort
'of merit. Nay, some without almost any merit. Your
'noblest Luther is soon followed by his ignoblest frightful
'Knipperdolling and John of Leyden![1] Such Parties of
'Moderate and Extreme, of Girondin and Mountain, as the
'French named them, could nowise fail in that grandest Re-
'volution the modern world had seen; properly the parent of
'all the Revolutions it has since seen and is yet to see: the
'Protestant Reformation. Not in the modern ages had such a
'Protest, or one at all like such, taken place before. The
'drugged, stupefied, prostrated Human Soul, starting up at
'length awake; swearing solemnly, in the name of the Highest,
'that it would not believe an incredibility any more. The
'beginning, you would say, of all benefit whatsoever to the
'poor Human Soul. Believing incredibilities; clinging spas-
'modically to falsities half-known to be false; saying to yourself,
'"Cling there, thou poor soul, thou wilt be drowned and
'swallowed of the devils otherwise!"—can there be conceived
'a more desperate condition? The human soul becomes a
'Quack soul, or Ape soul, in these desperate predicaments;
'gradually dies into extinction as a soul proper,—and instead
'of Men, you have Apes by the Dead Sea![2]

'But not to insist on that, consider how inevitable it was
'that after the Dissolution of Monasteries by Henry the
'Eighth and the Publication of Canons and Prayerbooks by
'Edward the Sixth, the great Protestant Reformation should
'not stop but proceed. The question always obtruded itself,
'When will you stop? For by this lightning bolt of Luther's,
'the divine-element vouchsafed us once more out of Heaven,

---

[1] John Beuckelszoon, head of the Anabaptists at Münster.
[2] See Sale's *Koran* (Introduction); or Carlyle's *Past and Present*, p. 190.

'there had been conflagrations kindled ;—nay, we may figura-
' tively say, subterranean coalfields kindled; deep answering to
' deep, and old dead things catching fiery life again from the
' re-awakened Heaven-element, as their way is in such cases!
' And formidable explosions had taken place; to be followed
' by far more formidable, up to the very formidablest, to
' Jacobinism itself ;—and in brief, there had, above ground and
' below, a series of electric and ignitory operations commenced,
' which could not by human or superhuman industry be made
' to terminate, till we had reached the eternal foundations
' again. A work for centuries; and one of the terriblest,
' though of all it is the indispensablest. O Prelate, Marprelate,
' you little know what you are tugging at !—

'Vesuvius in the sixteenth century, as I read, the old com-
' motions having sunk to rest for a thousand years or more,
' had grown green a-top. By the benign skyey influences
' continued for centuries, you saw a solid circular valley,
' verdant, umbrageous, a savoury pasture for flocks: but it
' had grown rough also with brambles, idle tangled thickets;
' populous now, for most part, with serpents, foxes, wolves.
' Such was the Roman Church; such in several respects, if you
' consider it. Firmamented into fair green compactness, on
' the bosom of Old-Judean and Old-European abysses, and
' explosions, once volcanic enough; till it had become green
' nutritive grass-sward, shelter for sheep and oxen ;—till it had
' become rough with briars and jungle, populous with wolves
' and foxes. The seasons and the ages circled on. The old
' subterranean coal-strata and electric reservoirs of the great
' Deep, had they renounced connexion with the Heavenly
' electricities, then; or only, to our poor eyes, suspended it?
' The fulness of time came; the day of "renewed activity"
' came: and where now is your circular grass valley on
' Vesuvius top? The lightning fell from Heaven, the electric
' fire-reservoirs of the great Deep, with smoke, with fire and
' thunder, loud, ever louder, awoke: sward and soil and jungle;
' oxen, wolves and serpents, and the rough valley altogether,

CHAP. III.] HAMPTON COURT CONFERENCE 27

'are blasted aloft into the immeasurable realms of air;—
'and in their stead, observe what kind of pumice-crater
'we have!'

Surely, my dark friend, this similitude does not go on all-fours, but halts dreadfully in one of its legs? He persists thus: 'It is the law of such explosions, when the lightning 'falls from Heaven across long sleepy centuries, and awakens 'the subterrene fire-elements; blasting your circular valley 'itself into air. The Soul of Mankind,—which has deep 'enough "strata," accumulated now for hundreds of thousands 'of years since we arrived on this Planet,—is it not essentially 'of that volcanic nature?' Similitudes that have to flounder along on three legs, flourishing the fourth by way of accompaniment, these also are not a pleasant spectacle! But to return to Hampton Court.

Certain select Prelates and other high personages, four select Puritans of chief quality, have met, convened by royal proclamation, to consider what they can do for perfecting the Divine Symbol or Church, here in England at present,—if it is not already perfect, concerning which point discrepancies exist. Does Symbol correspond with thing signified, as the visible face of man does to the invisible soul within him? Or are these pasteboard adhesions false noses which one would wish to pluck off? It is a question worth considering. Majesty himself will preside over these debates: for he is of lively accomplished understanding; and piques himself on his knowledge of Theology; which certainly, as the vital secret of this Universe, God the Maker's method of making and ruling this Universe, must be the thing of all others worth knowing by an accomplished man. Majesty, if it please Heaven, will regulate this high matter.

The Conference is in 'the drawing-room of the Privy 'Apartments' at Hampton Court: the room, or space, still there; but the actors and their actings,—ask not of them! They and the things they strove for, and the things they strove against, are alike unrememberable, though never so often repeated; of almost no interest to the living sons of men. Ancient choleric Whitgifts, younger choleric Bancrofts, grey spectral Bishops in considerable number, with their deans and satellites likewise spectral; spectral Puritans to the number only of four: it is all grown very spectral to us,—though we have still a kind of business there.

Whitgift, the venerable hoary Primate, still somewhat in dread of his 'Scotch mist,' may remain dimly visible to us; dimly the choleric Bancroft; Dean Overal, one day to be Bishop Overal, 'that prodigious learned man,' may likewise continue dim. Of Reynolds the chief Puritan, I have heard that he refused a bishoprick, preferring to be Head of Christ-Church College in Oxford, and apply himself to quiet piety and meditation. Another thing is perhaps still notabler: he was born, and grew up, a Papist; he had a brother who went into Protestantism: the two undertook to reason together, and did it with such effect that they converted each the other: logic, like ambition, vaulting too high, overleapt itself, or overleapt its *selle*, to this extent! John Reynolds is now not a Protestant only but a Puritan; considered to be one of the most learned men ever seen in this world; 'the very treasury 'of erudition,' 'his memory and reading near to a miracle.'[1] But indeed the 'learning' of these reverend persons generally is what we call prodigious: most praiseworthy; if not insight, then at least the sight of what others thought they saw into; which is an honest attempt towards insight! Man can do no more on that side than these good men, Puritan and Anti-Puritan, had generally done. Their learning is prodigious; the deep gravity of their existence is inconceivable to mankind in these shallow sneering days. Of Sparks, Knewstubs and the rest, so spectral is it, we shall say no word. 'There are three days of Conference, the 14th, 16th, '18th of January 1603-4,' so urges my erudite friend: the first a consulting day of Bishops and King only, with Puritans

---

[1] Wood, *Athenæ*, ii. 12.

CHAP. III.] HAMPTON COURT CONFERENCE   29

waiting in the anteroom; the other a pair of battle-days,
with Puritans summoned in to speak and fence for themselves;
but in our dim indolent imaginations it may be all massed
into one,—a spiritual passage at arms, worth noticing in ✕
English History.

And so the King sits jewelled and dizened, with diamond
hatband, in his chair of State; rich, we can suppose, as
Ormuz or Ind: on this hand, all in rochet, tippet, and
episcopalibus, Nine right reverend individuals, our Whitgifts,
Bancrofts, with seven bottleholders of the dean species; victory
threatening from their eyes: on that hand, in simple 'furred
' gowns like Turkey merchants or foreign Professors,' our poor
Four Puritans, Reynolds and Sparks, chief divines from
Oxford, Knewstubs and Chadderton, of the like quality from
Cambridge, not to speak of Scotch 'Mr. Galloway the
' Minister of Perth,' of whom not much is to be expected on
this occasion. Majesty is radiant, with diamond-buckled
hat, with wide-open glittering eyes and intellect: scattered
at due distances, in orderly groups, is a cloud of Peers, Privy-
councillors, and Official Persons, totally indeterminate to the
human mind,—among whom the ancient shadow of Chancellor Egerton, venerable man, with his shaving-dish hat and
white beard, and even with touches of ready wit still audible,
is faintly to be discriminated. It is a fact this Conference,
though now grown so chimerical; it lasted three days under
the sun: three days it occupied the drawing-room at
Hampton Court in the winter weather of 1603-4, while
England and the Earth were busy round it, and the Sun in
his old steady way was travelling through Capricorn above it;
—and it all looked solid enough at that time! The reader
can read about it in Dean or Bishop Barlow's coloured
Narrative, or in Scotch Mr. Galloway's anti-coloured one,
nay, in his Majesty's own 'Letter to Mr. Blacke'; and it will
remain in the highest degree spectral to him after all. The
generations and their arguments and battlements—O Heaven,

if the Bog of Lindsey did not receive them, condense them into something, where were we!

It must be owned, the claims of painful Dr. Reynolds and his Puritans are modest in the extreme. To be delivered from 'baptism by midwives,'—the very Bishops have conceded that; to be partially delivered from 'lay impropriation,' if it would please impropriation to render back 'the seventh part' of its church property for spiritual food to souls perishing; and then to be delivered from the pressure of the 'surplice' where it ties up frail human consciences useful otherwise; and to have a correct Translation of the Bible: the modesty of Marprelate, tending in any way towards the Eternal and the Veritable, through this huge element of rubrics, symbolics and similitudes piled high as the zenith over him, could hardly be more modest. It must be owned too that Bishop Bancroft, while the modest complaint was still going on, suddenly fell down on his knees before the King, begging that 'Schismatics be not heard against their Bishops,' and interrupted the painful Dr. Reynolds in mid career; and did again, falling on his knees, interrupt him; showing a sufficiently choleric temper of mind. Right reverend Whitgift too was choleric, apprehensive of the Scotch mist coming in on him.

His Majesty, however, gave small countenance to painful Reynolds and company; glad he, for his part, that he had now left the Scotch mist quite behind him, and got into the promised land, where no 'beardless boy in a pulpit' durst beard him; and on the contrary dignified Bishops and such like were here to honour him and call him the second Solomon. 'No Bishop no King,' said his Majesty more than once. And painful Reynolds going on to suggest, Whether it might not be well if the clergy were allowed to meet together, say once in three weeks, and have 'prophesyings' as in good Archbishop Grindal's time; meeting by deaneries, by archdeaconries, then by bishopricks, to strengthen one another's hands, and prophesy in various profitable ways?— his Majesty broke forth into sheer flame; declaring that 'this was Scotch Presbytery under a new colour, and agreed with Majesty as God did with the Devil,'—meaning as the Devil did with God. No more of that, good Doctor! 'There 'you shall have Jack and Tom, Will and Dick assemble them- 'selves, and at their wise pleasure censure both me and my 'council. Away, away, Doctor, wait seven years before ye 'speak of that. If ye find me growing lazy, and my mind 'getting short with fat, after seven years or so, then ye can 'try such a thing, for that will be the way to keep me in 'exercise! No Bishop no King!'—whereat the whole celestial Court shivers with glad rustle as of admiring mirth, and 'No 'Bishop no King' re-echoes applausive; and Reynolds and company are cowed into blank silence; and a Courtier says, 'It is now clear to him that a Puritan is a Protestant 'frightened out of his wits,' and another that Puritans, in their furred gowns of Turkey merchants, 'are more like Turks than 'Christians': and it is a titter and a snigger all over these, Courtly spaces; Majesty, like a far-darting Apollo, scattering his light-shafts in this exhilarative manner, to dispel the things of Night.

Reynolds and company are cowed into blank silence, almost into pallor and tremor; and right reverend Bancroft falling on his knees utters these words: 'I protest my heart melteth 'for joy that Almighty God, of His singular mercy, hath 'given us such a King as since Christ's time hath not been.' Right reverend, *my* heart, on the whole, doth not melt.— Likewise, in regard to that afflictive chimera which they call the *Ex-officio* Oath, venerable Whitgift, charmed beyond the limits to hear an approval of it, exclaims, 'Undoubtedly your 'Majesty speaks by the special assistance of God's spirit.' Think you so, right reverend? The *Ex-officio* Oath is a thing they try us with in their High Commission Court: Swear that you are innocent, or else be held guilty;—guilty surely, *unless* your conscience be elastic! Even Chancellor Egerton is heard admitting, 'He had never seen King and Priest so 'united as here.'

And, in fine, Dr. Reynolds being questioned, 'Have you 'anything more to say, Doctor?' answers, 'Nothing, may it 'please your Majesty.' And Majesty, thereupon rising, declares audibly, not without wrath, That these Puritans shall either conform, or one country shall not hold them and him! Dread Sovereign——?—And so, dispelled by the lightning-shafts of Majesty, these Puritans fly back into their caves; and the glittering bodyguards, shadows of high-plumed lords, long-skirted archbishops, professors in furred gowns, chancellors in shaving-dish hat, Hampton Conference in general, and Majesty with diamond hatband, become grey again, of an indistinct leaden colour, and vanish in the dusk of things.

Dull Mr. Neal informs me, The Puritans, at next Convocation, were loaded with abundant penalties, excommunications, ex-officios and what not; whereby some three hundred clergymen, pious zealous preachers of the Gospel, with consciences not sufficiently elastic, were plucked out as thorns from the flesh of the Church, such seeming evidently now to be the nature of them. The Puritans shall either conform, or withdraw to Chaos or Hades, by route of Holland, North America or what route they can. Bishop Bancroft, soon to be Archbishop, sings after his fashion, *Te Deum*, and is a busy man. For old Whitgift lay sick to death; and his Majesty coming to see him, he lifted up his old hand and eyes, saying '*Pro Ecclesia Domini*, For the Lord's Church!' and spake no words more in this world; and choleric Bancroft was Primate in his room. *Ecclesia Domini*: venerable pale old spectral Archbishop, Overseer of human Souls, under what inconceivable embodiments, 'congealed element piled 'high as the zenith over us,' does the Spirit of Man live bewildered in this world; and discerns its empyrean home either not at all, or in distortions and distractions beyond belief; now in white or black cloth-tippets, now in gilt log-palaces at Upsala, now in this now in that! Is not Chaos deep? is not the Grave greedy? And there is an 'azure of

'Infinitude' overspanning Chaos and the Grave, for all true souls of men.—— —Why does the poor Human Species quarrel with itself; why, in devout moments, sits it not rather, in sacred sorrowful communion one and all, with its harps hung on the willow trees, and weeps by the streams of Babel!—

But on the other hand, what if Puritanism would not quit the country, and go to Hades, either by way of Holland, or by any way whatever! Puritanism has a thing or two on the anvil before it go to Hades. Puritanism, as simple as it looks, is of a species his Majesty, for all his wide-open eyes and intellect, does not thoroughly discern. A species such as I have never yet known to go to Hades without doing a bit of work in this world; work not wholly mortal, nay, leaving a soul behind it that was not mortal at all! Simple Puritanism, capable of being cowed down by choleric Serene Highnesses, will break silence again, I think. There is that in it that speaks to the Highest in Heaven above; and will not, if necessity arrive, altogether tremble to speak to the High set on stilts at Hampton Court here!—

In fact, if his Majesty could see that epoch of his as we now see it, and what issue it has all had, it would astonish him. The times are loud, your Majesty, and then again they fall so dumb![1] What has become of all that high-sounding element of things, with its embassyings, intriguings, loud arguings, deep mysteries of state, which his Majesty presided over? It has proved a ceremonial mainly, an emptiness; the voice of it has gone silent, its bright tints deservedly have grown leaden. O, second Solomon, inspired to appearance by the spirit of God, what outcome has it all had; that same majestic English world of yours so dizened by the tailor and upholsterer, by the worker in cloth-tissues and the worker in word-tissues; which could reckon even a Bacon among its decorative tailors, very ambitious to handle a needle in that service,—what has the net amount of it turned out to be? Alas, your Majesty, almost nothing!

[1] As Goethe says.

There remains of it little that a modern man could lay his hand upon at once:—good Heavens, the main item of it is not Hampton Court with *its* extremely solid-looking phantasmagories, but perhaps — perhaps — the Bankside Theatre with its phantasmagories, professedly of pasteboard, got up for amusement of the gross million at a groat each! Heard human Majesty ever the like? From that chaos of loud-babbling figures gone all dumb, we have saved for ourselves— —Shakspeare's Plays. Verily that is the tangiblest item at this hour. Your embassies flying silver-winged, incessant, to all the four winds; your solemn jousts and tournaments, your favouritisms, caballings, sermons in the Star-chamber and vexations of spirit; your drinking bouts, dancing bouts, Count-Mansfeld fighting bouts, theologies, demonologies: they tumbled and simmered, wide as the world, high as the star-firmament; and the result that survives for us has been, are we to say,—these eight small volumes edited by Isaac Reed[1] and others? The oldest experienced King never heard the like!

Nay, your Majesty, there is another thing that yet survives for us, palpable in the life of us all; better even than Shakspeare; for by Heaven's blessing, it will be the parent of many Shakspeares and other Veracities and Blessednesses yet: I mean—alas, your Majesty, I mean this thing you have just flashed into quasi-annihilation with your royal sun-glances, and ordered to march straightway to Chaos, being inspired by the spirit of God. This thing called Puritanism, in its dim furred gown; this!

For it goes away abashed from your presence, being of melancholic modest nature; but not to Chaos or Hades; having appointment and business elsewhere. It goes to its chamber of prayer and meditation; to its writing-desk, to its pulpit, to its Parliament,—to the hearts of all just-thinking Englishmen. And singular to see, it returns ever back, with

[1] Critic and miscellaneous writer; born in London, 1742; died 1807. Edited the Works of Shakspeare, 1785.

its old Gospel-books, and old Lawbooks, and Subsidy-books; knocks ever again at the King's gate, saying, Shall our life become true and a God's-fact, then; or continue half-true and a cloth-formula? And ever its demands wax wider;—and your Majesty, in the Third Parliament, has to fly into mere wrath at Newmarket, and cry in an elevated shrill manner, 'Twelve chairs for the twelve Kings of the House of 'Commons,—they are Kings, I think, come to visit me!'[1]

Truly a Sovereign of England, second Solomon or other, who had read in his own noble heart what of noblest this England meant and dimly strove towards, would not have scouted Puritanism from him in that summary way. He would have said to himself: How now? Old traditional Decorum is good; but Sincerity newborn is infinitely good; Decorum divided from Sincerity will fare ill. This poor Puritanism, ragged contradictory as it looks, is a confused struggle towards God's eternal Verity,—wherein and not elsewhere lies the fountain of all blessedness for England and me and all nations and men. I will not cut it down, this poor Puritanism; I will guide it, foster it; try to make it my friend not my enemy. These poor scrupulous individuals shall go home to their places; shall preach abroad, among my English people, a Calvinistic Stoicism, which is deeper than Zeno's, which is deep as the Eternal, and will spring up in thousandfold harmonies, I hope!—A King who has in him the instinct to recognise such nascent heroisms in their incipient confused condition, and help them into birth and being, shall reign truly 'forever': a King that has not will reign falsely and but for a short time. Queen Elizabeth now dead, she too loved cloth and formulas; and could have held by the Old; but she felt in the heart of her country, feeling it first of all in her own noble heart, that the true vital pulse was Protestantism; and, with lifelong wise endeavour and valour, she said, 'Let us be Protestant then.' She, in a sense, reigns forever. She had a hero-heart of her

[1] See *infra*, p. 157 *n.*

own which could recognise heroisms. Heavens, had that Boy at Huntingdon but been *her* Son!—But a King who has no hero-heart, what to him are nascent heroisms springing never so authentically from the Eternal? They are ragged confusions, very criminal, rebellious; perverse world-tendencies which he will withstand. He stems himself in the breach against such; stands minatory there, with his pikes and cannons, his gibbets and white-rod ushers, a terrible spectacle;—and is washed away to the abyss, he and they!

Alas, your Majesty, never more, in any day of settlement, will Puritanism present itself with so extremely exiguous a bill of bookdebts as it has now done through the hand of Knewstubs and Reynolds! It will come, next time, not in doctoral furred gown alone; it will come in formidable Speaker's-wig withal, with Magna Charta and the Six Statutes and *Tallagio non concedendo* in its hand; with sword on its thigh; with drawn sword for sheer battle,—O Heavens, with headsman's axe, for regicide and one knows not what, never seen before under this sun! And Glorious Revolution Settlements, American Independences; nay, what say we, French Revolutions, very Jacobinisms,—there is no end of this Puritanism! For it holds, as I observed, of the Eternal; and will not go to Hades without its work done; nay, properly will not go to Hades at all, but live here on Earth forever, the soul of it blending with whatsoever of Eternal we have here on Earth, part of the indestructible perennial sum of human things.

Well, your Majesty, is not this world a catholic kind of place? The Puritan Gospel and Shakspeare's Plays: such a pair of facts I have rarely seen saved out of one chimerical generation. You say, 'We are an old and experienced 'King'; which is very fortunate. And again, '*Le Roy* '*s'avisera*, the King will take thought of it': really he should! This world is very wide, is deep beyond all plummets; has more in it, in Heaven and in Earth, than was yet dreamt of in your or my philosophy. A world ever young, as old as it looks; a world most feracious, most edacious; wherein the oldest experienced kings have been found at fault before now!

The following, by Smelfungus, seems more to resemble some sort of modern Puritan Sermon than a piece of History. In it there is no 'delineation of events'; but for understanding the spirit of what is delineated some readers may find it not without significance. Such as are already familiar with considerations of that kind may pass on, glancing all the more slightly. Our dark friend writes :—

'Descending into those old ages, we are struck most of all
'with this strange fact, that they were Christian ages.
'Actually men in those times were possessed with a belief that,
'in addition to their evident greedy appetites, they had
'immortal souls not a whit less evident; souls which, after
'death, would have to appear before the Most High Judge,
'and give an account of their procedure in the conduct of said
'appetites, with an issue that was endless. This, of which we
'have yet a hollow tradition, worse in some respects than none,
'was then a fact indisputable to all persons. Human persons
'all knew it well; only gross unhuman persons, and beasts
'destined to perish, knew it not. God's eternal Judgment-
'seat, awaiting all men above, was a fact as certain as the
'King's Court sitting here below in Westminster Hall. It is
'the vital fact of those old ages; which renders them, at this
'time, an enigma to the world. For the tradition of it has
'grown so hollow, it is worse in some respects than none.
'Sheer silence and ignorance, nay, atheistical denial once for
'all, how much better is it than canting sham belief and
'avowal from the teeth outward! In reality, what man
'among us, if he is not one of a million, can form to himself
'so much as an adequate shadow of that old fact?

'Worse in some respects than no tradition; and yet in
'other respects how much better, how invaluable in others!
'O cultivated reader, is it not worth while to hear of such a

'thing, even from the old dead ages, and as a rumour of what
'once was? That man's little earthly life is verily great,
'infinite; the shadow of eternities to him; whereby he will
'determine to himself the welfare or woe of eternities? A
'brief little drama on Earth, rigorously emblematic of eternal
'destinies in Heaven or else in Hell? The rumour still
'abides with us; let it still abide, were it only in a hollow
'doleful manner. Pure noble souls, with hearing ear and
'understanding heart, are sent occasionally into this world;
'these also here and there will hear it, and, with astonishment,
'will know it, will discern it; by these gradually the god-like
'meaning of it will be restored to us, never to be lost more.
'It is the work they have done in the Past Time; it is the
'work they have to do in all times. There will then be a
'heroic world, once again; much cant and much brutality,
'and miseries of many kinds, will then go their ways.

'Yes, out of all ages named heroic there has come to us
'some doctrine, feeling, or instinct equivalent to this; out of
'all ages that are not brutal, appointed to be forgotten,
'without worth or meaning for us. Ancient Heroisms had
'some intimation of it, had an instinct equivalent to it; the
'much nobler modern Heroisms had it made credible and
'indubitable to them. To History the purport of what
'highest Gospels we have had may be defined as even this,
'That Judgment and Eternity are not a hearsay, that they
'are a fact;—fit enough to kindle the inmost deeps of us!
'I say, without either an express doctrine, or a felt instinct
'expressed in rules of action to this effect, man is not himself;
'—he is, little as he may dream of it, a kind of enchanted
'monster. One has heard of a man very wretched because the
'Devils had stolen away his shadow: but here they have
'stolen his robes of light from him; he walks abroad, little
'knowing it, arrayed in the everlasting murk, a son of Nox
'and Chaos. He considers that his life was given him only to
'enjoy it, to eat and digest in it, to be happy in it. He is a
'ray of darkness become flesh. Noble deed or thought there

CHAP. III.]   HAMPTON COURT CONFERENCE   39

'is thenceforth none for him under these stars. His luckiest
'lot, were it not even this, to *return*, at his soonest, to Chaos,
'and report what a failure it was?

'For properly that outer fact of a Divine Judgment is
'the emblematic expression of this other internal fact, that
'man has in him a man-like sense of Right and Wrong.
'Right and Wrong; manfulness (*virtus*), or unmanfulness!
'A manlike sense, we say, and not beastlike: for the very
'beasts and horses know something of "morality," if this be
'"moral": To know that on this side lie hay and oats, and on
'that side lie scourgings and spur-rowels. But to a man, let
'him understand it or not, his being right or his being wrong
'is simply the one question. The most flaming Hell he will
'front composedly, right being with him; wrong being with
'him, the Paradise of Houris were a Hell.

'Yes, reader, it will require to be forever repeated till the
'obtuse generations learn it again, and lay it to heart and
'bring it forth in their practice again: man, very finite as we
'see him, is withal a kind of infinite creature. His little
'Time-life is a mysterious pavilion spread on the bosom of
'Eternities; there he acts his little life-drama, looked at, with
'approval, with rejection, by the Eternities and Infinitudes.
'Very certainly, let him know it or not, he does project him-
'self beyond all firmaments and abysses; has real property,
'more real than was ever pleaded of in law-courts, beyond the
'outmost stars. Either as an enchanted monster, forgetful of
'all this; or else as a man, encircled in celestial robes of
'light, and mindful of all this, does he, in every epoch, in
'every form of creed and circumstances, walk abroad; the
'enchanted thrall of this world, or else its heaven-sent king.
'A splendour of Heaven looks through all Nature for him,
'if he have eyes; if he have none, it is of course a dark-
'ness of Erebus. For Nature, say the Philosophers, is
'properly his own Self shadowed back on him; Nature is
'the product of his own thought: he, that poor little
'creature in round felt hat, is in a sense the "author" of

'Nature;—an Unnameable gave him that faculty of com-
'posing a Universe and Nature for himself, with those five
'senses of his, with that thinking soul of his.

'Encircle him visibly with that same celestial splendour
'which is native to him; in some way, let him understand
'indubitably at all moments that he *is* a man, that he
'does belong to the Heavens and Infinitudes, what a crea-
'ture is he! Difficulties, perils melt from his path, as
'vapours from before the face of the sun: difficulties, perils
'are not there for him; he can hurl mountains aside, and
'build paths across the impassable, march with spread
'banners through the Deathkingdoms, trample Death and
'Tartarus under his feet! I have known such, under
'various figures, at intervals in this noble world all along;
'and do, with continual gratitude, deeply thank the Heavens
'for them: Old Romans, Moslems, still more Old Christians,
'nay Puritans or modern Christians, "Believers," each after
'his kind. I have known Luthers, Mahomets, men "resigned
'to God," and not resigned to the Enemies of God;—in
'various forms I have known men come into this world as
'evident Sons of Light, born enemies of Chaos: men blazing
'with intolerable radiance; before whom all pedants, poltroons
'and the like beggarly persons had hastily to withdraw them-
'selves, hastily to shut their eyes, and procure if possible
'"improved smoked spectacles." For the radiance was in-
'tolerable as Heaven's own; it was the light of genius become
'fire of virtue and valour: intolerable enough; and sent
'oftenest, to this corrupt Earth, not with peace but with a
'sword,—nay, I believe, always with a sword among other
'things. For human figures of this kind shall we not per-
'petually thank the Heavens, as for their one favour; from
'and with which are all other favours; without which no
'other favour is possible, or indeed worth accepting if it were?

'But on the other hand, once hide this his celestial destiny
'from poor man; persuade him, by enchantment of whatever
'sort, that he has nothing to do with Heaven or the Infini-

CHAP. III.]   HAMPTON COURT CONFERENCE   41

'tudes, except to cant about them on ceremonial occasions,
'and for making assurance doubly sure, pray by machinery to
'them,—alas! Has the thinking soul any sadder spectacle
'in this world? Man has fallen into eclipse; the dragons
'and demons have, as it were, obliterated him. Yes, the
'Subterranean ones, tugging and twitching at his Light-
'mantle, have tugged it down with them; and he remains
'a mass of darkness, tenebrific, raying out mere darkness,
'greediness, baseness; with the figure still of a man, but
'unhappier than most animals and apes,—than all apes
'except those that sit on Sabbath by the shores of the
'Dead Sea!
  'There are many such; whole generations of such are, and
'have been, in this world: but they are a solecism, a futile
'monstrosity; worth no notice, as we said. Their glitter, so
'bright to themselves, is without brightness to any other.
'What is the brightness of rotting wood, so soon as morning
'has risen? Their doom is to be forgotten forever. How
'shall the soul of man take pains to remember what is intrin-
'sically trivial, undelightful, dead and killing to all souls?
'This is *un*related to the Eternal Melodies; this is discordant,
'related to the Eternal Discords! No soul of man will re-
'member it; will find any pleasure or possession in it.
'Melancholy Pedantry does its part, for a certain length of
'years, to the sorrow and confusion of the human mind: but
'Pedantry also has to terminate; its torpid volumes, no man
'reading or reprinting them, are gradually eaten by worms;
'the last dull vocable is eaten by some charitable worm, and
'the very echo of them vanishes forever. Such generations do
'and must fall abolished out of History; immense strata of
'them are at last found pressed together into a film. God is
'great.

  'But the truth is,' continues our severe friend, 'this King
'James having, with his royal radiance, scattered English

'Puritanism forth from his presence, and bidden it be gone to
' Chaos,—he has, so to speak, quitted hold of the real heart
' of England; is becoming more and more an alien, he and
' his, to what England means, and has in hest to do. This
' new Nobleness of England he has misknown, has taken for
' a thing ignoble. England nevertheless must do it; from the
' eternal kingdoms, from the foundations of the Universe,
' comes a monition to do it. The Law of Nature goes one way
' with us; our poor Sovereign Lord has set out to lead us and
' compel us on another. What can come of it? This poor
' Sovereign Lord, this poor Stuart Dynasty of Sovereign Lords,
' growing more and more aliens to the meaning of England,
' will occupy the throne of England,—but find one day that
' it is the Wooden-and-velvet " throne " merely, supported by
' certain constables and tax-eaters merely. All aliens come to
' be recognised for alien; and must depart, if not peaceably,
' then worse.

'Puritanism, heartfelt conformity not to human rubrics
' but to the Maker's own Laws,—what nobler thing was there,
' or is there? All noble things, past, present, future, are even
' this same thing under various conditions and environments.
' It is a kindling of the human soul once more into recog-
' nition of " God dwelling in *it*,"—recognition of its own awful
' godhead. All noble activities and enlightenments flow from
' this as from a light-fountain and life-fountain. Just social
' constitution, liberty combined with loyalty, privilege of par-
' liament and privilege of king, all practical veracities and
' equities,—these are but a small inevitable corollary from it,
' as all colours are a corollary from the sun. England will
' have to do this thing; this thing is in very deed the Voice
' of the Eternal to England, speaking such dialect as there is;
' and it must be done. Who will help England to do it?
' Who, heaven-sent, as a Pillar of Cloud by day, as a Pillar of
' Fire by night, will go before the destinies of England, to
' guide them, during his stage of it, through the undiscovered
' Time? Strong must he be; fit to march through very Chaos.

'He will have to defy the rage of Chaos; to advance with
'closed lips, with clear eyesight, through all yellings of mon-
'sters, athwart all phantasms and abysses. Strong as a
'Hercules, as a god. He, whether the gold crown be on his
'head or not, will be the real King of England. If the gold
'crown be *not* on his head, if the gold crown be on his enemy's
'head,—it will be the worse for the gold crown.'

CHAPTER IV

JAMES I

THIS King James, with his large hysterical heart, with his large goggle-eyes glaring timorously inquisitive on all persons and objects, as if he would either look through them or else be fascinated by them, and, so to speak, start forth *into* them, and spend his very soul and eyesight in the frustrate attempt to look through them,—remains to me always a noticeable, not unloveable man. The liveliest recognition of innumerable things, such a pair of goggle-eyes glaring on them, could not fail.

He is a man of swift discernment, ready sympathy, ready faculty in every kind; vision clear as a lynx's, if it were deep enough! Courtiers repeat his Majesty's repartees and speeches: was there ever seen such a head of wit? He, with his lynx eyes, detected in Monteagle's letter some prophecy of 'suddenness,' prophecy of—probable Gunpowder barrels; and found Guy Faux and his cellar, and dark lantern, his Majesty, I think, it chiefly was. He detected the 'Sleeping Preacher,' a sneaking College-graduate, of semi-Puritan tendencies, who pretended to preach in his sleep.[1] He was great in Law-suits, of logical acumen rarely paralleled; your most tangled skein of lawpleading or other embroiled logic, once hang it on the Royal judgment, he will wind it off for you to the inmost thrum. He delights in doing

[1] Stow.

lawsuits, presiding over conferences; testifying to himself and others what a divine lynx faculty he has. He speaks like a second Solomon; translucent with logic, radiant with wit, with ready ingenuity, and prismatic play of colours. Gunpowder Plots, Sleeping Preachers, what or whom will he not detect? No impostor or imposture, you would say, can well live before this King. None;—except, alas, that one Semi-impostor already lived *in* him, with a fair stock of unconscious impostures laid up: these from within did yearn responsive to their kindred who lived without! In this sense, impostors and impostures had a good time of it with King James: many bright speciosities were welcome; and certain rude noblenesses were indignantly radiated forth, and bidden go to Chaos.

But truly, if excellent discourse made an able man, I have seldom heard of any abler. For every why he has his wherefore ready; prompt as touchwood blazes up, with prismatic radiances, that astonishing lynx-faculty; which has read and remembered, which has surveyed men and things, after its fashion, with extensive view. The noble sciences he could, for most part, profess in College class-rooms; he is potent in theology as a very doctor; in all points of nicety a Daniel come to judgment. A man really most quick in speech; full of brilliant repartees and coruscations; of jolly banter, ready wit,[1] conclusive speculation: such a faculty that the Archbishops stand stupent, and Chancellor Bacon, not without a certain sincerity, pronounces him wonderfully gifted.

It is another feature of this poor king that he was of hot temper. A man promptly sympathetic, loquacious, most vehement, most excitable: can be transported into mere rage and frenzy on small occasions; will swear like an Ernulphus,[2] call the gods and the devils to witness what a life he has of

[1] 'He was very witty, and had as many ready witty jests as any man living, at which he would not smile himself, but deliver them in a grave and serious manner.'—Weldon (*Secret History of the Court of James I.*, Edinburgh, 1811), ii. 7.

[2] Whose Curse, a very comprehensive piece of 'swearing', indeed, is given in full in *Tristram Shandy*, Bk. iii. cap. ii.

it; will fling himself down and 'bite the grass,' say courtiers, 'merely because his game has escaped him in the wood.' Consider it: My game is gone, may all the devils follow it; and you, ye blockheads,—*maledictum sit!* And then, when the fit is past, how his Majesty repents of it, in the saddest silence, with pious ejaculations to Heaven for forgiveness! Poor king, his tongue is too big for him, his eyes are vigilant, goggle-eyes: physically and spiritually the joints and life-apparatus are ill-compacted in him.

Nor can we say, he has no heart; rather he has too much heart; a heart great, but flaccid, loose of structure, without strength: the punsters might say he suffered from 'enlarge-'ment of the heart.' His life expended itself in spasmodic attachments, favouritisms, divine adorations of this or the other poor undivine fellow-creature;—passionate clutchings at the unattainable; efforts not strong but hysterical. How he struggled for a Spanish Match;[1] how the passionate spasmodic nature of him cramped itself, with desperate desire, on this as on the one thing needful, and he was heard to say once with exultation, 'The very Devil cannot balk me now!' The one thing needful because the one thing unattainable. Alas, O reader, what is it to thee and me, at this date, whether the Spanish Match take effect or take no effect? Which of us, transporting himself with ever such industrious loyalty, into the then state of matters, would lift his little finger to attain that high topgallant of the Spanish Match and make a sovereign happy? The spasmodic endeavourings of that big royal heart which now amount to zero; the effulgences of that sublime intellect, comparable to Solomon's, which are gone all to rust and darkness, fill me with a tragic feeling. The Bog of Lindsey[2] is deep. The intelligence of man, when he has any, should not expend itself in eloquent talking, but in eloquent silence and wise work, rather.

His Majesty, with that peculiar 'divine faculty' of his, could not be expected to govern England, or to govern

[1] See *post*, p. 147.   [2] See *post*, p. 58.

anything, in a successful manner. Clever speech is good; but the Destinies withal are born deaf. How happy had his Majesty been, could he have got the world to go by coaxing, by brilliant persuasion, and have been himself left at liberty to hunt! We call his government bad, on all sides unsuccessful, at variance with the fact; the semi-impostor within him attracting all manner of impostors and impostures from without, and swearing eloquent brotherhood with *them!* Realities, of any depth, were an unintelligibility to him; only speciosities are beautiful. What trouble he had with his Parliaments! To the last it was an unintelligible riddle to him, what these factious Commons, with their mournful Puritanic Constitutional Petitions and Remonstrances could rationally mean. Do they mean anything but faction, insane rebellion, sacrilegious prying into our royal mysteries of State? Apparently not.

That this poor King, especially in his later years, took to favouritisms, is, as it were, the general summary of him, good and bad, and need not surprise us. With such eyes he could not but discriminate in the liveliest manner what had a show of nobleness from what had none. His eyes were clear and shallow; his heart was not great, but morbidly enlarged. Nay, we are to say moreover, that his favourites, naturally enough hated by all the world, were by no means hateful persons. Robert Car, son of the Laird of Ferniehirst, who quitted otter-hunting and short commons in the pleasant land of Teviotdale, to come hither, and be Earl of Somerset and a world's wonder had various qualities, I find, besides his 'beauty.'[1] Audacity, dexterity, graceful courteous ways; shrewd discernment, swift activity, in the sphere allotted him, had recommended Robert Car. Poor Car: had he staid in his poor homeland, hunting otters, or what else there might be; roving weather-tanned by Jedwood, Teviotdale, and the breezy hills and clear-rushing rivers; and fished for himself

---

[1] Robert Car (Carr or Ker) was created Viscount Rochester in 1611, and Earl of Somerset in 1613.

there, though on short commons, being a younger brother,—
how much luckier had he been, and perhaps we! Or he
might have gone abroad, and fought the Papists, under my
Lord Vere. In Roxburghshire, as an eldest son, as a real
Laird with rents to eat, he would have been the delight of
men.

As for George Villiers,[1] it is universally agreed he was the
prettiest man in England in several specious respects. A
proud man, too, rather than a vain; with dignity enough,
with courage, generosity; all manner of sense and manfulness
in the developed or half-developed state; a far-glancing man.
Such a one this King might delight to honour. Poor old
King, his own old dislocated soul loved to repose itself on
these bright young beautiful souls; in their warmth and
auroral radiance he felt that it was well with him. Crabbed
Cecil, Earl of Salisbury, had ended; advancing age and
increase of sorrow were coming on his Majesty, when he
betook himself to Car. These accursed Favourites, they were
called, and passionately said to be, several things; they were
properly Prime Ministers of England, chosen by the royal
'divine faculty,' such as it was. Bad Prime Ministers, very
ill-chosen;—but not the worst; I have known far worse.
We ourselves, who live under mere Prime Ministers chosen
by a Collective Wisdom and bursts of Parliamentary eloquence, have not we had worse,—Heavens, are we sure we
ever had much better! Prime Ministers are difficult to
choose. By kings unheroic, and by peoples unheroic, they
are impossible to choose.

How happy had it been for this King, could he have done
his duty without trouble, by eloquence of speech alone! O,
if the world would but go right by coaxing of it, by ingenious
pleading with it! Here is wit, here is jolly banter; sharp
logic-arrows, which give many a difficulty its quietus,—for

---

[1] Third son of Sir George Villiers of Brooksby, Leicestershire. He became
Viscount Villiers in 1616, and Earl of Buckingham, 1617.

the moment. Courtiers turn up their admiring eyes : a second Solomon, we vow ! But ever the difficulty awakens again, feller than before; it cannot be slain by logic-arrows. '*Beati Pacifici,* ' Blessed are the Peacemakers,' said his Majesty always. Yes, Your Majesty; but they will require other ammunition than clever speech, I am afraid. Fain would his Majesty have saved the Palatinate, how fain, could it have been done without stroke struck ! All vice had been far from him, had it not been so pleasant; all virtue near, except that it was troublesome. He would have promoted true religion, encouraged commerce, made a noble England of us, could it have been done by speech alone. O England, why wilt thou not go by coaxing ? Thou art like the deaf adder; listenest not to the voice of the charmer. Fact, it would seem, goes one way; I, and my Solomonisms, and courtiers with upturned eyes, go another. Since eloquent speech will not do it, what can we attempt ? Try it with ever new eloquence ;—and in the intervals, as much as may be, fly from it.

His Majesty, idle from the first, grew ever idler. He roved about in continual Progresses; he hunted greatly, as it were incessantly; his active history was one great hunt. Business, it is true, was neglected : but the semi-impostor within, responded to by plenty of impostors from without, declared it to be essential for 'the health of our royal ' person.' Consider, ye English People, if our royal liver got into mis-secretion ?—Certainly, your Majesty's health before all things; 'your Majesty is the breath of our nostrils !' His Majesty hunted much; and also, what was a natural resource for him, drank. His Majesty's drinking was considerable; moreover, it kept slowly but perceptibly increasing. Christian, King of Denmark, his royal brother-in-law,[1] came more than once to see him, with immense explosion of 'fire- ' works on the River ' and elsewhere; and the two Majesties had carouses together worthy of the old Sea-kings. Acrid

[1] James married, in 1589, the Princess Anne, sister of Christian IV., King of Denmark and Norway.

old Court-newsmen will apprise you how, before the Court masque got ended, the Majesties of England and Denmark were scandalously overcome with strong liquor; how even ladies of honour, and Allegorical Virtues, Faith, Hope and Charity, dressed for the nonce, staggered as they made their entrance, unable to speak their finishing parts, their tongue cleaving to the roof of their mouth; and in one dim hiccuping chaos, the worthships and worships of this lower world reeled eclipsed, as in disastrous universal twilight of the gods. What are we to think of these things, in Huntingdon,[1] for instance, and other such serious quarters! Alas, his Majesty's own royal conscience admits that it is scandalous; repents sorrowfully on the morrow, eager for soda-water and consolation.

It is also admitted that this King 'sold honours.' He was the first that started that branch of industry; sale of honours was a regular item in our royal budget during those years. He had a settled tariff of honours: so much for a Knight, so much for a Baronet, which latter was one of his own inventions; so much for Baronhood, for all kinds of Lordhood, up to Earlhood, which, it would appear, cost 10,000*l*. Whatsoever man, not entirely scandalous to mankind, will pay down 10,000*l*. can be made an Earl. Men disapproved of it, but men made purchases. Old Peers gloomed unutterable things, but had to submit in silence. The truth is, his Majesty was all along terribly in want of cash. He had withal a perpetual desire to oblige everybody, where it could be done with a mere garter, or slap of the sword. His temptation to sell honours was considerable. And yet,—alas, your Majesty, who are a wise old King, is not this same as mad an act as any king can do? The necessitous Indian, in like fashion, procures a brief warmth by burning his bed. Pay honour to whom honour is *not* due; it is an anarchic transaction every fibre of it: every such payment, on the part of any man, is a piece of

[1] Where Oliver Cromwell was living.

anarchy; a contribution to the great Bank of Social Falsehood, which if it go on accumulating will break us all. Nobility direct for cash, nobility in any way *by* cash, does it not mean now and forever a thing false? Does it not too fatally admonish us that Mammon is a great god; that he sits there as our great god, with diamond eyes, gold eyebrows, and belly full of jewels, awe-inspiring;—that certain greater gods, or were it even greater devils, strange Puritanisms, most strange Jacobinisms, Sansculottisms, will be needed by and by, to smite the crockery belly of him in pieces, and scatter him and his diamonds in a surprising manner!—

But in fact cash, all along, was the thing this King wanted; he could not help it. His revenues were great compared with Queen Elizabeth's: but Queen Elizabeth was thrifty,—she had it probably by nature. We of our royal bounty, again, are generous; a cheerful giver while we have it, to the worthy, to the unworthy!—King James's Parliaments, for various reasons, grew shy of furnishing him at such a ratio; his Majesty's necessities were habitually great. He had to subsist as a projector; from hand to mouth; his inspiring genii Hunger and Hope. By Benevolences, by forced loans, sale of honours, farming of Papist penalties, monopolies of gold and silver thread;—the very penalties on swearing were farmed; monopolies were thick as blackberries,[1] all farmed out for a consideration. His ways of raising money and of wasting it are a wonder to behold. On one Scotch individual called James Hay, called various things, called ultimately Earl of Carlisle, and married to Lucy Percy, daughter of Northumberland, he is computed to have spent first and last, 400,000*l.*; say a million and a half of our money. That was the money-price of Sardanapalus Hay and his services; probably the highest ever given for such a piece of goods. Hay was not without talent, expertness as courtier and clothes-horse: he went on several embassies, 'shook 'silver from his horse's hoofs' on the streets of Paris, riding

---

[1] Seven hundred of them, according to d'Ewes.

CHAP. IV.]   JAMES I   51

in state there,[1] that the populace and all persons might discern how regardless of expense he was. This King spent immensely on Embassies,—eloquent persuasion; which indeed was his one recipe for foreign affairs. By embassies, by progresses, by cheerful giving while we have it, our royal exchequer is perennially running on the lees.

Of this or the other person we hear it said, What an excellent man would he be, if he had but abundance of money! Yes, truly:—but the postulate is a very wide one. To have always money means in the long-run, mad as money and social arrangements are, that you do in some measure conform yourself to facts; that you do not entirely desert the laws of industry, veracity, self-denial and common arithmetic, on which, as on its central sanity, this mad world revolves, still keeping out of chaos! You do not forget these laws, you in a degree adhere to them; by that means some vestige of cash still remains with you. Forget them altogether, these central sanities, laws of self-denial, common arithmetic and such like,—there is no exchequer in the world but you will exhaust; Fortunatus's Purse alone would suffice you. It is even so. Fortunatus's Purse, that little leather pocket, in which, every time you chose to open it there lay ten gold coins, would subvert the laws of Moral Nature. Probably no such miraculous machine could be put into the hands of a son of Adam. Adieu then to all reformation, public and private! Adieu, ye central sanities; we can revolve forever in the superficial confusions. Injustice, madness, unveracity, shameless practical denial of the multiplication-table itself, does not now clutch me by the stomach, by the throat, and say, Thou shalt die or quit all that. No; I only hear of it from Moralists in Sunday pulpits, from demagogue orators or such like; and can contentedly go my way. So long as there are necessitous scoundrels in this Earth, cannot I hire flatterers, hire armies, keep down all demagogues; make Sunday pulpits, by much milder methods, temper themselves? I

---

[1] Wilson, in Kennet's *History of England*, ii. 704.

have but to dive into my Fortunatus's leather-pocket, and bring out always the ten gold coins. May the gods deliver us from any such miraculous implement, fit to overset the world!

When we say therefore that his Majesty is in perpetual want of cash, it is saying otherwise that his Majesty finds himself, after all, a kind of chaotic individual; not owned by the Veracities, as a Solomon should be, but disowned by them. Facts everywhere disowned him, much to his astonishment. Yet he struggled always, let us own, as his infirmities would permit. With eloquent speech, with every superficial assiduity, he tried to coax the Veracities; snarled in angry surprise, when they would not coax;—and anew tried them. Those vigilant glittering eyes, full of goodhumour, kindliness, jolly banter; that radiant wisdom secure that it is all-wise; that snarl, as of mastiff's swiftly passing,—poor Majesty! He was a man that hated trouble; idle, nay 'eloquently 'idle': in spite of black calumnies, what other vice had he? The summary of all his vices lay there, in that comprehensive one;—as the summary of all his misfortunes lay in want of cash. He had a most unquiet world to preside over; society all rent, or beginning to rend itself, in deep and ever deeper travail-throes: in this little Island of ours, multitudes of things confusedly germinating, which have since overshadowed the earth. A most pregnant, confused time; enough to astonish most Majesties. King of Puritanism? As the average of matters goes, we cannot expect such a thing. Puritanism, probably with struggle enough, will have to find its own King.

For the rest, let no man suppose that this King was a mere talking hypocrite; that he flung up the reins of government, like a modern Louis Fifteenth, in his Sybarite despair, and said, Go your own way, then! Far from it. King James, and this is the interesting peculiarity, never once in his remotest thoughts suspected that he was a Solecism. With his whole soul he feels always that he is Heaven-

appointed Governor of England; rolls his vigilant large
eyes, wags his eloquent large tongue, with real intent to
govern and guide it. There is a touching conscientiousness
in him. For indeed the fulness of time had not yet come!
Into no mind of man had it yet entered that this Universe
is an Imposture, an Uncertainty; that any man or king
can, otherwise than at his eternal peril, be a Solecism, and
empty anarchic Clothes-horse there. Comparatively, with all
its confusions, a lucky epoch that of James!

King James went in state to the Starchamber; pronounced
divine Discourses in the Starchamber; explaining to all
people, lords, commons, divines, lawyers and miscellaneous
persons, what their real duties were. He blew 'Counter-
'blasts against Tobacco'; he denounced Dutch Vorstius,
argued with Papist Bellarmine. How has he mastered the
mysteries of Kingcraft; written Basilicon-Dorons, that his
son after him might understand governing? He is near
going to war with the Dutch, he who all his days detested
war, because they hesitate to dismiss Vorstius, the mad Arian
who attempts to profess Divinity. He sent Bishop-Members to the Synod of Dort; longed for their despatches on
Vorstius, Arminians and the 'five points,' as for the water
of life; and when his Bishop-Members came home, he saw
them out of window, in a sad time, and said, 'Here come
' my good mourners.'[1] A King every inch, and even a kind
of Pontiff; a real Defender of the Faith; 'by which title
' he doth more value himself,' says his ambassador, 'than by
' the style of King of Britain.'[2]

With what unction does he discourse to Parliament also;
expounding, in affectionate allegories, that they are the wife,
and he the husband; that they must do no unkindnesses or
infidelities to one another. He feels himself as an immense
brood-fowl set over this England, and would so fain gather
it all under his wings. Cluck, cluck, ye unfortunate English;

---

[1] Fuller, *Church History of Britain* (London, 1837), iii. 282.
[2] *Ibid.* 251.

here are barleycorns, here are safe walks, if ye will but follow! Explosive, subterranean Papists, subtle Romish fowlers not a few, Puritan owlets, glede-hawks, vulture Vorstiuses are busy; but so too am I,—with my quick eyesight, with my prodigious head of wit. Why should a nobleman come idly hither to Court, and leave his own country unguided, uncheered; his chimney tops, the wind-pipes of good hospitality, smokeless among their woods? Why should a person of elegant appearance puff nauseous tobacco-smoke from him,—and even fill the cavities of his inner man with soot? If you dissect him, there have been known to issue, as I am informed, considerable quantities of soot.[1] Consider witchcraft too; beware of excess in witchcraft. O my people, do your duty wisely;—how fain would I too do my duty, were it not so troublesome! Hunting:—yes, but we are constrained to hunting for the health of our royal person. And drink:—we do take a little wine for our stomach's sake. Choose wise men:—and do I not, ye rebellious? I had crooked sorrowful Robert Cecil once; to me a great sorrow; and under him also you did nothing but croak. These brilliant young figures, they fly out as my angels, as my swift nimble scouts, seeking me the fit wise men; to me they make life easier; to you they are—agreeable, I would hope?

The trouble his Majesty had with his Parliaments is but analogous to what he had with all manner of Facts, everywhere. Not one Fact of them would go by coaxing; Parliaments are again a naked fact we have come upon, the summary of many facts. Through his English Parliaments there speaks again the reality of England to this King,—in a dialect extremely astonishing to him. Did not Heaven's Self and the Laws of Nature appoint me to

---

[1] 'Surely smoke becomes a kitchen farre better than a dining chamber, and yet it makes a kitchen also sometimes in the inward parts of men, soyling and infecting them, with an vnctious and oily kind of soote, as hath been found in some great *Tobacco* takers, that after their death were opened.' *Counterblaste to Tobacco* (King James's Works, London, 1616, p. 221).

be Sovereign, and general Parent Fowl over you, ye English? Have not I clucked as a most kind parent, struggling to cover you with my wings? And ye will prove mere rebellious cockatrices? Know that our royal breast contains anger withal; dreadful volumes of wrath, adequate to the dissolution of Nature in a manner! 'We think ourself very free and able to punish any 'man's misdemeanours in Parliament!'[1] From these Parliaments, in language of respect almost devotional, there comes truly a tone, lugubrious, low-voiced, unalterable; such as no second Solomon can understand. A croaking, tremulous, most mournful petition, ever repeated: That God's Gospel *be* attended to; that right be done according to the old laws; that eternal verity do assert itself veritably in all manner of temporal and other affairs. Dread Sovereign, enlightened Majesty, O that it would please your Majesty to put down Papistries, Spiritual Clothes-horses, blasphemous unveracities: it is the law of the Most High Maker; what will become of your Majesty's poor Commons, of your Majesty's Self and of us all otherwise! So pray the Parliaments ever more Puritanically.

What boots it? Knewstubs and Chadderton[2] were flashed back to Nox and Chaos, three hundred Puritan Night-owls scattered from their nests in the Parish Churches: and yet this strange Puritanism is spreading through all thinking souls in England! To the Country gentlemen it is grown natural; not a squire of them but has got the Bible-doctrine in his heart, or feels that he ought to have it, as the one thing needful. He has his Puritan Religion about him; as, in these days, our squire has his shotbelt and double-barrel. Low, tremulous, but bodeful as the voice of doom, rises the cry of the Bible Parliaments, waxing ever wider, ever deeper, through that Reign of James;—enough to drive a second Solomon mad, if he were to think of it! God's Gospel: Have we not got it, ye

[1] Kennet, ii. 741.   [2] See 'Hampton Court Conference,' *ante*, p. 24.

infatuated? Privilege, right according to law: Did any former king ever grant you the tithe of such Privilege? Will you yourselves be as kings, as gods knowing good and evil! Deep matters of State are far beyond your simple comprehension. We are an old and experienced King: are you advised of that? We think ourselves very free and able to punish any man's misdemeanours in Parliament. Shall we — dissolve Nature about your ears? We will to our hunting, and forget you! Let us forget you, ye infatuated; and live by monopolies, benevolences, sale of honours, and the general Grace of God!— —

Of a truth, King James had his own difficulties with the world; and also, it is to be admitted, the world had its own difficulties with King James. The Age of James, which we found lying dim, and of a leaden colour, in the Books of Dryasdust, is really in itself of dim nature; trivial, little worth remembering. An Age of tobacco and other kinds of *smoke*. An Age of theory without practice; old theory ceasing to be practicable, new not yet becoming so. Everywhere imminent, unconscious Decay struggles with unconscious Newbirth. Struggle and wrestle as yet all dark; inarticulate contention, smoky ineffectuality,—smoke without visible fire! Fire there is; but it lies deep under the fallen and falling leaves of a Past Time, which are not yet consumed, not yet understood to be consumable. What a most poor spirit has taken possession of your Bacons and Raleighs! Within high-stalking Formulas there walks a Reality fast verging towards the sordid. Hungry Valet-ambition, drunken brutal Sensuality abound, on this hand; and on that, empty Hypocrisy not conscious that it is such. Not conscious: if your Æthiopian never saw light, how can he surmise that he is black? He scorns the foul insinuation; has a vindictive feeling, as of injured innocence. Not the least fatal and hateful Hypocrisy is that same which never dreams that it is hypocritical.

Men wear bushel-breeches, filled out with bran, in that age; and so, you may figuratively say, do things. Such breeches are a world too wide for the shrunk shank, which is fast shrinking thinner and thinner, which really ought to be quitting the streets now, as no longer roadworthy! Much that fancies itself to be a dress is becoming a questionable masquerade. For there is a Reality in England other than the somewhat sordid one with high-stalking Formulas at Whitehall. A fire does exist; though deephidden under brown leaves and exuviæ, and as yet testifying itself only by smoke! Musical Spensers have sung their frosty Allegory of Theoretic Heroisms, Faery Queens; and lo, here is an unmusical Knewstubs and Company persuading every one that there ought to be a Practical Heroism. Rugged enough this latter, but noble beyond all nobleness. Not in frosty Allegories, in fantastic Dreamlands; but here in this Earth, say they, in this England,—at your feet, Peter, and at yours, Jack, —is a steep Path of Hercules, which does actually lead to the Eternal Heavens. That is news, old and yet extremely new; important if credible. Knewstubs knows it of a truth; reads it in his God's-Book, in his God-inspired heart;—and has one thing needful, that he may himself accomplish it. That he may himself accomplish it, this is the thing needful for Knewstubs; not, except as subsidiary thereto, that he may persuade all men or any man of it. The surer is he to persuade all men.

This was the unaccountable element in English affairs which a second Solomon had to face, and was altogether unable to understand,—which had not yet become thoroughly conscious of itself,—a conjuncture full of trouble to both King and People.

One merit can never be denied this sorry generation of James: That it is generating its Successor. When once our said smoke, which we see waxing ever thicker, catches fire and becomes flame, there will be a generation luminous enough.

CHAPTER V

BOG OF LINDSEY

[1605]

It is not naturally a romantic region, that Fen Country; for the lover of the picturesque there is little comfort in it. A stagnant land, grown dropsical; where the lazy streams roll with a certain higgling deliberation, as if in doubt whether they would not cease to roll at all, which, indeed, they occasionally do. The land-strata have not been sufficiently heaved up from the Ocean, say the Geologists, with much reason. The upheaval of strata from the ocean-bed may be in excess and give us Alpine snow-mountains, frightful Cotopaxis, Himalayas, with their cataracts and chasms; or in defect, as here, and give us quaking peat-bogs, expanses of fat mud and quagmire.

Not a land of the picturesque, we say; yet a land of some interest to the human soul, as all land is or may become. A gross, unpicturesque land, of reed-grass, weedy-verdure, of mud and marsh; where the scattered hills, each crowned with its Church and hamlet, rise like islands over the continent of peat-bog; and indeed do mostly still bear the name of *Ey*, which in the ancient dialect of all Deutschmen, Angles, Norse, or whatever they are, means *Island*. Coveney, Swavesey, Sheepey, Horsey, not to speak of Ramsey, Eel-ey or Ely, and so many other *eys* and *eas*,—they are beautiful to me, with their little Parish Churches in the continent of marsh there; better than picturesque. The leaders of your conquering Danes, East Angles or whoever they were, the captain of fifty, the captain of ten, had settled each on his dry knoll here, each with his merry men round him; and set to tillage, fishing, fowling, graziery and the peaceable cutting of peat. Prosperous operations, which in the course of fertile

CHAP. V.] BOG OF LINDSEY 59

centuries, have come to what we now see. The huts of his merry men are this hamlet, this town with its towers and markets; his private chapel, what is notablest of all, has grown to be this Parish Church! The merry men, I find, are still here, grubbing and stubbing in a very laborious manner; but the Captain himself has gone elsewhither, and is somewhat to seek nowadays! Meanwhile, we have it in indisputable rhyme that 'the monks in Ely were singing 'beautifully (*merry*) as Cnut the King came rowing through 'that quarter,' who straightway ordered a landing that he might hear them at their vespers,—the noble pious Cnut with an ear for *music* of every kind, and a soul!

> Merie sungen the Muneches binnen Ely
> Tha Cnut Ching rew therby.
> Roweth cnites noer the lant,
> And here we thes Muneches saeng.[1]

How the same King Cnut, storm-stayed at Soham, sat indignant in the imperfect frost, unable either to row or ride; with his Christmas coming on at Ely, in sight of him, yet unattainable: how he stormed and fumed; and did at last get through by help of a pikestaff and his own feet, guided by a happy peasant dextrous in bog-topography, to whom lands and quagmires were given for his service; and so kept

---

[1] This is the first and only surviving stanza of an impromptu song made by King Canute on the occasion of his visiting Ely, probably for the first time. As the King, accompanied by his Queen Emma, approached the church of Ely, he began to hear a kind of harmonious sound; drawing nearer and listening attentively, 'he perceived it to be the Monks in the Church singing their Canonical hours. The King in the joy of his heart broke out into a Song which he made extempore on the occasion, calling on the nobles that were about him to join in the chorus. This Song in the English or Saxon language . . . was long preserved by the Ely Monks, for the sake of the royal Author.'—Bentham's *History of the Church of Ely*, p. 95. The following is a Latin version of the stanza:

> Dulce cantaverunt Monachi in Ely,
> Dum Canutus Rex navigaret prope ibi.
> Nunc, Milites, navigate propius ad terram,
> Et simul audiamus Monachorum harmonium.

his Christmas at Ely after all: this and other the like facts are indisputable to Dryasdust.

Who knows what strange personages and populations have dwelt in this Fen country, since it first rose into the sunlight 'by volcanic agency,' or otherwise: Iceni, shaggy Fenmen, Norsemen; horrid Crocodile Ichthyosauri, wading in the mixed element! There have been Roman conquerors, East-Anglian conquerors, Danish conquerors in extreme abundance. Nay, holy Guthlac, when he fled away from men in his solitary boat and built a turf hut at Crowland, thinking he might have leave to pray there in the desolate swamp country, was beset with a populace of Devils, real Imps, the produce of Guthlac and this Fen region,—scandalous gorbellied, bowlegged, lobster-nosed little scoundrels, all dancing round him with foul gestures and cacklings; till he got them subdued by obstinate devotion and spade husbandry; and gradually a Crowland Chapel, and even Crowland Abbey sacred to Guthlac, was built there. Not to speak of devout Saxon virgins, kings' daughters some of them, 'and maids after 'twelve years of marriage,' flying through these watery wastes to escape the snares of the world; founding convents of Ely, —but for whom Cnut had never heard that music. Then also there were kings or kings' sons, lying sick to death; who, in the crisis of their agony, saw Shining Ones, clear presence of this or the other Saint, promising in audible sphere-music, celestial enough, that they should not die but live; who, thereupon, very naturally, decided on founding Abbeys, at Ramsey, or where they had the means. Strange enough productions of this Fen country;—foreign enough, to be bone of our bone! And here again, I apprehend, is a very strange production of the Fen country; this little Boy Oliver, whom we saw in a late Chapter, looking at the Hinchinbrook Phantasmagory, he himself a very real object! He too, under new guises, is of kindred to the devout kings' sons and persecuted virgins; perhaps also to Guthlac and his escort of Devils.

Be this as it may, one thing is certain: The progress of improvement being considerable in those days, there has arisen in Huntingdonshire and elsewhere some determination to have the Fen regions drained. An important speculation; how often canvassed at the fireside of Mr. Robert Cromwell and the Golden or Gilt Knight, among others! Speculative friends of agriculture see it to be possible; there has long been talk of it; ought it not now to be done?

Something from of old was done; something by her late Majesty; nay, by old Romans, by Norse, East Anglians, oldest Welsh Iceni and St. Guthlac;—no genuine son of Adam could live here without trying to drain a little, and make the footing under him firmer! Something was done; but alas, how little. Old works should be repaired; new greater ones attempted. Clough's-Cross bulwark with its wooden tide-gates and flood-gates, engineers are of opinion you could decidedly improve it. Morton's Leam, the old Bishop Morton's, could you not 'scour'[1] that, and make it run; to carry off the soaking Nen waters as it once did? Salter's Lode too, and so many other lodes and leams—but the Abbeys are all suppressed, given to the cormorants; and the Nen-deluges and several other things, ooze at their leisure, none bound to take heed of them.[2] The good old Bishop Morton, he had 'a brick tower' built for himself in those drowned regions: there on his specula commanding many a mile of wet waste, he surveyed with extensive view the domains of mud; and watched how, in the distance or near, his spademen in due gangs were getting some victory over it. Venerable good old man; a pleasure to me to see him on his brick tower there, though four centuries off! He, for one, I think, is a sane son of Adam; bent to conquer Chaos a little, on more sides than one. For I love to believe he was a good spiritual Overseer too, and did feats as Priest, as Pontiff and Lord Chancellor: a sworn enemy of Chaos, I do hope, whether it appeared as Lawyer's cobwebs, as

[1] Dredge. [2] Camden.

mud-swamps, or human stupidity, as Devil's disorder of whatever kind !—

And now his long good Leam, we say, lies stagnant, ineffectual; lapped in sedges and foul green slumber : that, at least, you could scour and set flowing. That and much else. These enormous Fens ought in short to be conquered. From the big Bog of Lindsey by Humber mouth, westward by Ramsey Mere, to Huntingdon, to Market Deeping in the head of Norfolk, what a tract of land to be gained from the mud-gods,—worth Sterling money if you had it ! Positively our River Ouse should not be left to run in this way, submerging whole districts : bank him, bulwark him, hold him up by sheer force ; and instead of mud and ducks, with summer hay, let there be cattle-pastures and corn.

Such is the talk of speculative friends of agriculture; such is the deliberate Public Report which the leading men in those Fen Countries, Sir Oliver and Mr. Robert Cromwell among others, after endless volumes of speech and inquiring, are now prepared to sign,—and will sign, 'at Huntingdon 'this tenth of May 1605,' legibly to Dugdale and others.[1] What speech and argumentative speculation they have had ; what personal inspection, ridings singly or in bodies, to and fro, enough probably to go round the globe, shall be left to the reader. Quantities of talk and vain riding are necessary; an obscure groping round the business, till once you get upon the business. So many vested interests to be conciliated ; town navigations along those sleepy Rivers; summer rights of pasturage and turf, winter rights of duck-fowling, with net, decoy-duck and cross-bow ! But the draining is decided to be possible. Pump up your leams and lodes, by windmill or otherwise, into this uplifted Ouse,—if we once had him lifted. It can be done 'without injury to any navigation,' say Sir Oliver, Mr. Robert, and fourteen others. They say and affirm that it can be done; but from the potential to the

[1] Noble's Cromwell, i. 83.

indicative mood there is always such a distance.[1] Before this possible thing can be done, what quantities of new vain speech must condense themselves, and ridings that would go round the world shrink into a point, '*the* point' as men call it!

'All speech,' exclaims Smelfungus in his dark way, 'is of
'vaporous character, and has to condense itself; speech and
'much else has to condense itself, in such confused manner as
'it can: these swampy Fen Countries are an emblem to thee
'of human History in general! The very meanings of speech,
'like the sound of it, do they not swiftly pass away? The hot-
'test controversial jangling which drives all hearts to madness,
'this too is a transient vibration in the lower regions of the
'atmosphere; this, too, if thou wait a little, will condense
'itself and not be. Vain even to print it and reprint it; its
'meaning for the heart of man is lost. That old brown stack
'of Pamphlets of the Seventeenth Century, full of hot fury
'then, is grown all torpid to us now, dead to us as ditch water
'and peat. Our loud words, our passionate thoughts, the
'whole world's angry jargon, how it hangs like a general cir-
'cumambient very transitory *air*; like a vapour mounting up
'a little way from the ferment of Existence,—then anon
'condensing itself, sinking quietly into the general Bog of
'Lindsey, to lie soaking there.

'How opulent, flourishing were those past generations;
'how silent, contracted now, compressed into black *caput*
'*mortuum*,—even as in Lindsey here! The generations were

---

[1] Nothing came of this speculation: it was not until 1629 that the first practical attempt to deal with the Great Level was made by Cornelius Vermuyden, a Dutch engineer. The opposition offered to the scheme by the neighbouring landowners, the fishermen and willow-cutters, was violent; and the engineer's plans were impracticable. It has been said that 'One of the principal labours of modern engineers has been to rectify Vermuyden's errors.' For a long time the business lingered. In 1649 an Act was passed for resuming the work under better auspices; a New Company of Adventurers was formed (of which Oliver Cromwell was a member), and proceeded vigorously with a New Bedford Level, —the one still existing. And in three or four years more the work was completed, after a sort. The Fen-office was burnt in the Great Fire (1666), and a complete account of the Draining of the Fens cannot now be written.

'like annual flowerages, the centuries like years. For them
'too, Life blossomed up, covered with verdure, with boughs,
'and foliage and fruit; and the sun and the stars shed on it
'motherly influences for a season, nourishing it sumptuously;
'and—and—the season once spent, all verdure died into
'brownness, fell away as dead leaves, as dead boughs and
'trunks; mouldering in huge ferment of decay; till it sank
'all as inarticulate rottenness, as black-brown dust, compressed
'by natural gravitation, and continued influence of weather,
'into the black stratum of morass we admire in these Fen
'Countries.—Yes, brother, the leafy, blossoming, high-tower-
'ing past century becomes but a stratum of peat in this
'manner; the brightest century the world ever saw will sink
'in this fashion; and thou and I, and the longest-skirted
'potentates of the Earth,—our memories and sovereignties,
'and all our garnitures and businesses, will one day be dug
'up quite indistinguishable, and dried peaceably as a scantling
'of cheap fuel. Generation under generation, even as here in
'the Bog of Lindsey, such is History; and all higher genera-
'tions press upon the lower, squeezing them ever thinner:
'how thin, for example, has Hengst and Horsa's generation
'become! About Hengst and his voyage hither, the greatest
'act of emigration ever heard of, you cannot distil a good
'written page from all the Nenniuses and Newburys: and our
'present inconsiderable paper Emigration Act, before we get
'it passed,—this, with the discussions on it, I suppose, might
'clothe St. James's Park in pica! Is not the Hengst-and-
'Horsa speech-vapour condensed into bog-moisture, to a
'wonderful degree?

'Melancholy, great: like the realms of the Death-goddess;
'—like the study of Rushworth and Company! How all the
'growths of this feracious Earth, what richest timber-forests,
'corn-crops, cattle-pastures, Periodic Literatures and Systems
'of Opinion, we have weaved upon it, do crumble fast or slow
'into a jungly abbatis, the living and still verdant struggling
'with the dead and brown; and at a certain depth below the

'present, all is become black bog-substance, all!' Or nearly all, thou dark Smelfungus! subjoin we.

'Vain to attempt reviving what is dead,' continues he; '*caput mortuum* will not live again. Have an eye for 'knowing what is extinct; it will stead thee well. How 'many interesting Neo-Catholic, Puseyite, and other plu- 'perfect persons, like zealous officers of a spiritual Humane 'Society, one beholds struggling, with breathless, half-frantic 'assiduity, with surgical bellows, hot-cloth friction, and gal- 'vanic apparatus, to restore you some vital spark which has 'irrevocably fled! Alas, friends, the dead horse will never 'kick again, except galvanically; never drag your waggon for 'you again. Try ye, meanwhile, what utmost virtue is in 'galvanism, unweariedly; till absolute putrefaction supervene, 'and galvanism itself produce no motion; and all men depart 'sorrowful, saying, "It is ended, it *is* dead!" Humane- 'Society galvanisers of this sort fill me with sorrow, but also 'with a kind of love. Idolaters,—yes probably: they are not 'innocent; but they are well-intentioned, and are they not 'unhappy? As for the other, vulture or vampire class, who 'have their own base uses in the matter; and scandalously, 'against Nature, keep the venerable Dead unburied that they 'may feed upon them: of these, not to speak things too 'savage, we will say nothing.'—

Our dark friend's concluding sentences are also notable: 'In the Bog of Lindsey,' says he, 'there lie wondrous animal 'remains. Huge black oaktrees; the white wood all gone; 'the incorruptible heart of oak, a venerable thing, alone re- 'maining. What fossil elks, enormous mammoths, of extinct 'species some of them, are raised from bogs. Such also in 'Historical Museums, belectured by fatal Dryasdust, I have 'seen,—figuratively speaking. A mammoth all gone to the 'osseous framework; its eyes become huge eyeholes, filled with 'the circumfluent clay. For it is all sunk in clay; down 'deep, in the dead deeps. Poor mammoth,—in its stomach, 'they say,—in the place that had been its stomach,—lay

E

'a bundle of recognisable half-eaten reeds. Reedgrass cropped
'in the antediluvian ages, with a tongue that had muscles and
'taste before the Deluge, but has none now. This mammoth,
'too, had its life. I tell thee, the world lay all green and
'alive round it then, and was not inert blind bog as thou
'seest it now. Not in any wise, thou fatal Dryasdust !—

'If History be the sister of Prophecy, if Past be Divine as
'Future, and Time on his mysterious bosom bear the two, as
'Night does her twins,[1] then History also is miraculous. Not
'lightly shalt thou persuade me to write a History of Oliver !
'Is it I that can bid full muscles, skin and life, clothe these
'dry fossil bones; the half-eaten reedgrass furnish itself with
'new gastric juices; and create an appetite under the ribs
'of death !'

CHAPTER VI

GUY FAUX AND THE GUNPOWDER PLOT

[1605]

WHAT is singular, the Dovetail Papers contain no account, or almost none, of the celebrated Gunpowder Treason. A curious proof, wonderful and joyful, how all dies away in this world,—battles as well as covenanted love, and how the bitterest antagonisms sink into eternal silence, and peaceably blend the dust of their bodies for new corn soil to the succeeding generations. Punic Hannibal and Roman Scipio are a very quiet pair of neighbours now. Guy Faux, who had nearly sent the British Solomon and all his Parliament aloft into the infinite realms by chemical explosion, has become, like Solomon himself, little other than a ridiculous chimera. 'I was gratified,' says Dovetail, 'on the 5th of
'November last, to meet an enormous Guy in the New Cut;[2]

---

[1] As represented by Thorwaldsen's celebrated *rilievo*, Night soaring heavenward with twins in her arms.
[2] A Street in London, joining the Waterloo and Blackfriar's Roads.

'got up with an accuracy of costume, in which this generation
'may surely pride itself. He seemed in stature about twelve
'feet or upwards; he was seated in a cart drawn by idle
'apprentices and young miscellaneous men, who shouted deep
'but not fiercely as they drew. The face, of due length, was
'axe-shaped as it were, all tending towards one enormous
'nose; the wooden eye looking truculently enough in its fixed
'obduracy from its broad sleek field of featureless cheek.
'Flood of black horsehair shaded this appropriate countenance,
'streamed copious over back and shoulders, and gave a tragic
'impressiveness to the figure. The white band was not for-
'gotten; nor square, close coat, with its girdle of black
'leather. The hat, about the size and shape of a chimney-pot,
'set in a pewter trencher, I considered to be of blackened
'pasteboard. To such length has useful knowledge extended
'among us; down even to the apprentices and burners of
'Faux. Thus travelled Faux in appropriate costume through
'the New Cut, few pausing to glance at him, still fewer
'offering any coin for the support of him. If here and there
'some passenger regarded him with a brief grim smile, it was
'much.... I passed along, musing upon many things. To
'such chimerical conditions do the sublimest Forms in History
'come at last; no bloodiest Truculence can continue terrible
'forever; how in this all-forgetting world do Angels of Doom,
'at which every heart quailed, dwindle into pasteboard Buga-
'boos; and does Thor, the Thundergod, whose stroke smote
'out Valleys of Chamouni, the angry breath of whose nostrils
'snuffling through his red beard, was once the whistling
'of the storm-blast over heaven, become Jack the Giant
'Killer. My Lord Montague of Boughton left 40$l.$[1] to keep
'alive the memory of this great mercy, while Time endured;
'and in a space of 240 years it has come to what we see!
'—There is no contest eternal but that of Ormuzd and
'Ahriman; the rest are all, except as elements of that, in-
'significant.'

[1] Collins.

Well, and are there in History many sterner figures than Guido, standing there with his dark-lantern beside the six-and-thirty barrels of gunpowder in Whinniard's cellar under the Parliament?[1] To such length has he, for his part, carried his insight into the true interests of this world. Guido is a very serious figure; has used reasonable effort to bring himself to the stickingplace and Hercules' choice of Roads. No Pusey Dilettante, poor spouting New Catholic or Young England in white waistcoat; a very serious man come there to do a thing, and die for it if there be need. Papal Antichrist, the Holy Father, whom Fate has sent irrevocably towards Chaos and the Night-empire, this Guido will recall again to light,—if not by Heaven's aid then by Hell's. He is here with his six-and-thirty barrels of gunpowder in Whinniard's cellar; to blow up King and Parliament.—It is remarkable how in almost all world-quarrels, when they came to extremity there have been Infernal Machines, Sicilian Vespers, Guido Powder-barrels and such like called into action; and worth noting how hitherto not one of them in this world has prospered.[2] No, my desperate friends, that is not the way to prosper. Can the Chariot of Time be stopt or hastened by clutching at its wheel-spokes in that mad manner? You may draw at the Chariot itself or draw against it; but do not meddle with its wheel-spokes. Besides, in all cases, I consider the Devil an unsafe sleeping-partner, to be rejected, not to be admitted at any premium; by whose aid no cause yet was ever known to prosper.

A changed time truly, since Guido Faux was a figure of flesh and blood steering his wild way between Heaven and Hell; instead of a pasteboard one travelling the New Cut to collect Anticatholic pence for fireworks! A most truculent fact that of Guido, if we will meditate it. Gentlemen of

[1] The cellars under the House were let to coal-dealers, etc.
[2] So also with the modern dynamitards.

honour, of what education, reflexion, breeding and human culture there was going, have decided after much study to solve the riddle of Existence for themselves in this manner. 'Heard are the Voices,' speaking out of the Eternity to man that he shall be a man; and it is in this way that Guido Faux and Company interpret them. They have communed together by word of mouth and glance of eye; have clubbed money, sworn on the Evangels; and Jesuit Garnet,[1]—many looking askance on the business, has said, 'Well-done.' And so King and Parliament are to fly aloft, and papal Antichrist is to be recalled again to light.—Reader, it was not a Drury Lane scenic exhibition to be done by burnt cork, bad Iambics, and yellow funnel-boots, this of Guido's; but a terribly pressing piece of work not to be got done except by practical exertion of oneself! I have a view of the renting of Whinniard's cellar; the landing of those six-and-thirty casks of gunpowder there. Living Guido stands there, a tough heart beating in him, dark-lantern and three matches in hand;[2] and there will be a fireblast and peal of Doom, not often witnessed in this world; and one Parliament at least shall end in an original manner! And Papal Antichrist, the Holy Father, shall resume his old place, and England unite herself with the old Dragons, instead of the new-revealed Eternal God. Had not his Majesty, seemingly again by special inspiration, detected in this dark mystery the faintest light-chink ever seen,—an ambiguous phrase in a letter,[3] fit for such a pair of vigilant quick-glancing goggle-eyes; and, pressing forward, torn out the whole fiery secret of it—to the wonder, the terror, the horror and devout gratitude of all men. Flagging imagination, in this new element of ours, can do no justice to it, need not try to conceive it; imagination even of Shakspeare cannot. Faux lies in stern durance; austere, lynx-eyed judges round him, with their racks and interrogatories, their feline lynx-

[1] Henry Garnet, Provincial of the Jesuits in England.
[2] *State Trials*, ii. 201.   [3] See *ante*, p. 43.

eyes, as it were all pupil together, dilated into glow of rage and terror; able to see in the dark. Three-score [1] Apostolic young gentlemen ride with the speed of Epsom through slumbering England, into Warwickshire, designing as they profess to hunt there. The Warwickshire 'hunt' ascertaining how the matter is, swiftly dissipates itself again; with terror lest they themselves prove cozened foxes, and experience not what the hunter but what the chased fox in these circumstances feels. The three score Apostolic young gentlemen have to gallop again for life, for life; the Warwickshire Posse Comitatus galloping at their heels. And 'on 'the edge of Warwickshire at Stephen Littleton's house,' O Heavens, while the poor fellows dried their gunpowder, it caught fire, scorched two of them almost to death, or into delirium. And the others 'stood upon their guard,' as hunted human truculences chased into their last lair might; and Sheriff and Posse had a deadlift effort to make; and their faces are grimed with powder-smoke, bathed in sweat; and faces lay grim, minatory in the last death-paleness in Stephen Littleton's house there;—and they were all killed or else taken wounded, and then hanged and headed. And horror, wonder, and awe-struck voice of thanksgiving rose consentaneous from broad England, and the Lord Montague founded 'an endowment of 40*l*. (annually) that the memory ' of the deliverance might be celebrated, in all time to come, ' in the town of Northampton.' And in English History there was never done a thing of graver tragic interest than this which Dovetail now sees reduced to pasteboard in the New Cut. What dust of extinct lions sleeps peaceably under our feet everywhere! The soil of this world is made of the dust of Life, the geologists say; limestone and other rocks are made of bone dust variously compounded.

But was not this a notable counterpart to the Hampton Court phenomenon; that in its dreary grey, not yet got to the length of being luminous; this in its expiring splendour,

---

[1] *State Trials*, ii. 211.

going off in a flash of hell-fire? One would have thought his Majesty had got enough of Papism;—England, in general, thought very heartily so. His Majesty had no hatred of the Pope, except as a rival to King's Supremacy; had at one time wanted a Scotch Cardinal. His Majesty did find good, when a certain old negotiation with the Pope came to light, to lay the blame of it on Secretary Elphinstone, the Lord Balmerino;[1] to have Balmerino condemned to die, and then pardon him again. A Scotch Cardinal would have been a sort of conveniency, he thought. Kings are peculiarly circumstanced; especially kings that know not the heart of their Nation, Ormuzd from Ahriman.

[1] Sir John Scott of Scotstarvet says that Elphinstone (Lord Balmerino) 'was in such favour with King James, that he craved the reversion of secretary Cecil's place, at the king's coming to the Crown of England, which was the beginning of his overthrow; for the said secretary Cecil wrought so that, having procured a letter which had come from King James, wherein he promised all kindness to the Roman See and Pope, if his holiness would assist him to attain to the Crown of England;—this letter the said secretary Cecil showed in the king's presence in the Council of England; whereupon King James, fearing to displease the English nation, behoved to disclaim the penning of this letter, and lay the blame thereof on his secretary, whom a little before that he had made Lord Balmerino: to whom he wrote to come to court; where being come, for exoneration of the king, he behoved to take on him the guilt of writing that letter.' *The Staggering State of the Scots Statesmen* (Edin., 1754), 59-60.

The King took immense pains to prove that he had had no hand in writing this letter; that the signature to it had been got surreptitiously; and there is evidence, independently of Balmerino's confession which might have been a forced or bribed one, to prove pretty certainly that James was, technically at least, innocent of this particular charge. The king, however, had written compromising letters to the Cardinals and Italian Princes; and in his 'Premonition to all the most mighty Monarchs, Kings, Free Princes, and States of Christendom,' which appeared some time afterwards, he does not even mention Balmerino's Confession. Professor Gardiner (*History of England*, ii. 34) says: 'It is possible that, by the time that book appeared, James had remembered that the signature of the letter to the Pope was but a small part of the charge against him, and had become unwilling to call attention to the fact that, at all events, he had ordered letters to be written to the Cardinals.'

CHAPTER VII

KNIGHTING OF PRINCE HENRY

[1610]

BEN JONSON'S MASQUES

ON Wednesday the 30th of May, 1610, or Thursday the 31st, Prince Henry, hope of these Lands, was created Knight of the Bath; he, and certain other highly select persons: with an explosion of rich silk dresses, cavalcadings, naval combats, peals of ordnance, and 'most stately Masques,' enough to darken the very face of the Sun.

For Norroy and Clarentiaux and the proper Upholsterers were busy; and dignitaries, and Lord Mayors and Lord Mayors' barges, and 'fifty-four of the Companies of London,' all puffed out in scarlet and the usual trimmings. And there was riding in state to Richmond on high horses, and sailing in state from Richmond in gilt barges; and more than once 'the River was in a manner paved with boats.' And 'at Chelsea there was a Dolphin upon whom sat 'Neptune, and upon a Whale,' presumably of leather, 'there 'sat a Watergoddess; both of whom made certain Speeches 'unto the Prince,'—Mr. Inigo Jones and rare Ben Jonson, incited by the authorities, having done their best. And then the young Knights, with his young Highness, 'walked round' this chamber, and afterwards round that; and sat 'in white 'linen coifs,' and again 'in grey cloaks,' poor young gentlemen; and then rose, and went to prayers; and had spurs; and redeemed their spurs 'with a noble each to the King's 'Cook, who stood at the Chapel door with his cleaver in his 'hand';—went to prayers, we say, and to dinner, and finally to sleep, in a most surprising manner;[1] London and the contemporary populations looking on with breathless veneration.

This immense event, and explosion of events, enough to

[1] Stow, 899.

CHAP. VII.] KNIGHTING OF PRINCE HENRY

deafen England,—who is there that would reawaken? It shall sleep well amid the brown leaves and exuviæ; wet condensed portion of the Bog of Lindsey, with one tear of ours added to it,—forever and a day. Alas, standing there in a bewildered manner 'at the Chapel door in Whitehall,' beside his Majesty's Cook with the gilt cleaver; bewildered; jostled by so many shadows, we have to ask: In these boundless multitudes crowding all avenues, is there no soul then whatever whom we in the least know? None or almost none; they are leaden shadows to us. Sardanapalus Hay, yes he steps out a new-made Bath Knight, pays his gold noble among the others; he is there,—whom one does not want to know. 'Master Edward Bruce' too, a handsome Scotch youth, Master of Kinloss, like to be Lord of Kinloss in the Shire of Fife; he is there,[1] a shadow less leaden than the others. His new spurs, his proud-glancing eyes do lighten on us somewhat,—with a tragic expression: he shall die in duel this one;[2] it is sung by the Fates. And 'Master 'William Cavendish,' heir-presumptive of the Shrewsburys at Worksop, heir of Welbeck, Bolsover and much else; an elegant youth, brimful of accomplishments and teachable sciences; he also takes a kind of colour; him we shall meet again. The rest——Heavens, how they have vanished, with their fresh-coloured cheeks, bright clothes, breathless veneration; and are silent; all but a doomed few who roam, yet for a season as shrieking ghosts, in the Peerage-Books and torpid rubbish-mountains of my erudite Friend!—— But truly the explosion itself was audible and visible, nay, as it were, tangible to all England, that Summer of 1610: for you had to pay your dues on the King's son being knighted; —wherein, however, his Majesty instructed the bailiffs to deal gently for peace's sake, and be lax rather than rigorous. It appears likewise that 'Sir John Holles[3] of Haughton was 'made Comptroller of the Prince's Household'; an appointment none of us can object to.

[1] See list in Stow, p. 901.   [2] See *post*, p. 99.   [3] See *post*, p. 202 *n*.

But the thing I had to remark above all others was, that Ben Jonson composed the Masque.[1] O Ben, my rare Friend, is this in very deed thou? There in the body, with thy rugged sagacities and genialities; with thy rugged Annandale face and unquenchable laughing eyes;—like a rock hiding in it perennial limpid wells! My rare friend, there is in thee something of the lion, I observe:—thou art the rugged Stonemason, the harsh, learned Hodman; yet hast strains too of a noble softness, melodious as the voice of wood-doves, fitfully thrilling as the note of nightingales, now and then! Rarer union of rough clumsy strength with touches of an Ariel beauty I have not met with. A sterling man, a true Singer-heart,—born of my native Valley too: to whom and to which be all honour![2]

Ben made many Masques; worked in that craft for thirty years and more, the world applauding him: he had his pension from the Court, his pension from the City;—if you have leather Dolphins afloat, you must try to get a little music introduced into them withal. Certainly it is a circumstance worth noticing that surly Ben, a real Poet, could employ himself in such business, with the applause of all the world; it indicates an Age very different from ours. An Age full of Pageantry, of grotesque Symbolising,—yet not without something in it to symbolise. That is the notable point. Innumerable Masques and masqueradings; a general Social Masquerade, it almost seems to us, with huge bulging costumes and upholstery, stuffed out with bran and tailors' trimmings: yet within it there still is a Reality, though a shrunken one, an ever farther shrinking one. Ben Jonson, Francis Bacon, and other such can still work as tiremen for it. How could it stand on its feet otherwise? A Social Masquerade fallen *altogether* empty collapses on the pavement, amid the shrieks of the bystanders,—as in these last times of ours we see it sorrowfully do! To the heart of

---

[1] Called 'Prince Henry's Barriers.'
[2] Ben himself was born in Westminster; his Grandfather, in Annandale.

Ben, of Francis, and of all persons, here was still a real King and a real Prince; whose knighthoods, cavalcadings, and small and great transactions, the Melodies and Credibilities had not yet disowned.——

I myself, under certain conditions, have often assisted at Ben's Masques; looked at the quaint Court, in their fardingales and stuffed breeches, treading solemn dances, 'flying out 'in winged chariots' or otherwise;—and endeavoured to make acquaintance with a fair friend or two on such occasions. Lucy Percy I have seen, though she saw not me: the paragon of women; sprightliest, gentlest, proudest; radiating continual soft arrows from her eyes and wit; which pierce innumerable men,—pierce Sardanapalus Hay for one. Anne Clifford too, a somewhat stern young maiden, full of sense, full of heart and worth; whom I think a certain young Sackville of the House of Buckhurst—'O Mistress Anne!'—is sometimes glancing at. These I have seen at Masques of Ben's; much admiring. The Masques themselves were not undelightful to me.—

But certainly of all Ben's Masques, the one I should have liked to see had been that one given at Holmby Castle in Northamptonshire seven years ago,[1] when Queen Anne first came southward out of Scotland, and the little Prince [Henry] with her, then a small boy. For there issued Satyrs singing from the real bosquets of Holmby Park, and Queen Mabs discoursing, not irrationally, as her Majesty and little Son advanced; and 'two bucks,' roused at the right moment, were 'happily shot,' real bucks which you could dine from: and then on the morrow, there appears a personage called NOBODY; he is to speak some prologue to a general voluntary morricedance of the Northamptonshire Nobility assembled there; and his complete Court-suit is,—let any and all readers guess it,—

---

[1] This was the Masque called 'The Satyr.' Carlyle has noted in his copy of Jonson's Works (Barry Cornwall's Edition, London, 1842): 'This' [*The Satyr*] 'must have been presented at *Holmby* to Queen Anne as she came from Scotland with the Prince.'

'a very large pair of breeches buttoning round his neck, and 'his hands coming out at the pockets.' My rare friend!—Prince Henry was there, a boy of eleven years.[1] Prince Charles was not there: he, too, will get to know Holmby and its Bosquets, by and by, perhaps?—

Consider also how the 'wit-combats at the Mermaid' were even now going on! For the divine world-famous 'Elder Dramatists' were as yet new Dramatists, obscurely gliding about, as mere mortals; in very rusty outfit, some of them; lodging in Alsatia, by the 'Green Curtain at Shoreditch,' Blackfriar's Playhouse, or God knows where. London with its half-million population found some hutch, garret or rusty cranny somewhere, for the lodging of these among others. And at the Mermaid, of an evening, we assemble, if we have any cash. And there are Ben and William Shakspeare in wit-combat, sure enough; Ben bearing down like a mighty Spanish War-ship, fraught with all learning and artillery; Shakspeare whisking away from him,—whisking right through him, athwart the big hulk and timbers of him; like a miraculous Celestial Light-ship, woven all of sheet-lightning and sunbeams! Through the thick rhinoceros skin of my rare Ben there penetrated strange electric influences; and he began to wonder where that pricking of his fell came from! He 'honoured William Shakspeare, on this side 'idolatry, as much as any man.' These are the wit-combats at the Mermaid;—and in two years now they are to cease; and that divine Elder-Dramatist Business, having culminated here, is to decline gradually, and at last die out and sink under the horizon, giving place to other Businesses, probably of graver nature. In 1612,[2] the man Shakspeare retires to Stratford-on-Avon, into a silence which no Dryasdust or obscene creature will ever penetrate;—as it were, a kind of divine silence, and mute dialogue with Nature herself, before departing; sacred, like the silence of the gods!—These are

---

[1] Born, 1592.
[2] Collier's *Life of Shakspeare* (London, 1844), p. 232.

the wit-combats at the Mermaid of an evening, if you chance to be an Elder Dramatist, and have any cash left.

Thus, at any rate, have we got Prince Henry Knighted; one piece of loud labour is not to do again. It was consummated on the evening of Thursday, 31st May, 1610.

Prince Henry, besides being Prince of Wales and Knight, is at present the hope of the world. Some seventeen years of age; really a promising young person,[1] in a world prone to hope. Courageous, frank, serious; not so disinclined to Puritanism, they say. He has a Sister, Princess Elizabeth, now budding into most graceful maidhood; indisputably the flower of this Court. A most graceful, slim, still damsel; with her long black hair and timid deep look,—not without the dash of Gypsy-tragic either. She has something of Mary Queen of Scots, I think, this charming Princess, though not the Papistries, the French coqueteries; and may grow yet to

[1] 'See description of him in Harris,' Carlyle has noted here. Perhaps the reference is to the following, by Sir Charles Cornwallis, quoted by Harris (*Life of James I.*, London, 1814, i. p. 295):—' He was of a comely, tall middle-stature, about 5 ft. 8 in. high, of a strong, straight, well-made body, with somewhat broad shoulders, and a small waist; of an amiable majestic countenance, his hair of an auburn colour, long face and broad forehead, a piercing grave eye, and most gracious smile, with a terrible frown; courteous bearing, and affable; his favour like the sun, indifferently seeming to shine upon all :—naturally shame-faced, and modest,—most patient, which he showed both in life and death. Dissimulation he esteemed most base, chiefly in a prince; not willing, nor by nature being able to flatter, favour, or use those kindly who deserved not his love. Quick he was to conceive anything; not rash but mature in deliberation, yet most constant, having resolved. True of his promise; most secret, even from his youth : so that he might have been trusted in anything that did not force a discovery; being of a close disposition not easy to be known or pried into : of a fearless, noble, heroic and undaunted courage, thinking nothing impossible that ever was done by any. He was ardent in his love to religion; which love, and all the good causes thereof, his heart was bent by some means or other (if he had lived) to have shewed, and some way to have compounded the unkind jars thereof.

' He made conscience of an oath, and was never heard to take God's name in vain. He hated Popery, though he was not unkind to the persons of Papists. He loved and did mightily strive to do somewhat of everything and to excel in the most excellent,' etc.

be Queen of Hearts, if not otherwise a Queen. We have to regret, yet not with an impious unthankfulness, that the Royal Family amounts only to three: Prince Charles and these two. Their Royal Mother, blond and buxom, much given to Masquing, flaunts about ' she and her maids all like ' Nereids, Hamadryads and mythological Nymphs"[1]; a Princess of considerable amplitude of figure, massiveness of feature; philosophic indifferency, good humour and readiness of wit.

Little Prince Charles, it appears, has thoughts of being Archbishop of Canterbury: there is in him a lachrymose solemnity which perhaps might be suitable there. For the rest, he stands badly on his legs, poor youth; shambling somewhat. Likewise, if it ever come to preaching, he will stammer. The Destinies know!

CHAPTER VIII

MATERIAL PROGRESS IN ENGLAND,—IN LONDON ESPECIALLY

[1610-1620]

But England withal is producing something else than Duels[2] and Court-Masques; England, if we knew it, is a very fertile entity in those ages; all budding, germinating, under this Court-litter,—like a garden, in the Spring months, hidden under protective straw! Let us recognise also how true,

---

[1] Wilson, in Kennet, ii. 685.
[2] In a portion of the MS. preceding this chapter there is given a series of Duelling Anecdotes: (1) Sir John Holles of Haughton and Jervase Markham; (2) The Croydon Races, where James Ramsay, of the Dalhousie Ramsays, switched the crown and face of Lord Montgomery, Earl of Pembroke's brother, and the peace was with the utmost difficulty kept; (3) Sir Thomas Dutton and Sir Hatton Cheek.—These anecdotes were printed in *Leigh Hunt's Journal*, Nos. 1, 2, and 6 (1850); and were afterwards (1857) included in Carlyle's Collected Works under the title, 'Two Hundred and Fifty Years ago—a fragment about Duels.' See *Miscellanies*, vi. pp. 211-27 (Liby. Edition).

CHAP. VIII.]   MATERIAL PROGRESS   79

within its limits, is this motto of his Majesty, 'Blessed are
'the Peacemakers.' Gardens and countries cannot grow if you
are continually tearing them up by the ploughshare of War.
Let them have peace; peace even at a great price. If it be
possible, so far as lies in you, study to live at peace with all
men.—In fact the progress of improvement, everywhere in
England, especially in London City; 'the unimaginable ex-
'tension of buildings,'[1] and clearing away of rubbish encum-
brances, 'greater during these last twelve years than for
'fifty years before,' fills my ancient friends and me with
astonishment.

Moorfields, for example, did you know Moorfields before
the year 1606? From innumerable ages, the ground lay
there a wilderness of wreck and quagmire; stagnant with
fetid ditches, heaped with horrent mounds, hollow with unimaginable sloughs, the 'general laystall' of London, and
cloaca of Nature;—so that men, with any nerves left, 'made
'a circuit to avoid it'; the very air carrying pestilence. Thus
had it lain, from the times of William Redbeard, of Sweyn[2]
Double-beard, or far earlier; and the skilfullest persons pronounced all drainage of it impossible;—nevertheless see now
how possible it is. 'Sir Leonard Holiday,' our estimable
Lord Mayor, and 'Master Nicholas Leate,' wealthy Merchant: in the general peace and prosperity, these estimable
citizens decided on draining Moorfields, even contrary to
possibility; and, with the windiest Force of Public Opinion
blowing direct in their faces, calling it '*holiday* work' and
other witty names, they proceeded to get spademen, crafts-
men, proper engineers, and from their own pockets 'made
'large disbursements';—and now you see the work is done!
Instead of Nature's cloaca you have comfortable green
expanse, smooth-nibbled, trodden firm under foot; waving
with hopeful tree-avenues, 'those most fair and royal walks';

[1] Stow, 1021-2.
[2] 'Sven Tvae-Skieg (Twa-Shag, or Fork-beard) Canute's Father; Danish
King;—who lies buried at Gainsborough,—says my erudite friend.'—T. C.

the Force of Public Opinion blowing on it now as a soft zephyr, thankfully, wooingly. Thanks to brave Holiday, to brave Leate; who made 'the disbursements' of money and of courage! Here truly is now a beautiful promenade and artillery-ground; where citizens can take their evening walk of meditation; where on field-days, trained-bands and grand military musters can parade and exercise themselves.

Smithfield, still earlier, has ceased to be Ruffian's Rig; Smithfield in these years is getting drained and paved:[1] firm clear whinstone under your feet; and in the centre a reserved promenade 'strongly railed,'—which, the authorities consider, may be useful as a market by and by. For, indeed, what with carts, what with stalls and new produce, and the tumult of an ever-increasing population, the market streets on market days are becoming as it were impassable. Cheapside, Gracechurch Street, Leadenhall,—look at them on a market day; a hurlyburly without parallel! There are the country carriers, packing, unpacking; swift diligence, thousandfold messagery looking through their eyes; there are the market-stalls, the garden-stuffs, the butteries, eggeries, crockeries; the pigdroves, oxen-droves, the balladsingers, hawkers: 'What d'ye 'lack, What d'ye lack?' It is a hurlyburly verging on distraction; and will actually require new marketplaces, in Smithfield or elsewhere.

But truly, if we should speak of the 'unimaginable ex-'tension' and improvement of this London generally, could Posterity believe us, O my ancient friends? Yet it is a fact. By 'St. Catherine's and Radcliff,' what masses of new buildings; like a town of themselves. See, the Strand, with its row of Town Manorhouses, opens out fieldwards; the miry ragged Lane of Drury has become a firm street, fit for persons of distinction. Northampton House, or Northumberland House, at the end of Whitehall, rivals palaces. By St. Martin's Church, meanwhile, Holborn seems stretching out a limb to Charing; St. Martin's puddle-lane is now an elegant paved

[1] Finished in 1615. Stow, 1023.

CHAP. VIII.] MATERIAL PROGRESS 81

street; as if London and Westminster were absolutely coalescing! What will the limit of these things be? Cheapside paves its house-fronts with broad flagstones;—O Posterity, it is within men's memory when there was an open blacksmith's forge on the North side of Cheap; men openly shoeing horses there. And now it has broad flag-pavements, safe from wheel and horse, even for the maids and children;—and there runs about on it one little Boy very interesting to me: 'John 'Milton,' he says he is; a flaxenheaded, blue-eyed beautiful little object; Mr. Scrivener Milton of Bread Street's Boy: good Heavens!

In brief, flag-pavements are becoming general; and, at least, the 'high causeways' everywhere are getting themselves carted away. 'From Holborn, from the Strand, the Barbican,' from all manner of places go causeways carted off; and the doorsills of mortals see the light. Nay, in these years is not indomitable Sheriff Myddleton digging his New River;—leading that poor river, contrary to the order of Nature, not into the Sea but bodily into human throats! He has got past Theobalds with it, the indomitable man, visible from the King's windows; on 'the 29th day of September, 1613,' he opens his sluices at Islington itself with infinite human gratulation, explosion of trumpet-and-drum music, marchings with spades shouldered, and even, I think, some kind of thanksgiving Psalm, 'as they saw the waters come gushing in.' Truly this London threatens to reach half a million, to be one knows not what! His Majesty issues Proclamations about it, Proclamation on Proclamation that no new houses be built, for it is growing to be a wen.

These things his pacific Majesty sees with pleasure; gives them eloquent permission: he is right willing to give or to do, for all good things, whatsoever will not trouble him too much! He has 'settled Ireland,' they say; by exertion, or by happy luck and forbearance of exertion, he has got, for the first time in recorded History, the bloody gashes of Ireland closed. Rabid carnage, needful and needless, has

F

ceased there; the kind Mother-earth gratefully covering it in; grateful that her Green Island is no longer dyed with horrid red. Ireland, once in the course of ages, has peace. The waste fertilities of Ulster are getting planted with useful Saxon Londoners, useful Danish Scots. Where royal Shane O'Neill, son of the Mudgods, 'ancient' enough, I doubt not, ancient as very Chaos;—where Shane O'Neill roamed, not long since, with bloody axe and firebrand, with usquebaugh, and murderous bluster and delirium, or 'lay rolled up to the neck in mire to cool his drink-fever,'[1] like a literal wild Boar with the addition of whisky and human cunning, —peaceable men now drain bogs, sow wheatfields, spin yarn; 'Coleraine and little Derry, now become London-Derry, are 'their capitals.' May it long continue! These things his pacific Majesty has done, or with approval and convenient furtherance, seen his people do. He is right willing to give every good thing a pat on the back; what inexpensive Charter, Patent or such like it may wish for, he will cheerfully grant.

How willing was he to have seen Silkworms introduced into this country, could a Patent have done it! He encouraged the planting of mulberry trees as the food of silkworms; to 'the ingenious Mr. Stalledge' and another he granted 'a 'Patent for seven years,' encouraging them as he could, to import mulberry-seeds, to raise trees out of them, and plant the same. In all Shires of England the mulberries are planted;[2] at Stratford-on-Avon, says fond tradition, Shakspeare planted a mulberry. Old mulberries still stand here and there in England: planted indisputably by sons of Adam; not indisputably by Shakspeare, by Bacon, still less by Queen Elizabeth, by Sir Thomas More! They yield their

---

[1] Kennet (ii. 409) says of Shane O'Neill: '*A man he was who had stained his hands with blood, and dealt in all the pollutions of unchaste embraces; and so scandalous a glutton and drunkard was he besides, that he would often lie up to the chin in dirt to cool the feverish heats of his intemperate lust.*' (The italics are Kennet's.)

[2] Stow, 894.

sorry berries ever since to this day; but the Silkworms did
not follow: owing to climate or other causes, there came no
silkworm culture into England.

On the other hand, Alum, says my ancient friend, will
succeed. In Yorkshire and elsewhere men are busy digging
Alum; in Yorkshire 'Sir John Bourchier, Sir John Fowlis,'
have Alum-pits; are roasting, steeping the rude clays of
Bridlington, in hopes of getting Alum. Alum is verily
there; but the skill to extract it is rather behindhand: let
us send for Germans, for High or Low Dutchmen, born to
the business; they will teach us a new process! The harsh
styptic Alum, invaluable mordant for dyers, is dug by the
newest processes from Bridlington earth to this day. For a
people that weave, there ought to be Dyers, to be alum. By
Heaven's blessing we can now dye our own cloths; need no
Flemings in Pembrokeshire or elsewhere, to teach us that
secret.

Certainly the Cloth-manufacture does thrive. In Stroud-
water and the Western valleys, white woollen webs, finer than
togas of Roman Senators, stretch openly on tenterhooks; a
goodly spectacle, as you issue from the Cotswold Hills. Leeds,
Yorkshire, Lancashire itself are beginning to excel in woollen
webs. In most English Towns are weavers, are clothiers; the
wives of farmers set their maids to spin on winter nights. Colchester serges are a fabric known to mankind and womankind.
Reading Town clatters multifariously with looms; the stew
of fullers is in it, the hum of old women and spinning-wheels.
There was old Mr. William Laud,[1] dead a few years ago,
what a quantity of 'looms he kept going in his own house';
the jangle of them wont to awaken young Master William, of
a morning, and set him to his parsing-books! Young
Master William is now Dr. William; a small lean man of
forty; President of St. John's College, Oxford, Rector of this,
Vicar of that; King's Chaplain, with hopes to rise at Court
and become great. The jangle of those paternal looms in

[1] Heylin, *Life and Death of W. Laud* (London, 1668), 46.

Reading, buried now under what other jangles, and deafened for the time, lives yet in an obscure way in the memories of Dr. William!

Old Mr. Laud the Clothier at Reading:—nay, was there not, long since, a Jack of Newbury, known in Storybooks, in authentic History? A Weaver Jack comparable to Robber Johnny of Gilnockie: he, by mere weaving, did keep five score of men in his hall; for the king's service too, on occasion! The very Scots are equal to manufacturing. Look at Fife, how it spins linen; Flemish Dutchmen invited over by these Stuart Kings, having taught the trade there. Dunfermline Town, though the king sits no longer in it drinking the blood-red wine, can weave linen shirts;—will teach the very Ulstermen and Irish to make linen.

In many or most English Towns are clothiers, we say: but Gloucestershire, with its Cotswold fleeces, bears the bell; the Manchester wool-*cottons*, I think, are not in such demand as formerly.[1] Nevertheless, Lancashire, Yorkshire, though their wool is half hair, are strangely distinguishing themselves in the coarser fabrics. They weave; they dig alum;—the 'Sheffield Whittles,' with their keen edge, meet me in many markets. Hold on, ye Yorkshire men, ye Lancashire wizards and witches: who knows how far it may carry you! Litherpool, corruptly called Lirpool, Lerpool and Liverpool, has built new fishing-boats, increased its traffic with Ireland: a thriving little village;—may come to rival Chester yet, in the Irish trade and other things! There stands, in a decayed, honeycombed state, a kind of royal castle at Litherpool; 'under keeping of the Lords of Sefton,' this long while: a range of huts, and even houses and warehouses, runs along the Mersey beach there. Sandy heights, sandy flats; scraggy bent-grass far and wide, interspersed with bogs and moory pools; beaten with wild rains;—not a favourable locality, but it may come to something. From 'Chatmosse' and other places a respectable 'unctuous turf' is dug.[2]—O my

---

[1] Camden (Lancashire). [2] Camden.

erudite Friend, what things are growing, under the Whitehall phantasmagory and dead Court-litter thou so pokest in!

CHAPTER IX

SPIRITUAL PROGRESS

[1609-14]

THE AUTHORIZED TRANSLATION OF THE BIBLE (1611)
INTERCOURSE WITH AMERICA AND INDIA

PRECIOUS temporal things are growing [in these years of peace]; priceless spiritual things. We know the Shakspeare Dramaturgy; the Rare-Ben and Elder-Dramatist affair; which has now reached its culmination. Yes; and precisely when the Wit-combats at the Mermaid are waning somewhat, and our Shakspeare is about packing up for Stratford,—there comes out another very priceless thing: a correct Translation of the Bible; that which we still use. Priceless enough this latter; of importance unspeakable! Reynolds and Chadderton petitioned for it, at the Hampton-Court Conference, long since; and now, in 1611, by labour of Reynolds, Chadderton, Dr. Abbot, and other prodigiously learned and earnest persons, 'forty-seven in number,' it comes out beautifully printed; dedicated to the Dread Sovereign; really in part a benefit of his to us.[1] And so we have it here to read, that Book of Books: 'barbarous enough to rouse, tender enough 'to assuage, and possessing how many other properties,' says Goethe;—possessing this property, inclusive of all, add we, That it is written under the eye of the Eternal; that it is of a Sincerity like very Death; the truest Utterance that ever came by Alphabetic Letters from the Soul of Man. Through which, as through a window divinely opened, all men could look, and can still look, beyond the visual Air-firmaments and mysterious Time-oceans, into the Light-sea of Infinitude,

[1] Fuller's *Church History* (London, 1837), iii. 227-45.

into the stillness of Eternity; and discern in glimpses, with such emotions and practical suggestions as there may be, their far-distant longforgotten Home. Emotions and practical suggestions, naturally of most transcendent kind!—And so, the mimic Shakspeare Dramaturgy having gone out, there is another coming, I perceive, whose thunders and splendours are not mimic! In this also the English shall essay themselves. There are Realities which dwarf all Dreams, in this Life of ours; Acted Poesies which reduce all Spoken or Speakable to silence.

Again, may we not call this a germ; this notable little twig of English History, shooting forth in the year 1609;— springing up among the ephemeral dockweeds and luxuriances, perhaps as a mighty Cedar, as an everlasting English Oak to overshadow half the world! By a lucky chance we catch sight of it through the old Logbook of the Ship Sea-venture; Silas Jourdan, the Mate, having been kind enough to jot it down. Discernibly enough, in the summer days of 1609, a Fleet of eight ships from the Port of London is traversing the Atlantic, on a remarkable errand. Eight of them; the chief ship that same Sea-venture, wherein sails Captain Newport, sail Commodore Somers, General Gates, commanders of the whole; a right seaworthy ship of three hundred tons: the Fleet, O reader, is an Emigrant Fleet, bound—to Virginia! Beautiful, is it not, in the waste solitudes of the Atlantic, in the depths of the old centuries, there? Let us step on board with Silas Jourdan, and see how they get on.

For a week or two, says Silas, we had pleasant weather; all right till we reached the Latitude 30°, on the 25th July, when 'a most sharpe and cruell storm' began upon us, threatening nothing short of destruction. The tumbling, the raging and the roaring; mere Chaos broken loose, and your poor small wooden ship, small human crew at wrestle with it,—readers can conceive. Through night and tempest, the winds and fiends of Chaos piping on us! Our ship wears heavily, pitches like a thing driven by devils; springs a big leak. To the pumps, all hands to the pumps! On the morrow morning, where are our seven comrade ships with their Emigrants? All gone; to the sea-bottom or elsewhere: far and wide, in the lurid tempest-light round the horizon, all is empty, mere tumbling water-mountains, wild-piping winds. And the leak does not abate on us; the leak gains on us: All hands to the pump, yarely my men! For three days we pump, and bale with all our 'kettles, baricos and 'buckets'; feeling that we must beat this leak or die. And still the leak gains, and still the wind rages; we, pumping desperate, run blindly before the wind.

What boots it? The leak gains on us, the grim horizon is empty but of tumbling sea-monsters; the ship is filling, sinking: we, at any rate, are dying of sixty hours' fatigue. God in His mercy receive our souls; for our bodies here there is not now any hope. Silent are the pumps, all hands have quitted the pumps; have—gone to bed; dropt down anywhere into very stern sleep. The sinking ship drifts before the wind; Admiral Somers sits wakeful on the poop, where 'he has sat these three days,' Captain Newport too; awake they, saying little, as is like. We are drifting towards death, then. At this hour, in the Middle Aisle of Paul's, they are talking, promenading! Merry England, rugged Mother Earth, farewell forevermore.

See, there under the lee, is there not land; at least rocks, and spray deluges? O heaven, on the chart in these latitudes, is no land but Bermudas; it is Bermudas, the ever-vext Bermoothes! Islands inhabited by mere Demons; where it thunders and lightens, pours down rain and storm forever; and on the black tempest, which the thunderbolt illumines blue, seamen have seen hags riding. Nay, the very Islands shift their place, dancing hither and thither: sailors sent to visit them have sought, for weeks, in vain; could find no Island, only tempests, blue lightning magazines, and images of forked Demons. Such is the ever-vext Bermudas, towards which we are now driving; fatal Isle of Devils!—Nonsense! cries Somers, cries Newport: Or if it were? cry they; a man must have a heart in him to defy the Devils! Cheerily, all hands, O again all hands; and I take the tiller in the name of God!—

O reader, this poor foundering Sea-venture was driven into the 'only inlet' of these rockbound Isles, such being the Divine Will. She bounded in at the top of high water; soused down between two crags, as in a natural dock, and lay there; every soul getting out safe. Their shipstores, 'meal' and so forth, were drenched with brine; but they had saved their lives, man, woman and child. They found a land with no Devils in it, except of their own bringing: a land overgrown with bushy vegetation, 'mulberries, pears, palmettoes, 'stately cedar-trees'; a frondent wilderness rich in fruit; tropical Autumn wedded to Spring. Fruit enough: and what was far better,—plenty of wild pigs ran squeaking in the thickets waiting to be shot and cooked. Better roast-pork, eaten with acidulent tropical fruits, was not often dished to man. These pigs dwelt there, and had been fattening themselves :—' undoubtedly the product of former 'shipwrecks'; in some former shipwreck the ancestors of these had swum ashore, meaning to be ready there. We found 'hawks' also, of an ornamental nature; and 'abundance of 'tobacco.' What could man require more? A new English subject was born to us in this Island, and we called him 'Bermudas.'

Stout Sir George Somers, our noble Admiral, decided on building us a new Ship; and did in the space of fifteen months, with unwearied toil and patience, very destitute of iron and other necessaries, build a Ship of thirty tons; and therewith carried the main body of us to Virginia, after all; where we found the seven comrade ships had arrived,—and need enough of them and of us. Courage, stout Sir George; thou too art doing a bit of English History;—these very pigs of the Bermudas, swimming ashore from shipwreck, were doing somewhat! The reader will be struck to learn that Sir George returning to Bermudas, on a future year when all this was over, to supply Virginia with pork, did gather pork and salt it; but also, alas, did eat roast-pig in over-abundance, and died of a surfeit of roast-pig. Brave man; of large appetite and large heart: let the earth of these Bermuda Islands, no longer 'Islands of Devils,' but human 'Somers 'Islands,' lie light on him: and his memory be not unvenerable to us![1]—

As for Virginia, this fine settlement, since it was first planted, in 1587, 'with above a hundred persons, men, 'women, and children,' has been much neglected. Not till 1606, hardly till this fleet of 1609, was there any effectual remembrance of it by its Mother; and what these hundred persons have done with themselves in the interim would be painful to consider. But here with Somers and his Fleet came help; new settlers, artificers, commanders, all things necessary; sent by the Virginia Company and his Majesty in Council;—and Virginia Shares, we may hope, have now reached par! For renowned Captain Smith, too, has been 'up at the Falls'; has founded Jamestown; has conquered King Powhattan, the pipe-clayed, shell-girdled Majesty, and taken his Daughter Captive,—whom one 'Mr. Rolf, a young 'English gentleman,' is found audacious enough to marry. 'Marry a Princess?' His Majesty [King James], I understand, had thoughts of punishment: but reflecting that she was only a pipe-clayed Princess, flatfaced, with probably some ring or doorknocker through her nostrils, and no trousseau or wardrobe but a scanty petticoat of wampum, he perceived that the case was peculiar, that there was room for extending the royal clemency. Audacious Rolf retains his Princess; generates half-caste specimens, with manifest advantage to all

[1] *A Discovery of the Bermudas, otherwise called the Ile of Divels, by Silas Jourdan.* London, 1610 (Reprinted in *Hackluyt*, v. 555: London, 1812). —Stow, 1019-20.

parties: and, on the whole, Virginia, I think, will come to something, and the shares rise to par or higher!—

Nay, looking into other old Logbooks, I discern, in the Far East too, a notable germination. By Portuguese Gama, by Dutch and other traffickers and sea-and-land rovers, the kingdoms of the Sun are opened to our dim Fog-land withal; are coming into a kind of contact with it. England herself has a traffic there, a continually increasing traffic. In these years,[1] his Majesty has granted the English East India Company a 'new Charter to continue forever'; the old temporary Charter having expired. Ships, 'the immense 'Ship, Trade's-Increase, and her Pinnace, the Peppercorn'; she and others have been there; in Guzerat, in Java, in the Isles of Ternate and Tidore, bringing spicy drugs. At Surat and elsewhere, certain poor English Factories are rising,— in spite of 'the Portugals of Goa.' Nay, in 1611, there came Sir Robert Shirley, a wandering, battling, diplomatising Sussex man, 'Ambassador from Shah Abbas the Great'; and had a Persian Wife, and produced an English-Persian boy,—to whom Prince Henry stood godfather.—Shah Abbas, Jehangire, Great Mogul, and fabulous-real Potentates of the uttermost parts of the Earth, are dimly disclosed to us; Night's ancient curtain being now drawn aside. Not fabulous, but real; seated there, with awful eye, on their thrones of barbaric pearl and gold :—is it not as if some rustle of the coming epochs were agitating, in a gentle way, those dusky remote Majesties! The agitation of 'the Portugals 'at Goa,' on the other hand, is not gentle but violent.

For lo, we say, through the Logbook of the old India Ship Dragon, in the three last days of October, 1612, there is visible and audible a thing worth noticing at this distance. A very fiery cannonading, 'nigh Surat in the Road of Swally.' It is the Viceroy of Goa, and Captain Thomas Best. The Viceroy of Goa has sent 'five thousand fresh men, in four great 'Galleons with six-and-twenty lusty frigates,' to demolish

---

[1] 1610, Camden (in Kennet, ii. 643). 'May, 1609,' says Stow, 994.

Captain Thomas Best and this Ship Dragon of his,—in fact to drive these English generally, and their puny Factories, home again, out of his Excellency's way. Even so :—but Captain Thomas Best will need to be consulted on the matter, too! Captain Thomas Best, being consulted, pours forth mere torrents of fire and iron, for three days running; enough to convince any Portugal. A surly dog; cares not a doit for our Galleons, for our lusty frigates; sends them in splinters about our ears; kills eighty-two of us, besides the wounded and frightened! Truculent sea-bear, son of the Norse Sea-kings; he has it by kind! The Portuguese return to Goa in a very dismantled manner. What shall we do, O Excellency of Goa? Best and his Dragon will not go, when consulted! O Excellency, it is we ourselves that will have to go!—This is the cannonade of Captain Best, 'General 'Best' as the old Logbooks name him; small among sea-victories, but in the World's History perhaps great.[1]

Captain Best, victorious over many things, sends home despatches, giving 'a scheme of good order' for all our Factories and business in the East; sails hither, sails thither, settling much;—freights himself with 'cloves, pepper' and other pungent substances, and returns happily in 1614. The Great Mogul had a 'Lieger' or Agent of ours, for some time past; and now, in this same year, 1614, Sir Thomas Roe goes out as Resident Ambassador. The English India Company seems inclined to make good its Charter! His Majesty, in all easy ways, right willingly encourages it.

American Colonies, Indian Empire,—and that far grander Heavenly Empire, kingdom of the Soul eternal in the Heavens: is not this People conquering somewhat for itself? Under the empty halm, and cast-clothes of phantasmagories, under the tippets, rubrics, king's-cloaks and exuviæ, I think there is a thing or two germinating,—my erudite Friend!

[1] Orme's *History of Hindostan* (London, 1805), 330 *et seqq.* Stow, 994.

CHAPTER X

PAUL'S AISLE: PAUL'S CROSS

[1610—1615]

DAILY 'about eleven o'clock,' it is the custom of all cultivated persons, ' principal gentry, lords, courtiers and profes-' sional men not merely mechanic,' to meet in Paul's Cathedral, and—walk in the Middle Aisle till dinner time, about twelve. After dinner they return thither ' about three, and walk again ' in the Middle Aisle till towards six.' There they roll hither and thither, daily; exchanging salutations; ' discoursing ' of news, business,' and miscellaneous matters;—the many-voiced hum of them yet audible in the mind's ear. In these very days, are they not talking of Ravaillac, Rue de la Ferronnerie, and the murder of Henri le Grand? What will that Scarlet Woman, sitting so on her seven hills and sending out her Jesuit militia, come to! Our Paris Letters say he did it with a knife, and stabbed twice, standing on the hind-wheel of the carriage. The king exclaimed, 'I am hurt'; and at the second stroke, died[1]: *Linquenda tellus et domus!*—'I, ' Francis Osborne, an observant youth, spending three-fourths ' of my year in London, discourse of the worthiest persons, and ' news from the fountain-head': 'I had come up on some pro-' mise of court-preferment,' which alas, proved rotten mainly!—

And at Paul's Cross hard by, from your raised pulpit ' roofed with lead,' raised on steps like some big Spiritual Sentry-box, you have sermon frequently, on weekdays or other · you sit on benches, in most rapt silence, under the open canopy there; detect Puritanical tendencies now and then, Papistical now and then. Over in Cheapside, meanwhile, the shop-apprentices are crying, 'What d' ye lack?

---

[1] Friday, 14th May (24th by the then English style) 1610. Osborne, *Historical Memoirs*, p. 209. Hénault, *Abrégé chronologique*, p. 585.

CHAP. X.]   PAUL'S AISLE: PAUL'S CROSS   93

'What d'ye lack?' Old London, with its old shop-cries, its old 'shrill milk-cries,' and foolish and wise discoursings of the human windpipe, is very vocal: Labour's thousand hammers also fall in it, with multitudinous tumult, unnoticed by Dryasdust!—Silent in the Tower sits Raleigh, sit my lord Northumberland and others: it was the Lady-Arabella[1] Plot, the Gunpowder Plot, what Plot one knows not. Tough Raleigh is writing his *History of the World*; hemmed in by strait stone-walls. And at Court Attorney-General Bacon is clearly on the rising hand; a useful Court-lawyer, 'with an eye like a viper.' And in many Church-pulpits an alarming Puritanic tendency is traceable; in others a Papistic. And at Lambeth, choleric Bancroft is waxing heavy, verging to his long sleep; like to be succeeded by solid Dr. Abbot. And, on the whole, is not motley very generally the wear, for men and for things? They have their exits and their entrances; they dress themselves in what fig-leaves and ornamental garnitures they can; and strut and fret their hour. If the somewhat paltry Stage of Life were *not* an emblematic one, who, on such salary as there is, would consent to act on it? Not I, for my share. But it is and remains emblematic enough; very wonderfully and also fearfully emblematic! Paltry loud-babbling Time, mirrored on the still Eternity, is no longer paltry; and poor mimes, seemingly mere clothes-screens dressed out of Monmouth-Street,[2] *are*, if they knew it, either gods or else devils!—

[1] Arabella Stuart, Daughter of Lennox (Darnley's younger brother), and Cousin to King James. In May 1610 she married William Seymour, who was of Tudor blood and might in certain contingencies have claimed a right to the Crown of England. The young couple were both cruelly and unjustly treated by the King: after imprisonment, escape and recapture, and incarceration in the Tower for four years, Arabella died insane, 1615. See *Letters and Life of A. Stuart*, by Elizabeth Cooper.

[2] Now called Dudley Street, long noted for its second-hand-clothes shops.

CHAPTER XI

DEATH OF PRINCE HENRY: MARRIAGE OF PRINCESS ELIZABETH TO THE PALSGRAVE

[1612-13]

MEANWHILE the news are bad. On Thursday, 29th October 1612, Lord Mayor's Day, there is a grand to-do in Guildhall; German Prince, Elector Palsgraf, and other high dignitaries, secular and clerical, dining with the new Lord Mayor there. An explosion of princely and civic gratulation and good cheer; radiant enough, if we had time to reawaken it. The Archbishop of Canterbury, good George Abbot, the last of the Souls' Overseers is there;[1] Palsgraf and he talk Latin to each other all the afternoon, much to the admiration of the citizens. Bishop of London too is there,—one King, of whom little is known; a 'pious man,' employed in Weston's affair.[2] Prince Henry, alas, is absent,—he would have come, but has fallen suddenly ill: this princely corporation dinner is chequered by that one shade of sorrow; but we struggle to suppress it.

As to this handsome young Count Palatine, Palsgrave as they call him, he is a handsome man; lodges in Essex House; expenses all defrayed by his Majesty; we understand he is come about marrying the Princess Elizabeth. He comes from Heidelberg, from Munich far beyond seas; is of the progeny of 'Otto von Wittelsbach,' of one knows not whom; is Count Palatine of the Upper and Lower Palatinate: a Serene Highness whom singular destinies await. His progeny, by Protestant Settlements, glorious Revolutions and such like, do now govern these Islands; are the present agreeable Family of Hanover whom we all know. He speaks in Dutch Heidel-

---

[1] Stow, 1004, but the paging is wrong thereabouts.—T. C.

[2] He exerted himself to induce Weston to plead at his trial for complicity in Overbury's murder. See *infra*, p. 112.

CHAP. XI.] DEATH OF PRINCE HENRY 95

berg Latin to Archbishop Abbot this day at the Lord Mayor's Feast; says his Highness (Prince Henry) had a game of tennis, whereat his Highness got heated;[1] George Abbot, in Cambridge dialect, 'hopes in God it will pass quickly, and 'come to nothing!'

Alas, it passed quickly, but took the young Prince along with it. On 'the 6th November between seven and eight,' at his Palace in St. James's, he died. The sorrow of the population is inconceivable by any population now. This, then, is what it has come to. Our leather dolphins at Chelsea, and all our stately Masquings, the glory of this Earth; and all our high hopes for a reign of Gospel Truth and real nobleness in England, vanish so between seven and eight in the dim November evening; choked in damp death forever. He was made a Knight, we saw; but it availed not. A wise, brave youth for his years; he scorned many honourable clothes-screens, male and female, of his Father's Court; yet in a discreet, reticent manner; from boyhood he had admired the Great Henry[2] of France,—whispers go that he was cognisant of the Henry's Grand Scheme, and had determined to be king of Protestantism. He was of a comely, tall middle-stature, five feet eight, or so; beautiful, shaped like an Adonis, of an amiable majestic countenance; the hair auburn, the eyes deep and grave, with the sweetest smile in them, with the terriblest frown. So say the Court newsmen, with the handkerchief at their eyes.[3] And he lies there dead,—vanished forever. He has had two appearances in this History; an entrance and an exit: happily if also unhappily no intermediate performance was required of him: applauses therefore are unmixed; he lies there a beautiful ideal youth, consecrated by the tears and sorrowful heart worship of all the world. The Lord Mayor's feast is sorrowfully clouded;—all feasts are sorrow-

[1] *Pictorial History of England* (London, 1840), iii. 51.
[2] *Henri quatre*, who had prepared a splendid army of 30,000 men, and was thought to be on the point of setting out at the head of it to make war against the Pope and his dominions.
[3] Sir C. Cornwallis, in Harris, i. 295. See *ante*, p. 77 *n*.

fully clouded: broad Anne of Denmark weeps once more from the bottom of her Mother's heart as she hoped never to have done; paternal Majesty does not weep, but his thoughts, I believe, go wandering over Time and over Eternity, over Past and Present, in a restless, arid, vague, still more tragic manner, and discern at glimpses what a sorry Rag-fair of a business this of Life and its Eloquences is:—what a frivolous play-actor existence we have at Whitehall here, with the Furies looking through the arras on us; what a sorry business this of unheroic Human Life with its Court Masques is! Let us forget it, your Majesty. Music, then; new Masques, and ceremonials; let the business of the State go on; marriage of the Palsgrave as one of the first of its businesses.

The sorrow of the population (as we said) is inconceivable to any population now. As yet the whole nation is like the family of one good landlord, with his loyal tenants and servants round him; and here is the beautiful young Lordship and Heir Apparent struck suddenly down! Who would not weep? We, had our time been *then*, should have wept too, I hope: but it is too late now. So fair a flower of existence is cropt down; the hope of Protestantism snatched sternly away: we reflect that Prince Charles will be King, not Archbishop now, but King; which may produce results.

There goes a report of poison; report that the Spaniards and Jesuits have done it,—nay, still blacker reports that Somerset Car whom he hated,—that a paternal Majesty, struck with jealousy:—reports which are not now worth naming.[1] But indubitably enough the Funeral on Monday, 7th December,[2] as it winded on with its high hearse and waxen effigies, with the sable principalities, with divers Bishops and Marquises, Earls and Barons, all in crape, and the gentlemen

---

[1] The prince it would seem, died of typhoid fever. See Dr. Norman Moore's Pamphlet, 'The Illness and Death of Prince Henry, Prince of Wales—a historical case of typhoid fever,'—St. Bartholomew's Hospital Reports, vol. xvii. Stow says: 'He died of a popular mallignant fever, which raigned that yere in most parts of this land.'—*Chronicle*, 1004.

[2] Stow, 1004.

CH. XI.] MARRIAGE OF PRINCESS ELIZABETH 97

officials of the King's chapel 'singing very solemnly as they
'marched,' was one of the saddest sights. The hearts of all
men are darkened. Guy and his fellow Fiends were for
blowing up his Majesty and High Court of Parliament; do
they mean to try it now another way? A Spanish warship,
I hear, 'has arrived,' in what port is uncertain, wholly
freighted with pocket pistols. Such is the rumour in these
days. Short pistols, to be distributed each to its due truculent Papist assassin, all over England; truculent Papists
shall wear them in their pockets; shoot with them each his
distinguished Protestant man. 'A black Christmas,' they
say, 'will make a bloody Lent.'[1] How little know we what
our fathers suffered! We walk lightly over the graves and
martyr-struggles of our fathers; but, indeed all the conquests
of this world are the fruit of martyrdom; in all the noble
possessions of this world lies unrecognised the heart's-blood
of a heroic man. Courage! His Majesty prohibits by a
Proclamation[2] the wearing of any pistol that will go into a
pocket at all,—any pistol the barrel of which is not fifteen
inches long or thereabouts: will this pacify you?

As to the Marriage of Palatine Serene Highness and
Princess Elizabeth,—it happens on Shrove-Sunday the 14th
February, 1612-3, 'St. Valentine's Day,' says old Stow.
Considering what destinies came from it, let us look at the
phenomenon one moment. The Bride was all in white; her
train borne by twelve bridesmaids, the beautifullest and noblest,
all in white; on her head was a golden crown: her black hair
streamed gracefully down to her girdle, which was of pearls
and diamonds. In fact she was all of pearls, and herself one
beautifullest pearl,—a Mary Queen of Scots, without the
Popery, come again,—and made a radiance round her, says
old Wilson, like the Milky Way. She was led to the Altar,
in Whitehall Chapel it was, by two bachelors: young orthodox, austere Prince Charles, and old nefarious Howard, Earl

[1] Wilson, 62.   [2] *Ibid.*, 63.

of Northampton; a crypto-papist too; and from the Altar by two married persons, whose names I forget.[1] At the Altar, while Archbishop Abbot did his functions,[2] she blushed like Aurora, but smiled withal; nay, there went flashings of the morning-light of joy from her fair young face, which seemed ominous to Arthur Wilson. Majesty himself is there, looking vigilant-impatient, with open eyes and sardonic under-jaw; Queen Anne too, is there,—little charmed with the match. Goody Palsgrave, she calls her, Goody who might have been a Queen, with due management. She will be a Queen of Hearts, at any rate,—and give rise to the present agreeable family of Hanover.

The Old Chronicler feels all the tailor stir in him at thought of the 'Masquings' and 'Processionings' with their velvet, Mechlin lace and cloth of gold;—transitory all as the brightest flash of morning succeeded by laborious rainy day.[3] The Procession and Masque of the young Lawyers which came along the Strand by torchlight, and up the River in illuminated royal barges, throws the old heart almost into ecstasy. For they did ride as Moriscos,[4] Indian kings, Moguls or other truly exotic characters; escorted by savages with gilt rods, by hairy anthropophagi and men whose heads do grow beneath their shoulders: all with torches; all caparisoned, high-prancing through the Strand by night, to the astonishment of all mortals.[5] Such then were young gentlemen of the Inns of Court; a class much given to Masquing. Was William Noy there, for instance? Good Heavens, they will grow to be old gentlemen these; and get into quite other Masques,—into long wigs and red cloaks some of them,— and sit as judges, Shipmoney judges, and Attorney-Generals; dried specimens of Humanity, tough as leather tanned for thirty years! Noy has a Christmas pie sent up yearly by his

[1] Duke of Lennox and the Earl of Nottingham.
[2] Stow, 1005.　　　　　[3] *Ibid.*, 1006.　　　　　[4] Moors.
[5] The young Lawyers' Masque, called 'The Masque of the Inner-Temple and Gray's Inn,' was written by Francis Beaumont; and was presented on Saturday 20th Feb. 1612-3 in the Banqueting-House at Whitehall.

good Mother: for Noy too had a Mother; and there were once smiles to him and human tears; and he was not always of leather,—not of leather tanned for thirty years.—

In brief the Elector Palatine and beautiful Electress, after festivities like those of Ahasuerus, were dismissed in the beginning of April;—shipped at Rochester; and with a train of festivities and triumphal arches, continuing still over the West of Europe, making their path a kind of temporary Valhalla or Vauxhall, did get at length to Mannheim; there happily and unhappily to hold Court levees, produce sons and daughters, and mingle as they might in the great growth of sublunary things. Fair days to them, to the young Queen of Hearts especially.

CHAPTER XII

DUEL—SACKVILLE AND BRUCE[1]

[1613]

On an Autumn afternoon in August 1613, two young gentlemen each attended by an official-looking person, are riding at a slow, steady pace through the Eastern Gate of Antwerp, proceeding first by broad highways and then by remote byways towards Bergen-op-Zoom. They ride at some distance apart these two pairs of persons, yet scrupulously observing one another; turn after turn through the green meadows, the hindmost pair follows accurately the leading of the first. What do they want in Bergen these two young gentlemen with their attendants? In Bergen nothing, but in the road towards Bergen much. The March-line of the States territories and the Arch-Duke's lies here in these green sequestered meadows; as near that as may be they would find some quiet spot: there if a deed of blood chance to be done

---

[1] Edward Sackville, afterwards 4th Earl of Dorset, born 1591, died 17th July, 1652. Edward Bruce, 2nd Lord Kinloss.

in the one country, the survivor has but to step across into the other and he is safe. Peaceable cattle graze in these meadows, peaceable Tenier's boors are getting their ale or after-dinner nap in these painted cottages;—not of peace is the errand of these two young gentlemen. Their attendants are two silent Surgeons or Barber-Surgeons, for a Surgeon in those days is but a Subaltern, and shaves. Their errand I think is of a duel. The foremost of these two young gentlemen is the Honourable Edward Sackville of Buckhurst Knowle, etc., is younger brother of the Earl of Dorset, grandson to Buckhurst with his Ferrex and Porrex,[1] great in Queen Elizabeth's days, as fair a piece of young manhood as you shall readily fall in with. The hindmost of them who keeps such strict eye on him, is of Kinloss in Fife; the Lord Bruce of Kinloss; also one of the prettiest young men. What rage and fire swells in these beautiful young faces, all silent, shaded with their long brown hair. Apollo piercing the Python Serpent looked somewhat so, one fancies:—two Apollos in modern Spanish hats and set on horseback there. My young friends, I doubt you have mischief in your eye.

To this day I could never discover exactly what the cause of quarrel was. The likeliest seems that it was a sister of the Lord Bruce's,—alas, this Sackville is seductive enough,—a sister of Lord Bruce's, and then some former tiff of controversy, soldered up by intervention of Friends, wherein the Lord Bruce, feeling that it was questionable, had said, 'He 'gave his hand then, but his heart he reserved and did not 'yet give.' Accordingly, from Paris in June last, he wrote to Sackville the most courteous, the most fierce of letters soliciting a meeting as the chief of all earthly blessings and charities to him, to which Sackville as courteous and as fierce, gave swift and brief assent, and so they arrive in the Netherlands rendezvous at Antwerp, and the Seconds match their swords, and the Lord Bruce indicates that the Seconds

[1] *The Tragedie of Ferrex and Porrex*, by Thomas Sackville, Lord Buckhurst, 1st Earl of Dorset (Lond. 1571, 16mo.).

CHAP. XII.] DUEL—SACKVILLE AND BRUCE 101

shall not attend them, but only two Surgeons, for he is bound to do or suffer what no Second could witness without interfering,—bloody intentions, bloody and butcherly as Sackville's Second said; but intentions, which being reported to Sackville, awaken such a humour in him that he starts up from the very dinner-table saying, 'Be it now then!' And so they are riding in byways among the green meadows between Antwerp and Bergen-op-Zoom, the two angriest young figures in the Low Countries that afternoon. Some two miles they have ridden, and found nothing quite satisfactory: but human nature cannot long endure such riding: Sackville draws bridle, pointing to a wet meadow, private, though wet, says, 'This will do,' and the Lord Bruce answers, 'Why not 'this?' The two Surgeons therefore retire to a distance; 'interpose not between us as you love your lives, but leave us 'to do our will on one another,'—and so now: 'At your 'service, Sir.' 'At your service, my Lord.' We doff our doublets, Spanish hats; the meadow is water to the ankles; but the drawn swords glitter in the sun; we are to strive here for the greatest prize.—Sackville whose description no Homer could excel shall report the rest:—

'And there in a meadow, ankle deep in the water, at least, bidding farewell to our doublets, in our shirts we began to charge each other, having afore commanded our surgeons to withdraw themselves a pretty distance from us, conjuring them besides, as they respected our favour or their own safeties not to stir, but suffer us to execute our pleasure, we being fully resolved (God forgive us!) to despatch each other by what means we could.

'I made a thrust at my enemy, but was short, and in drawing back my arm I received a great wound thereon, which I interpreted a reward for my short shooting; but in revenge I pressed into him, though I then missed him also, and then received a wound in my right pap, which passed level through my body almost to my back. And there we wrestled for the two greatest and dearest prizes we could ever expect trial for,—honour and life; in which struggling, my hand having but an ordinary glove upon it, lost one of her servants, though the meanest, which hung by a skin, and to sight remaineth as before, and I am put in hope one day to recover the use of it again. But at last breathless, yet keeping our holds, there passed on both sides propositions of quitting each other's swords, but when amity was dead, confidence could not live, and who should quit first was the question! which on neither part either would perform; and restriving again afresh, with a kick and wrench together I freed my long captive weapon. Which incontinently levying at his throat, being master still of his, I demanded if he would yield his life or his sword? Both which, though in that imminent danger, he bravely denied to do. Myself being wounded and feeling loss of blood, having three conduits running on me, began to make me faint, and he courageously persisting not to accord to either of my propositions, remembrance of his former bloody desire and feeling of my present estate, I struck at his heart, but with his avoiding missed my aim, yet passed through his body, and drawing back my sword repassed it through again through another place, when he cried: "Oh, I am slain!" seconding his speech with all the force he had to cast me, but being too weak, after I had defended his assault, I easily became master of him, laying him upon his back, when, being upon him, I redemanded of him if he would request his life? But it seems he prized it not at so dear a rate as to be beholden for it, bravely replying he scorned it! which answer of his was so noble and worthy, as I protest, I could not find in my heart to offer him any more violence, only keeping him down till at length his surgeon, afar off, cried he would immediately die if his wounds were not stopped: whereupon I asked if he desired his surgeon should come? which he accepted of; and so, being drawn away, I never offered to take his sword, accounting it inhumane to rob a dead man—for so I held him to be.

'This thus ended, I retired to my surgeon, in whose arms after I had remained a while, for want of blood, I lost my sight, and withal as I thought my life also; but strong water and his diligence quickly recovered me; when I escaped a great danger: for my Lord's surgeon, when nobody dreamt of it, came full at me with my Lord's sword; and had not mine, with my sword interposed himself, I had been slain by those base hands, although my Lord Bruce, weltering in his blood, and past all expectation of life, conformable to all his former carriage, which was undoubtedly noble, cried out, "Rascal, hold thy hand!" So may I prosper as I have dealt sincerely with you in this relation.'[1]

'So may I prosper as I have dealt sincerely with you in 'this relation.'—Whereat the Universal Benevolence Society, the Abolition of Capital Punishment Society, the All-for-

[1] Collins, *Peerage of England*, ii. pp. 153-7 (London, 1812). A long narrative of this Duel was first printed in the *Guardian*, Nos. 129 and 133.

Sugar and Syrup Society wring their hands; and the Select Anti-Twaddle Society calls attention to it as a thing not without meaning. 'Rascal, hold thy hand'; reflect well on that, you will find withal an epitome of many great things there. For rage does dwell perennially as a submarine fire element in the most flowery benevolent soul of man, and all his reason and all his civilisation shine out consecrated when he can, instead of being madly wielded thereby, manfully wield it; and like a god launch and check the very thunderbolts. For thunder exists, must exist, and lightning in a summer sky is very different from hell-fire in the murk of Chaos;— and, in short, the Select Anti-Twaddle Society advises the All-for-Sugar Society to take care in these times that their Sugar be not Sugar-of-lead.

CHAPTER XIII

SHAKSPEARE'S DEATH—CERVANTES—KEPLER

[1616]

But what is this that is passing in these very hours westward in the centre of England, at the Town of Stratford-on-Avon?—Stratford is peaceful this day, hammering, sawing, weaving, following its daily business for most part. But there lies in it, taking his departure for an unknown Land, a mighty man. William Shakspeare in these hours is dying. Twenty-third of April, 1616, if there be faith in monumental brasses, which for once we will thank. While Oliver Cromwell enters himself in Sidney Sussex College, Cambridge, William Shakspeare takes his leave of this world. Dim are now those once bright eyes, heavy with the long sleep; the radiant far-darting soul, now weary and fordone, painfully with tired wing is weltering through dark rivers of Death towards unknown Shores. Earthly Dramaturgies are done; in huge torch-dance all the Figures of this world, snakehaired Furies, azure angels roll away. Coulisses, backscenes, footlights, dropscenes of this terrestrial theatre spin and tumble to annihilation; and the Divinities and Silences and Eternal Realities supervene. There have been many Shakspeares of my kindred,[1] silent ones and other;—but thou art known to me; take thou my spoken blessing. My Shakspeare, brightest creature known to me in all this world, Adieu! Anne Hathaway's tears drop fast, her face is all bewept, and the tears of young Judith fall fast: and Shakspeare is away! Exit Shakspeare, enter Oliver. Wit combats at the Mermaid are all over, and quite another set of combats are to begin. These things happen in England in one day.

Nay, far away,—for I love to follow the celestial Lightbringers of this world, wherever Ass Dryasdust and his multitude of oiled paper lanterns, and illuminated hollow turnips will allow me,—far away in the heart of Spain, there too they have been lodging an Angel unawares, in rather a sorry manner. Miguel Cervantes; he too is just dead, after a brave and weary life,—precisely ten days ago. Twenty-third of April 1616, so in words say the Spanish Registers; and Chevalier Florian will persuade me that it was the same day as Shakspeare's and Oliver's; forgetting the difference of Old Style and New. A fortnight since, while Dorothy Cromwell at the West end of Huntingdon was getting Oliver's linen ready, my poor brave Miguel, sick of dropsy, worn out with toil, had borrowed himself a horse and ridden out to see the green young leaves and bright Spring sky once more, before he died. A kindlier, meeker, or braver heart has seldom looked upon the sky in this world. O my brave Miguel, when I think of thee fighting Turks at Lepanto, struggling like an unsubduable one, seven years against captivity among the Moors; struggling all thy years against poverty and misrecognition and hard luck; and writing at last *Don Quixote,* 'our sunniest and all but our deepest

---

[1] 'Yes, this Shakspeare is ours; we produced him, we speak and think by him; we are of one blood and kind with him.'—*Lectures on Heroes,* p. 133.

'modern Book'; sitting maimed, forsaken, old, and in jail,— I could blush for my own beggarly complaining,—I have to say to myself remorsefully, self-contemningly, 'Silence!' From Miguel come no complaints; from Miguel came often thanks, gushing forth full of gratitude for the day of small things. A born indefeasible gentleman; whom you recognise as such under every conceivable defacement, says one. Yes! a born indefeasible Beam of Light, say I; which could not be defaced; which struggled upward victorious through all elements of fortune, purifying all, not pollutable by any. How Heaven's light will upwards! Noble Chivalry is out now, cannot live now except as in self mockery; let it live in that way, since in no other; and we have a 'Knight of the 'Sorrowful Countenance,' and a Squire of the fat Paunch, and, amid Yanguesian Carriers and Maritornes Hostelries and all the uglinesses of the Earth, with Delirium and broken bones at the bottom of them, such glimpses of Elysian scenes and bright Boccaccio Gardens, and figures with their hair flowing down like sunbeams,—as were seldom given before in this world. Honour to Cervantes; apotheosis to him, if there were any sense now of what was godlike, what was manlike!
— —He has ridden out, I say, to take one other look at the azure firmaments and green mosaic pavements, and strange carpentry and arras work of this noble Palace of a world, which is his more than another's; one look more, which proved his last. 'On his way back to Madrid, in company with
'two of his friends, they were overtaken by a young student
'on horseback, who came pricking on hastily, complaining
'that they went at such a pace as gave him little chance of
'keeping up with them. One of the party made answer, that
'the blame lay with the horse of Don Ml. de Cervantes, whose
'trot was of the speediest. He had hardly pronounced the
'name, when the student dismounted, and touching the hem of
'Cervantes' left sleeve, said, "Yes, yes! it is indeed the maimed
'" perfection, the all-famous, the delightful writer, the joy and
'" darling of the Muses!"—You are that brave Miguel!'

'In a few days more he had forever paid farewell to jest-
'ing, farewell to merry humours,—to gay friends, and had
'entered that other life, where he realised his last desire to
'see his beloved one happy there.'— —Such things befall
contemporaneously in this world.

Human Blockheadism strives to bore us with innumerable
Spanish interests, of long-faced Philips in their velvet mantles,
thick-lipped Infantas, Treaties, Marriage-treaties, and I know
not what: but this, very strangely we discern, is becoming
as it were the one Spanish Interest: this is the Voice of the
entity called Spanish Nation in our Universe, a day, as I
discern, is coming when it will be all dumb but this;—as the
land of Greece now is, a waste of bewildered ruins, nothing
surviving of it but the voice. Happy the Nation that has
once spoken!

Good Heavens, my erudite Friend, how dark, dead and
void is all that Europe, which lay then sunny, leafy, busy
every corner of it in those Summer months while Oliver is
grappling towards study of the Tongues under Dr. Howlet!
It is gone to brown ashes and mere Rymer's *Fœdera*,[1] meseems; it is vanished all away. The Leipzig Fair was holden
twice annually, with chaffering and weighing, bargaining, and
paying of moneys; but the merchants and pedlars with their
booths and bales have gone their ways again. Solemn
Majesties all along from Spain to Sweden, a fair sprinkling
of them all, on thrones as rich as Ormuz, with their treaties,
war-treaties and marriage-treaties, festivities and finance-
schemes; not to speak of innumerable little German Dukes,
with their sixteen quarterings, their stiff Kammerherrs and
thickquilted ceremonials,—Good Heavens, they are gone like
ghosts, with an unmusical screech; and we hasten onwards
through the Death-kingdom, refusing to be instructed of
them. Life is short, my erudite Friend; and Art is long;
it is not with vanished clothes-screens and poor extinct oil-
lanterns, but, if possible, with Heroes only, and what of

[1] *Fœdera*, etc., in 20 voll. folio, by Thomas Rymer, London, 1704-35.

heroic they have left, that I will concern myself. They and their works:—why, it is properly all that this world has. The rest—Chaos has it: thou blockhead, why wilt thou bewilder us with Chaos a second time? Was not *once* enough? Miguel Cervantes is worth all the Philips and one to boot.

What the Ericson Vasa people are doing at Stockholm, I will not inquire; a brave race, sons of heroic Vasa who rose and freed his Country; and true Protestants, who will be ready when wanted. Far off in the East, however, I remark one Figure, in threadbare gabardine, with haggard face, ploughed seemingly with many toils and tribulations, but with eyes in which, amid sorrow and despair, beams deathless hope, beams victory over all things: resident about Vienna: but often hovering hither and thither as necessity drives: the name of him is Johannes Kepler, Almanack maker to the Kaiser's Highness. Yes, reader, of whatever class, trade or character thou be, thou canst take a look at that one;—why, man, it was he in a manner that brought thee thy breakfast out of China this morning, that taught thee rightly what o'clock it was; the very nautical almanacks to this day are made by him. He is the Imperial Highness's Almanack Maker; has strange astronomical and other apparatus: old Sir Henry Wotton, going to 'lie abroad'[1] for his Majesty, saw his Camera Obscura and him, face to face; thought this Kepler a very ingenious person. He has to shew Camera Obscuras, write Almanacks, be servant of all work, lest bread itself fail him and he be reduced to water. His salary is 18*l* Sterling a year; and they pay it him dreadfully ill. He has to go to Regensburg, to solicit the Imperial Diet. 'Noble Lordships, serene Highnesses, Principalities and Powers of sixteen quarterings, pay me, of your innate nobleness, my 18*l*!' Of late years they have paid

---

[1] 'Sent to lie abroad,'—as an ambassador; a witticism of Sir Henry Wotton's. See *Life* of him by Isaac Walton; *Reliquiæ Wottonianæ*, p. 300; and Carlyle's *Frederick the Great*, i. 329-30.

him terribly ill,—and his great heart,—for the man has a great proud heart withal,—is almost getting weary of it. A small salary when so irregularly paid:—but Johann has done a bit of work; that is his comfort. Reader, he has followed the motions of the star Mars ('*De Motibus Stellæ Martis*') and discovered them! For long lonesome years, in spite of loneliness, discouragement, scolding wives, and very hunger; with a tenacity like death, he has followed this Star Mars, gone through his calculations seventy times, looking up with a cheery smile into the face of Hunger itself: saying, 'O 'Hunger, do not kill me till I find this Star Mars!' By Heaven, I say he has found it; and I cry victory with him to this hour. Here are the eternal Laws of the Planetary motions: [in ellipses, with the sun for focus, describing equal areas in equal times, with the square of the periodic time proportional to the cube of the mean distance from the sun]; it was so the Maker from the first appointed these shining things to move. I have found it, exclaims Johann; and you do not understand it: you are not like to understand it for a long while. Never mind. If God Almighty waited for six thousand years for one to see what He had made, cannot I wait a century or two for one to understand what I have done? Yes, my brave one!

CHAPTER XIV

EFFECTS OF COURT DOINGS ON THE MINDS OF IMPARTIAL ENGLISHMEN

INTO all prudent households, into all wise hearts reading Controversial Divinity in England, and intent to govern their life on some God's truth there, what sorrowful rumours and reflexions are those that the course of royal affairs, of politics foreign and domestic, sheds abroad every where in those days! Pious Mr. Robert Cromwell, pious Dr. Beard the schoolmaster are shocked in Huntingdon. Sir Oliver himself, though of hopeful secular nature, and bound to Majesty by knightship and otherwise, sometimes knows not what to say. From Court there seem to come almost no news that are not more or less distressing.

Guy Faux and Company on the point of exploding Protestantism out of England by one infernal shot of gunpowder; this, since the project failed, was not the worst news. That an English King should still favour Papistry, find in the Pope nothing unpardonable but his claim of a supremacy over kings,[1] and still struggle to connect himself with Spanish Infantas and the other rubbish of heathen Babylon; blind to the Gospel of Heaven, to the 'Life of Immortality' anew 'brought to light,' as we may say, in all serious English hearts: what are men to think of this? The King of England sits on his august throne, raised aloft, conspicuous to all men as the illustrated symbol, the beautiful and almost beatified epitome of our general English Existence and Endeavour: and these are the news he sends us? Favouritisms, frivolities, foolish profusions and forced loans; monopolies, unjust taxations, open sale of honours, open neglect of business; drinking-bouts, court gallantries, Overbury Murders; Spanish Matches, lost Palatinates: abroad or at home, disgrace, disaster, fatal ineffectuality in whatsoever we do or attempt!

To us of the 19th century, seeking for some History of England, these things, as the *pabulum* of loud rumour and of sorrowful reflexion to contemporary English hearts, have still a kind of meaning; in such sense they are still faintly memorable to us,—hardly in any other sense. Indirectly and by reflex they have in this way some relation to the History of England; but directly and as intrinsic facts, they have almost none. What History of England lies, or can lie, in all that? The truth now is visible to every one, which then no one could see or surmise, that this King James, and his

[1] James's Speech to his First Parliament. Wilson (in Kennet) ii. 671.

works and mis-works, are not the History of England at all, but something other than the History of it;—that 'this King 'James, who sat on the throne of England, and did consume 'the taxes, and command the constables and armed men of 'England, was at bottom *not* King of England, as he seems to 'be, but well-accredited Sham-King only; that, alas, this royal 'man was no Chief Hero of England, but was Chief Chimera 'of it rather!' as our dark friend[1] says. The more is our sorrow, in all respects. No wonder his history has grown chimerical; would this were the worst result of such chimeraship! As a chronological milestone, and also as a fountain of loud rumour and sorrowful reflexion to contemporaneous believing men, King James must still have some purpose in English History: in these capacities the surliest modern must accept him, since it has so pleased the Fates.

To ourselves, except in these two relations, as time-milestone and as fountain of rumours, King James, Solomon of these Islands, shall be in great part indifferent; our History could otherwise afford to leave him in the dim vaporous state, a hazy, chimerical and indeed incredible and impossible person, as other Sovereigns, Solomons, and royal sublimities, in the pages of our English Dryasdust, are. Why summon spectres from the vasty deep of Dryasdust, unless one have business with them? Innumerable bright-tinted personages and occasions, solemn ceremonials, deep strokes of King-craft; rises and falls of Somerset Car, of Buckingham Villiers, Overbury Murders, trials of Lady Lake: let this all or almost all remain of an indistinct leaden colour for us; in the infinite leaden haze which goes down to Chaos, Nox and the primeval Dark, let it dimly hang and hover for us. Spectres, spectres; all living significance of which is gone and returns not! Let them roam there in great part invisible on the torpid Rubbishmountains; shriek, at as rare intervals as possible, dolefully, unintelligibly, on the viewless winds.

The tragedy of Overbury; beautiful Robert Car of Fernie-

[1] Smelfungus.

CHAP. XIV.] EFFECTS OF COURT DOINGS 111

hirst, beautiful Frances Howard of the House of Suffolk, fallen into the snares of the Devil, into Westminster Hall and the malediction of gods and men: it was all loud in that time, it has become low in this.

Viscountess Purbeck, for cause of gallantries, is to stand in a white sheet, with lighted taper, and do penance, at St. Martin's; let her duck into some Savoy Ambassador's, frail female, and escape from the big beadles, by a hole in the garden wall,[1]—with small notice from the readers of these pages. She was daughter of Coke upon Lyttleton; married to some unfortunate madman, brother of George Villiers; and fell, sinful and sinned against, as flesh in these circumstances may. Beautiful George Villiers, beautiful Robert Car, nay crooked Robert Cecil himself, cunning Earl of Salisbury: they were Prime Ministers once; but, except perhaps as subsidiary 'chronological milestones and fountains of rumour,' they are as good as Nonentities now. Lord Chief Justice Coke, Coke upon Lyttleton, is out; and Chancellor Bacon, Baron Verulam, Viscount of St. Albans, Augmenter of the Knowledges, is in[2]: to us, at this distance, how can it be vitally important? These are not cardinal events, not properly events at all; these are but as chief appearances, phenomena more or less empty; and concern the reality little. All these, in deference to Dryasdust, let us know, but be careful not to mention. We know them, Dryasdust, in the travail and torpor of our souls we have got to know them; and they are worth nothing to us. Carefully dressed cucumbers, thin sliced, the vinegar, the pepper, and all else complete upon them; and now this last duty remains for us, That we faithfully throw them out of window!—Two facts, nevertheless, selected from the Papers of my dark friend, I wish to retain here:—

'Raleigh, Cobham and others,' says he, 'are condemned at 'Winchester[3]; for over strenuous opposition politics, "plotting '" to bring in the Lady Arabella,"[4] and one knows not what:

[1] Weldon, *Secret History*, i. 446.
[2] See *post*, p. 140, *n.*
[3] See *infra*, p. 130, *n.*
[4] See *ante*, p. 93, *n.*

'they are all out to be beheaded, an immense multitude is
'assembled to look on; but John Gibb, his Majesty's Scotch
'valet, having ridden all night, gallops in at the very nick of
'time, strange haste looking through his eyes, and produces a
'sign-manual,—a kind of pardon, to be received with shout-
'ings. Kind of pardon, which was but a respite and perpetual
'imprisonment; whereby Raleigh got to the Tower, and writes
'us a History of the World, before dying: poor Raleigh!'
'—And again, this also I discern: 'Robert Devereux, an
'Eton boy, is playing at shuttlecock with Prince Henry;
'Prince Henry, the hope of England, says in his anger at
'something that went wrong in the game, "It is like the son
'of a traitor,"—the father of this Robert having as is well
'known lost his head. "Son of a traitor"; whereupon
'Robert did, with his battledore, smite the royal bare crown
'of Prince Henry, and draw royal red blood from it;—rash
'youth, prefiguring for himself an agitated, probably disloyal
'future. The King, however, got him wedded to the fair and
'false Lady Frances Howard, of the House of Suffolk: wedded,
'but, alas, in form only; it is an unrecordable history; and
'gave rise to the poisoning of Sir Thomas Overbury.' These
facts, though small, we will retain.

CHAPTER XV

THE OVERBURY MURDER

[1612-1616]

ENGLAND meanwhile is ringing from side to side, not in the most edifying manner, with the rumour of the Overbury Murder. It is three years since this foul villany was done;[1] for two years it had lain concealed, sounding only in vague popular rumour; and now last Winter the cloak was torn

---

[1] Overbury died, 15th September, 1613.—Somerset's Trial was 25th May 1616.

CHAP. XV.] THE OVERBURY MURDER 113

away from it, and the subaltern actors in it were all before Christmas got hanged. Stupendous, unutterable; which Dryasdust in the wearisomest foul old details and objurgations strives to utter. 'As if this,' says Truepenny, 'were the 'History of England in those days!'—

Overbury, a Gloucestershire gentleman and scholar, with good talent, figure and manner, but with arrogance and contentious vanity more than proportionable, had made acquaintance long since with Robert Car now Earl of Somerset. The son of Ferniehirst was not to spend his days peaceably hunting otters in the streams of Teviotdale, nor was Thomas Overbury to write dull Tragedies alone. They had made an intimacy, I think, in the Court of France, while they were both as pages learning manners there in the year 1604.[1] Car rose to be royal Favourite, Overbury naturally joined him: at bottom one finds that Car was Chief-Secretary of State; and Overbury, a man prompt with his pen, was in an unofficial way managing Secretary under him. They in their fashion, with the aid of Royal Solomon, old crooked Salisbury and a Privy Council, managed the affairs of this Country, better or worse. In occasions of real strait, old Salisbury and real Experience intervenes; on other occasions, as of the Digby Embassies, the Hay Embassies, Spanish Matches and such like, above all in the 'granting of suits,' it was little matter how the business was managed. For certain years these two did it, better or worse; Car Somerset walked before his Majesty with white rod, as Bacon pathetically says; radiant he as the chief of all the celestial Planets, and Overbury is his Moon.

Precisely in the time while Overbury formed his first intimacy with Scotch Car in the Court of France at Paris, the beautiful little Fanny Howard, Treasurer Suffolk's second Daughter, of the best blood, of the beautifullest face and figure you could find in all these Islands, was betrothed to young Robert Devereux, son of the last great Essex, himself

[1] *State Trials*; 'Nine years since.'

H

Earl of Essex, restored in blood and fortune;[1] the same whom we saw smiting Prince Henry on the royal crown with his racket for calling him 'son of a Traitor.'[2] These two are betrothed, nay, I think married, though as yet under years, Essex hardly above thirteen, the lady some months younger. Old Salisbury, they say, advised it, his Majesty approved, thinking doubtless it would be a benefit for both, such a combination. Alas, it proved far otherwise! The young Earl was sent upon his travels, till the years of boyhood should be over: he returned a handsome, likely youth of eighteen, found a right blooming bride, who however, did not smile much upon him: by the malison of gods and men, by conjurers at Lambeth, cunning women at Suffolk House—who knows? By perverse, capricious imagination,—surely by perverse accursed Art and human manufacture, when beneficent Nature had done her part,—there could still no marriage be; and protesting against old crooked Salisbury, mere unblessed mysteries and tragedies supervened! Dryasdust imperatively demands that I should fold him up here; bury these records of his, as our old German Fathers would have done, in the deepest discoverable Peatbog, and drive down a stake of oak through them. To me it is very clear, the young Frances Howard, Lady Essex so-called, proud, capricious, passionate and foolish, had turned her ambitious thoughts aloft, had decided on marrying a heavenly Planet, and fixed on Scotch Car as the palpable chief of these. 'Am not I the fairest damsel in England? This 'Robert Devereux with his big fat cheeks and heavy jaws, with 'his wheezing voice and proud sulky temper—Besides he is 'forced upon me; it was not I that chose him! The foremost 'man in all the world—ah, it is not sulky, thick-voiced 'Devereux, the Lord of Essex; it is radiant Scotch Car of 'Rochester! all-powerful he on Earth, the cynosure of England,

---

[1] Robert Devereux, 3rd Earl of Essex, became commander of the Parliamentary Army at the beginning of the Civil War. He was a man of great courage and inflexible honour, but was far from being a successful general. See *Cromwell's Letters and Speeches*, i. 201-2.

[2] See *ante*, p. 112.

'whom very dukes wait upon as a divinity,—by the very gait
'of him a god.' Saw the eyes of young foolish woman any
nobler figure of a man? 'Tall is he, strong and swift, graceful
'of look; how fierce and gentle, like the swift greyhounds of
'Scotch Teviotdale, which doubtless is a Parish of Fairyland!
'The cynosure of English eyes; whom the proudest Howards
'worship even as flunkies or valets: him, ah, could I have
'him!'—So spake the eyes and thoughts of the poor foolish
young woman in the old Soirées of that time, in a somewhat
radiant manner; and the eyes of Scotch Car, nothing loth,
could not but somewhat radiantly respond.

The eyes of Car respond; but find Overbury thinks far
otherwise. A man of insolent ways, who hates the House of
Suffolk in all its branches; of braggart thrasonic disposition,
to whom, in his boundless selfconceit, it seems as if Car indeed
were the chief man of England, but *he* the real Car, he the
real working Undersecretary, reading all his Embassy despatches, suggesting all the replies. Of *him* there is too little
notice taken; not on him fall those radiant glances from the
Daughter of the House of Suffolk; falling on another they
are not beautiful to him. Rude counsels, remonstrances
couched in the guise of friendship, largely tinctured with
insolence and acrid selfconceit; these now are frequent from
Under Secretary Overbury to Supreme Secretary Car. 'I
'made you,' they almost seem to say; 'that foolish wanton of
'the House of Suffolk shall not unmake you; I will not allow
'it:' Car smiles as he can; keeping down many things; finds
it nearly unsupportable. For the man is insolent; treats my
Lady of Essex as if she were a ———. Good heavens!
One night very late, in private in the Gallery at Whitehall,
Car coming home past midnight, finds Overbury with bedroom
candle in hand: 'Where have you been so late?' 'Pooh;
'out on my occasions.' 'I see it, that base woman will undo
'you.' 'Who knows?' 'In that course I will not follow
'you.' 'Quit *her*?' 'Yes, if you do not quit that unmen-
'tionable, look you stand fast.' 'Stand fast?' answers

Rochester. 'what is to hinder me? I think my own legs
'are straight enough to stand on. Suppose you went to bed,
'noble knight?'—And they part thus in a flash of fire. Of all
which the unsatisfied, distressed, almost distracted, foolish
young Lady of Essex is informed. For Car and she have secret
intercourse, swift correspondence, secret as the gods; meet
in farmhouses between this and Hampton Court[1] on signal
given,—meet where they can, poor creatures, being grown
desperately beautiful to one another. This sulky, thick-voiced
Lord of Essex, shall he lie forever like a gardener's mastiff, in
front of Hesperides apples, himself not eating fruit? The
malison of Heaven lies on it, sure enough. And it is so this
Overbury speaks; and the earth is full of eyes and ears. 'Get
'Overbury put away,' cries Frances Lady of Essex, in a shrill
inspired manner; him away, my Sungod; thou canst subdue
him, thou;—to the Tower with him, to Russia with him,
to the Nether Fiend with him, till the gardener's mastiff
be driven out, and then! — — Overbury does land in
the Tower. I think a Russian Embassy was proposed to
him first; but he declined it, or on second thoughts they
advised him to decline it, thinking the Tower would be
better. And so he sits in the Tower (22nd April, 1613);
and the gardener's mastiff shall be poked out from that lair
of his, and our perilous adventure launch itself.

And so now straightway the poking out of this Gardener's
Mastiff, suing of Divorce for Nullity, proceeds apace; an unspeakable operation, recorded voluminously in Dryasdust,—
which demands from all men to be buried in the deepest
attainable Peatbog, with a stake driven through it. Enough,
the Lady Frances is divorced, forever free of sulky Essex[2]; the
Gardener's Dog poked out, departs, not altogether unwillingly,

---

[1] State Trials, ii. 920.

[2] 'Perceiving how little he was beholden to Venus,' Essex after the divorce
went abroad to 'address himself to the court of Mars,' in other words to learn
the art of war in the Low Countries. He returned, and married again in 1630-1.
But his second wife, pleading on the same grounds as his first had done, also
obtained a separation from him. See Masson's *Life of Milton*, ii. 154.

I think, though in a disconsolate manner, with his hair up and his tail between his legs. Keep your Hesperides Apples in the Devil's name; they were never of my choosing;—only I was set to watch them, and I have done it. This is ended on the 25th September[1]; and there is nothing comfortable in it except that brave George Abbot, Archbishop of Canterbury, considerably the bravest Archbishop I have known since that time, refused to have any trade with it. Though named in the head of his Majesty's Commission, he said resolutely, No. Other Bishops and learned Doctors sit,—and solicit now to be buried in Peatbogs,—but one Chief of Bishops does not sit: honourable mention to him. He is of Puritan tendencies, say some: his House at Lambeth is all alight in the dead hours of darkness; and I am told that he has Puritan Divines in conference with him there! distressful to Court: silenced Preachers some of them, secretly indifferent to surplices some of them: with these does an Archbishop consort! What can you expect? Scotch Privy Councillor, Sir George Hume, Earl of Dunbar, first recommended him, I hear; found him a wise religious man,—did not ask sufficiently what he thought of surplices. And so Lambeth Palace, you perceive, glows in the nightwatches with men consulting about mere piety, careless of surplices. And at Oxford the Brother of this Abbot, Head of a House there, and like to be a Bishop, snarls on William Laud for semi-papistry, reproves him in open convocation for the space of half an hour. And George Abbot, Head of Christ's Church in England, he, for one, will have no hand in the Lady Frances Howard's business, not even though the King command him;—he thinks it will be safer not.

All this while Overbury lies in the last impatience in the Tower; persecuting Rochester with letters; thrasonically exalting his past services, throwing out dark hints that he will do a mischief yet, if he be not attended to. A mischief: for he has secrets of Rochester's: secrets or a secret, which Dryasdust to small purpose at this distance beats his poor

[1] *Pictor. Hist.*, iii. 54.

brains to discover. Was it the poisoning of Prince Henry? Dark suspicions of that kind are afloat; to which his Majesty, had he been a loving parent, might have attended more. Nay, was it some unutterable business, conceivable in foul imaginations, but to be kept forever unspoken, especially by Majesty and Rochester? Dryasdust, thy imagination is most vile, thy intellect is most dark; thou unfortunate son of Nox. It is likely this Under-secretary Overbury in a seven years intimacy with such an Upper-secretary, might know many secrets, not quite convenient to be discovered! What they were, we none of us shall ever know in the least,—and some of us do not care in the least, would not give a doit to know completely. I prithee, close the lid of that foul fancy of thine; it is malodorous; the nostril is afflicted by it; the lungs taste poison from it. I would not give thee half a doit for all the interpretation thou wilt ever throw on these matters; it should be other knowledge that we seek in the midst of poisons and malodours! Silence, thou son of the Cesspools! Very clearly Overbury in the Tower continues importunate, insolent, of a most intemperate tongue; and a proud, hothearted, foolish young woman knows of it;—and is consulting conjurers in Lambeth, and has Procuress Turner, and Apothecary Franklin, many bad men and cunning bad women at her bidding; and is now within sight, almost within grasp, of Rochester Car, the Teviotdale Sungod,— wading towards him with open arms and heart half or wholly mad, through rivers of tribulation, crime and despair. Overbury had better not thwart such a humour, if he knew it. Nay, she has an Uncle, old Volpone Northampton, he too knows of it; he too, for his own objects, wishes that she may attain her Sungod, and make all the Howards great. Overbury calls her base woman, openly declares his hatred of all Howards. Such sport will he spoil; and thrasonically declares it: 'When will you bring me out? you dare not 'keep me here?' For the man's voice is still intemperate. Better cut him off by poison? Slow poison, suggests Mrs.

CHAP. XV.] THE OVERBURY MURDER 119

Turner, Earl Northampton, or the Devil through some other agent; and in the third week of his imprisonment the slow process is begun. Overbury's tongue continues as intemperate as ever; but there is a new keeper appointed for him, a new Lieutenant of the Tower appointed;[1] Northampton beckoning mysteriously, they mysteriously responding; Overbury's friends are all excluded, his father and mother persuaded home again; and Procuress Turner, with apothecaries, with rosalgar and corrosive sublimate and white arsenic in small quantities, are sapping and mining.

It was about the end of Summer when the unspeakable Divorce case ended, and foolish hot-hearted poor young Lady Frances got free of Essex; saw herself advancing through the River of Horrors towards the land of Everlasting Sunshine; towards the Teviotdale Sungod, namely. By Heaven I could pity the poor young wretch; struggling so towards a heaven; which proved such a heaven! I cannot slay her without tears. It is a case for George Sand and the French Romances,—if not rather for the old Teutonic Peatbogs. Of such stuff are we all;—and when such stuff gets uppermost in any of us, Eternal Justice bids inexorably that it be put down again;—if not by wigged judges, hangman, and gibbet, then by unwigged Lynch and his rifle: down, one way or other, it must and shall be put. Nature and Destiny and all the gods have inexorably said it, and if the wigged judge, as I say, will not do it, Lynch will have to do it; and also to send the wigged judge by and by into limbo, or some repository of old wigs: such judge, I should say, is not long for this world!—Overbury takes a deal of poisoning; the process being slow.[2] He has had as much as would poison twenty men, say apothecary Franklin and Keeper Weston. At length on the 15th September 1613, he dies—all covered

---

[1] Sir Jervis Elwes was installed as successor to Sir William Wade in the Lieutenancy of the Tower.

[2] Some affirmed that the poison sent for Overbury was withheld from him for a time.

with blotches, a miserable, tragic object, fit for French Romances; and is huddled that same day into a deep grave within the Tower; and so we smooth the Earth-mound down, close, close, and begin to look about us now for our rewards. The river of Horrors is now waded; heaven is now here— such as it is.—Overbury's death is 15th September, Rochester Somerset's wedding is 26th December.

On 26th December, many things being now annihilated, two Lovers are made happy: Majesty assisted and all the Court Galaxy of Stars: a wedding of unimaginable pomp; coranto-dancing, masquing, and deray,—such pomp as never even Chelsea saw when the leather Seagods spake in verse. Poor fool Frances, poor fool Rochester have their heaven; and, I find, take up their lodgings at the Cockpit in St. James's. Northampton and the Howards strike the stars.— But let us hasten. Northampton soon dies; all men do so soon die! The Howards are all since dead, and no star shifted from its place. *O curas hominum!* Overbury is buried deep; but murder, they say, will out. Popular rumour, sounding into all quarters and crevices, sounds at length into some ear that can give response. It is evident! His Majesty not without a love of justice, not without a terror of appearing unjust, summons all the Judges, Coke upon Lyttleton at their head; Majesty says passionately: Foul murder! search it out; God reward it on me and mine, if I screen any murderers. And so last Autumn and Winter from October on to Christmas 1615, there was an investigating, a deponing, pleading and empanelling, and the whole foul matter is brought forth into clear daylight before God and the country; and the gallows is not idle. First Weston, Overbury's appointed keeper in the Tower, is tried; on the 19th October 1615, he,—and he will not plead or speak Guilty or Not-Guilty, being urged to silence by high persons in the Cockpit, as is like. Coke upon Lyttleton explains to him that the Law can make a man plead: that the Law can squeeze him by hyper-Bramah presses, feed him on 'water from the nearest puddle,'—render him very glad to plead. Go to your cell again, my man Weston; and consider that. Weston on his next appearance pleads; Apothecary Franklin, driven by conscience, peaches; Weston peaches; is found guilty,—sent swiftly to the gallows. Concerning whom I observe only this: Two gentlemen ride up to him on the ladder at Tyburn,—seem to speak words with him; one of which gentlemen, I seem to myself to know. Heavens, he is Sir John Holles, whom I saw fencing in Sherwood Forest, many years since, spoiling Jervase Markham in one important particular.[1] He is father of the boy Denzil; has Denzil at College somewhere; a prosperous gentleman this John; Markham has never forgiven him. He from his saddle speaks earnestly to Weston that he would revoke his confession, his accusation of great persons: 'What ho, Weston, wilt thou die, doing thy kind 'masters a disservice?'—'May it please you, I am going to 'be hanged, and seem now to be my own master. Think 'you, worshipful Sir John, will the Grand Headmaster, Maker, 'Creator and Eternal Judge of us all, like me better for going 'to Him with a lie in my mouth? Worshipful Sir John, if 'you ever come to be hanged yourself—!' Weston dies sticking to his confession; worshipful Sir John Holles and the other gentleman are tried at criminal Law,[2] get thrown into the Tower, for this service; but ere too long get out again. Fain would worshipful Sir John Holles have done my lord of Somerset a service, but he could not, Death and the Devil were too strong.

Franklin too is hanged; though he peached it could not save him. The light of day breaks in and ever in upon this dark business; and now London rings with it, and England rings with it; foolish countenances are agape and foolish

---

[1] See Carlyle's *Miscellanies*, vi. 214-18.
[2] Sir John Holles, Sir John Wentworth and Mr. Lumsden were summoned to the Starchamber for having by this proceeding 'traduced the Publick Justice.' *State Trials*, 13 James I., 1615, No. 110.

tongues go wagging, happily all silent now.—How often have I too seen a sooty smith with forge-hammer grounded under broad black palm, with wide eyes and mouth stand swallowing a tailor's news! The Bog of Lindsey has it now. —Forward! Mrs. Turner is tried and hanged; a truly wretched female who once saw better days, a Doctor's or Chirurgeon's widow it would seem; but destitute of money, which my Lady of Essex is well supplied with; 'was my Lady ' of Essex's servant, had no way of living but through my Lady ' of Essex';—and therewith burst into tears. Lynch himself would have compassion; but Lynch would have something else withal! One good effect of Widow Turner's hanging I consider to have been the disuse of yellow starch. Idle blockheads, forever changing modes, disfiguring their poor unfeathered bodies, had fallen sometime since into discontent with their circular ruff, or linen neckgear, as not yet imposing enough, and thought the effect could be aided, were it starched yellow. Yellow starch accordingly, for it and for all linen got up in mode. For Man in dressing his skin adumbrates unconsciously his inner self, and comes out very peculiar at times. At times I liken him with Butler *Hudibras* to dog distract or monkey sick. Widow Turner being a person of respectability, though at Tyburn, could not but appear in yellow ruffs duly got up; whereupon all the world indignantly scoured its ruff white again. O Widow Turner, Widow Turner, the getting up of that yellow ruff, the night before Tyburn! And thy long ride through London streets, and through this world generally; and respectability in yellow ruff to be devoured by Hemp and Death! Justice inexorably hangs thee, but there are tears in her eyes. And Sir J. Elwes, Knight; he too is tried; defends himself, 'Thou canst not say I did it'; the jury find that he looked through his fingers, that he aided and abetted; he too is hanged. His speech I have read in Dryasdust; an affecting speech on Tower-hill, from the Gibbet-ladder: he confesses all; too ambitious, I wanted to be up in the world, forgot the Law of God; a great sinner, was a gambler too; vowed once, 'may I be hanged if I gamble more'; I gambled more, and see God is just; the King and his Laws are just. Guilty, I, before God and man. Ye friends—I see many friends, there, there, there,—thanks to you! Pray for me! Sir Maximilian Dallison, we have gambled much together; I charge you give it over. Sir M. Dallison answers from horseback that he will. And now the cap being fitted, Elwes says these words: 'O Christians, pray for me, who 'shall never more behold your faces!' The Christians pray for him; who would not? His two servants stand bitterly weeping at his feet. The hangman does his office; and it is ended.

These are edifying things for England; edifying to comment upon by the Winter fires of the year of Redemption 1615! They whom the King delights to honour, pity they had not been honourabler. The foremost of all England, beautiful by nature, doubly beautiful by art, there are they traced into hand-in-glove commerce with blackartists, swindlers, procuresses, corrosive sublimate, treachery and murder: the Devil, it would seem, has his Elect. What Chadderton and Knewstubs, virtuous bible-reading Squirarchy and the painful praying Ministry thought of these things? The shadow of these falls into every thoughtful heart in England.

Oliver is hardly warm in Cambridge till there come tidings that my lord of Somerset and my lady of Somerset are themselves arraigned. In Westminster Hall; 24th May 1616, she; 25th May, he. I will not dwell upon it; would I could bury it in the bottomless Bog of Lindsey where its home, in spite of mortals, yet is. The fated Frances Howard; fair, false, an angel of Heaven, yet with the glare of Hellfire in the face of her. A doomed one. I think Helen of Troy was probably not fairer; Clytemnestra little guiltier; Medea of Colchis little fataler. Tragedies could be written of her: but it skills not. The History of

James's Reign generally has been written as if by mutinous valets; rioting in flunky saturnalia, the Master being gone. They worshipped this goggle-eyed Scotch Majesty as a visible god while alive among them, the proudest saying, 'Here is 'skin and soul to boot, much at your Majesty's service: this 'poor skin of mine, would it please your Majesty to have it 'flayed, tanned in any way, and made into boots for your 'Majesty's wear?' And Majesty once gone, they burst out into undisguised insolence of Flunkyism; no lie too black for them, no platitude too gross.—Frances Howard appears at the Bar in Westminster Hall: Lords all in ermine, scarlet, Attorney Bacon in black silk, with eyes like a viper. Serjeant Montague with black patch on his crown; Chancellor Ellesmere with shaving-dish hat; Coke upon Lyttleton; there are they all; and the fatal Medea-Clytemnestra Howard 'with 'bare axe borne before her;' trembling very much. She is in black of the finest, or superfinest, hoops, ruffs, with white 'cobweb lace,' chimneypot chaperon or hat of I know not what felt or chip: a beautiful pale trembling Daughter of the Air,—of the Prince of the Power of the Air. They read her indictment; at the name of Weston she gave way to tears, she lifted her fan, screened her face with it, and wept till the indictment was done. Guilty: she pleads Guilty. Guilty? He with the viper eyes had a speech ready, which will not be of use then![1] Frances Howard, what hast thou to say, etc.? A voice of the smallest, not audible in Court, till he of the viper eyes repeats it, answers: 'My Lords, I can 'much aggravate, but nothing extenuate my fault. I desire 'mercy, and that the Lords will intercede for me to the King.' Sentence is pronounced: 'That you be hanged by the neck 'till you be dead; and the Lord have mercy upon your soul.'

Next day appears my Lord of Somerset. Superfinest satin doublet, velvet cloak, eyes sunk and face very pale. 'Not guilty, my Lords,' says Somerset: and defends himself against Bacon of the viper eyes, not without acuteness, not

---

[1] See Bacon's Works, Birch, iii. 493.

without dignity. His Majesty was in some terror he ' might
' fly out,' being very hot of temper, and blab Court secrets:
but he did not. Who can say I knew of Overbury's poisoning? This thing was unknown to me, and that thing.
There were others to poison him, I suppose. They whom he
had injured beyond forgiveness might poison him, perhaps:
was I to be his shield? It was a duel they had with him.
In his heart lurks that insinuation; but openly on the tongue
only this, 'I knew it not.' On him, too, the sentence is
passed, ' Be hanged till you be dead,' etc. This, on the 25th
of May, 1616.

And so the Tragedy is ended then? Justice done: a land
cleansed of blood? Alas, his Majesty was a Rhadamanthus,
but in theory only. Weston said, ' I see they will catch the
' little flies, but the big ones shall escape.' Even so, his
Majesty pardoned fatal Frances, pardoned the husband of
fatal Frances; emits them in succession with due pauses
of years and sums of years, from their imprisonment in
the Tower.[1]

They quit the Tower; but they are very miserable. Their
daughter and only child marries the Earl of Bedford's son
and heir: they fall sick, have fallen poor, obscure:—fall very
miserable: handsomer had Rhadamanthus done his part and
ended them at once!

CHAPTER XVI

KING JAMES'S DISCOURSE IN THE STAR-CHAMBER

[1616]

THOSE dreadful Overbury-Somerset affairs being well over,
and the parties either hanged or lodged in the Tower, his

[1] 'The Earl and his Lady were released from their confinement in the Tower
in January 1621-2, the latter dying 23rd August 1632. . . . The Earl of
Somerset survived his Lady; and dying in July 1645, was buried in the church
of St. Paul's, Covent Garden.'—*State Trials*, ii. 966.

Majesty thinks he will relieve his royal heart by a bit of good public speaking. He proceeds, on the 20th of June, 1616, to the Star-Chamber, and to the assembled Peers and Judges there pronounces with a most earnest face, and energetic Northern accent of voice, his world-famous 'Discourse in the Star-Chamber';[1]—intimating to all ranks of persons in this country how their respective duties are to be done. As a universal Brood-hen and most provident assiduous Clucker, does this great Monarch gather the three Nations under his wings, and cluck-cluck to them: lulling, admonishing, caressing, reproaching them. He thinks, after these commotions, it will have a good effect in composing the general mind a little. A kinder heart beats not in any man or clucker; think also what a flashing fury there is, should danger, disobedience, or any devilry occur! A most vigilant, vehement, Royal Clucker, rolling large eyes on every side of him; coercing, compescing; ready, if need be, to fly out in flashes of fury, with his feathers up, and voice at a mere screech! Dread Sovereign! For we are an old and experienced King. And consider, Master Brook, whether it be a light matter to lead some millions of people, and be clucker over them?

This world-famous Discourse can still be read in King James's Works; but I do not much advise the general reader to try it. Heaven knows, the British Nation did and does ever need to be admonished, rebuked, guided forward by some King! Some greatest man, who, with gold crown on his head, and bodyguard round him, or totally without any such appendage and mark of recognition, is King of the country; is, I say, and remains King, the other King socalled being merely one of shreds and patches, with much broken meat, expensive cast apparel, and waste revenue flung to him, but with no real authority in this world or in any other,—a Morrice-dance King, most beautiful to the flunky; most tragic, almost frightful to every thinking heart. The

---

[1] 'Made a very fine Speech,' says Camden.

CHAP. XVII.] BURNING OF THE PLAY-HOUSE 127

peculiarity of this King James is that he assumes the part of a real King, not in the least suspecting that he has become a sham-King. Hence our laughter at his cluck-clucking, which were otherwise very venerable. Nowadays your Sham-king knows his trade too well: it has been followed for above two hundred years now, and he ought to know it a little.

CHAPTER XVII

BURNING OF THE NEW PLAY-HOUSE IN DRURY LANE, A PURITAN RIOT

[4th March 1616-7]

ON Shrove Tuesday the 4th of March, 1616-7, there assembled in several quarters, many disorderly persons of sundry kinds, among whom were very many boys and young lads:[1] these assembled themselves in Lincoln's Inn Fields, Finsbury Field, in Ratcliff and Stepney Field; wherever young persons were met for mirth of Shrovetide; singularly consentaneous groups of illegal young men; and some infectious notion getting abroad among them, they in their respective localities took to pulling down the houses of ill-fame of this Metropolis, determined that London should be rid of one abomination at least. Houses of ill-fame they violently smashed to ruin; the doors, windows, all frangible materials of them; tumbling out the accursed furniture of them, scattering many a terrified Doll Tearsheet and brassfaced Mistress Quickly amid shrieks and howls. Mere victualling houses, Taverns for strong drink, they, fancying these too might secretly be houses of ill-fame, took to smashing. Thou shalt not suffer a Devil's servant to live. What is this sale of strong waters; whom does it benefit, if not Tearsheet and Quickly, Sathanas and Company? A man selling liquid madness by the gill, ought

[1] Stow, 1026.

to look in God's Word; see whether there, or elsewhere out of Tophet, there be any warrant for him! Begone ye Missionaries of Insanity, ye recruiters for Bedlam, ye brass-faced, detestable Quicklys, ye unfortunate females generally and unfortunate males! Audible shriek rises from amid the general hum of London; Doll Tearsheet weeping; brandy-faced Quickly herself grown pale. Sir F. Michell, the Knight of Clerkenwell; he drives a pretty trade, I am told, he the *un*worshipful protecting bordels in that dense quarter of the City, negotiating with Council-boards to wink at them: but to-day he is powerless to protect, — glad if he can protect himself.

What a sound rises to us, reaches even to us, out of that Shrovetide in old London! The riotous young populace goes about with some voice, not of the 'Five Points' Weekly Intelligencer, but of the Christian Scriptures, in its head; says inarticulately, in a voice audible though mixed with mere riotous mischievous ingredients,—voice semi-animal, as like a billow as a voice,—'Servants of Satan, depart! It is you 'that bring God's curse upon us, you that ought palpabliest 'to depart! Away!'—Puritanism has spread downwards to the populace; our Apprentice riots are getting Puritan! Wait a little, my pretty young ones; grow to strength of bone; many a one of you will get a Gospel matchlock to carry yet, with bandaliers, with bullets in your cheek;[1] and have a juster mark than poor Doll Tearsheet to aim at. You will see the Devil's Own drawn out rank and file, with banners spread, lintstocks kindled, in full strength and truculence: at *them* you shall make a dash,—if it lie in you!

These riotous young persons, scum of the population with some dash of the Christian Scriptures in it, were of course visited by Dogberry and Verges, nay, by the worshipful Sheriffs of London and such constabulary force and united

---

[1] In default of *pouches* the soldiers in those days carried a supply of bullets in their mouths.

CHAP. XVII.] BURNING OF THE PLAY-HOUSE 129

Justices of Middlesex as they could muster: but them they 'resisted and despitefully used,' not valuing them a rush. Go home, ye worshipful Sheriffs; we say certain avowed Devil's servants shall presently depart. Towards night they decide on a very extraordinary, new step, decide on checking. or stopping the progress of the Legitimate Drama! Believe it, Posterity: Shakspeare is not yet dead a year, and James Shirley is a lad at school, and Ben and Beaumont and many rare friends of mine are in their prime, when this riotous assemblage pours itself towards Drury Lane; operates with crowbars on the fair new Playhouse lately builded there. With crowbars, with sledgehammers, extempore battering-rams,— torches too in the distance seem possible to me. What floods of tin armour, paper crowns, pasteboard Tempest-Islands and the vasty fields of France, pour themselves from the upper windows; with clangour frightful to consider!

'Stop them, stop them, ye joltheads!' His Majesty is supping hard by in Somerset House, in solemn State that evening with the jolly broadfaced Queen Anne, whom it is rare for him to visit; making a right merry Shrovetide; when this insane clangour of the destructive populace invades his ear. They are pulling Drury Lane to pieces; Dogberry and Verges and the Constabulary Force are in flight, and the Sheriff they have resisted and despitefully used! Out with the Trainedbands; let the Lords of the Council proclaim instant Martial-law: so orders the angry Parent-fowl; by my soul we will stop them, if our feathers once rise. Martial-law, I believe, means very rapid hanging; I believe, almost on the spur of the instant. A stringent riot-act. The illegal populace hears word of it; rapidly ebbs home; leaving the Legitimate Drama to its fate. Majesty held his solemn supper with the broadfaced jolly one; a high Lady of considerable substance bodily and spiritual, not without decision, goodhumour and motherwit, whom I rather like, though her face is freckled, and her Danish hair too blond for me. His Majesty, the populace having ebbed home again, was pleased,

I

nay delighted. Somerset House, says he, in some pause of the coranto-dancing and comfit-eating, this is called Somerset House, but in honour of my beloved Queen and this night, I will that it be henceforth called Denmark House. We will drink prosperity to Denmark House, if you please!—responded to with loud acclaim; drunk I suppose, with gusto by every one from the Queen to the meanest of her subjects. And so ends Shrovetide, 1616-7. This Puritan riot I thought good to take a glance at.

CHAPTER XVIII

BACON

AT London on the 7th day of May, 1617, observe a thing worth one slight glance from us. Sir Francis Bacon, he whom we saw with the liquorish brown eyes pleading as Attorney General in my Lord and Lady of Somerset's case,— he is now made Lord Keeper, High Chancellor, or whatever name they give it; and is this day astonishing the London Public and the Middle Aisle of Paul's by his 'mighty pro- 'cession,' as the admiring Dryasdust calls it, 'on the first day 'of Term.'[1] A procession and cavalcade such as new Lord Keepers are used to give; but this is far mightier,—very grand indeed;—starting I know not where, consisting of I know not what; caparisoned grand horses, caparisoned grand men, long-gowned Law Lords and sublime Lord Keeper with his purse and great seal; learned Serjeants, horse-cloths, trumpets, tabards and trumpery: one of the sublimest Processions; which the Middle Aisle generally must admit to surpass most things. This new Lord Keeper, I find, is fifty-four years of age; and the high topgallant of his

[1] The Great Seal was delivered to Sir F. Bacon, the King's Attorney, aged fifty-four, on 7th March, 1617; 'solemn Procession in mighty pomp' took place on the first day of Term, 7th May. Camden.—Bacon had been made Lord Chancellor on the 7th January, 1616-7; and six months later he was raised to the Peerage under the title of Lord Verulam.

fortunes, fruit of endless industries, and assiduity fit to attain the amaranth crown and cap of immortality, is now attained. There rides he sublime, with purse and big seal; shall have the beatitude of sealing into authenticity the behests of George Villiers and James Stuart, the Dread Sovereign. Next year they make him Baron Verulam. There rides he for the present, with his white ruff, with his fringed velvet cloak and steeple hat, and 'liquorish viper eyes'; a very prosperous man. O Francis Bacon, my Lord of Verulam, if they had appointed one the Lord Keeper to the Chancery of Heaven, as I have known it happen to some, so that one could seal into authenticity the behests of God Almighty instead of George Villiers' behests,—it had been something! There is in this Lord Keeper an appetite, not to say a ravenousness, for earthly promotion and the envy of surrounding flunkies, which seems to me excessive. Thou knowest him, O reader. he is that stupendous Bacon who discovered the new way of discovering truth,—as has been very copiously explained for the last half century,—and so made men of us all. Undoubtedly a most hot seething, fermenting piece of Life with liquorish viper eyes; made of the finest elements, a beautiful kind of man, if you will; but of the earth, earthy; a certain seething, ever-fermenting prurience which prodigally burns up things:—very beautiful, but very clayey and terrene every thing of them;—not a great soul, which he seemed so near being, ah no!

The King discovered Bacon's large genius and also its intrinsic hollowness; the many coloured lambent light as if from Heaven, and also how it was in good part a light not from Heaven at all, but from the earthly market-place with its fish-oil lamps and curiously cut and coloured glasses;— alas, a light not even of honest fish-oil: how beautiful to some eyes is the light of fish itself in a certain state of forwardness! Putridity, O Dryasdust, is not without luminosity, nay, radiance of a sort; and one day thou wilt discover that Prophets are other than inspired shop-keepers;

that *Novum Organum* teaching us how to discover truth is good, but that a poor John Kepler making out by natural *Vetus Organum*, by the light of his own flaming soul, in hunger and obstruction, after *experimentum crucis* seventy times repeated in the heart's blood of the man, the greatest discovery yet made by man, the laws namely of the Heavenly stars, was worth, even for scientific purposes, a horse load of Organums! This Bacon, with his eye like a viper, is nevertheless a pretty man shining out of the dark place; a man in whose light I have sought for guidance but not hitherto found any. The dark places of my destiny were not made clear to me by these many-tinted flickering transparencies. In such moods and stern necessities that lie in the path of men, the transparencies, the augments of the sciences, O my Lord Chancellor!—Does your Lordship think the sciences can be augmented effectually by an augmentation of shop-drawers where one reposits them; better methods of labelling, of mixing, compounding and separating,—by any augment of machinery whatever! Such augments shall be welcome, but not the welcomest at all! The spirit of sincerity, of self-sacrifice, of common honesty, my Lord; these once shed abroad, we shall have augment of the knowledges and other good things; not otherwise, I believe. Knowledges are attained by the flaming soul of man writing its knowledge formulas in its own heart's blood; only Pedantries, drowsy pretentious Ineptitudes, Dryasdustisms, are attainable otherwise. It is of the former that Prophets have always prophesied from their Pisgah-heights, not of the latter. Call you that a Pisgah? I call it a common Hampstead Hill, where will lie a broken-down Chancellor gone to ashes in his own phosphorescence; ruined by ambition, secularity, insincerity, and at last bribery and common want of cash: a sight tragic to see.

How can a great soul like Bacon's worship a James; spend itself in struggling to gain the favour of a James? Patience, reader; he is the last such. Our next great soul is a

Milton; he will prove unbuyable by your Jameses; unbuyable enough! . . .

His Majesty being absent in Scotland when Bacon was appointed Lord Keeper, he (as I find recorded in the mutinous-flunky pages of Dryasdust), being left with some chief authority, played the amazingest tricks:[1] slept in the King's beds, held levées, tried so far as he could what real-imaginary sovereignty was. For which they shoved him almost into annihilation, the real Sovereigns did, at their return: and he had to do obeisance to George Villiers, and cry, with what of nobleness he could, 'Have pity on me, thou 'mighty one!' Much whereof I do not care to believe. But true enough the hatred borne to this man, by high and by low, seems very great. Alas, in fact this great man is of flunky nature. . . . Let us leave him, let us leave him, wish him big revenues, big stacks of lawpapers, old hats, marine stores,[2] cast-apparel and unrivalled shop-lists: out of such came never any word of life, nor will. Seekest thou great things, seek them not. There, whither thou strivest, it is even as here, not a whit better. Stand to thy tools *here*, and be busy for the Eternities; and noble as a Protestant Hebrew, not base as a Whitechapel one.—Enough of Bacon.[3]

---

[1] Weldon, *Secret History of the Court of James I.*, i. 438.

[2] Worn-out tackle and other odds and ends for sale in second-hand shops at Sea-ports.

[3] The above reflexions on the author of the 'Novum Organum' will seem to many excessively severe; but they do not exceed in severity what Weldon, Wilson, and others have put on record regarding Bacon. 'He was,' says Arthur Wilson, 'the true emblem of human frailty, being more than a man in some things, and less than a woman in others. His crime was Briberie and Extortion, . . . and these he had often condemned others for as a *Judge*, which now he comes to suffer for as a *Delinquent*: And they were proved and aggravated against him with so many circumstances, that they fell very foully on him, both in relation to his reception of them, and his expending of them: For that which he raked in, and scrued for one way, he scattered and threw abroad another; . . . This poor gentleman, mounted above pity, fell below it: His Tongue, that was the glory of his time for Eloquence (that tuned so many sweet Harrangues) was like a forsaken Harp, hung upon the Willows, whilst the waters of affliction

CHAPTER XIX

THE KING'S JOURNEY TO SCOTLAND

[1617]

SHROVETIDE riots and festivities, Francis Bacon's Lord-keepership, and Oliver Cromwell's return from Cambridge, kindling up the dark void of Dryasdust a little, one begins to discern that, even now in these weeks,[1] his Majesty made a Royal Progress into Scotland; his first thither, since we saw him fire the shot on Berwick Walls, and also his last.

It is indisputable his Majesty visited Scotland; but by itself it has ceased to be very memorable. There are healthy human memories withal; let them be thankful that they have a talent for forgetting. Magniloquent loyal Addresses more than one, on this occasion, full of drowsy Bombast, like tales told by an idiot, I have read, and will not remember. History, human Intelligence, has to stand between the Living and the Dead. The Addresses to Royalty in that age are perhaps the drowsiest of all on record. They are very false, we may say they are the first really false loyal Addresses delivered by

---

overflowed the banks. And now his high-flying *Orations* are humbled to *supplications*, and thus he throws himself, and Cause, at the feet of his Judges, before he was condemned:' [Here follows the Humble Submission and Supplication of the Lord Chancellor to the Right Hon. Lords of the Parliament]... 'Though he had a pension allowed him by the King, he wanted to his last, living obscurely in his lodgings at Gray's Inn, where his loneness and desolate condition, wrought upon his ingenious, and therefore then more melancholy temper, that he pined away. And had this unhappiness after all his height of plenitude, to be denied beer to quench his thirst: For having a sickly taste, he did not like the beer of the house, but sent to Sir Fulk Grevill, Lord Brook, in neighbourhood (now and then) for a bottle of his beer, and after some grumbling the Butler had order to deny him.' *Life and Reign of James I.*, 159-61.

Spedding's *Letters and Life* of Lord Bacon, which Carlyle read in later years (1861-74) a little modified his opinion of the great but erring genius; though he never became one of Carlyle's heroes or great men. See, also, *post*, p. 170.

[1] The King set forward on his Journey into Scotland about four o'clock in the afternoon, March 14th, 1617.—Camden.

English persons, but they do not yet feel that they are false, nay, they as it were unconsciously lament that they are false; and accordingly inflate themselves into bombast, now grown very sorrowful to us.[1] Our Loyal Addresses, in the progress of things, have long since recognised themselves as false,— they know better now than to go into bombast. They say, We too are tales told by an idiot; God help us, man surely was not meant to do aperies and tales told by an idiot;— but they shall at least be done *without* the sound and fury,— in a very gentle style, a style conscious that it cannot be too gentle.

His Majesty's businesses in Scotland, doubt it not, were manifold.[2] Festivities, huntings, bombast Addresses, these are pleasant pastime; and for the earnest hours of a Solomon there are thrums enough gone a-ravelling to knit up in such

---

[1] As a specimen of the style of these addresses take the following extract from that delivered by the Deputy-town-clerk of Edinburgh to king James on the occasion of the above visit: 'How joyful your majesty's return (gracious and dread sovereign) is to this your majesty's native town, from the kingdom due to your sacred person, by royal descent, the countenances and eyes of these your majesty's loyal subjects speak for their hearts. This is that happy day of our new birth, ever to be retained in fresh memory . . . acknowledged with admiration, admired with love, and loved with joy, wherein our eyes behold the greatest human felicity our hearts could wish, which is to feed upon the royal countenance of our true Phoenix, the bright star of our northern firmament, the ornament of our age, wherein we are refreshed, yea revived with the heat and beams of our sun. . . . The very hills and groves accustomed before to be refreshed with the dew of your majesty's presence, not putting on their wonted apparel, but with pale looks, representing their misery for the departure of their royal king.'—R. H. Stevenson, *Chronicles of Edinburgh*, p. 137.

[2] 'His chief object in visiting Scotland was to effect the complete establishment of the Episcopal form of church government, and to assimilate the religious worship of the two countries. Without the least spark of religious zeal, James was most determinedly bent on the subversion of the Presbyterian system, the spirit and form of which he detested more than ever, as inimical to his notion of the divine right of kings, and their absolute supremacy over the church as well as state. From the time of the controversy with the English Puritans at Hampton Court, he had been devising how he should fully restore episcopacy to Scotland. . . . Soon after, the bishops, who had never altogether ceased to exist in name, were re-established in authority and in revenue,—that is, to the extent fo the power of James and his slavish court.'—*Pictorial Hist.*, iii. p. 64.

a country. Those old Church-lands; seized really with an unspeakable coolness by our hungry Vicekings or Aristocracy here, when the Nation set about reforming its Religion: had the hungry Vicekings before all men the clear right to them? A cooler stroke of legislative trade I have not seen anywhere, —nor had my friend Knox seen anywhere. Majesty thinks the Headking might as well have these lands back again to himself. This Church too, besides its poverty, is all out at elbows every way. A ragged, ill-tempered kind of Church; much given to censuring persons in authority; never duly reverent of the Earthly Majesty, shadow of God in this Earth. They ought to have real Bishops, they ought to have Surplices, ceremonies; it would bind them to good behaviour. No Bishop, no King. His Majesty in secret, I discern, is preparing the Five Articles of Perth;[1] emblematic of good ceremonial; five Articles, unrememberable though oft committed to memory; in two years more, by packed Assemblies, and other kingcraft methods of hook and of crook, he will get those Five Articles, and see visions of Scotch Bishops, though still only stuffed-skin Bishops,—Tulchan[2] Bishops as the Scots called them.—Gently, your Majesty!— — Dr. Laud, a small chaplain, lean little tadpole of a man, with red face betokening hot blood: him I note there authentically as Chaplain to the King. These preparations for the Phantom Bishops, stuffed surplices, he in a subaltern way discerns gladly. Surveying this savage country with attentive view, he can discern as yet no 'religion' in it, none. Such is his verdict. You will seek between the Mull of Galloway

[1] The Five Articles of Perth are given in full in Spottiswood's *Church of Scotland*, p. 538 (Edition, 1655). Condensed they are as follows: (1) The Communion to be received kneeling. (2) In case of illness and necessity the Lord's Supper to be administered in private houses. (3) Baptism, *ditto*. (4) Various Fast Days to be observed. (5) Children to be brought to the Bishop for a blessing.

[2] A Tulchan is a calf's skin stuffed with straw, and set beside a cow to make her give milk; and a Tulchan Bishop, one who received the Episcopate on condition of assigning the temporalities to a secular person.—*Jamieson*. See also Carlyle's *Cromwell*, i. 44.

and John of Groat's, inquiring after such an article, in vain, for what I could see. 'The churches are as like barns as ' churches'; there is not a surplice in the country; I question if there be a tailor in the country that could cut you a decent surplice. The tradition of religion seems lost.—No religion in this country, think you, Doctor? There are men living here that have heard John Knox. They have a notion here that man consists of a soul as well as of a body with tippets. I am sorry to find they have 'no religion,' Doctor! The little redfaced screechy Doctor takes his first survey of this country.

His Majesty, as I bethink me, returned from Edinburgh (it was now grown Autumn) by the pleasant Western Road, by Drumlanrig and Dumfries, at which latter Burgh, very interesting to me otherwise, it was our lot to suffer by a sleepy mass of bombast promulgated at the old Port on Lady Devorgilla's old Nith-Bridge (blessings on her Lady-heart, she built a bridge there, some five hundred years ago, and founded Abbeys and Balliol College at Oxford, and her footprints in this world are still lovely to men and gods): a somniferous Town-Council harangue, I say, got up by some extinct Dominie Sampson of the neighbourhood, with steam almost at the bursting point, whom I do not bless; and pronounced at the old Nith-Bridge Port by ancient Provost and civic authorities, and a wondering ancient population, — very wonderful to me.—Ye Eternities, ye Silences! Nith River rushes by brown from his mossy fountains, singing his very ancient song, and the salmon mount in Spring;—and a Burns has been there;—and the Exits and the Entrances are in fact miraculous to me. Nith River rolls;—and the River of Existence rolls: to the Sea, to the great still Sea! Mr. Rigmarole, somnambulant charmer, have you any notion of the really miraculous?— —His Majesty does on this happy occasion present the Dumfries Population with a miniature bit of ordnance in real silver, saying, 'Shoot for it annually,' and encourage the practice of weapons. Which 'Siller Gun' and annual practice of shooting did accordingly continue itself almost to our own days. Scotch readers know *The Siller Gun*, by a Dumfries Native named John Mayne, a small brown Poem-Book, not without merit: as good as some Ostade Picture of poor extinct burghers and their humours; to be hung in the corner, and looked at, not without emotion. These burghers, too, are all vanished and become transfigured; their three-cornered hats, their old hair-queues, are already acquiring some preternaturalism for us. Their noise, their loud vociferation, and ha-ha-ing on that Siller-gun day, is it not all gone dumb? Ye Silences, ye Eternities! This was the chief trace his Majesty left in Scotland for the Writer of these pages!

CHAPTER XX

THE BOOK OF SPORTS

[May, 1618]

His Majesty was always fond of Archery, of manly sports and recreations. Coming[1] into Lancashire, his princely bowels are touched with two things: the sorrowful temper of the Protestant people, especially their sad way of spending Sunday, and the considerable number of Papists who deny the King's Supremacy. Two indisputable evils. These Papists deny our Supremacy; are dangerous fellows; they were near blowing us up with Gunpowder a little while ago. And our Protestants, alas, they are all Puritan; they spend the Sunday in mere readings of the Word, in mere meditations on Death, Judgment and Eternity. Much revolving in his royal heart these indubitable evils, his Majesty discerns that both may be helped, and new stimulus given to Archery withal and manly sports, by one wise stroke of legislation. He promulgates in Lancashire his Royal Proclamation per-

[1] On his return from Scotland.

mitting manly sports on Sunday after church service, commanding all ministers to say that they are permitted. Poor Majesty, a well meant stroke of legislation, but the unsuccessfullest I ever heard of. Horror, abnegation, despair, execration fervent but unspoken, seizes the heart of all Bible Christians in England. Has not God above written, Remember the Sabbath day to keep it holy; and here your Majesty bids us make it unholy? Archeries, Church-ales, football, leapfrog, dancing and Church-farthing—are these the ways of sanctifying a Sabbath of the Lord?—'Tush, 'tush,' snarls his Majesty, 'ye understand little of it!' These Church-ales, leapfrog and such like, do not ye perceive I grant them to nobody *till* he has attended Church-service? Is not there an encouragement to Protestant Church-going? You have no legislative acumen, you! The Papists used to have a merry Sunday; but see, now they dare not sport openly. My Sport Book says expressly it is this sad Puritan Sabbatism that deters weak vessels from conversion to Protestantism in those parts. They dare not be converted to passing the Sunday in that manner! It is too gloomy for them. Let me introduce a little football, encourage Protestantism, open a smoother road Heavenwards, and become a noted 'Easy-'shaving shop.'—This is the far-famed Book of Sports, published 24th May, 1618, received with horror, with speechless but felt execration, by all Bible Christians in England. I know not if even the surplice Christians thought much good of it.[1]

[1] Neal (*History of the Puritans*, ii. p. 115) says the Book of Sports was drawn up by Bishop Moreton. Archbishop Abbot disapproved of it, and refused to allow it to be read in the Church at Croydon.

CHAPTER XXI

EXECUTION OF RALEIGH

[1618]

On the morning of 29th October, 1618, in Palace Yard, a cold morning, equivalent to our 8th of November, behold Sir Walter Raleigh, a tall greyheaded man of sixty-five gone. He has been in far countries; seen the El Dorado, penetrated into the fabulous dragon-realms of the West, hanged Spaniards in Ireland, rifled Spaniards in the Orinoco;—for forty years a most busy man; has appeared in many characters: this is his last appearance on any stage. Probably as brave a soul as lives in England;—he has come here to die by the headsman's axe. What crime? Alas, he has been unfortunate; has become an eyesorrow to the Spaniards, and did not discover the El Dorado mine. Since Winchester,[1] when John Gibb came galloping [with a reprieve], he has lain thirteen years in the Tower; the travails of that strong heart have been many. Poor Raleigh, toiling, travailing always; in Court drawing-rooms, in Tower prison-rooms, on the hot shore of Guiana; with gold and promotion in his fancy, with suicide, death and despair in clear sight of him: toiling till his 'brain is broken'[2] and his heart is broken: here stands he at last; after many travails it has come to this with him.

Yesterday, after consultation of the Judges, he appeared in the King's Bench in Whitehall to say why he ought not to die, being doomed fifteen years ago, and only respited by John Gibb, not pardoned? Hard to say: he said what he could. Chief-Justice Montague, a very ugly function for him, had to sit there and answer that it was all naught. To the Gate-

---

[1] Where Raleigh's trial had taken place in November, 1603. He was charged with 'treason,' convicted, sentenced to die. A reprieve came from the king, by the hands of John Gibb, in the very nick of time, and Raleigh was committed to the Tower, there to remain during his Majesty's pleasure.

[2] This expressive phrase is Raleigh's own in a letter to his wife.

house this night, to the scaffold on the morrow.—Here accordingly what a crowd of human faces, all unknown to me! Oliver from some of the Law-offices in Chancery Lane, come truanting hither? It may be; it is not certainly known to me. Earls of Arundel, Northampton and Doncaster in a window. Earl of Clare; our old friend John Holles—Heavens, what a morning! Raleigh's Death-speech, Raleigh's Life History, is inarticulate tragedy itself to us. (Why has none yet loved this Raleigh; made a musical Hero of him? He is a great man.) He raises his voice that the Earl of Arundel and others looking from their window may hear him; they say, 'Nay, we will come down to you, Sir Walter'; and they come down. He has smoked his last pipe of tobacco by candle-light this morning; drunk a cup of sack, saying, 'Good liquor, if a man might tarry by it.' With a stern sympathy John Holles, the tawny, deep-eyed Earl of Arundel, and the assembled thousands listen to him. Bess, his faithful Bess, with her orphan, sits weeping in secret,—one orphan here amid a very stern world; my brave first-born lies buried in Guiana, slain on the other side of the world; and Walter, their father, is to die! It is eight of the clock; a cold November morning;—and the speech ended. 'Would 'you wish to go down and warm yourself a little?' said the sympathetic sheriff. 'Nay, good friend, let us be swift: in a 'quarter of an hour my ague fit will be upon me, and they will 'say I tremble for fear.'—Here is the greatest sacrifice the Spaniards have yet had.

CHAPTER XXII

COURT PRECINCTS—TOURNAMENTS, ETC.

[1621]

D'Ewes had his eyes about him; a brisk young gentleman going about Town; brings comfortable proof to us that the grass was green in those days too. In galooned or plain breeches, with satin or coarser doublet, in cuerpo or with Spanish cloak, busy or idle, men do walk on legs; women, in small steeple hats, in fardingales, in bands yellow starched or otherwise, are somewhat interesting to them. Conceive it, reader! It was not dead, a vacant ghastly Hades, filled with Dryasdustism, with Rymer's *Fœdera* and Doctrines of the Constitution,—that old London;—it was alive; loud-voiced, many-toned, of meaning unfathomable, beautiful, wonderful, fearful. God had made it too,—it was and is not; and we, issuing from it, are, and shall soon not be.

D'Ewes, for one thing, we find goes much to Tournaments. Sublime Tournaments, of frequent occurrence, are the cynosure of intelligent curiosity: there, in all their caparisons and glory, and horse trappings, are the gods of this world to be found. Dryasdust is aware of that Tilt-Yard; there, just behind our present [Horseguards?][1] stands that sublime establishment, of figure somewhat uncertain to me, stands the Tiltyard of King Henry; stands the Cockpit, too, not now a place of cocks alone, but a residence of Car-Somersets, kings' favourites, and Cocks of Jove. These and much else stand there; and 'across the head of King Street' runs an arch and covered passage leading from St. James's Park into the Privy Gallery of Whitehall; and trucks and street passengers rolling freely under the feet of the king, when he chooses to issue in that way. And as yet there is no Parliament Street. Parliament Street is the esplanade of Whitehall and the thoroughfare from King Street to Charing Cross; and Privy Gallery is at the end of it; and Canonries of Westminster, and Cannon Rows behind the Privy Gallery are—I know not what; and Palace Yards, and Passages to Lambeth Ferry. And Westminster Bridge is not, and Whitehall Bridge is. And outward in front of Whitehall and the Banqueting House, spreads some dignified esplanade, with gilt-railing, I doubt not, and Courts of yard; the trucks and cars and street-

[1] In turning the page Carlyle omits some word here, probably 'Horseguards.'

passengers rolling freely in front from King Street to Charing Cross and the Strand. And Royal Whitehall is like a kind of City in itself; the king's household and all manner of courtier persons having their apartments there. And it is all of figure very uncertain to me. For it is all vanished, by fire and otherwise; and only the Banqueting House of Inigo Jones yet stands, got into strange new environment. The fashion of this world passeth away.

What Processions to St. Paul's; what Tilts and high-flown Tournaments, not in the least memorable to me. Take this one seen through the eyes of D'Ewes, and multiply it by as many hundreds spread duly over the dead centuries as your imagination will conveniently hold :—

' *Monday, 8th January* 1621-2.—In the afternoon I went to the Tilt-yard, over against Whitehall, whence four couples ran, to shew the before-mentioned French Ambassador, Cadnet, and divers French Lords that came with him, that martial pastime. Prince Charles himself ran first, with Richard Lord Buckhurst, Earl of Dorset, and brake three staves very successfully. The next couple that ran were the beloved Marquis of Buckingham and Philip Lord Herbert, Earl of Montgomery, younger brother of William Herbert, Earl of Pembroke; but had very bad success in all the courses they made. Marquis Hamilton, a Scotchman, and the King's near kinsman, with Sir Robert Rich, Earl of Warwick, performed their course almost as gallantly as the Prince and Earl of Dorset; but the last couple did worst of all, almost not breaking a staff.

'After this, most of the tilters, except the Prince, went up to the French Lords in a large upper room of the house standing at the lower end of the Tiltyard; and I crowding in after them, and seeing the Marquis of Buckingham discoursing with two or three French Monsieurs, I joined to them, and most earnestly viewed him, for about half an hour's space at the least; which I had opportunity the more easily to accomplish because he stood, all that time he talked, bareheaded. I saw everything in him full of delicacy and handsome features; yea his hands and face seemed to me, especially effeminate and curious. It is possible he seemed the more accomplished, because the French Monsieurs that had invested him, were very swarthy, hard-favoured men. That he was afterwards an instrument of much mischief, both at home and abroad, is so evident upon record as no man can deny; yet this I do suppose proceeded rather from some Jesuited incendiaries about him, than from his own nature, which his very countenance promised to be affable and gentle.'[1]

Thanks, worshipful Sir Simonds ; a man that has eyes and a pen, it is pity he does not take a sketch or two as he passes along through this variegated life-journey. I love measurements by the foot-rule; I love practicalities, Doctrines of the Constitution, arguments by logic, computations by arithmetic; but, alas, these of themselves will do little; these of themselves become brown parchments, torpid Dryasdustisms, dead marine stores, purchaseable bad-cheap at sixpence the ton.

Would to Heaven this seeing Knight, travelling about in that age, were now at my bidding! Thou shouldst go for me, worshipful Sir Simonds, to look on this man and on that. What is Rare Ben saying to it? Tell me what kind of lair he lodges in, that lion-hearted one; mastiff-hearted; irascible, so jovial, faithful; an honest English Spiritual Mastiff. Where is it; what sort of room is it, how many chairs,— what stockings has the Rare Ben on? Is his wife mending shirts? O D'Ewes—!—But the place I would gladliest of all send worshipful D'Ewes to is the Church of St. Giles's Cripplegate, on the morning of 22d August 1620. There is a wedding going on there; I know it yet by the old Parish Books. Oliver Cromwell to Elizabeth Bourchier, daughter of Sir James Bourchier of Felsted Essex. Even so: it is my old friend Oliver who, by time and industry, has brought it thus far. Much has passed in this King's reign; and here too is a thing that has come about: Nollkin, the little bony-faced Boy that went about, in child's cap and breeches, gazing on the Scotch Majesty at Hinchinbrook,[2] has grown to the height of five feet eleven or so, a substantial man of his inches, and is here acquiring in marriage a very great possession, a good wife! We saw him last in the Church-yard burying his Father. The wide rolling river of Existence pauses not; the genera-

[1] Sir Simonds D'Ewes, extracted from *Biog. Brit.*
[2] See *ante*, p. 15.

tions die and are born, let the King do as he will. What this Oliver was like?—O, D'Ewes! what countenance *he* wore, what boots, band, doublet, sword and velvet coat *he* had on! An authentic shadow of the look of that Transaction in St. Giles's Cripplegate, would have worth for me. Mr. Cromwell in the bloom of youth cannot be considered beautiful; but no ingenuous man on the morning of his marriage can well be without beauty. A rugged substantial figure; with modesty, ingenuousness and earnestness, strength of pious simplicity, which is the strongest of all, which I take to be the beautifullest of all. He has dark hair, of the olive black common in England; grey, earnest eyes, beaming very strangely this morning; a nose of fair proportions, inclining decidedly to the left,—not too accurately bisecting the face in the way Painters so dislike. A mouth big enough, none of your poor thin lips; compact, yet extensive, expansive; room in it for all manner of quivering and curling, for fervour, for love and rage, for prayer and menace : a face to me very beautiful, Mr. Palette. Of the Bride I will say so much : her look is what the Scotch call *sonsy* ;[1] caps, cambric ribbons and equipments all betoken an ingenuous wholesome character.

CHAPTER XXIII

JOHN GIBB

[1622 ?]

ONE day at Theobalds his Majesty discussing weighty affairs of State, bethinks him of a certain bundle of Papers, reports or such like of some Public functionary, which will be of essential service to him. He calls for them ; to his astonishment they are not to be found. With waxing impatience he summons this person and that to no purpose ; summons John Gibb, his faithful Scotch valet, who has

[1] Sonsy=well-conditioned, good-humoured, sensible, engaging.

K

attended him out of Scotland, faithful as the shadow to the Sun, and never been found wanting: 'Where *are* those 'Papers?' 'Your Majesty, I know not, I never had them.'— 'Nonsense, I gave them to you; find them, or by——!' His Majesty begins to swear horribly, to rage like the cave of Æolus, threatening to dissolve Nature or eat the carpets from the floor. John Gibb falls on his knees, calls Heaven to witness, as he is his Majesty's faithful slave to death, that he never saw these Papers, never saw them, or heard of them, is ignorant of them as the babe unborn. The cave of Æolus rages with horrible oaths, more dreadfully than ever, rages, stamps, smites the kneeling Gibb on the breast or abdomen with his royal foot! There is life in the humblest oyster, in all living things. John Gibb starts to his legs in silence; in silence issues from the royal presence, beckons his horse from the stable, and mounts, determined to ride to the end of the Earth rather than remain. No sooner is Gibb gone in this manner than some Secretary or Subaltern Official aroused in his closet by the bruit that has everywhere arisen, hurries to the royal presence with the papers in his hand, saying, 'May it please your Majesty, *here*! Your Majesty 'gave them to me!' 'And where is John Gibb?' cries his Majesty. John Gibb has ridden towards the end of the world. Pungent remorse convulses the royal breast into new tempest or counter-tempest. 'Ride, run,' cries his Majesty, all in frenzy, 'bring me back John Gibb or I will 'die. Ride, I say; tell him I will not break bread till I see 'his face again; he will kill his King if he returns not. 'Ride like the wind, and the whirlwind!'—Poor Majesty; the Equerries riding like the whirlwind, overtake John Gibb in a very stern humour about Tottenham Cross, on his way to London; conjure him, not without difficulty, back again; his Majesty blubbers over him in an uncontrollable tempest of tears, O Gibb, O Gibb, falls down on his knees to him, to John Gibb, swears he will never rise again till Gibb forgive him. Think of it; it is very unmajestic, and yet I have known pattern characters of the Solomon and other sorts, who never in their lives were equal to such a thing! I consider his Majesty a good man wrong placed; the function of him was to be a Schoolmaster not a King; he should have been bred up rigorously to command that infirm temper; there in a calm manner how beautifully had he taught the young idea how to shoot, and been respected in his parish!

CHAPTER XXIV

THE SPANISH MATCH[1]

[1623]

We can form no image of the just horror with which our ancestors of that age regarded Spain. Spain, the eldest son of the Man of Sin; chosen champion of Antichrist, whose function is to be the enemy of God. Very potent; yes, the sun never sets on his Empire; among the kingdoms of this world he is greatest; sits there on his Ormuz and Golconda throne, warring against the Most High. To the beast soul he is as a God; what can withstand him and his treasure-heaps and millions of armed men? asks the beast soul. But woe to the man soul that considers him as such. Falsity seated on twenty Golcondas, dost thou think it can prosper? I think it cannot. In God's Scriptures, in all printed and not yet printed Scriptures, I read his doom. He wars against the Most High, and cannot prosper. His doom is certain, if ever any's was. God shall arise to Judgment, the hour continually draws nigh. They shall perish by the brightness of His coming,—stricken with intolerable splendour, they shall vanish to the Night and to the den of Eternal Woe.

A terrible entity this same Spain. Its gloomy wing overshadowing one half the globe; a dark Western world with its El Dorados, Romish Inquisitions, monopolies, and horrid

[1] The proposed marriage of the Prince of Wales to the Spanish Infanta.

cruelties. A Western Hemisphere given to Antichrist, the Enemy of God. There, in those dark countries, in those dark gold mines worked by the blood of poor black men, are forged the war-armaments, the infernal thunder, with which Antichrist persecutes the Saints of God. A dark world, from which none yet has dared to tear away the veil. Our Drakes and Frobishers lifted the veil; valiantly ventured in, illuminated with English cannon-fire those kingdoms of Night; brought home rich prizes, gleams of practical Romance. A true Wonderland, that Western Region; splendent with jewels and gold, where mercy and justice never come. Whose veil is wonder and darkness; whose God is the Devil.

So far as I can discern, the whole foreign policy of James consists in soliciting alliance with this potent, world-rich, wondrous, but infernal country. 'Conservatism,' yes holding by what is already established, what has money in its pocket,— even though the Devil be partner in the concern. The whole English Nation thinks not so. It says from the depth of its heart, No partnership with the Devil. His Majesty who has such a wondrous head of theological wit, hopes partly, I suspect, to *convert* this Spanish Devil. Dreams to that effect soothe the royal conscience. If we were once united in league of amity, who knows what light I might throw on Religion, too, for that great king, nay, for the Pope himself? The Pope is not so bad, if he would give up meddling with the Supremacy of Kings. I have certainly in theology an acumen that seeks its fellow. The Pope and we might join halfway; the unspeakable miseries of Europe healed. — — Perhaps the soul of all James's policy was this Spanish Match. What a thing will it be for England to have the richest country of this Planet at its back, and probably heal up the Reformation split itself in Europe !

Deep stroke of kingcraft ! Can anything be more unprosperous ? As unlucky as the Book of Sports for turning [Catholics in] England to Protestantism ; as the settlement of the Scotch Kirk by putting Tulchan Bishops over it ! His wise Majesty, most eloquent of living kings, is not wise to discern the true Grand Tendency, I think. Eloquence, kingcraft, are good; but it is vain to try the Laws of Nature with such alteratives. The Laws of Nature, the Law of Right and Truth, the Eternal Course of things, may it please your Majesty, is steadily flowing otherwise; which no Second Solomon can counteract. If all this that you are so eloquently pleading, assiduously establishing, should happen *not* to be the truth, what a crop of dragon's teeth will you have been sowing broadcast, all your days! Swashing and sowing, with that eloquent tongue and mind of yours, mere dragon's teeth, which rise up as armed men! Woe to the king who cannot discern amid the topcurrents, backwaters and froth eddies what the grand true tendency is. He is no king, but a stuffed king's Cloak merely, a Tulchan king; a king of shreds and patches, that will be torn up yet and flung into the fire.

The Puritan Mob at Drury Lane had some significance; much more, and to the like effect, the Mobs at the Spanish Ambassador's. As in a faint whisper, the cardinal movement of the English mind does there speak to us. I find two Spanish Mobs in these years; riotous, violent, indicative.

First Spanish Mob is 12th July, 1618; second is 3rd December, 1620. We are reduced to read the thought of England in dumb hieroglyphics, in popular commotions, how we can. There are of us that remember the Armada yet; and the giant ships, with big bellying sails, like big vultures sent of the Devil to pounce upon us. The Gunpowder Plot, and lit match miraculously snatched from it, is yet young. Both Houses and your Majesty in the middle of them, were near springing skyward on that occasion. The Scarlet Woman that sitteth on her Seven Hills, making the kingdoms drunk with the wine of her abominations—we know her, we have to all eternity rejected her. Not with Nox and the clammy putrescence of the Dead and Unbelievable, will we of England take our lot. Away with that; it is disowned of God, it has become unbelievable to men. Our part is Forward, not backward!

Of this poor king's Parliaments we have yet said nothing. A singular Entity these English Parliaments; almost as unknown to us as the Spanish Main. Horse-loads of writing on them, too; but writing which no man can read, which no man can remember when read. From 400 to 600[1] human individuals assembled there under complex conditions to consult concerning the arduous affairs of the kingdom, at a distance of two hundred years and more, dull enough at first, they are become ditchwater, Stygian Marshes and death-pools for the intellect of man. Sleep well, ye old Parliaments, till the general Trump of Doom awaken you, and then in a very summary manner; for to gods and men you have become dead, clammy, noisome,—'dead for a ducat!'

We find however, that the Spanish Match and the constitution of Puritan Parliaments are intimately related to each other. Had there been real Kings still in England, instead of Sham-kings fancying themselves real, and Sham-kings knowing that they are sham, how different had been the development of English Parliaments; how different the whole History of the world! Parliaments in old times had agreed well with kings; as realities do naturally with things real. Had the Captain of the English people, he who with big plumed hat and other insignia stood there to guide the march of England through the undiscovered Deep, but known in verity what the real road was, and been prompt to take it always wisely, and say, 'Hither; *this* way, ye brave!' what need had he to quarrel with his Serjeants and Corporals? The Serjeants and Corporals and all the Host down to the meanest drummer, all but some few mutineers, easily repressed,

[1] Rushworth states that the original members of the Long Parliament (1640) were exactly 500 in number. Forster says there were between 3 and 400 members in the Parliament of 1628. In James's Parliaments the number would be still smaller; but in the above estimate Carlyle may have had both Lords and Commons in mind.

had answered as from of old, 'Yea, Captain; Forward, and 'God save you! we follow always!' But when your chief Captain took the Spanish Match, Antichrist and the Devil and all the dead putrid Past which had still money in its pocket, to be the road;—which was *not* the road; which the Eternal had declared in written Hebrew words, and in Divine instincts, audible in all true English hearts, to be the road to Ruin temporal and eternal,—what could your poor Corporals, Serjeants, Drummers and the Host in general do? They had to pause in sorrowful amazement, to wring their hands, cry to the gods;—stretch their old Parliamentary Formulas; in some way or other contrive not to go Devil-ward!—Alas, good kings for the ever-widening Entity called English Nation were difficult to get; the Earth is importuning Heaven at this hour everywhere with the question, How shall we get them? Brothers, by knowing them better. They were there, if you had had eyes to recognise them,— if you had been real God-worshippers and not Tailor-god worshippers. If you had been real worshippers of God, would you not have recognised the Godlike when you saw it in this world? What was the use of all your worship other but even that same? It was for that end alone; for that simply, and no other that I could ever discover. Alas, the Moslem and others have said, God is Great. But this English People is beginning to say, Tailors Shutz and Company are great. Do you call that bit of black wood God? indignantly asks my friend Mahomet. You rub it with oil, and the flies stick in it, you stupid idolatrous individuals. Do you call that Plumedhat and Toomtabard a Captain? We know not what to call him, answer the English sorrowfully. Human nomenclature has not yet mastered the significance of him. His name is—Toomtabard, the Deity of Flunkies. Woe is to us, and to our children. Yes, it had been all otherwise had they found good kings, kings approximately good. Kings approximately good had never gone into Spanish Matches; had known Puritanism for the noblest; rude as it was; and there would have been no Spanish Matches, no misbred Prince Charles, no Oliver Protector, but only Oliver Farmer, no rebellious Parliament, no American Revolution.—The Supreme Powers willed it otherwise.

The reader therefore understands why, in August, 1623, bonfires blaze and steeplebells ring joyful all over England for the Prince's return from Spain. An unspeakable mercy; the dark Maelstrom of Antichrist has not sucked into its abysses this hopeful Prince. Thank Heaven, we have our own again; and no thick-lipped Infanta, Austrian Daughter of the Devil. Ding-dong, therefore; ding-dong;—and let us dance about the bonfire! Such a gleam rises all through England in these harvest months, struggling up under the harvest moon some short way towards the stars. Veritably as a kind of twilight in the black waste night, I still discern it; let the reader consider it well.

Posterity, says Lord Keeper Finch discoursing to the Parliament, will consider the thing incredible. Posterity, which never wants experience of distraction in the sons of men, does still make shift to believe it,—has ceased now altogether to care a straw for it. They went, they took post through France, this sublime young Prince, sublime young Duke; under name of Jack Smith and Tom Smith; in big black wigs, scattering store of money; and their attendant and factotum was Richard Graham, a shifty Border lad, used belike to Border reiving; once a lad in Buckingham's stables, but advanced gradually, so shifty was he, to be Equerry, Spanish Factotum, Sir Richard, and a prosperous gentleman,— not extremely beautiful to me. True there is merit in him, he subsists to this day; some toughness of vitality, a merit of being able to subsist,—such as the Whitechapel Jews manifest: none of the highest merits, though an authentic one.

The details of this sublime expedition in the common Dryasdust are very unauthentic; borrowed mostly from

Howell's Letters.[1] James Howell, a quickwitted, loquacious, scribacious, self-conceited Welshman of that time. He was presumably extant in Spain during these months; his Letters were put together above twenty years afterwards. Letters partly intended, I think, as a kind of Complete Letter-writer; containing bits of History too, bits of wit and learning, philosophy and elegant style; an elegant reader's vade-mecum; intended, alas, above all, to procure a modicum of indispensable money for poor Howell. They have gone through twelve editions or more: they are infinitely more readable than most of the torpid rubbish, and fractions of them, if you discriminate well, are still worth reading. These are the foundations whereon our accounts of this sublime Expedition rest. Very unauthentic; but in fine we care nothing for the business itself. Alas, the one interest in it is this most authentic fact: That the bells all rang in England when it ended in failure.

CHAPTER XXV

JAMES'S PARLIAMENTS

PARLIAMENTS keep generally sitting during this king's reign; Lords sit, and Commons too, as they have done since Henry III.'s time, granting supplies, attending to grievances; a great Council of the Nation; not a little mysterious, ignorant even themselves of what meaning lies in them. There let them sit, consulting *de arduis regni concernentibus*, etc.,—deep down in the Death-kingdoms, never to be evoked into living memory any more;—not till an abler Editor than this present make his appearance, or a public better disposed.

James's First Parliament, nearly blown up with gunpowder once, sat, nevertheless, long;—seven years, unscathed, from

---

[1] 'Howell is very questionable,' says Carlyle in a marginal note on a page of his copy of the *Pictorial History of England*.

the Spring of 1604 to the Spring of 1611; doing the arduous matters of the kingdom the best it could. Not wholly to his Majesty's satisfaction;—as indeed, what Parliament, representing a real England, could agree with this king, who represented an imaginary England? At Hampton Court Conference and on other occasions, we have seen his Majesty refuse to recognise the meaning of this real England, the highest purpose it had, the dim instinct of it, unuttered, unutterable, but living at all hours in every drop of its blood. We have elsewhere shown the progress and effect of this. In brief, his Majesty, little as he dreams of it, has long since divorced himself from England; goes one way, while England goes another.

His Majesty had by this time taken up with beautiful Robert Car; already made him Rochester;—had decided to try another way for supplies. The Parliamentary way is barred for the present: there is instead within reach the way of benevolences, of selling monopolies, titles;—his tonnage and poundage,[1] many perquisites, purveyances;—one could try benevolences; in some way live without continual contradiction. For three years his Majesty tries it; a difficult way this too; cumbrous, confused, unfruitful: shall not we try a Parliament again? Alert Car and others revolve it in their minds; say they will 'undertake' to get a compliant Parliament; by their interest in Shires and Boroughs, by their unrivalled skill in managing Elections, the majority shall be secure and devoted to his Majesty. Try it, then. They try it, and fail. The Second Parliament of James, 5th April 1614, called the Undertakers' Parliament, got on as ill as possible. King's favour for the Scots, Recusants, Monopolies, etc., etc., being the burden of their song; it was suddenly dissolved, says Camden, 7th June—not one Act passed: and

---

[1] As these terms are often misunderstood, it may not be amiss to say that Tonnage meant a certain duty or impost on each *tun* of wine; and Poundage *ditto* on each twenty shillings' worth of other goods. Weight was not a consideration in the computation of the tax.

all their proceedings declared null and void. This was the Undertaker Parliament—not as if the Parliament had belonged to the burying profession, and sat all in black, with Cambric weepers—no, but because men 'undertook' for it that it should be compliant. Wherein, as we see, they signally failed. There was a terrible moroseness in this Parliament; their appetite for Popish Recusants was keen. 'They all 'took the sacrament in St. Margaret's,' as the wont was; 'none refused it'; no Papist could be detected by that test. They were dissolved suddenly after two months, and not one Act passed.

Monopolies again, therefore; tonnage, poundage, purveyances, benevolences; monopolies have increased to the number of seven hundred. So we weather it, through Overbury Murders, Bacon Keeperships, till Somerset is sent away, till the Palatinate is on fire, till a new world has come, with difficulty ever increasing—and we decide at length to try a new Parliament, 30th January, 1620-1.

On 30th January, 1620-1, after two adjournments, the king goes in state to open this, his Third Parliament.

Very dim, we have said, are these Parliaments: dim and musty all the records of them. Escaping out of that impalpable dim-mouldering element, how glad are we to catch this concrete coloured glimpse, through a pair of eyes that still see for us! Sir Simonds D'Ewes, a brisk Suffolk gentleman, of dapper manners, of most pious most polite, high-flown Grandisonian ways, amazingly learned in the law and history of Parliaments for so young a man:—he, we perceive, has come up to Town, got a convenient place, and is there for all ages, or as many ages as will look. We extract his own words, with many thanks to him:—here it all is, as fresh as gathered:

'1620-1. There had long since writs of summons gone forth for the calling of a Parliament, of which all men that had any religion hoped much good, and daily prayed for a happy issue. For both France and Germany needed support and help from England, or the true professors of the Gospel were likely to perish in each Nation, under the power and tyranny of the Antichristian adversary.

'I got a convenient place in the morning, not without some danger escaped, to see his Majesty pass to Parliament in state. It is only worth the inserting in this particular that Prince Charles rode with a rich coronet upon his head, between the Serjeants at Arms, carrying maces, and the Pursuivants carrying their pole-axes, both on foot. Next before his Majesty rode Henry Vere, Earl of Oxford, Lord Great Chamberlain of England, with Thomas Howard, Earl of Arundel, Earl Marshal of England, on his left hand, both bare-headed. Then followed his Majesty, with a rich crown upon his head, and most royally caparisoned.

'I, amongst the nobility, chiefly viewed the Lord Seymour, Earl of Hertford, now some eighty-three years old, and even decrepit with age. He was born, as I was informed, the same day King Edward the Sixth was ripped out of the Lady Jane Seymour's womb, his aunt.

'In the King's short progress from Whitehall to Westminster, these passages following were accounted somewhat remarkable. *First*: that he spake often and lovingly to the people, standing thick and threefold on all sides to behold him: "God bless ye! God bless ye!" contrary to his former hasty and passionate custom, which often in his sudden distemper, would bid "a pox," or "plague" on such as flocked to see him. *Secondly*: though the windows were filled with many great ladies as he rode along, yet that he spake to none of them but to the Marquis of Buckingham's mother and wife, who was the sole daughter and heiress of the Earl of Rutland. *Thirdly*: that he spake particularly, and bowed, to the Count of Gondomar, the Spanish Ambassador. And *Fourthly*: that looking up to one window, as he passed, full of gentlewomen or ladies, all in yellow bands, he cried out aloud: "a pox take ye! are ye there?" —at which, being much ashamed, they all withdrew themselves suddenly from the window.—Doctor Andrews preached in Westminster Church before the King, Prince, and Lords Spiritual and Temporal.

'Being afterwards assembled in the Upper House, and the King seated on his throne, he made a pithy and eloquent speech, promising the removal of Monopolies, of which there were at this time 700 in the kingdom, granted by Letters Patent under the Great Seal, to the enriching some few projectors and the impoverishing all the kingdom besides. Next, he promised, with his people's assistance, to consent to aid the King of Bohemia, his son-in-law, and not to enforce the Spanish Match without their consent; and therefore in conclusion desired them cheerfully and speedily to agree upon a sufficient supply of his wants by Subsidies; promising them, for the time to come, to play the good husband, and that in part he had done so already. I doubt not, however, these blessed promises took not a due and proportionable effect,

CHAP. XXV.]   JAMES'S PARLIAMENTS   157

according as the loyal subject did hope; yet did King James (a Prince whose piety, learning and gracious government after-ages may miss and wish for) really at this time intend the performance of them.'[1]

Thus goes King James to open his Third Parliament. The Sermon by Dr. Andrews, sublime as a Second Canto of Childe Harold, shall remain unknown to us; unknown what passes in the sublime Parliament itself, or known only as a hum of many voices, crying earnestly in such English dialect as they have: 'Dread Sovereign of this English Nation, lead ' us not to Antichrist and the Devil. Dread Sovereign, our ' right road is not Devilward, but Godward: woe's me! we ' cannot, nay, must not, go to the Devil!' In dim Parliamentary language, engrossed on the old Records, incredibly diffuse, and almost undecipherable for mortal tedium, this is what I read,—this and nothing more. Majesty quitting D'Ewes's field of vision has got into the hands of Dryasdust, and merges into the eternal dusk, vanishing from the cognisance of men.

PRAGUE PROJECTILES—BEGINNING OF THE THIRTY-YEARS' WAR

[1621]

Something I would have given to be at Newmarket, when the Deputation from the Commons came to him in 1621. His Majesty's old eyes flashed fire; and there burst from him, with highly satirical snarl, not unbeautiful to me at this distance: 'Twelve chairs! Here are twelve kings come to ' visit me!'[2] The quarrel I will trouble no man with; all

---

[1] D'Ewes's *Autobiography* (Lond. 1845), i. 169 *et seqq*.
[2] Carlyle here quotes Arthur Wilson (see his *Life and Reign of James I.* London, 1653, p. 172): 'The King entertained their messengers very roughly; and some say he called for twelve *Chaires* for them, saying here are twelve *Kings* come to me.' According to another report the King called 'Bring stools for the ambassadors' (see *State Papers Dom.*, cxxiv.,—Chamberlain to Carleton, 15 Dec. 1621): 'It seems they had a favourable reception, and the king played with them, calling for stools for the ambassadors to sit down.' The majority of later historians have accepted Wilson's report without question. But whether

men, as I have often done, would straightway forget it. The record stands in Arthur Wilson; read, whoso is of power to take interest in it. The Commons, with awestruck thought, sat trembling, yet obstinately quiescent. Our formula stretched, so far, must not contract itself again? No, not unless his Majesty could take into the course of going Godward,—which I fear is not likely! Devilward, said the instincts of them all, we cannot go. His Majesty, now growing old, fonder of peace than ever: what can he do but yield?

The truth is his Majesty is growing old, and tribulations are thickening on him. The Spanish Match cannot make right progress; perverse men, perverse events, all England, nay, all Europe is turning against it. What hum is this in the Middle Aisle of Paul's; dim image to be gathered there of a world-contest going to take arms again? Couriers in those months of Summer, 1621, going and coming very thick on the business of the Palatinate. Such a world hum I have never yet heard in the Middle Aisle. Battle of Armageddon coming on! You that have hearts in your bodies; you that love bright honour; you that worshipped the Lady Elizabeth when she went in diamond brightness and long black hair a daughter of the galaxy, a Protestant Mary Queen of Scots, a young Elizabeth Queen of Hearts!—Or shall we give the story in connected manner, as an eye-witness looking his best from two centuries off records it for us?

Wilson's or Chamberlain's account is the more correct, or whether there is much truth in either, is very uncertain,—and very unimportant. Wilson, however, records another story which has some interest in this connexion: he says that when the king (soon after his return from Scotland in 1617) was about to leave London for Theobalds early on a Monday morning, his carriages passed through the City on Sunday with a great deal of clatter and noise during Divine Service. The Lord Mayor hearing of it commanded that the carriages should be stopped. Complaint was made to James. 'It put the King into a great rage, swearing he thought there had been *no more kings in England but himself;* yet after he was a little cooled he sent a warrant to the Lord Mayor, commanding him to let them pass, which he obeyed.'—Wilson, *Life and Reign of James I.*, 106, or Kennet, ii. 743.

THE THREE PRAGUE PROJECTILES

If England itself shall be dim for us under James, how infinitely dimmer the rest of the world! Henry of Bourbon with his *Henriades* shall rustle on unheeded; unheeded also the German Kaisers and their debateable *Reichstage*. A mighty simmering darkness,— wide as the living Earth, deep as the dead Earth. Deep, the very thought refuses to sound it: where did man begin? Night-Empire; Hela's Empire,—Dryasdust, vexer of minds, let these be respectable to us.

And yet across the hazy European continent is not this a phenomenon worth noting; this projection of three human respectable individuals from the Castle of Prague? Visible to us, lucent across the dusk of ages? Three respectable individuals; they descend violently from a window, as inert projectiles do, accelerative law of Gravitation acting on them, velocity increasing as the time, space as the square of the time, in a truly frightful manner! Whence? Whither? These are the questions.

The Bohemians are a hot-tempered, vehement, Sclavonic people, given to Protestantism almost since the time of Wickliffe, and involved in continual troubles on that account. Of martyred Huss and the wars that rose from the ashes of Huss; of Zisca and his fighting while alive and his skin bequeathed to be a drum that he might still help to fight when dead; of these, a century before the time of Luther, all men have heard. And now, a century after Luther, it is still a trouble and contention, in that hot Sclavonic country, concerning Protestantism. The German Kaisers keep their word ill with these Bohemians; the German Kaisers are false feeble men, in straits from without and from within; the throne of the Scarlet Woman, built upon confusions, is not easy to hold up. How Kaiser Rodolph quarrelled with Matthias, and Matthias with Rodolph, and signed treaties and broke them, and again signed and confirmed them, and harrowed the poor Bohemian Protestants now this way, now that, were long and sad to say. The Bohemians got a kind of Magna Charta, *Majestäts-brief*, in 1609,—three years after this they got Matthias for their king. Do we not know that Rodolph sat surrounded with astrologers, fire-eaters, and jugglers, while Kepler the Astronomer, going over his calculations seventy times, having a pension of 18*l*. which was never paid, had to die broken-hearted and as it were unjustly starved? It is the same Rodolph, and Matthias is his brother. Wonder not at the state of *Böhmenland*. Rodolph at signing of the last treaty did not write upon the paper, so much as splash upon it, so angry was he; and dashed his bonnet on the ground at his brother's feet, poor man, stamping in much rage,—and happily died very soon. And now Matthias Kaiser has made a Catholic Ferdinand his king of the Romans, king of the Bohemians, and Bohemian Magna Charta is again openly violated in the teeth of your Imperial word and signature, and Protestant churches pulled down by subaltern Jesuit Officials, servants of the Devil; and the Bohemian humour is harrowed up once more, and fretted to the flaming point, and the Estates have assembled, and Prague streets are swarming with an angry armed population,—who have agreed on one thing, That the Honourable the Herr Wilhelm von Slavata and Javeslav von Martinitz, the two chief incendiary officials who betray Bohemia, shall be sent out of the country. These two Privy Councillors, Slavata and Martinitz, shall brook the Bohemian Privy Council no more, but seek an establishment elsewhere. It is the 23rd day of May, 1618, when matters have come to this pitch in Prague. The Deputation of Estates, Count Thurn and other dignitary patriots at their head, have gone to Palace State House of Prague, armed population crowding at their heels to hear the Imperial rescript, to answer it by announcement, That Martinitz and Slavata shall pack and depart. The Summer sun shines

CHAP. XXV.] JAMES'S PARLIAMENTS 161

without; debates in the interior Council Room most probably run high; the agitated multitude on Prague streets watch and gaze expectant; Posterity two centuries off and more gazes expectant: See at last! an upper window of the high State House, sixty feet or so, suddenly opens its folding leaves; suddenly a four-limbed projectile body bolts forth, committed to the law of Gravitation, to a desperate fall of sixty feet: it is the Honourable Herr Javeslav von Martinitz, lights happily on a dung heap, plunges to the neck therein, unhurt, but dreadfully astonished. And see again a second precisely similar phenomenon: it is the Honourable Herr Slavata; he falls not so soft; is unkilled but lame I doubt for life. And, see, finally a third: Fabricius Platier, the Secretary of these two, he also takes the frightful lover's-leap; —lights happily on the dungheap, he; gathers himself together, and having steeped and washed himself makes off to Vienna to report news. The Bohemian land and Diplomacy is thus cleared of these three sooner than was expected. This is the 'Whence?' of that extraordinary descent of human projectiles still visible through the dusk of centuries. As to the 'Whither?' of it, that is a much longer story.

These three human beings, flung out into the murky sea of European things, raise commotion of billows, eddies, tides and swelling inundations, which extend into all regions, for the sea itself is no common sea, but a miraculous living one. Not Bethlen Gabor in Transylvania, not Richelieu in France, no king of Denmark, Sweden, Poland; least of all a king of England, nor any living man, can escape the influence of it. There come new Bohemian Elections of a king to go before them; they unhappily elect Friedrich;[1] and he unhappily accepts. There come Battles of Prague, frightful Defeats of Prague: Friedrich the king sat at dinner with his Queen and

[1] Called derisively by the Germans the 'Winter-König' (Winter King), meaning to imply thereby that he was a mere snow-king, very inert, very soluble, and not likely to last long. He was crowned at Prague, 4th Nov. 1619. See Carlyle's *Friedrich*, i. 329.

Court, during this Prague Battle; but the musket volleys came too near, breathless messengers rushed in, king and queen had to spring to horse without packing their goods, and gallop,[1]—her Majesty rode behind the Earl of Dorset (Sir Edward Sackville)—they all galloped towards Holland; the royal pair towards mere disaster, obstruction, and want of all things. Six months of royalty brought loss of the Palatinate itself, and a life all bound in shallows and misfortunes. It involved our poor Solomon in Spanish treaties, in endless embassies, in life-long effort to recover this Palatinate by kingcraft without Battle. Impossible: for Germany, Catholic against Protestant, is all gone to battle; it is a universal European war of Protestant against Catholic once more: unhappy Europe! And Gustavus comes in, and on the other hand Wallenstein with his Croats, with his Pappenheims and Tillys: it is what they call the Thirty-Years' War, the war of Protestantism, hardly exampled for misery and desolating violence in these new ages. New truth when it comes into the world has a stormy welcome, for most part. The old foolish world, it will not learn that Divine Truth comes out of Heaven, and must and will by eternal law rule here on Earth: admit the new Truth, it is as sunlight, blessed, fruitful for all; resist the new Truth, it has to become as lightning, and reduce all to ashes before the blessedness can arrive. This war of Protestantism with its flaming Magdeburgs, its gloomy Tillys, Pappenheims, its murderous murdered Wallenstein, is wastefuller than even the war of Jacobinism has hitherto been in these new ages. And so there is at last the war of the Reformation to be fought. Murk of Hell is to rise against Bright of Heaven, and try which is stronger. In death-wrestle, grim, terrible, world-wide, for a space of Thirty Years. Our Fathers!— neither was your life made of down and honey! History could summon remarkable English fragments from that German scene of things; but will not at present, being bound

---

[1] Sunday, 8th November, 1620. *Ibid.*, 331 n.

elsewhither. This Protestant war of Germany is as the loud prelude of a Protestant war in England. From a worldwide orchestra, with battle trumpets, cannon thunders and the crash of towns and kingdoms, rises the curtain of our smaller but still more significant English Drama. In Germany it asks but that, for the present, it may be allowed to live and continue. God's Bible, *is* not that the real rule of this world, with its depths and its heights, its times and its eternities? Universal Protestantism has already answered Yes, and seems to think the matter finished: but here is an English Puritanism rising which says: In the name of God, let us walk by it, then, and front all the times and the eternities on it! Protestantism was to have its Apotheosis in England,—to rise here into the eternal, and produce its Heroes like other divine *Isms*.

Noble Englishmen of warlike temper, not a few, I see fighting in this German scene; Scottishmen a great multitude: whither better can a noble-hearted young man go? To the souls of Protestant men it is the cause of causes. Shall God's Truth, indubitable to all open hearts, survive in this world, or be smothered again under the Pope's cloth chimera, incredible to all but half-shut hearts,—frightful, detestable to all but such? Truly a great question. For as yet there is no babble of toleration and so forth, alas, there is yet no Exeter Hall Christianity, but quite another sort; doubt and indifference do not yet say to themselves, How noble am I; don't you observe how I tolerate? But the toleration there, and always, meant by good men, was tolerance of the unessential, total eternal intolerance of the other; vow like that of Hannibal to war with it forever . . .

And so Bohemia is coming to the crisis (May, 1620); couriers fly and have long been flying. Archbishop Abbot has written like an English Protestant man and Chief

Priest;[1] the Parliament like Englishmen have spoken and voted. 'Desert not our own flesh and blood, dread Sove-'reign; desert not the cause of God on this Earth!' Embark on the cause of God,—good bottom that, your Majesty! Lo, we are all here to follow you through Life and Death, and to defy the very Fiends on that. 'Take the van of it,' cries Abbot; cry the heart of England, the Parliament and all authentic voices of England. Take the van of it, fear nothing; with faith, with sober energy defy all things; unfurl the flag of England in this time of doubt and dread, to the expectant Nations; let it float on the heaven's winds, proclaiming to all kingdoms, sublunary and subterranean, 'Lo! Hither, ye oppressed; we are for God's cause, we; ' God's cause is great, the Devil's cause only looks great!'

The poor pacific king is in sad straits; and will be forced to consent in a small degree. They will force him to go voluntarily!—And so, on the 11th day of June, audible, I daresay, to Simonds d'Ewes, audible to learned Camden, my truly estimable friend, ' the drums beat in the city.' Yes, to a certain extent I still hear them. 'Rat-tan-tan, rat-tan, ' rodody-dow: any young man that has a heart above slavery, ' that has a heart to fight for Christ's Gospel and the Lady ' Princess far away amid the German Popish Devils! Princess ' Elizabeth, Queen of Hearts, Queen of Bohemia too!'—Enlist ye expectant stout young men, city apprentices, street porters,

---

[1] 'This Prelate (Abbot) being asked his opinion as a Privy Counsellor, while he was confined to his bed with the gout, wrote the following letter to the Secretary of State, 12th September 1619: "That it was his opinion that the Elector should accept the crown; that England should support him openly; and that as soon as news of his coronation should arrive, the bells should be rung, guns fired, and bonfires made, to let all Europe see that the king was determined to countenance him. . . . It is a great honour to our king to have such a son made a king; methinks I foresee in this the work of God, that by degrees the kings of the earth shall leave the whore to desolation. Our striking in will comfort the Bohemians, and bring in the Dutch and the Dane, and Hungary will run the same fortune. As for money and means, let us trust God, and the Parliament, as the old and honourable way of raising money."' *Cabala*, i. p. 12. (Quoted by Neal, *History of the Puritans*, ii. p. 118.)

draymen and others, who stand there in your leather or woollen jerkins with hearts not disinclined to blaze in this matter.— Or, rather, on the whole, perhaps, do not enlist. Your cause is the best a human soul could wish : but your Supreme Captain, alas, he is a Plumed-hat and Captain's Cloak hung on a long pole, at the service of all the thirty-two winds. He cannot lead, or command to be led, towards victory in any enterprise. Good Generals, if he do choose them he will desert them ; bad generalship, bad lieutenantcy, bad serjeantcy, an issue futile, not effectual. On the whole I will not enlist, much as I long to do it. — —

A certain proportion of men do nevertheless enlist ; good Generals are to lead them : Generals Vere, Earl of Oxford, my young Lord of Essex.

They got into Bohemia ;—sailed from Gravesend 22nd July, 1620 ; we sent them off with many blessings, warm tears. They got into Bohemia, but it proves as I said : they were not supported. With grim energy, dumb, making no proclamation of themselves on the page of History, they fought there, and stood at bay in Frankenthal, like invincible English mastiffs, begirt with clouds of Spanish wolves, cut off from all help. Frankenthal stands in the pleasant Rhine country,—dost thou know it, idle English tourist of these days ? Know that the 'Siege of Frankendale' was once world-famous ; that the brave died there, unconquerable and without renown. Indisputably enough, there stand they, the truehearted, mastiff-faced ones, with their steeple hats, matchlocks, and unimproved artillery service ; grimly at bay against Europe in general ; and cannot conquer, will not be conquered,—and die : Trafalgar victory, Blenheim victory, and and I know not what victories, not one of these had more valour at the gaining of it.

CHAPTER XXVI

GLIMPSES OF NOTABLE FIGURES IN JAMES'S PARLIAMENT OF 1620-1—ACTS OF THE SAME—BACON—MONOPOLISTS

In this shadow of a Parliament sitting as in Hades, I, with a strange emotion, notice faces not entirely unknown to me. The blooming broad face of John Pym, Member for Chippenham or Tavistock,[1] a young Somersetshire gentleman, much distinguished at Oxford; learned Latin Tutors, Fathers of Nonsense Verse, have written him Delight of the Muses, a very Ingenuity of a Boy: '*Lepos puelli, deliciæ Musarum.*' He has now been in the Inns of Court, become learned in Law, sits in Parliament; has got, or hopes to get, solid Official employment; speaks well—what is far more, thinks and means well : the stuff of a first-rate Senator, I should say, lies in Mr. John Pym. Look in his face; there are in it the lineaments of a very rhinoceros, such a field of cheeks, such a cliff of brows; the hair carelessly dishevelled, the eyes as if weary and yet unweariable. He believes, every fibre of him, in God's truth; reads the same out of Hebrew Gospels, out of English Parliament Rolls ;—leaves, wherever he is reading, the Untrue in a good measure lying as if unread. Cobweb does not stick to him :—what an advantage in readers ! A rational, pertinent man : I observe they often put him on Committees, though young : his word is modest, sagacious, elucidative of the matter in hand.

Then there is the silver-toned Sir Benjamin Rudyard (from Wilton), an elegant young gentleman about Town ; on whom Ben Jonson has congratulatory Epigrams ; most strange to hear Gospel-texts, and mellifluous Puritanic preaching from a young gentleman with that cut of beard, in ruffs of that quality ! How serious is the face of young Sir Benjamin ; yet

[1] He preferred Tavistock next Parliament.—*Commons' Journals*, i. 681.

CH. XXVI.] GLIMPSES OF NOTABLE FIGURES 167

with delicate smiles on occasion! The grave, the awful, is well divided in these men from the ludicrous, the insignificant. Man is as the chameleon; takes his tone from the circumambient element: now sniffing, sneering as a humbug in the midst of humbugs, struggling the best he can to be king of his humbug Universe; now silently praying, mellifluously preaching as a devout Puritan in James's Parliaments; much overshadowed with the awe of his condition; with the elegant starched ruffs, with chosen phraseology, vanity cut of beard, struggling to be king of *his*, which is a very different one! What contrasts!

Sir Thomas Wentworth,[1] of Wentwoodhouse in Yorkshire; him, too, I notice there. A tall young gentleman, of lean wiry nature, of large jaws, and flashing grey eyes: commemorative now and then of the Gunpowder Treason,[2] of matters dangerous to religion and liberty; for the rest, inclined frequently to have the matter referred to a Committee. A proud young man; in whom slumbers much fire,—to be developed one way or the other.

Sackville, Sir Edward, he whom we saw staggering, bleeding, near dead by dead and gory Bruce, in the meadows of Tergose,—whom the dying Bruce opened his eyes yet to save, and with his tongue waxing motionless said: 'Rascal, hold 'thy hand!'—This Sackville has come back from the Antwerp meadows, from Frankenthal, and much miscellaneous roving and hard service; and sits here, a most pertinent composed Member of Parliament, ripening towards official and other destinies. Beautiful the women call him; beautiful the men. Eloquent, too, by no means destitute of eloquence, of fruitful insight, of heart-veracity, which is the mother of eloquence. I hear him say, this pink of chivalry and fashion, 'The passing-bell ringeth for religion.'[2] Obscene Papal spectra in Three Hats, Austrian Kaisers, dusky kings of Spain, and all the

[1] Created Earl of Strafford, 12th January 1639-40.
[2] *Commons' Journals*, i. 655-6.

Heathen are raging: dusky infinitudes, stirred up by that fall of the Three Prague Projectiles ;—and dim oceans, do make a roaring: threaten Sackville that they will engulph the last fragment of Protestant firm land. The passing-bell ringeth for religion;—now, if ever, let our Dread Sovereign endeavour to get out his war-tuck, and lead England on! Alas! the war-tuck will not out; hardly do we see a glimmer of the blade of it (as at Frankenthal last winter), when it is rammed home again; and we try the way of negotiative ambassadors. Sackville, meanwhile, is very loyal; would not touch upon the Sovereign's prerogative for untold gold. 'Had I as many ' voices as Fame is fabled to have, this your Remonstrate ' Petition which toucheth on the Royal Message, should not ' get one of them, Mr. Speaker !'[1]

Of older venerable persons, who rather hold by the Past than tend to the Future, I say little. Learned Serjeant Crew, one day to be Speaker Crew,—how strange, almost preternatural, to hear him talk of the woman of Tekoah: of an issue of blood which we will heal by touching the hem of King James's garment! He says it with the earnestness of an old Prophet, this learned Serjeant,—as, indeed, serjeants themselves were still in earnest; even Noy has his Bible in his pocket, and would shudder if he thought he was not God's servant, but only Mammon's;—nay, Coke upon Lyttleton—let profane chimerical mortals in wig and black gown, now grown so chimerical, take thought of it!—Coke upon Lyttleton, when our Session ends, and we all rise to be prorogued for a month, uplifts the Litany.[2] Sir Edward Coke desired the House to say after him, and he recited the Collect for the King and his children (from the Gunpowder Treason version): 'Almighty God, who hast in all ages ' shewed thy power and mercy in the miraculous and gracious

---

[1] 'Sir Edward Sackvyle said, "Had he as many Voices as Fame is said to have, should not have one of them, this Clause of the Prince's Marriage."' —*Commons Journals*, i. 655.

[2] *Ibid.*, i. 629.

'deliverances of thy Church and in the protection of righteous
'and religious Kings and States professing thy holy and eternal
'truth, from the wicked conspiracies and malicious practices
'of the enemies thereof,' etc. etc.—Is not this one Fact inclusive of innumerable multitudes of Facts?

Thus they in their ancient Parliament, sitting there in their steeple hats and Spanish cloaks; in presence of God and King James:—the venerable and unintelligible men. The passing-bell ringeth for religion, the swelling seas of Antichrist and foul damnable Error, will lick out the stars of heaven; and the Dread Sovereign will not be incited to take note of it:—what, and what in the world shall we do? 'I hope,' observes an honourable Baronet,—the name of him is Philips,[1] but who has any chance to remember it?—'I hope 'every man of us hath prayed for direction before coming 'hither this morning!'[2] Good Heavens! I too could reverence a Parliament of that kind, and think it might be good for something. The same honourable Baronet listens with unspeakable reverence to Coke upon Lyttleton and the precedents; but says, withal, more than once, 'If there be no 'precedent, it is time to make one!' This is his opinion, Sir Robert Philips's,—an answer to his prayer, I could almost say; such a superhuman audacity is required for it!—

The spectre of that steeple-hatted Parliament, in its dread reverence, in its dire straits, balancing itself on old precedents as on a Bridge of Azraël,[3] with long pole loaded with Serjeant's lead at each end, shuddering to advance; and Philips and necessity saying: Thou must!—is venerable and pathetic to me. Itself so pale, quaint, steeple-hatted, shadowy, its dire writhings grown sport to us;—the foremost vanguard of innumerable extinct Parliaments that have not even a spectre

---

[1] Forster (*Life of Eliot*), i. 94. The *Commons Journals*, i. 658, attribute a similar remark to Sir G. Moore, also: 'Sir George Moore "hopeth every man here hath prayed for direction."'   [2] *Ibid.*, 658.

[3] Azraël is the Angel of Death; the Bridge is by some called Tchinavar. See, for example, Voltaire's *Zadig*, chap. ii. *Cf.* 'The Brig o' Dread' of Scotch ballads.

left,—down into the deep night of Saxon *Were-moot*, of Spear-councils on the coast of the Baltic, older than Hengst, than Odin;—O Heavens! is not the Past a divine Book, unfathomable, awful, inclusive of all divine Books whatsoever? Inspired penmen have been dreadfully wanting.

This spectral Parliament, all pale to us, but some young faces, the Pyms, Wentworths, etc., that have the hue of Life still in them,—did several things, which are memorable to Dryasdust rather than to me. It is the Parliament that overhauled poor Chancellor Bacon. Alas, what a change since we last saw him, riding in purple cloak from Chancery Lane.[1] They have in this earnest Parliament,—meaning something far other than improved shop-lists, and augments of the sciences, meaning fair-play namely, and God's Justice on Earth,—got their claws upon the sublime Chancellor, and will do him a mischief. They have indisputable traces of a thing or two,—a purse delivered by the Lady Wharton, a purse by Mr. Egerton;[2] in brief, they have detected this poor Chancellor to be a hungry Jew of Whitechapel, selling Judgment for a bit of money: they twitch the purple cloak off him, all the learned wigs, patch-coifs, and trappings off him; and say, with nostrils dilated in disgust: Go! He goes, one of the sorrowfullest of all mortals, to beg beer in Gray's Inn,[3] to augment the sciences, if from the like of him the sciences have any augment to expect!

On the whole, this earnest Parliament is vehement upon swindlers, monopolists, corruptionists, foul-players in general; has got its claws upon the seven hundred monopolies, for one thing. May it prosper! Good luck to this Parliament! With what a shrill tone it denounces your Sir Giles Mompesson, hauled down from his bench;—for he was an Honourable Member this Giles. He has had monopolies of gold-thread, which was mere pinchbeck thread; of ale-houses, of lobsters,—and what not? He was deep in the seven

---

[1] See *ante*, p. 130. [2] See Spedding, *Letters and Life*, vii. 252 *et seqq*.
[3] See *ante*, p. 134, *n*.

hundred monopolies; treated the field of trade as if it had been a hunting-field, and all men that sewed gold, all men that drank ale, or ate a lobster, as if they had been royal game, for which he had a licence; vexing them with his attorney hunting-beagles. And he got himself elected by 'a rich 'country gentleman.' Behold him now, hauled down from his bench, laid on the flat of his back; figuratively speaking, the claws of the Parliament fixed in him; its fierce beak denouncing him with considerable shrillness, making ready to rend him! A Committee on him; sharp searching questions on him; sharp eyes and beaks upon him. Sir Giles flies; escapes from the Commons' Serjeant with slippery dexterity; escapes hastily beyond sea, wings his obscene flight, with plucked feathers, into outer darkness. Mompesson, we regret to say, is gone; but Michell, his main Attorney, him we have safe in the Tower; he, I expect, will not go for a few weeks yet! Sir Francis Michell, unworshipful knight, living by the Doll Tearsheets in Clerkenwell, by the bullies of Alsatia, by lobsters,—a putrid eye-sorrow on this earth;— the reader saw him once at the sack of Drury Lane Playhouse: the reader perhaps will not grudge to see how a Puritan House of Commons deals with a gilt scoundrel when they catch him. I copy part of the sentence: old Stow or Howe, old Arthur Wilson, Chronicle-Baker and the whole world saw it done. First his spurs knocked off by the servants of the Earl Marshal, and thrown away.[1] 'Then the silver 'sword' (which ought to have been gilded, says Mr. William Camden[2]) 'is taken from his side, broken over his head, 'and thrown away. Last of all they pronounce him no longer 'to be a knight, but a knave, as was formerly done to Andrew 'de Herclay, when he was degraded by Anthony Lucy.'— This done;—Sentence:

'To be taken back to the Fleet Prison, and confined there 'in the place called Bolton's Ward.' Yes, through Bolton's Ward, too, we obtain a stern glimpse into old tragic doings.

[1] Stow, 1034.   [2] Camden, *Annals of James I.* (16th June 1621).

The state of the Fleet Prison itself is examined in this Parliament; Bolton's Ward and other things come to light in a very unsatisfactory manner. There they lie, the poor prisoners, in this or the other Ward, prisoners for debt or misdemeanour in this world; eighteen on one mattress, twenty-four on another; harsh Warden charging twopence a night. . . . If you do not pay, you are turned into other far worse Wards, left there to consider yourself. There used to be a kind of slit, or open barn-window, through which poor prisoners consulted with their friends or lawyers; the tyrannous Warden has walled it up beyond human height, reduced it to a pigeon-hole far up; there now only falls in on us some melancholy ray through the pigeon-hole overhead,—disclosing darkness visible. No wonder men get discontented, irreverent of persons in authority, and require to be roused at night and clapt into worse Wards. The worst of all the Wards is Bolton's. Bolton, a man unknown to me, seemingly of truculent humour, was clapt some years ago into a certain bed-ward one night, he and another; for bad conduct, as is like. In the gloom of the night Bolton's truculent humours surged up, not a whit appeased; the damp black stones round him, on these he could not vent his humours; and there was in this ward, besides himself, but one comrade. Bolton, it is like, has been gruff to the human comrade, the human comrade gruff to him: on the morrow morning Bolton was found there alone; Bolton, with glaring blood-shot eyes, quite private by himself; the human comrade lay dead and murdered on the floor there. Bolton, doubt it not, was hanged; and the place ever since is called Bolton's Ward; a Ward as squalid as any, and now with two ghosts in it over and above. It is here that Francis Michell, vender of monopolies, swindling attorney that decreed injustice by a law, once prosperous scum of creation, sits with his spurs hacked off, and all prosperity fled far from him, considering the vicissitude of things.

And on the morrow morning we behold this phenomenon,

very singular to us, through the little chink in the murk of centuries. An unspurred knight of the rueful countenance, 'with a paper on his breast and back that pointed at the 'foulness of the cause,' mounted on what leanest spavined garron was discoverable, with his face to the tail, with the tail in his hand, led by the hangman, equitating as on hot iron, in a shambling, high-pitching, excited spavined manner; escorted by great and small from Palace-yard to 'Finsbury 'Prison,' amid the curses and the howls and laughter of mankind. Clear enough there; clear as sunlight through this identical chink effected by the Commons' Journals for us in the leaden murk of the old dead times. Halting Punishment has found thee, right unworshipful ! thee for one: ride there, in a halting, high-floundering excited and spavined manner, whither thou art bound ! The modern reader looks on it, too, with a grim smile; and yet with a sigh. The modern reader thinks: Why cannot I have one of my monopolists, my air-monopolists, my food-monopolists, my prosperous scums of creation,—decreers of injustice by a law,—shaken out from his Longacre respectability, and shown as what he is, set even on such a Rosinante to ride with his face to the tail? By Heaven, modern reader, thou wilt get such a thing when once thou hast well deserved it. At present thou knowest not Right from Wrong, as thy fathers did; thou knowest it not at all, except as a horse knows it,—thou unhappy!

This Parliament made a public clearance of monopolists, unjust Chancellors, attorney swindlers, in greater and lesser wigs, not without success: but one laments soon to see it get into fearful flat contradiction with the Dread Sovereign himself. Inevitable: the Dread Sovereign set to govern England, and here is England not minded, not capable of being minded, to be governed so. The Dread Sovereign wants a Spanish Match for England; England, by laws older than any Parliament Rolls, cannot wish any Spanish Match. England must adhere to Christ's Gospel, and have the true God for Patron.

The true God joined with the Spanish Mammon, his Majesty will have. In brief, these Commons have concocted an humble and humblest Petition; and, lying flat on their faces, touching the hem of his Majesty's garment, earnestly, as with tears, entreat him to have regard to the same. The bleeding condition of the Palatinate, of the Protestant Gospel, has struck them; they glance even at the Spanish Match, and pray God and the King that there might be a Protestant Match, instead. Popish Matches are bad, whisper they to one another within their Parliament walls. We knew a Papist woman at Acton, she had children whom her Protestant Husband insisted to breed as Protestants:—the frantic Papist mother killed them, rather.[1] Good cannot come of any Papist Match; let us make our Petition, let us touch the hem of his Majesty's garment. Impossible! cry others, cries Edward Sackville, for one. These are high matters of State: —had I as many voices as Fame has, this clause should not get one of them![2]

Whereupon, his Majesty hearing what was toward, writes a severe admonitory Letter:[3] his hunting at Newmarket is quite spoiled; he refuses to receive our Deputation of Twelve, to read their Petition at all: we have to send express and recall them on the Eastern Counties' Road. What is to be done now; in the name of wonder and terror, what? Why, at worst, nothing may be done; perhaps that is the best of all. This Parliament, so to speak, strikes work; sits there for certain days expostulating, arguing, convincing itself that it cannot in these circumstances go on with any Bill.[4] Admonitory high Letters follow:—'An old experienced King,' etc., 'very free and able,' etc.—Dread Sovereign, we read these Letters, and again read them, and ever again: but to

---

[1] *Commons' Journals.* [2] See *ante*, p. 168.
[3] Of date 3rd December 1621.
[4] 'And the House finding it a great discouragement to them to proceed in any business when there was so great a distance [divergence] betwixt the King and them, . . . thought they had as good do nothing, as have that they do undone again.'—*Wilson*, 172.

go on with any Bill is impossible. We have struck work, with or without foresight, we have stumbled on that plan, and sit here doing nothing; the world all buzzing round us. A wonder, a wonder! a Parliament that does not get on with Bills! It is the most ominous attitude I have yet seen in England: touching to the mind from this great distance of years. Not that trivial insolence or any light sputtering is legible on those old steeple-hatted faces: ah, no! clouds of dark sorrow, of awe and dread, which they are driven by necessity to front;—outer clouds and some inner eternal Light; stern, red-cloudy beckonings of a Day that is yet below the horizon, loaded perhaps with thunder! I hope no man of us but has prayed for direction before coming hither.—What boots it? A strike of work in any king's Parliament, if the men have come hither with prayer, is serious. His Majesty, after certain high Messages and certain low but obstinate answers, consents to receive our Deputation of Twelve. . . . The Deputation was received, but the breach was not healed. The Commons made a protest[1] that it was their ancient and undoubted birthright to enjoy 'the Liberties, 'Franchises, Privileges and Jurisdictions of Parliament,' and 'that the arduous and urgent affairs concerning the King, 'State, and the Defence of the Realm, and of the Church of 'England and the making and maintenance of Laws, and 'redress of mischiefs and grievances which daily happen within 'this Realm, are proper subjects and matter of counsel and 'debate in Parliament.'—Sackville and the State Servants who sit before the Speaker gainsaying what they could within doors, reporting to Majesty without. His Majesty, now come as far as Theobalds, hears that the Protest is engrossed on their Records. Majesty thereupon comes galloping up to Town; tears out their Protest with his own hand (30th December, while the House is prorogued); and, on the 6th of January 1621-2, dissolves this Protesting Parliament.

[1] Protestation of the Commons concerning Privileges. *Parliamentary History*, i. 1362.

Such a Parliament I never before saw in England;—a Parliament that struck work. Clouds of lurid sorrow on their old faces, luridly illuminated by some light still below the horizon, lurid symptoms of a Day not yet born, but like to be very stormy. I hope none of us awaits it without prayer; —it will be better not!

SIR EDWARD COKE IN JAMES'S PARLIAMENTS—ENGLISH LOVE OF PRECEDENTS

The quantity of intellect, struggling under elements grown opaque to us, which reveals itself to us in Sir Edward Coke, fills us with amazement. Never wanting with his sharp jest, with his witty turn; learned, how learned! in records;— 'he knoweth all the Books.' His argument, grown now entirely opaque to all mortals, flashes in the astonished eyes of contemporaries like a light-beam, like a lightning-bolt. ' It is not under Mr. Attorney's cap to answer that!' saith he.

The cause of Liberty, I have heard, is much indebted to Coke. If that be synonymous with the cause of Parliament, as for the moment it doubtless was, the debt is probable. In the stretching of Precedents, which he has of all sorts and ages, dug up from beyond Pluto and the deepest charnel-houses and extinct lumber-rooms of Nature, which he produces and can apply and cause to fit by shrinking or expanding, and on the whole to suit any foot,—he never had a rival. Whatever the old Parliaments had done, when they were all Lords and Barons, with armed England at their back, whom none that would live in England could venture to gainsay at all,—this our learned friend asserts to be competent to 'Par-'liament' still; now when we are poor Commons paid by our boroughs: when we are mere learned serjeants and inconsiderable knights of the Shire.

One of the most surprising features of these English Parliaments and of this English People, is their veneration of precedents. Their worship of the past;—which is indeed one of the indispensablest features of a great soul, in a Nation as in a man. He that cannot persevere, that is not bound by the law of his nature to persevere, how can he ever arrive? Habit:—it is the law of habit that makes roads everywhere through the pathless in this universe; wheresoever thou findest a made road, there was the law of habit active,— honour it in its degree. Granted the road is not the best, yet how much better is it than no road! 'Had you seen it 'before it was made';[1]—and what toil General Wade had with it!—For indeed the History of the Past is the real Bible. So did the God's will which made this universe manifest itself to usward: even so, if thou wilt think of it. That is the true series of Incarnations and Avatars. The splendour of God shone through the huge incondite Chaos of our being, so, and then so; and by heroism after heroism, we have come to what you see. The Bible of the Past; rich are they that have it written, as some old Greeks, old Hebrews and others, have had. But looking in Collins's Peerage and the illegible torpid rubbish-mounds of Dryasdust, I am struck dumb. English Literature, if literature mean speaking in fit words what the gods were pleased to act, as I think it does and must,—is a thing yet to be born.

'God is great,' say the Moslems: Yes, but Dryasdust also and human Stupidity are not small. It, too, is wide as Immensity; it, too, is deep as Hell; has a strength of slumberous torpor in it, the subduing of which will mean that the History of this Universe is complete. *Dummheit*:—there is something venerable in it. In its dark belly it swallows all light-beams and lightnings: they are all, as it were, welcome to it. With some celestial coruscations, huge as

---

[1] 'Had you seen this road before it was made,
You would lift both your hands and bless General Wade!'

A doggerel couplet said to have been written at an inn in Glencroe in the Scottish Highlands, though it smacks more of the Emerald Isle.—It is cited by Carlyle in *Dr. Francia* (*Miscellanies*, vi. 77), and often elsewhere.

Ophiuchus,[1] you illumine for a moment its cavernous immensities, wondrous, terrible; you display its black sooterkins, its brood of dragons;—and straightway all again is peaceable and dark. The gods will never conquer it, says Schiller, and say I.

[1] Ophiuchus, the serpent-holder, a constellation in the northern heavens.
'Like a comet burn'd,
That fires the length of Ophiuchus huge
In th' arctic sky.'—MILTON, *Par. Lost*, ii. 708-10.

PART II
IN THE REIGN OF CHARLES I.

CHAPTER I

CHARLES AND HIS QUEEN

KING CHARLES, supreme Sovereign of these kingdoms by 'right of sixty descents,' he too, is not without his difficulties. His sixty descents, and the right grounded on them, do indeed remain unquestionable to all creatures; this man, somewhat knock-kneed, tongue-tied, of a hasty temper and stuttering speech, derives his existence such as it is from entirely antique Ferguses, Malcolm Canmores, indisputably from Robert Steward and Elizabeth Muir of Rowallan, a lady of contested virtue, which however no one yet contests.[1] Indisputable King of England. Here as he stands on his more or less splay-footed basis, no wildest mortal dreams of questioning that he, Charles Stuart, has the right, the might and divine vocation from above, to furnish guidance for this people of England. Yet is his position not without complicacy; not without its abstruse sides,—as indeed it reaches into the vague on all sides, and had better not be questioned, if it could be avoided.

This King is of fine delicate fibre, too fine for his place, and would have suited better as a woman. With Queen Bess for a husband how happy it had been! There is a real selectness, if little nobleness of nature in him; his demeanour everywhere is that of a man who at least has no doubt that he is able to command. Small thanks to him perhaps;—had

[1] 'The royal line, as used to be well known, had, or was passionately supposed and passionately denied to have had, a kind of flaw in the very starting of it, "Elizabeth Muir," the mother or grandmother of them all in that line, being by some considered an improper or partially improper female, whose children came *before* marriage! We will hope otherwise.' *From unused MS. of Carlyle's 'Cromwell.'*

not all persons from his very birth been inculcating this lesson on him? He has, if not the real faculty to command, at least the authentic pretension to do it, which latter of itself will go far in this world.

Hammond L'Estrange, a learned gentleman in those days, asks, 'Was there ever a fool that stammered?'[1] If stammering be the infallible proof of wisdom, this king is wise. He has a hauk, a stutter in his speech, a regurgitancy, as if his thought went too fast for his tongue. Everywhere a hasty man, brooks no delays, no formalities that stand between him and his purpose, rushes on, often enough with more sail than ballast. Not an eloquent man, though a vehement; I have read many hundreds of his Speeches and letters, till the tone of them has grown familiar to me:[2] 'Sirs, Sirs, have a care 'how you with——withstand a King!' his fine hazel eyes flashing almost with rage the while, for he is of a choleric turn. A somewhat too headlong man. Did he not, for example, dash off incognito to Spain, to look after his (intended) Spanish bride himself; the negotiations proving tedious? he went with Buckingham, as Jack Smith and Tom Smith, disguised in enormous wigs;—a feat, which, says Speaker Finch,[3] posterity will rank among fables. He came nevertheless; came, saw and conquered *not*,—returned

---

[1] 'Since there was never, or very rarely, known a fool that stammered.' *Reign of King Charles I.* (Lond., 1656), p. 2.

[2] Carlyle had also read the *Eikon Basilike* (attributed by some to Charles, by others to Gauden) and thus records his impressions of it in a pencil note probably written at the British Museum :—' *Eikon Basilike*; a beautiful piece of sincere cant; nearly the most beautiful I ever saw. Which by no likelihood, except in an age all of cant, could have been believed to be genuine. Few paragraphs of it but denounce its falsity, its absolute incredibility as the writing of King Charles,—or indeed of any other man whatever, who was other than the *mime* of a man. Very practical-looking!—King Charles throughout as this poor *Eikon* represents him, has nothing to say except, "Am not I the most faultless of men and martyrs? Was there at any time in any case blame found in me? A good man surely;—O Lord, Jidst thou ever chance before to make one as good! Make me better if possible." It is the *ne plus ultra* of Phariseeism. Perhaps at bottom there are few untruer books. Enough of *it!*'

[3] Rushworth, i. 205.

home without his Infanta, near wrecked in the Bay of Santander. The brown beautiful Infanta, beautiful though her lips were somewhat large, blushed beautifully when she saw him on the *Prádo*, again fled, beautifully screaming, when he leapt the garden wall to have a word with her; but it came all to nothing; the blushings, the beautiful screamings wasted themselves fruitless, swallowed in the inane; alas! The Infanta got another husband; this Prince another wife,[1]—for I saw him coming with her up the River Thames towards Whitehall, in gilded barges; and he had taken her out to view that mighty London of two hundred and twenty years ago,—a notable place of half a million souls, with Shakspeare's Theatre at the Bankside yonder and much else; but a sudden shower, splashing impetuous out of heaven, drove him and her below deck again, and the London of two centuries ago dips under cloud from us. O Speaking Shakspeare, O ye dumb half million. Is not *Time* the miracle of miracles? Fearful and wonderful?

A beautiful little creature she, too, if the Ritter Van Dyke lie not to us, beautiful and sprightly with her bright hazel eyes, with her long white fingers, and dainty looks and ways, the Daughter of the Great French Henry, but born to a fate not happy. She, like him, was unfortunate in her religion. For there landed with her at Whitehall stairs, there went to live with her at Denmark House (Somerset House now named) a retinue of Jesuits, of tonsured priests with pyxes and Popery equipments according to contract, and began to play tricks before England and high Heaven. They began, and ended not; it was the root of infinite sorrows to her. Why did not the Solomon of England choose a Protestant wife for his son? There was no Protestant woman visible to Solomon of adequate divinity of lineage in those days, so failing the Infanta of Spain, he chooses her Majesty of France,—the

---

[1] Henrietta Maria, daughter of Henri IV. and Marie de Médicis; born 25th Nov., 1609; married to Charles (by proxy), 1st May, 1625; arrived in London, 16th June of the same year; and died, 31st August, 1669.

unfortunate Solomon, no headstrong Saul, no reckless Rehoboam, could have chosen worse. For the priests, we say, Jesuits, Legates, etc., whose name is legion, begin and could never end, and walk as a real demon-host, a legion of obscure spectres, enchanters and unruly goblins through the whole history of that period, troubling as goblins do and must, the solid minds of Englishmen. They were Priests of the Infallible Church : they were Frenchmen, sons of that *Belle France que nous aimons tous.* Goblin troops of Recusants gather to their chapel in clear daylight. They set the poor young Queen to do a penance, walk barefoot all along the Strand from Somerset House to the Abbey of Westminster, carrying a big wax candle, we suppose, and wrapt in sheet of sackcloth, in the hope of propitiating Heaven by that means. In the certainty of alienating Earth at least ! The headlong young King took a sudden resolution, sent sailing barges to wait at Somerset House, sent officers with cash : paid up these French incomers, male and female, priest and lay, suddenly one morning, their arrears to the utmost penny; ordered them to pack up, one and all, and sail home again, without word spoken.—Inexorable! They went, with objurgation, imprecation, with female hysterical noises and emotions, —all swiftly conveyed beyond the Nore, no heart pitying them.[1] The poor young Queen, when his Majesty went to tell her in Whitehall, flew into such a tempest as none of us had seen hitherto,—quite driven beyond the vaporific point, the apartment not really able to contain her, poor Queen ; for she ' smashed the window glass with her little fist,' and skipped about entirely in a mænadic state. Can rages of that magnitude dwell in celestial minds ? Such tempest in a Queen, most perilous, momentous then, though shrunk now to small dimensions, and raging now with beautiful distinctness as a mere tempest in a teapot, the old Annalists do through their miraculous spy-glasses indisputably exhibit to us.

[1] With the exception of a few of the Queen's personal attendants, they were all expelled in August 1626.

CHAPTER II

CHARLES AND HIS PARLIAMENTS

This King's power we said was indefinite, whereby he thinks it infinite. He is astonished at his faithful Commons that they will not, his irrefragible reasons once nay twice and three times laid clearly before them, grant him supply for his occasions! Sunbeams are not clearer to his eye than those reasons to the royal mind. And his power if not infinite is indefinite which is so like infinite. . . . And on the other hand, these Commons have an antiquity to go back upon; have an authority which is also indefinite. Old learned and thrice learned Cokes, little short of the owl of Minerva in learning, quote precedents of Henry vi. and Richard ii. (weak kings both), crabbed Latin out of Bracton, Fleta and one knows not where; dive down into a bottomless antiquity, a dust-vortex of learned tradition whither the eye dreads to follow them, and return with wise saws and antique instances, and speak with vehemence, one might say, with insolence. Prerogative of Majesty, Privilege of Parliament, these are two indefinites apt to mistake themselves for Infinitudes; they dwelt far enough apart in the old times, each in its venerable Indefiniteness or Indefinitude, raying out an infinite respect towards one another, and now by the progress of things they have become closer, they have come in contact, and indefinite so differing from infinite, it is like to be collisive, I fear. How unhappy for venerable Indefinitudes when they have to come closer and define themselves. A king was once a great truth. A king was once the strongest man, raised aloft on bucklers with clangour of sounding shields and sounding hearts from all the people. His Parliament in those times was simple enough, a festivity of all his Vice-kings, Barons, Jarls (strong men), Leaders (Ducs) whom he had made Lords of Land; they came to keep their Christmas with him, and many is the royal flagon of good liquor, the loin of good roast meat they have consumed at his table in this very Westminster Hall. Assiduous Seneschals and Sewers, with white aprons and eager assiduity, hurrying to and fro, torches blazing on these learned walls, copious oil lamps, and log fires blazing, the frost of Christmas bolted out of doors, all frost and darkness hanging over you like an infinite cloak, not uncomfortable to think of. A most ruddy potent blaze of life and Christmas cheer, and such talk in Norman Saxon! This was the original kind of Parliament as the human eye, piercing the opaque eclipse of Dryasdust, discerns it; a highly eligible kind. For every measure was debated on, both sober and then in a kind of mental elevation; you saw both sides of every object, and tried to hit the middle of it.

But since that time the Parliament has greatly altered. The Parliament does not meet now in Westminster Hall for Christmas festivities and consultation over wine; far different. This Parliament is now divided into two Houses, and consults in a jejune manner. Strangest of all, the dumb Commons have got to have a voice in it; have come these three centuries or more, and grow yearly more important, more importunate. For the king's Peers that used to sit in Westminster are now by no means the only Vice-kings in this Britain. Fighting has given place to trading, ploughing, weaving and merchant adventuring. It might be these Peers of the king would decide on a thing, and now, as times are turned, it could *not* be executed. Wherefore others also must be asked for their assent.

Very greatly too has this acknowledged Strongest, King as they call him, altered since those old days. Not now lifted on the bucklers of men; which was always a contentious business: he is accepted through sixty descents, and the virtue of Elizabeth Muir; all men joyfully with assured heart exclaiming, This is he, this infirm, splay-footed one; he is our acknowledged Strongest. This is he! Men and brethren, this! 'Yes, he,' answer they with one voice, 'he is 'our acknowledged.' And it is wonderful, to us nearly unimaginable, what divinity does still encircle this infirm king of the composite order, and the proudest heart veils itself awestruck before the glance of his eye; and he is considered the Lord's Anointed; and to himself and others appears terrible and inexorable. Man is a creature of much Phantasy and little understanding, his approximatings, his amalgamations of the true and false, call it rather the Eternal and the Possible, are sometimes surprising. The remedy is, If this Strongest prove altogether intolerably weak, it has been our use from of old, driven to it by stern necessity, to cast him away and get rid of him, were it even by the fieriest methods. For the law of the Universe is inexorable: the equation, not exactly soluble by any human Algebra, is meanwhile a most exact thing in Practice and Fact and does assert itself continually in gradual circuitous ways, in swift paroxysms, notable to all persons.

King James prospered ill with his Parliaments, but it is nothing to this of Charles. We saw King James with 'Twelve Chairs here!' 'Twelve kings come to visit me, I 'think'![1] and that magniloquent snarl and glance of the royal eyes, not destitute of claims to human sympathy from us. In fact, English Parliaments are England in epitome, brought face to face with the king: if the king be minister of the dumb heart's-purpose of England, Parliament will be as oil upon his head; if he be minister of some quite different purpose, and have in his royal heart parted quite away from the dumb heart of England, England must needs, in some more or less dumb way, were it only by sobs and dumb groans, in a very inarticulate manner, signify the same to him. For it is inevitable. And if there were no Parliament, or a Parliament that pretends to be satisfied with him, the fact were no whit altered.—That he has got off the rail-tramroad, and is travelling towards perdition; this fact, if not attended to, will have to announce itself in a still fataler manner.

[1] See *ante*, p. 157, *n*.

CHARLES'S FIRST PARLIAMENT

[1625]

Charles's First Parliament met on 18th June, 1625, soon after his accession;—his Father had died on the 27th of March preceding. His Majesty with impetuous haste signifies that he is in a war by Parliament's direction, of Parliament's seeking; that Parliament has one thing to do: grant him supplies straightway. Parliament does grant two subsidies, the amount of which is unknown to Dryasdust and me; but inadequate for his Majesty's occasions.[1] The Parliament cannot afford above two subsidies for the present; has recusants to complain of, crypto recusants; learns with a horror very natural to it, that the king has lent his ships to the French to fight *against* Protestantism, against the Protestants of Rochelle![2] As the pestilence is raging, we adjourn the Parliament to Oxford, rising after a session of four weeks.

That loan of ships to the French is a fact which all men see with their eyes; which his unfortunate impetuous Majesty, tied up by treaties, misled by negotiations and so forth, tries to explain, but cannot satisfactorily. Palpable to all mortals is the fact: even English warships, equipped by the toil and gold of England, manned by the oak hearts of England, sailed away for the French coast, and there learned that they were meant not 'for Genoa,' but against Rochelle, poor Protestant Rochelle;—and they went, after struggling enough, the English ships went, though not

[1] The two subsidies amounted only to about £140,000.
[2] Rochelle was the stronghold of the Huguenots under the duke de Rohan and his brother the Prince de Soubise. Being comparatively powerless on the sea, Richelieu, for the French Government, claimed the loan of eight ships from England by a clause in the marriage-treaty of Charles and Henrietta Maria. Charles and Buckingham succeeded for a while in deceiving the English people and even Pennington, the captain of the 'Vanguard' of the little fleet, by pretending that it was destined against Genoa, the friend and ally of Spain.—See Forster, *Life of Eliot*, i. 322, *et seqq.*

one English sailor would go with them,—or rather there was *one* solitary gunner that went,—and he, we are happy to learn, was shot by a bullet from Rochelle; the rest resisted all bullying, cajoling,—preferred stepping ashore in a foreign port [Dieppe], begging their way homewards—go they would not. And then the English ships [manned by Frenchmen] cannonade the poor Protestants; the guns we founded with our own brass go to *that* use. Who can grant subsidies? Who knows to what war they will go, whether to any war? 'It is the Duke of Buckingham's doing; he misleads the good 'young king.'—He wants money, this Duke, and is very uncertain about his war: he said once in Mr. Strode's hearing, 'Grant four subsidies, and choose your own war!'—The Parliament reassemble at Oxford, 1st August, with the Rochelle ships and cannonadings, and the cry of all England dinning in their ears; and are not very immediate with their supplies. Supply my occasions, says his Majesty; says and reiterates in message after message, supply my occasions, and be swift about it. The Parliament is slow about it; gets into petitioning about Religion, first of all. Will you supply my occasions? asks his Majesty more impetuously than ever: —the season is going, near gone! Will you, yea or no? The Commons, with sad thoughts, know not what to answer; will perpend this religious matter first. Dissolve them; send them home again; make Oxford and us clear of them :—after a Session of eleven days. Alas, this young Majesty is too quick! Has Solomon left a Rehoboam? How his Majesty sent out for benevolences, forced men to give him free gifts, to etc., etc., and imprisoned them when they demurred, my readers, Dryasdust and the whole world know.

It was in this Parliament that Lord-keeper Williams (Bishop of Lincoln, who succeeded Bacon) first, taking the measure of England, of himself, of the Duke of Buckingham and this Parliament and things in general, found that it were well if he threw off the Duke's livery, and set up for himself. It is well known, and was doubtless often repeated by the braggart Welshman himself, how the two took counsel together, and came to high words on the matter. There are grievances in England, which ought to be redressed, thinks Williams. Reverend, what language is this? Do you also mean to join with the factious Puritan Party? Think what your footing is, my Lord-keeper, in this court of his Majesty! I will stand on my own feet, said Williams, and try to get justice done. Buckingham's face flashes fire. Then, look you stand fast, answers he :—the smoking controversy ending in clear flame.

Williams has been very useful to Buckingham; who knows to what lengths he has used his quick wit in serving him! The Spanish Ambassador, for instance, had a cunning plot of the most dextrous engineership, all primed and charged for Buckingham; ready to explode in James's time ;—the Lord-keeper Bishop, by dim scouts, prying in the very brothels for him, found it out in time; the consecrated Bishop, in a case of necessity, communicated with unfortunate females; distilled the due intelligence from them. Thus did he save his Duke.[1] But now the little Bishop Laud, of Bath and Wells, is coming in. He seems to be getting superseded; whereat his Welsh blood takes fire :—he resolves to throw off the Duke, as above said, and set up for himself.

CHARLES'S SECOND PARLIAMENT
[1625-6]

CAPITAL in this way [2] coming in with difficulty . . . we summon a new Parliament in February of next year, 1625-6.

---

[1] This refers to Lafuent's and Carondelet's plot to overthrow Buckingham in 1624. Carondelet's mistress was in the pay of Williams, and discovered to him that a secret interview had taken place between James and Lafuent, at which the latter had done his utmost to ruin the favourite in the king's estimation. Williams first made known his discovery to Prince Charles, saying, 'In my studies of Divinity I have gleaned up this maxim, "It is lawful to make use of the sin of another. Though the devil make her a sinner, I may make good use of her sin."'

[2] By Privy Seals, Benevolences, Forced Loans, etc.

We ourselves, all in white satin, were inaugurated, crowned at Westminster, successfully; but the Parliament—why, it took to censuring poor Richard Montague our Chaplain, Pym drawing up a long indictment of him;[1] took to censuring Buckingham, nay, impeachment of him, Bristol and he entering upon long arguments, and your Eliot, your Dudley Digges and others came up to the Lords' House with an impeachment of the Great Duke. Vain all our management, our letters, messages, our speaking at Whitehall, Buckingham's speaking; our sending Eliot and Dudley Digges to the Tower and emitting of them again: mere impeachment is the end of it; and when we for the last time send peremptory word, 'Supply us quickly or —— —!' they answer by a 'Remonstrance' about Papists and other confusions;—and we have to dissolve them as if with a flash of fire;[2] and take to loans again, to alienating of royal demesnes, to farming out of Jesuit Recusants, shifts painful to the royal mind!

CHAPTER III

CHURCH PROVOCATIONS—MONTAGUE—MANWARING

[1627-8]

DID you hear of the Canon of Windsor's 'New Gag for *an old Goose*'? Yes, and of the '*Appello Cæsarem*':[3] but I will say almost nothing of them. Goose and Gag, Cæsar and the Appeal to Cæsar are alike dead, dead ;—let them sleep in peace for evermore. Conceive that the Goose is quacking, hissing; that the gagging of it did agitate the inmost soul of England: but that it is all now gone into the preterite, into the plupreterite tense, and ought not to disturb any innocent son of Adam any more. Sons of Adam are born for other pur-

[1] Rushworth, i. 209-12.   [2] On 15th June 1626.
[3] Kennet, iii. 30.

poses than to pore over shot rubbish, and get into jarring with one another about marine stores.¹ These few facts, three old buttons, excerpted from the mouldering rubbish, let them suffice, and more than suffice, for afflicted human nature in our day: 'Gag for the New Gospel' was a Papist Book that came out against Protestantism about 1624—or three or four years ago,—how lively, talented, hissing with vehement satirical meaning every line of it; now dead as the dust of king Harry, who 'loved a man.' Richard Montague, a Cambridge man, of what breed I know not, had got to be Canon of Windsor, Fellow of Eton, Rector of I know not what, and Chaplain to his Majesty; a prosperous reverend man, replenished with fat livings, with College-fame for acumen and academic lore, blooming with a kind of flush vigour verging almost towards insolence of soul, as a man in those prosperous circumstances may. Ten years ago, young Mr. Selden published his Book on Tithes, thinking tithes to be probably not of Divine origin; and got into trouble enough on that account. Richard Montague was one of the many who smote into rubbish this pernicious tenet; Selden was covered, if not with contempt, yet with the king's censure; and Montague got in tolerably swift succession the fat livings and church-decorations above enumerated. Well, some year or two after Selden was reduced to rubbish, there came out another book, called 'Gag for the New Gospel,' a Papist Book, as we have said, against Protestantism. Richard Montague took his pen again; and I will believe, with a beautiful vein of academic acumen, of flush vigour, and perhaps a certain dash of prosperous flunkyism, wrote his 'New 'Gag for an Old Goose,' not only confuting the Papist to the requisite extent, but cutting withal into the sides of Puritanism, when it happened to stand in the way of his flourishings. He has a heavy polemic sword, and swings it recklessly; learned Pym knows with what vehemence; not I, having never opened one of his books, nor ever in the least

¹ See *ante*, p. 133, *n*.

meaning to do so,—horrible is the thought to me! But they grumbled at him in James's last Parliament; gave him over to Abbot, last of the Archbishops, who rebuked him with due severity;—whereupon the Windsor Canon went home to his stall, much discontented, and never once came to visit his Archbishop any more. On the contrary, he sets to work, clutches his pen or polemic sword, unsubdued, writes another Book 'Appello Cæsarem,' in defence of himself as is evident; which Book, which two Books, and the general procedure of this Richard Montague, Windsor Canon, proved 'highly dis- 'tasteful' to the Commons in Parliament; filled the two first Parliaments of Charles I. with considerable clamour, and in England occasioned much distress:—the Goose, the Gag, Cæsar and the Cæsar Appealed, being all yet in their plenitude of life, not yet flung out as shot rubbish, but throbbing with blood in every vein, with agony and rapture lying in every fibre of them. Such was then the general constitution of this country. What a change!

Many clergy and other men of genius answered the Canon Montague; learned laity, too; young Mr. Rouse of Truro, among others. How Goose, and Gag-goose Montague, hissed and sounded for a space of five or six years through this realm of England; was brought to the Commons Bar (7th July 1625),[1] sentenced to be fined, incapacitated, to be, if not drummed out of the ranks of the Spiritual army, at least ordered sternly to keep quiet, and fall into the rear rank there; all this the world shall learn from Dryasdust,[2] not from me. And how the king at one time designed letting the Common law take its course;—whereupon, the little Bishop of St. Davids, one Dr. Laud, beginning now to be busy at Court, 'sees a cloud rising,' jots down in his Journal, 'I see 'a cloud rising.'[3] Be of courage, my little shrill Doctor! Clouds indeed,—one knows not what clouds. But cannot

---

[1] *Commons' Journals*, i. 806.   [2] Rushworth, i. 605.
[3] 'He said: "I seem to see a cloud arising and threatening the Church of England."'—Rushworth, i. 199.

you write to the Duke of Buckingham; in straits he might be a present aid?[1]—Enough; this Montague, censured in two Parliaments, keeps all his places; in these very days, I hear they are about giving him the Bishopric of Chichester (14th July, 1628).—Enough of Richard Montague, and more than enough:—meantime let no man confound him with [James] Montague Bishop of Winton, Editor of the immortal Works of King James.—

It will be proper also to jot down with extreme brevity the exact essential facts concerning Dr. Manwaring. Dr. Roger Manwaring, of whom I know nothing,—minister of Guy Mannering for anything I know,—is Chaplain in ordinary to his Majesty, and enjoys the Vicarage of St. Giles's in the Fields, where he occasionally preaches;—the place is still in the fields, not yet among the Seven Dials, as modern readers will recollect:—and a sweet breath of new hay comes in upon Dr. Roger, as he preaches.

Dr. Roger, while the Loan was going on, and many persons refusing, and getting pressed as seamen, was called to preach before his Majesty, on 4th July, 1627; and saw good then to set forth and elucidate by learned arguments and triumphant pulpit eloquence, that refusing of his Majesty's Loan, to supply his Majesty's just occasions, was a thing comparable to the worst actions on record; to Core, Dathan and Abiram's action,[2] for one, to Theudas's and Judas's, and I know not whom and what,—a thing damnable, in short. This was on 4th July, 1627, at Whitehall in the County of Middlesex. Finding great applause, he when his turn next came round, on the 29th of the month,[3] repeated the same doctrine with enforcements and embellishments, proving clearly to all Courtier persons that by refusing his Majesty's Loan, you not only subjected yourself to the Star Chamber, but to Damnation itself. These things he preached in his Majesty's Chapel in Whitehall, in the glowing days of July, 1627: giving great

---

[1] Letter given in Rushworth.
[2] Their rebellion against Moses, see Num. xvi. 1-36.   [3] Rushworth, i. 594.

satisfaction to the minds of Courtier men. One may hope promotion will visit this Dr. Roger. Among the various species of the genus Flunky, is not truculent flunky one of the ugliest ? Do but further dress him in Priest's garments, make him solemnly take God and men to witness that he is, for his part, and will daily through life be, a consecrated antiflunky,— to render him perhaps the ugliest spectacle this beautiful, blue, patient heaven overspans in our poor world! Doctor Roger's sermon is accepted at Whitehall, and occasionally heard during the sultry days, amid the breath of new hay.

CHAPTER IV

BUCKINGHAM AND THE ISLE OF RHÉ[1] AND OTHER DISCOMFITURES

[1627]

ALAS, the king's loans did not answer! The Duke of Buckingham came home hardly saved from out of the salt-pits of the Isle of Rhé; one of the most draggled conquered heroes ever seen in England. I know the salt-pits of Rhé, and the world knows them. Beautiful Buckingham stood up in his boat, with drawn sword, as his men disembarked on the mud-beach of Rhé Island, and valiantly dislodged the French therefrom :—he was a fearless young gentleman, too, but had no military knowledge whatever; in fact, he was like that celebrated fiddler,—he did not know whether he could fiddle or not, but would now *try*! I noticed him at a later period of the season, sitting in his tent in his nightgown, with sand in his dishevelled hair, distraction clouding his beautiful brow: Fort St. Martin cannot be taken, cannot be breached, scaladed, mined, by a man that till now has never tried; and as for starving, they have smuggled provision ships over the bar;

---

[1] Buckingham had sailed from Portsmouth on June 27th, 1627, and arrived on 10th July at St. Martin's, a fortified Town on the Isle of Rhé, which lies close to Rochelle.

the sentries stand 'with legs of mutton on their pike-points.'
Fort St. Martin is unattainable ; the young General sits there
in his nightgown, clutching his dishevelled hair, by the night
lamp, to no purpose. In a few days more, I see him breaking up
his camp; marching by narrow causeways, French pikes pricking him frightfully in his rear ; salt-pits on each hand of him,
indefensible bridges, fierce struggling, fierce, but fruitless, and
2000 brave men buried in the bogs,—and only the sea and
English ships with any hope ahead. He got on board, a much
altered man. Bright as a new gold coin, all heavy gold he
came ; tarnished as a piece of dis-gilded copper, now visibly
copper, he went ; and gallant Sir John Borroughes and two
thousand and odd brave Englishmen lie buried in the bogs.
And Rochelle and French Protestantism was left in despair.
All England was waiting to rewelcome him with curses not loud
but deep. So that, riding through a town 'on the south
'coast,'—which town my Dryasdust omits to name,[1]—the
gallant young Earl of Denbigh, his nephew, proposes to change
cloaks with him, that he be not massacred ; which generous
proposal the Duke, a fearless man, declines. In this nameless
town he was not massacred—not there.

Our wars were most unfortunate, our treaties proved all
futile or worse, we meant to assist the Protestants, to recover
the Palatinate, and alas, our assistance was mere hindrance,
our embrace was as the clasp of one taken with the falling
sickness, dangerous. Eight of our ships sent against poor
Protestant Rochelle . . . And then our new armament, and
armaments, under Cecil, under Denbigh, under Buckingham,
to Cadiz, to relieve Rochelle, to the Isle of Rhé, or where-
ever it might be ; which of them has had the smallest success?
A good many thousands of heroic English souls have vanished,
their bodies disastrously left in several lands and shores, in
mound heaps round the German hospitals, in Salt-bogs in the
Isle of Rhé ;—happiest they that could see the face of Tilly

[1] Plymouth was the name of the town.

and his Pandours, for they at least died fighting, though in vain. Mansfeld led a force to the Low Countries;[1] none would allow them to land: they died by ague and scurvy on the swampy coasts of Holland. Morgan led a force to join the King of Denmark, and Tilly cut the King and them to pieces; Morgan after a siege of Stade has to surrender, and return with the skeleton of regiments[2] . . . Cecil sailed to attack Cadiz, spent biscuit, courage, powder and many a brave life, and returned home with disgrace and a minus quantity on board. We have quarrelled with France, gone to war, and agreed again: it mattered not; our peace was almost worse for a man than our war. Buckingham for instance and the Isle of Rhé.

Alas, it will not do. Forced Loans come in with difficulty, with endless contentions, obstructions, imprisonments of contumacious town and country gentlemen; and yield with all our patents, and rents of Jesuit penalties, a most scanty return. . . . What is to be done? Sir R. Cotton is sent for and consulted, all the oracles consulted, sing 'Summon a 'new Parliament; and at whatever cost agree with your 'Parliament.' A Third Parliament is summoned; meets on 17th March, 1627-8,—Oliver Cromwell, burgess of Huntingdon, one of the Members.

CHAPTER V

CHARLES'S THIRD PARLIAMENT—FIRST SESSION

[1628]

YEARS of dim, leaden haze, wherein History yields us nothing but Death and Torpor, and dust and ashes, we will leave behind us. What boots it? Let it lie all dead, quiet in the realms of Hela; Memory is not possible, unless Oblivion keep pace with it. Let us look, if possible, with our own eyes into Charles's *Third* Parliament; one summer

[1] January 1624-5.   [2] Stade surrendered to Tilly, 27th April, 1628.

morning of the year 1628. The reader will be willing; how willing, if with his own eyes he could there *see* anything! History, delineation, talk of any sort whereby nothing can be seen,—let us not augment the mass of it,—which threatens to equal the mountains.

Honourable gentlemen rise early in those years: shortly after seven in the morning, prayers are over in the House, the Speaker set, and business under way. Very edifying to see the honourable gentlemen wending rapidly along, with the morning sun still level; hastening, if they catch the chimes of Margaret's;—for if too late, you are fined twelve-pence for the poor. They come from Drury Lane, from Martin's Lane, King Street, Holborn, and other fashionable quarters; the Lords come from their Town-houses mostly along the Strand;—what they breakfasted upon,—except that they have generous wines, jolly English Ales, solid English sirloins and unadulterated bread,—I do not know. Breakfasted they have; four millions of English souls have breakfasted and got to work in various ways; and here we are, in the old Hall of Westminster, on the 5th of June 1628, while the chimes of Margaret's have not yet sung half-past seven.

Ask me not to tell thee what the crowd consists of. Men of business, men of idleness, men of curiosity; Lawyers, walking here till their cases in the Courts come on,—earnest in conversation with their clients—about causes which are all settled now. Eager *quidnuncs* come to catch at the fountain-head what is the news. It is a noisy quick-simmering place, and a strange hum rises from it, of which, happily, we know not one word. The June sun shines on Palace Yard, makes even Palace Yard beautiful. Father Thames flows gushing on, and much water has run by since then. I seem to catch the sound of Burlamachi, of Dalbier, Trailbaston—Burlamachi, a Lombard, as I guess, from Lombard Street, has the Serjeant's summons, about shipping cannon against law, about buying great saddles, German lances,—must come here to answer it. He is among this crowd even now. It does appear his Majesty had decided on having 1000 German horse, heavy horsemen with big swords and unknown speech; knowing men whisper, what they dare not say, that it was for the purpose of coercing such English as would not lend upon benevolence. Colonel Dalbier and Scotch Balfour, Sir William,—they were to command, to enlist the men, to choose the horses. Burlamachi by warrant and sign-manual was to have the furnishing of them in the markets of North Germany. What were they meant for, those 1000 horse under a foreign German, a foreign Scot, with this Lombard for purseholder? If not for an actual Trailbaston business, then for what? One's blood runs cold! *Trailbaston* was the old law of Norman Game-preservers, to coerce the Robin Hoods and such like, by swift military execution, if nothing else would do it; but we,—we thought we had got a Parliament law! I hear the name of Manwaring mentioned also: —Manwaring (of whom we have briefly noted the business elsewhere[1]) had his quietus yesterday, or what will lead to his quietus. Mr. Pym gave it him home to the heart yesterday, I hear it whispered; his accusation is all engrossed on vellum, and the Lords, I think, will accede.[2]

Petition of Right, Petition of Right; this, too, I hear much murmured of. I am told his Majesty's acceptance of it on Tuesday last was hardly satisfactory. He accepted it; but with a certain vagueness. I hear the Commons are dissatisfied; and have spoken to that effect,—if a man may dare to murmur that he knows such a thing. Petition of Right, I incline to consider, the greatest thing since Magna Charta. What is it but Magna Charta itself, and the Six Statutes reconfirmed? Magna Charta has had to be confirmed thirty times already; and this is the thirty-first? O Mr. Rigmarole! what a Parliament this might have been! These Trailbastons, these forced Loans, and tyrannous proceedings, not of his

[1] See *ante*, p. 194.   [2] Rushworth, i. 597.

Majesty, God forbid!—but of certain ill-advised persons, who misled his good heart,—are all done away by this Petition. It was the doing of Sir Edward Coke; thanks forever to Coke upon Lyttleton! Were you there on the 1st of May, when the 'great silence' took place? Our House was busy on the Petition, considering what could be done in the alarming invasions of our liberty; the King sent a message: Take my royal word, there shall be no more of all that. You will take my royal word, or will you not?—whereupon ensued 'a 'great silence,'[1]—very natural. Many knew what to think, but none what to say. At length, with the humblest prostrations and expressions, these respectful Commons craved leave to *take* his Majesty's royal word, to write it down, namely, upon parchment, in due form of a Parliamentary Bill, that it might remain clear to all the world, and to a grateful Posterity when perhaps a less excellent King might be reigning—in other words, to go on with our Petition of Right. This is the Petition of Right: it grew up under the cunning hands of venerable Coke upon Lyttleton; he worked it upon the potter's wheel of a debating House of Commons, spun it aloft into this beautiful piece of porcelain law-symmetry, which we hope may be the Palladium of our liberties. No Englishman to be imprisoned without *habeas corpus*; no Tallage to be conceded; no nothing:—a brief document and a beautiful;—which has cost us two months, come through many perils from the potter's-wheel of the Commons, from the furnace-kiln of the Lords;—and the King's acceptance of it was thought to be somewhat of the stingiest. He did not say: *Soit droit fait comme il est désiré*:—he said: it should be law but—but:—why did his Majesty introduce any 'but'? An excellent Parliament, Mr. Rigmarole;—but it is said they are to be prorogued on Wednesday next.

But let us, in Heaven's name, try if we can get into the interior of the Parliament itself; look about and see if there is anything discoverable there. A strange, dim old place;

[1] Rushworth, i. 553.

very invisible, yet very indisputable. There is no disputing of it: here are the Rhadamanthine *Commons Journals* proving to the latest posterity that it is a real corporeal entity, no fiction of the brain, but a creation of the Almighty Maker. Look on it, reader, with due earnestness; it will dawn on thee as a visible or half-visible ghost, one of those strange Parliaments of the Past, which are not, and which were;—the perpetual miracle of this our Life on Earth.

Yes, here I see is learned Serjeant Finch, as Speaker;[1] his face nearly hidden from one by his wig. Hidden mostly by their wigs, sit near, in front of him, his Majesty's select councillors, such of them as have got selected: a Secretary Cook, a Sir Humphrey May, Chancellor of the Duchy, and others: dim rudiments of a Majesty's Ministry such as we now have: they as yet sit sparse and feeble 'in front of the 'Speaker'; mostly hidden from all mortals, so to speak, by their official wigs. To all mortals they are and have long been mere human official wig-bearers, not worth discriminating or distinguishing;—as such let them to all Eternity continue!

And over in the general amphitheatre of benches,—well, is it not a sight!—there they sit, all clothed and banded, the honourable Puritan gentlemen, most grave thoughts under those steeple-hats of theirs. Our old friends in the 'Twelve 'kings' Parliament,[2] most of them I still see here: these, and sundry whom I note as new. Old Sir Edward Coke, tough veteran, one rejoices to see still in his place; they have pricked him as Sheriff, they have tried various tricks to keep him out, but could not, so learned was he in precedents, a man of the toughest fibre, of quickest wit, not to be easily balked in the laws. Mr. Pym, still in the Puritan interest, manages most of our complaints against the Manwaring and Priestflunky species: a man rising, growing; as the healthy oak does; a man you may well call robust. Trumpet-tongued Sir Benjamin [Rudyard?], still on the side of Court. Decisive Wentworth wishing to have Committees appointed; staunch

[1] Collins, ii. 232.   [2] See *ante*, p. 157.

for Protestantism and Privilege of Parliament; but always with method. It is inconceivable what he has had to suffer down in Yorkshire, in county business, in Elections, from the Savile genealogy there: how they have thwarted and spited him, and striven to make him small among his neighbours;—a thing he cannot brook. Do they know what stuff he is made of, this young Wentworth? He is full of energy, he is full of method; deny him not the first necessity of man, that of expanding himself, of growing bigger,—he must do it, must and will, in a noble or ignoble way. I notice Mr. Coryton, also, my esteemed young friend from the west,[1] Mr. Strode, esteemed young friend Mr. Denzil Holles, old Earl's[2] favourite son,—inherits plenty of the family irascibility. Here is a Sir John Hotham, too, from Yorkshire,—rather a poor-looking creature? says the reader. Yes, on his countenance I read pruriency enough, ill-tempered vanity enough,—a stamp of Fate?—much desire to distinguish himself, and small ability to do it;—that is stamp enough of Fate, I think. Fate, the Devil, or whatever we call it, has ear-marked or brand-marked that man, legibly to intelligent minds, 'The Devil his.'—

Mr. Hampden—ah, yes! hail to you, Mr. Hampden; right glad to see you here again! He sits there in the purest linen, clear-combed, close-shaven, his mouth, somewhat thin in the lips, is very carefully shut, his bright eyes are radiantly open. Don't you think the lips a trifle too thin? My beautiful Mr. Hampden! His mother has never yet got him a Peerage; he himself begins to have other views: he, too, is growing bigger, and has to do it, but I hope in a noble way. Fiery Eliot is there, speaking like pistol-bullets; his very silence eloquent. Our young friend Sackville,[3] Duel Sackville, is become Duel Dorset, by his brother's death, and gone to the House of Lords; but I notice, home here from the German wars,

---

[1] Cornwall.

[2] John Holles, father of Denzil, became Lord Houghton in 1616 (having bought a Peerage for £10,000), and Earl of Clare in 1624. He died in 1637.

[3] See *ante*, pp. 99, 167.

CHAP. V.] CHARLES'S THIRD PARLIAMENT 203

another manful young gentleman, Ralph Hopton, Sir Ralph they call him, of whom in coming years we shall know more. And seated on the intermediate degrees, lost in the general crowd of steeple-hats, what face is yonder?—The same we saw last in Cripplegate Church, eight years ago, in wedding raiment beside Elizabeth Bourchier,—Mr. Oliver Cromwell, Burgess for Huntingdon! Yes, sure enough, there sits he; confabulates at times with cousin Hampden; he has been living, been doing and endeavouring all this while, though we saw nothing of him! Doing and thinking—who knows how much! 'What am I? What is this Universe? Whence ' came I into it? Whither am I bound in it?' These dread questions fell deep on the great silent soul; stirred it up well nigh to madness. Doctor Simcock has told friends of mine that he suffered under terrible hypochondria, and had fancies about the Town-cross. No wonder. These questions are insoluble, or the solution of them is a miracle to us: they are great as our soul is great, accurately of the same size. To 'Apes by the Dead Sea' this Universe is an Apery, a tragic humbug, which they put away from them by unmusical screeches, by the natural cares for lodging, for dinner and such like; but to Men it is an awful verity, of which some solution is indispensable!—In brief, my brave Oliver, after much wrestling to solve it, has laid hold of the Puritan Gospel, wherein he finds the question answered; after long hearsay, it became a Divine fact for him, and he stands from henceforth with the Eternal stars above him and the murky waters safe under him, on this firm ground, with a Hitherto shalt thou come, but no farther.—It is a victory like few. Noble as the gods is he that hath gained it!

The Order of the Day on this Tuesday of June, 1628, is the Declaration to the King. The House was yesterday in Grand Committee, gradually building up its Declaration to the King. A work of delicacy and difficulty, but imperative to be done. It behoves a faithful House of Commons, now when Mass-Priests swarm among us, and are setting up a College in Clerkenwell, here at home; when abroad the Three-hatted Man of Sin is a-tiptoe on his Mountain of Idolatries in the Romish Babylon, summoning all servants of the Devil in cowl or crown, by insidious plot or open violence, to tread out God's light on this Earth; when the passing-bell ringeth for religion, and also for liberty and right; when men are maltreated against law, and our trade and substance are decaying visibly, and our counsels, foreign and domestic smitten with futility, and even English fighting is become as mock-fighting, except that we ourselves are slain and sunk in salt-pits, and disastrous quagmires, and scandalous Turk-Pirates are grown familiar with Laver [?] Point, and the Nore buoy, and capture our ships in our own waters; and from all the people struggles wide-spread, inarticulate, a sound of sorrow and complaint,—which some one ought to change into a voice:—in such circumstances, it behoves a House of Commons mindful of its mission registered, not in the Rolls Chapel alone, but in the Chancery of Heaven, to venture on doing it. We dare not say it! We are very miserable!

The House is to meet this morning at seven of the clock; the Order was, the Grand Committee and business of the Declaration shall be proceeded in at eight. No business of greater delicacy could be given to men reverent to his Majesty as to the visible Vicegerent of God,—and not with lip-reverence but heart-reverence; and yet the invisible God himself must have His Truth spoken;—at thy peril hide it not!—The modern reader will do well to understand that such, in very sober truth, was the temper of this Parliament; that mimicry of reverence either to man or to God had not yet come in. The distractions of this heavy-laden Earth were not yet completed; quacks were not raised by general acclamation anywhere to ride and guide the business of this Earth, but there remained in man a clear sense for quacks and for the Eternal doom of quacks;—a great hope consequently remained. This House of Commons will go forward in its Declaration with all reverence, yet with all faithfulness; I hope none of them have come hither without prayer for guidance.[1]

Alas! before ever we get into Grand Committee, hear Speaker Finch with a message from his Majesty: Finch, of whom I see little but the wig, has been with his Majesty over night; as his wont is too often for a faithful Speaker;—and now this is the message: That we are to be prorogued in eight days; that we ought to get on with our Bill of Subsidies, and not take up new matter: that, in fact, his Majesty 'requires us' to abstain from such new matter, and especially from all new matter 'which may lay any scandal or aspersion 'on the State-government or Ministers thereof.'[2] Here is the King's message. We shall not need to go into Grand Committee, then, to give voice to the dumb sorrow of the people, and the word of the Lord that has come to us. Our treading of the Bridge of Dread will not be called for. We are to lay no scandal on the State Government or Ministers thereof. I command you, says the God's Vicegerent, with brief emphasis, that on that subject you be silent. Such a message, we may hope, never before came to any House of Commons.

Will the modern reader believe it? can he in his light, innocent, mimetic mind, bring the matter in the least home to himself? This House of Commons, men of English humour and rugged practical temper, did, at hearing of this message, burst, not into Parliamentary Eloquence, but pretty generally into a passion of tears! It is the incrediblest of all entirely indisputable facts. Honourable Yorkshire Burgesses, learned Serjeant Members, have written authentic note of it, historic Rushworths put it in print, and the MSS. themselves moulder, still decipherable, in the British Museum. Charles's Third Parliament, on Thursday the 5th of June, 1628, at hearing of the above message, sat with

[1] See *ante*, p. 169.   [2] Rushworth, i. 605.

consternation on every face, and could not speak for weeping.

Sir Robert Philips rises :—This, if ever any was, is a case for making a precedent, if there be none ready made. Philips in broken words attempts to utter his big thought. Is it so, then? There is to be no hope, then, after all our humble and careful endeavours towards God and towards man; and no hope of rectifying these miseries, seeing our sins are many and great. Yes, it is our sins, I consider. I surely am myself now, if ever at any moment, wrought upon and tempted to sin. To the sin of impatience, poor Sir Robert means. 'What was our aim, but to have done his 'Majesty service?' says he; but the big tears burst forth,— except in that way, his big thought can find no utterance; he sits abruptly down. Oliver, I think, is pale in the face, and Mr. Hampden's lips are closed like a pair of pincers. Pym speaks; but Pym, too, breaks down with weeping. It is such a scene as I never saw before.

Fiery Eliot rises, in his eyes, too, are tears, but lightning also; our sins, he says, are exceeding great; if we do not speedily return to God, God will remove himself farther from us. Sir John thinks, surely there must have been some misreport of us to his Majesty· what did we aim at, but to vindicate the honour of his Majesty and of our country? 'As to his Majesty's Ministers, I persuade myself, no Minister 'how dear soever can'—Here the Speaker, feeling that a certain high Duke is aimed at, starts from his Chair,—tears in his eyes also;—says, 'There is a command laid upon me, '—I must forbid you to proceed';—and Sir John, as if shot, plumps down silent.

And old Sir Edward Coke rises, Coke upon Lyttleton, tough old man, here in one of the last of his forensic fields, his old eyes beam with strange light, his voice is shrill, like a prophet's: 'Mr. Speaker, I——p——'! By Heavens! that tough old visage, too, is getting all awry, dissolved into weeping! Sir Edward, 'overcome with passion, seeing the desola-

'tion likely to ensue, was forced to sit down when he began
'to speak, through the abundance of tears.'[1] We were much
'affected to be so restrained, since the House in former times
'had proceeded by fining and committing John of Gaunt, the
'King's son, and others, and sentenced the Lord Chancellor
'Bacon.'[1]—Old Coke weeping, the House all weeping; it is
such a scene as I never saw in any House of Commons. So
deep the two reverences lie on the old honourable Gentleman,
—such a clash does the collision of the two reverences make
when they hit together! The King, God's visible Vicegerent,
commands us to desist; the invisible God himself, dumb
England, and the voices of our Fathers from the Death-
kingdoms of the Past, and the voices of our children from
the unborn Future, bid us forward. We are come to the
shock of conflict, then,—here is the actual clash of long-
threatened war; and it is we that have to do it, the stern
lot was ours. Very terrible this hour,—the child of centuries, the parent of centuries. 'Apes by the Dead Sea'
would not weep at such an hour; they, with unmusical
screech, would whisk out of it, and be safe: but Men have
to front the hour; woe to them if they make not their post
good!—therefore does this House of Commons weep,—
'besides a great many whose grief made them dumb.'

Yet some, says Mr. Alured the younger, bore up in that
storm.[1] Mr. Kirton says: 'He hopes we have hearts and
'hands and swords, too; he hopes we will not be trodden
'down into the mud without a word or two with our enemies,
'without a stroke or two with them!'[2] Dangerous words, like
a glow of sheet-lightning across the weeping skies. Mr.
Kirton's words being complained of, the House of Commons,
on the morrow, upon question, with one accord did vindicate
the same. 'In the end they desired the Speaker to leave the
'Chair,' 'that they might speak the freer and the frequenter,
'and commanded that no man go out of the House, upon pain

[1] Rushworth, i. 609.
[2] *Commons Journals*, i. 909.

'of going to the Tower. Then the Speaker humbly and
'earnestly besought the House to give him leave to absent
'himself for half an hour, presuming they did not think he
'did it for any ill intention; which was instantly granted
'him.' Sir Edward again rises, his voice firmer this time, he
says: 'I now see God hath not accepted our late smooth
'ways; in our fear of offending, we have not dealt sincerely
'with the King. We should have laid bare these miseries to
'the roots, and spoken the truth. We have sinned against
'God therein.'—Old Sir Edward, actual Coke upon Lyttleton,
thinks he has sinned against God. 'Therefore, I,' says the
tough and true old man, 'not knowing whether I shall ever
'speak here again, will speak freely; I do here protest that
'the author and cause of all these miseries is the Duke of
'Buckingham!'[1] Yea, yea! cries the voice of all the world,
breaking the dread silence with acclamation: 'which was
'entertained and answered with a cheerful acclamation of the
'House, as when one good hound recovers the scent, the rest
'come in with a full cry.' And we now vote, not only, that
our Declaration shall go on, but that the Duke of Buckingham
shall be expressly named in it; we will solemnly point him
out; him, as the bitter root of all these sorrows; let us
please God rather than man! And so, now our eyes are dry,
just as the vote is passing, Speaker Finch comes back upon
us, after an absence, not of half an hour, but of three whole
hours,—for the chimes of Margaret's are now ringing eleven
—and informs us that we are to rise straightway, and no
business farther in House or in Committee, by us or any part
of us, to be done this day. 'What are we to expect on the
'morrow,' says Mr. Francis Alured, 'God of Heaven knows.'
Dissolution, most probably, and confusion on the back of
confusion! Sir, let us have your prayers, whereof both you
and I have need.

This is the Session 5th June, 1628: which History thinks

[1] Rushworth, i. 609-10.

good to take notice of, as of one of the remarkablest Sessions rescued from the torpid rubbish-mounds of Dryasdust, and set it conspicuous, as on a hill. No modern reader ever saw a House of Commons weeping. What spoonies! says the modern honourable Gentleman: Why did they weep? O modern honourable Gentleman, I will advise thee to reflect why;—reflect well upon it, and see if thou canst find why. It may chance to be of real profit to thee. Men in these days do not usually weep; the commonest case of weeping is that of the schoolboys whom you have cut off from their bun. The loss of one's bun, whether baked bun or other, is still a serious calamity: schoolboys, enamoured young gentlemen, romantic young ladies, and such like, do yet weep for the loss of their several sweet buns;—but it is justly thought improper in men. Men do not usually weep; men usually are not in earnest enough for weeping. 'It is a touching 'thing,' says Diderot (of his Father) 'to see men weep.' I call it a scandalous condition of affairs, in which one cannot weep except for the loss of one's bun: very scandalous, withered and barren, indeed :—the sign that soul has now become synonymous with stomach; which state of matters may the gods speedily put an end to for evermore! With stern satisfaction one discerns that if the gods do it not, the Devil will do it, before long!—

The Parliament, as we know, was not dissolved on the morrow: contrariwise, the King changed his hand, and determined to conciliate these Commons; weeping Commons, that dry their eyes with a Nation ranked behind them, reverent to man, but reverent before all to God, are a thing to be conciliated, if one can. Buckingham himself, a man not without discernment, advises it. His Majesty, with such softest speeches as he had, anxious to soothe, and to get his Subsidies, studies to mollify. For we meet on the morrow, which is Friday, and go on with our Declaration, and justify even the words of Kirton, about swords and our enemies' throats. On Saturday, his Majesty assembles us; with a kind short speech, much to the purpose, confirms our Petition of Right, passes it in the usual way of Bills, with all formalities of sanction, ' Let right be done, and *Soit droit fait comme* '*il est désiré.*' To the joy of all men; to the illumining of London again, had not the night been Saturday. We may pray our thanks on the Sabbath, but not illuminate.

If the Commons would now pass their Subsidy Bill, and go about their business! The Commons have their Declaration to perfect first; they have the Trailbaston, foreign Dalbier and Burlamachi to see into. Conciliatory Majesty annuls the whole Trailbaston business, discharges Dalbier, Burlamachi, Balfour, and all German horse whatsoever:—orders the proper authority to sell off the great saddles, disperse men, horse and all by the rapidest mode it can, and let the Trailbaston drop forever and a day,—the Trailbaston for one thing. Our Commons go on with their Declaration, debating daily with closed doors: the Subsidy-bills, for all our hurry, cannot be hastened beyond their own tortoise pace. And London simmers, deep and huge, round them; all dumb to us, to itself all-eloquent; hears, with a bright flash in every eye, that the Duke is actually to be named. Let him look to it. London has no *Times*' reports, Hansard's Debates: but what the Parliamentary sympathy of London was, rude dumb actions do still speak. For example:—Who is this coming out of the Tavern in Old Jewry on the evening of the 13th day of June, Friday evening? It is little more than a week since the noble House of Commons sat all weeping; and now the Duke, yes the Duke, is to be named. Do you see that scandalous old man?—an old man and an old sinner, Duke's Devil,[1]—Dr. Lamb the name of him. A warlock, they tell me, a dealer with unclean spirits, himself, sure enough, a most unclean spirit,—tried for life before now; his crimes shameful and horrible, his defence cynical; that of a beast, not of a man. Pity they did not hang him

[1] H. L'Estrange, 87.

CHAP. V.] CHARLES'S THIRD PARLIAMENT   211

then! A catspaw of the Duke; that is worst of all. He, denizen of dark scoundreldom, deals with unclean spirits, with scandals and abominations, to help the Duke. Enemy of God and of England, servant of Duke and the Devil. Why has he emerged from the deep of scoundreldom into daylight this blessed June afternoon? He has been at the play in Shoreditch this very afternoon—at the play. We copy the rest from historic Rushworth:

'At this very time, being June 18,[1] 1628, Doctor Lamb so-called, having been at a Play-house, came through the city of London; and being a person very notorious, the Boys gathered very thick about him; which increased by the access of ordinary People and the Rabble; they presently reviled him with words, called him a Witch, a Devil, the Duke's Conjurer, etc.; he took Sanctuary in the *Windmill* Tavern at the lower end of the *Old Jewry*, where he remained a little space; but there being two doors opening to several Streets out of the said House, the Rout discovering the same, made sure both doors, lest he should escape, and pressed so hard upon the Vintner to enter the House, that he, for fear the House should be pulled down, and the Wines in his Cellar spoiled and destroyed, thrust the imaginary Devil out of his House; whereupon the tumult carried him in a crowd among them, howling and shouting, crying: a Witch, a Devil; and when they saw a guard coming by the order of the Lord Mayor for the rescue of him, they fell upon the Doctor, beat him and bruised him, and left him for dead. With much ado the officers that rescued him, got him alive to the Counter; where he remained some few hours, and died that night. The City of London endeavoured to find out the most active persons in this Riot; but could not find any that either could, or, if they could, were willing to witness against any person in that business.'[2]

Here is an end to Doctor Lamb,—a man I never saw before. A most ugly weather-symptom, for Duke and Duke's Patron;—a protest not spoken in Grammatical Parliamentary Remonstrance, but written in violent mob hieroglyphics; which, nevertheless, it would beseem a wise King to interpret well. The King interprets that it is violent spirits in the Commons who stir up all this; makes double haste to

[1] 18th in Rushworth is a mistake or misprint for 13th.
[2] *Collections*, i. 618.

quicken the Subsidy-bill, and get the Commons sent adrift.—
Declaration has the best heat in the Parliamentary oven;
Subsidy-bill is baking very slowly. Declaration is presented,
is accepted with sniffing politeness; Subsidy-bill is still un-
ready. Patience, three days! Finally, mere Speaker Finch
and Official men reporting that the Subsidy-bill, though not
handsomely ready, may now be eaten, hastily his Majesty
quenches his Parliamentary oven: in plain language, in a most
hasty, flurried manner, prorogues the Commons, namely;[1]
not even thanking them for his Subsidy-bill. The Subsidy-
bill, we said, was ready, though not handsomely ready: the
Tonnage and Poundage Bill was not ready at all. This
latter, meanwhile, as an indispensable item of our finance,
we determine to use, nevertheless. The London Magistrates
are fined heavily for Doctor Lamb: the Commons' Members
are all home in the counties: Mr. Cromwell, I think, at
Huntingdon, reports the course of matters with due reticence
and pious reflection to Dr. Beard, and other judicious persons,
that have a claim to that privilege. His precise words are
lost to us; but the meaning of them is very plain to us and
every person for a thousand years or so;—all England *meant*
what this Mr. Cromwell was now meaning; and saw itself
reduced to express the same in a dreadfully audible manner
by and by! Puritanism shrank out of sight very submissive
at the Hampton Court Conference, in furred gown, four-and-
twenty years ago: but out of being it could not shrink;—
nourished as it was from the eternal fountains, and commanded by God himself to be. It was, in furred gown, very
submissive twenty-four years ago: but behold it now as a
Parliament all in tears, with tough Coke upon Lyttleton,
himself unable to speak,—yet urged on by the thought of
offending God. A Parliament all drying its tears, in the
name of God venturing to name the Duke; the very populace
in chorus, after its own rude way, pouncing upon a Doctor
Lamb. A spirit wide as England, seemingly; deep as the

[1] On 26th June, 1628.

world! If I were his Majesty, I would try to reconcile myself to this spirit;—try to become Captain of it, as the likeliest way. His Majesty, a man of clear insight, but none of the deepest, determines on attempting to subdue it. The Destinies of England ordered that this English King should have no sympathy with the heart-tendency of England, therefore no understanding of it; that he should nickname it Puritanism, mutiny, 'violent spirits,'—and try whether he could subdue it.

CHAPTER VI

POPULAR DISCONTENT ON THE PROROGATION OF THIRD PARLIAMENT—BUCKINGHAM—FELTON—ROCHELLE, ETC.

[1628]

THUS is the Parliament sent home again; and, as Mr. Strode says, a slight put upon it in print. For his Majesty causes his Prorogation Speech to be printed;—issues, likewise, a Proclamation whereby the blame is shifted from his shoulders, and laid upon ours. His Majesty also saw good, in respect of the Reverend Roger Sycophant Manwaring,—brought to his knees in the House of Commons and sentenced to heavy penalties,—his Majesty sees good to forbear the same; sees good on the contrary to confer on Dr. Sycophant the rich living of Stanford Rivers in Essex, with dispensation to hold that of St. Giles's, the while:—there can Dr. Roger preach his Court doctrines, in town or country, much at his ease. His Book,[1] I think, is burnt according to sentence; and Proclamation is issued, to talk no more about it; which stops on the threshold a host of learned Anti-Roger Books and Pamphlets just coming out; and, as we in Whitehall hope, finishes off this Reverend Dr. Sycophant affair in a judicious manner. Court Chaplains, minor Canons, any able

[1] Consisting of the two Sermons of July 1627. See *ante*, p. 194.

Gospel Preachers who will preach that men, if they do not lend us money on royal summons, will be damned—ought not they to have encouragement? Bishop Neile, Bishop Laud, the Right Reverend Fathers, are of that opinion. On which ground, too, Canon Montague, he who for five years has lived in hot water on our account, has gagged old geese and ganders in such masterly style, and been censured and badgered,—Canon Montague, we decide, shall have a Souls'-Overseership; he, if any, is fit to oversee souls:—if souls cannot get to heaven following Canon Montague, what chance have they otherwise? So it is decided. The See of Chichester falling vacant in these weeks, we settle, by *congé d'élire* and *nolo episcopari* and the other forms, that Canon Montague shall have it. These things a realm of England has to witness, while the yellow corn is rustling in the harvest sun of this year 1628: honourable gentlemen, following their reapers, flying their hawks in their several counties, have to hear of these things:—and answer them with an expressive though inarticulate 'huh!' variously accented.

It is Buckingham that has done it,—Neile and Laud, his spiritual bottle-holders; servants of the Scarlet Woman, thrice scandalous flunkies of the Man of Sin. Shall England be trodden down, then, into temporal and eternal ruin? Not our 'trade' only, but our salvation, the Gospel of the living God given up for a Devil's Gospel of Rubrics, of Mammon, of Flunkyism; England and all its children forsaking the Laws of God, and staggering down and ever down towards their, in that case, very inevitable goal, the Devil! Mr. Kirton hopes we are Englishmen; hopes we have hearts and hands, and sharp steel withal, to have a word or two with our enemies first, a stroke or two with them. Alas, how our fathers felt in those things, is all unknown to this more unfortunate enchanted generation; quack-ridden, hag-ridden, hell-ridden, till it has forgotten God altogether, and remembers only the cant of God; and now lies choking in a grey abyss of Inanities and vain Vocables, as in the exhausted bell of an air-pump,—and will either awaken soon, or perish for evermore. We are still more unfortunate!

Lieutenant Felton, walking in those old hot days on the shady side of old London streets, is grown as grim as Rhadamanthus; thinking of this state of affairs, thinking what, in these circumstances, a just man, fearing God and hating the Devil, ought to do. A short, swart figure, of military taciturnity, of Rhadamanthine energy and gravity; on him more than on most this universal nightmare crushing down all English souls, sits heavy. O that the gods would tell this heavy-laden soul what he, for his part, ought to do in it! The gods, or else the devils, perhaps will. Passing along Tower Hill, one of these August days, Lieutenant Felton sees a sheath-knife on a stall there, value thirteen pence,[1] of short, broad blade, sharp trowel-point, and very fair temper and dimensions,—made of an old sword, I think,—the glitter of it flashes into his eye, and into the eye of his soul, as a Heaven's response; a gleam of monition in his great darkness. He pays down the thirteen pence, sticks the sheath-knife in his pocket, and walks away.

Meantime, we hear from Rochelle that matters there are coming to extremity. King Louis, Cardinal Richelieu, with big Bassompierre and huge-whiskered hosts, have beleaguered it, begirdled it, are staking up with piles and booms the very harbour; they write to us for help, these poor Protestant Rochellers, 'with their tears and their blood.' Yes, in us there is help! grimly mutters Felton, grimly mutters England. Our eight warships sent to batter them, which every man deserted except one gunner, who was shot,—in these there was a very singular 'help'! And the great Duke's generalship in Rhé,—his expenditure, discomfiture, 2000 left in the brine-bogs,—was not that a help for you?—My Lord of

[1] The price is variously given: some say tenpence, others say sixteenpence, others a shilling.

Denbigh[1] went again this summer; his big sails they saw from the walls, looking wistfully—but nothing more. He could not get in;—him, too, they found a broken reed. Their tears and their blood—poor Rochellese! O England, England! And the Duke is going again; brave men once more are to be led by *him*. The Duke will try a second time whether he can play on the war-fiddle:—good Heavens! the patience of gods and men had need to be great!

Buckingham actually is going; busy, he, at Portsmouth; and the king is with him in these August days, getting ready a right gallant sea-armament, putting forth the whole strength of England. If he can relieve Rochelle, it will be an immense relief to himself withal. He must do it, he must try to do it. The weight of a Nation's scorn and silent rage is not light upon a proud heart. Buckingham, in the centre of a gathering sea-armament, with impatient French Soubises, hasty Sovereign Majesties, difficulties, delays, and every conceivable species of refractory official person, is one of the busiest men in all the world. On the Saturday morning, August 23rd, my Lady Denbigh at Newnham Paddox in Warwickshire, the sister of the great Duke, has a letter from her brother . . . ' Whereunto all the while she was writing ' her answer, she bedewed the paper with her tears; and after ' a most bitter passion [of weeping], whereof she could yield no ' reason but that her dearest brother was to be gone,—she fell ' down in a swoon. Her letter ended thus: " *I will pray for* ' " *your happy return, which I look at with a great cloud over my* ' " *head, too heavy for my poor heart to bear without torment;* ' " *but I hope the great God of Heaven will bless you..*" '[2]

Precisely about which time, I discover a swart, thick-set figure riding into Portsmouth; taciturn, of Rhadamanthine gravity. Lo! it is Lieutenant Felton, he that bought the sheath-knife on Tower Hill, for thirteen pence. Going to Rochelle, perhaps? He was near drowned last time in the

---

[1] Buckingham's brother-in-law.
[2] *Reliquiæ Wottonianæ* (Lond. 1685), p. 235.

salt quagmire there. He rides into Portsmouth, and is lost in the general whirl of men.

Whether Buckingham has had his breakfast, or is only going to have it, whether he is entering into this dark passage or coming out of that dark passage, and how, in short, the matter was, my erudite friend is ignorant. Several different witnesses report each individual circumstance in a different way; and I reconcile myself without difficulty to be ignorant. The house is whirling with officials, menials, military gentlemen, naval gentlemen, with every conceivable business, including that of breakfasting and bartering. The Rhadamanthine Felton is elbowing about among the others. M. De Soubise has been arguing, talking loud with the Duke this morning, some thought in anger, but it was only the French excited manner: the Duke is now barbered, is breakfasted or about to breakfast, at any rate is come down stairs, and is stepping along, speaking into the ear of Sir Somebody,[1] a military gentleman unknown to me, who with low *congé*, takes his leave; the next moment there is a shriek from some strong voice. The Duke it is:—the Duke ineffectually grasping at his sword, staggers back, two serving-men, hastily rushing up, he staggers into their arms; he tugs at a knife sticking in his left breast, tugs it out, and a torrent of lifeblood with it; and groaning only 'The villain hath killed 'me!' sinks down into swift death;—from the pinnacle of England swiftly down into the bottomless deep forever. His poor Duchess running out in morning deshabille, looks over the stair balustrade,—what a sight! They lay him on a table; they leave him there:—he is dead, he is the pinnacle of England no more.

Felton did not hide himself: Felton, hearing them say it was the Frenchmen, said calmly: 'It was I:'[2] a methodic

[1] Sir Thomas Fryer, one of Buckingham's favourite Colonels: a 'short man.'
[2] Felton withdrew to the kitchen after the dastardly deed; and some say that hearing the people cry out 'A Frenchman! A Frenchman!' and mistaking this cry for 'Felton! Felton!' he *then* surrendered himself.

Rhadamanthine man! In his hat they found a bit of writing, in case they had killed him straightway, to explain that a man could sacrifice his life in a good cause.[1]

The king was at prayers at Southwick;[2] the messenger, arriving, found the whole Court in chapel on their knees; he stepped over kneeling figures, stepped up to his Majesty and whispered; his Majesty, without change of face, continued praying. Some say he wept duly afterwards; to us it shall remain indifferent. On the morrow, Bishop Laud and Bishop Neile, just engaged in consecrating Canon Montague at Croydon, hear the news;[3] certainly with due sorrow, they,— for it is most momentous. An electric stroke, awakening all England into horror, into reflexions profitable or unprofitable.

At bottom this, too, was as a voice of protest, saying, O King, quit not the Law of God, lest the Devil's Law come upon us! An illegal, unparliamentary protest; as ineffectual as the legal Parliamentary had been. Puritan England could give Felton's action no approval; the grim deed changed nothing, took away nothing except in a shocking manner the lives of two poor men. Alas, if you are going to kill and abolish, it is the Sham-king of England that you must abolish from the face of poor England, to get the true king there; and assassin knives are not the road to that! The road to that, it also will have to be trodden? and in the course of years and the course of centuries we may arrive. Felton's protest, one of many, went for little. Our fleet, too, all ineffectual as if Buckingham's self had led it, sailed for Rochelle in a few days; could not relieve Rochelle, could not get across the Richelieu boom; could only come its ways home

---

[1] ‘ "That man is cowardly base and deserveth not the name of a gentleman or Souldier that is not willinge to sacrifice his life for the honor of his God his Kinge and his Countrie." Lett noe man commend me for doinge of it, but rather discommend themselves as the cause of it, for if God had not taken away o^r hearts for o^r sinnes he would not have gone so longe unpunished—Jo. Felton,' were the words on a paper pinned into Felton's hat.

[2] Four miles from Portsmouth.

[3] Rushworth, i. 635.

again. The townsmen saw it from the walls fade over the horizon; then opened their gates to the king's mercy, who did prove merciful. A ghastly population worn to shadows, the third soul only surviving, the rest dead of famine, desperate labour and sorrow:—so ends Protestant Rochelle; it is to be called Borgo Maria, in honour of the Queen Mother, our Queen's Mother, too. Ah, Guy Faux did not then perambulate the New Cut, a mere guy, as now: he was a ravening devil then, drunk with the blood of brave men! I hate him as the friend of Darkness, the cowardly slave of the Past, struggling to believe incredibilities, to cramp, handcuff, and mutilate his own God-given soul,—a most beggarly trade;— but it is with no perfect hatred; it is with a kind of sorrow rather, mainly with a kind of ennui. Men's one request of him is that he would cease to bore them; good Heavens, let him cease to bore us: on his own side of the pavement how free shall he be! he shall most freely live while there is a gasp of breath in him—were it for three centuries yet, as M. Jouffroy[1] counts.

Felton in his prison was visited by numerous friends; sternly reasoned with by friends and by foes. Solemn Puritans convinced him that he had done wrong; that his soul was too dark and grim; that the gleams of that sheath-knife, illuminating his inner chaos, was a light of Satan. Bishop Laud sternly demands his accomplices, his prompters. 'I had, 'and needed to have, none. In my own heart I thought to do 'God service. I now find it was a temptation of the Devil. 'My life is forfeited to the Law justly, to Man's Law and 'God's Law. As to accomplices, I have none—none!' 'If we 'put you to the rack, you will name them,' said Bishop Laud. 'Alas,' answered he, 'in the extremity of pain, I may name 'any one—I may name your lordship, for that matter!' Laud is for venturing on the rack, nevertheless; 'it must have been

---

[1] Théodore Simon Jouffroy (1796-1842), philosopher, and author of many works,—*Mélanges Philosophiques, Cours de Droit naturel, Cours d'Esthétique*, etc. Translator of Dugald Stewart and Thomas Reid.

'the Parliament that set this man on.' The rack, answer the Judges, is not permitted by the Laws of England.[1] Felton cannot be racked as Guy Faux was.

On the 27th November, Felton is brought from the Tower to Westminster Gatehouse, takes his trial at the King's Bench; *guilty* by his own confession: Doom, Death at Tyburn. He laid his right hand on the bar, saying: 'My 'Lords, I have one other request: Will your Lordships add to 'my sentence that this hand, which did an act abhorrent to 'God's Law, be smitten off from me before I ascend the 'gibbet? It will be a satisfaction to my mind!' The Law of England, again consulted, says that there is now in it no such doom.[2] Felton dies at Tyburn on the 29th a grimly pious death in the sight of all men. His dead body is carried down to Portsmouth; hangs high there. I hear it creak in the wind through the old ages. An old almost forgotten tragedy. Clytemnestra's was not grimmer: and the Earth now covers it, as she does so many.

King Charles, in this excited condition of the English mind, sees good to put off the re-assembling of Parliament a little. Not while the news of Rochelle is fresh, not till Buckingham's death have become a familiar fact, and Felton have swung for some weeks, and we have got on our course again, let Parliament re-assemble. I have one glance more to give into this Parliament. We saw it weeping; we shall now see it dry-eyed.

---

[1] The judges unanimously declared that the use of the torture had been at all times unwarrantable by the laws of England.—*Pict. Hist. of England*, iii. 138.

[2] 'Mr. Justice Jones answered that the law and no more should be his, hanging and no maiming.' Forster, *Life of Eliot*, ii. 373.

CHAPTER VII

CHARLES'S THIRD PARLIAMENT—SECOND SESSION

[FEB.-MARCH, 1628-9]

STORMY CLOSE,—SPEAKER FINCH HELD DOWN IN THE CHAIR

CHARLES, it is very visible, had done his best to conciliate this Parliament; was conscious of a great effort for that purpose. Too 'conscious' of it, indeed: it was *his* best that he had done. There lay a rent between them, which he or they had little notion of; rent daily widening into an impassable chasm. The fact is: They were England, wanting to be governed and led; he was King and Governor, not of them but of a theoretic England, lying in cloudland, in the brain of his Majesty and some particular men.

By many messages, the king, bridling his quick, imperious, impatient humour, had tried to soothe this Parliament, and get his Subsidies, his Tonnages and Poundages, handsomely out of them: handsomely is better than unhandsomely. The royal choler spurts up through the conciliatory messages, like the chafing of a curbed steed; the paw of velvet, stroking you so gently, had an impatient set of talons in it! This the Commons felt; and, better than his Majesty, discerned the meanings, tendencies and probable issues of it :—with sadly presaging soul. We saw the whole House in tears towards the end of last Session. Let us now see the whole House dry-eyed, their eyes not weeping now, but blazing ;—which indeed is the next consequence of such tears.

The Tonnage and Poundage, that sheet-anchor of royal Finance, has taken a sad course. The King thought and thinks it his without grant of Parliament: the Commons have again and again demonstrated, voted, not in the least to his Majesty's conviction, that it is *not* his; that it is theirs, and shall be his when they give it him. Tedious debates, raking up of precedents, splitting of Constitutional hairs. Do the Commons mean to say we can or shall do without our revenue of Tonnage and Poundage? His Majesty prorogued Parliament last Session, the Tonnage and Poundage Bill not passed, only advancing with an intolerable slowness towards passing,—and decided to levy the Tonnage and Poundage, without a Bill, as usual.

Constitutional men and merchants refuse to pay; their goods are seized, they are haled up to the Council; have *ore tenus* to stand. Richard Chambers had a cargo of grograms coming in from Bristol. 'Tonnage and Poundage for 'them?' 'No,' answers Chambers, vehemently 'No.'—And before the Council says vehemently that England is growing intolerable for a mercantile man, that in Turkey itself merchants are not screwed as they are here.[1] Rash words: for which the said Richard had to stand examinations, to pay fines, to lie in prison;—the first of a lifelong course of tribulations, of Tonnage and Poundage martyrdom, to the said Richard. Merchant Rolle's goods, too, have been seized; Rolle, is an Hon. Member;[2]—and when he pleaded to the Customhouse men, saying, 'Am not I an Hon. 'Member?' they answered, 'If you were the Parliament itself, 'we must do it.' Besides, the Petition of Right has been wrong engrossed in the Record Office, has been wrong printed. It is engrossed, it is printed, not as we ordered and anticipated, with his Majesty's second clear conclusion and complete answer, but with his first hesitating, incomplete, and altogether dubitable one. The Printer says he had 1500 copies printed with the proper second answer, but was ordered to cancel these. Only three of them got into circulation; it is the Petition with its first answer that now circulates; an altogether lame and impotent Petition. Wherefore are these things?

[1] Rushworth, i. 639. State Trials, iii. 373.
[2] John Rolle, Member for Kellington.

The Parliament meets, as we can imagine, in no sunny humour. His Majesty expects to have his Tonnage and Poundage made into a Bill; the Commons have first of all to inquire strictly how Tonnage and Poundage have come to be levied, and Hon. Members to be coerced for it, without any Bill. Likewise, what the history of Roger Manwaring, Rector of St. Giles's has been, since we sentenced him last Session? The history of Sibthorp, Vicar of Brackley. The history of Canon Montague, whom we by solemn judgment covered under a bushel, and who now sees himself Bishop Montague, and set on a hill. Religion does not seem to be in too good a way. The Church presided over by Neile and Laud fails to give universal satisfaction: are there not causes of some dissatisfaction in the State of England? Space enough for controversy between a King of those humours and a Parliament of these? The debatings, searchings for precedents, stretchings of old forms in the new necessities,—the summonings, the royal messages, the questionings and canvassings, the speakings and silences; the mood of mind within doors and without;—let the reader conceive them even in a vague manner! 'Pass me my Tonnage and 'Poundage Bill,' reiterates his Majesty, 'Pass it, and then, 'there will be no brabbling about it! Chambers and Rolle 'will pay their Customs when the Bill is passed, and say 'nothing—Pass it, I say!' The Commons consider that—they have an admirable reticence in them, these Commons—they consider that — that — it will be better to consider the state of Religion first; that the state of God's Church among us is of more pressing moment than are his Majesty's Tonnage and Poundage. We will take the two together; but have our Grand Committee of Religion sitting as the first and main business. '*A Jove principium,*' quote they: begin with Heaven, if you want to have anything blessed on Earth. 'Grant me patience!' cries his Majesty, fuming and chafing. 'Ye Commons, pass me my Tonnage and Poundage!' Patience, your Majesty, O patience, curb them not too tight, these Commons of England; they should be ridden with a strong yet gentle bridle-hand. 'Methinks I see a cloud'; so do I, your Grace!

It was on the 11th of January, 1629, by our reckoning, while this Grand Committee is sitting, that Mr. Oliver Cromwell, Member for Huntingdon, driven by zeal for God's House, made his first speech in Parliament, declaring on the authority of Dr. Beard how 'flat Popery had been preached by Dr. 'Alablaster at Paul's Cross.'—A first appearance in regard to the temper of that Parliament no less than to the person of the speaker.[1]

Flat Popery, Doctor Beard said. Manwaring, whom you sentenced, is gone to Stanford Rivers. Montague, whom three Parliaments solemnly decreed to cover under a bushel, that he might not pervert men, is Bishop of Chichester by Neile's procurement, he is set on a hill. 'If these be the 'steps to Church preferment, what are we to expect?'[2] The Honourable Member sits down with glowing face and eyes;

---

[1] *Letters and Speeches*, i. 65.
[2] So ended Cromwell's first Speech according to *Parliamentary History* (on the authority of Crewe); but in a report of the speech by Nicholas these words do not occur, whence some historians conclude that Cromwell did not speak them on this occasion. Omissions are common in reporting, interpolations or additions are comparatively rare; and the reader may judge for himself whether it is not quite as likely that Nicholas, who reported the first part of the Speech very fully, failed to catch the conclusion as that Crewe added to the Speech words that were not spoken! What motive could he have had for making such an addition? 'If these be the steps,' etc., appears to have been a common enough expression, made use of by more than one honourable member on more than one occasion. Carlyle makes a further interesting reference to the subject in another part of this MS., where he writes: ' "If these be the steps to promotion [*sic*] what are we to expect?" floats on the whirlwind of Tradition like that other speech written down one knows not when first or where first by the phantasm Nennius: "*Eu Saxones nimith eure saxes!*"—Winged words have verily a singular power of flying, support themselves through dense and rare, through the dark bewilderments of savage centuries, and arrive clear, fresh and still on wing here at our own door even now.'—For *Eu Saxones*, etc., see Nennii *Historia Britonum* (Londini, 1838), p. 37; or *Six Old English Chronicles* (London, 1848), p. 405.

CHAP. VII.] CHARLES'S THIRD PARLIAMENT   225

happy that, under never such obstructions, he has got a bit of his mind spoken, a fraction of his message done in this House, whither England has sent him to speak for her. Veteran Sir Robert Philips does not compliment the young Member 'on 'his speech,' bless the mark! but he follows up the young Member's meaning;—*does* yea to it, which is better than *saying* yea. Mr. Crewe has taken down the young Member's words;—in the *Commons Journals* of that day, 11th February 1628-9, is this entry: '*Ordered*, That Dr. Beard of Hunt-'ingdon be written to by Mr. Speaker, to come up and testify 'against the Bishop; the order for Dr. Beard to be delivered 'to Mr. Cromwell.'

These words of the young Member for Huntingdon, 'Flat 'Popery,' and 'what are we to expect?' shall stand as the epitome to us of that Grand Committee; its doings and debatings in those weeks thereby rendered dimly conceivable to us. Bishop Neile and Bishop Laud are named as the grand fomenters of that anti-English, anti-Gospel tendency in the Church of this country; solemnly named and complained of by the Commons of England; let them think of that! Not lightly or factiously, but solemnly, as an act of real sacredness. Select readers, patient of old verity buried in dead torpid phraseology, who may read this Resolution[1] will find, after repeated perusals, a strange tremor of a nobly pulsing heart still traceable in it: profound reverence to God's Anointed, but still profounder reverence to God; and simple-hearted, wise and genuine old fathers, standing solemn, sorrowful, as with eyes wet and yet stern, between these two contradictions. For the hour in this world's history has arrived. You, will you serve Christ or Antichrist? meaning withal: You, will you serve Truth or Falsity in the cast-clothes of Truth? Do you know in your hearts, with joy and awe, that the Present also is alive; or do you know only that the Past *was* alive and that you are dead clock-work set in motion by the Past? Heavens, what shadows and con-

[1] Against Jesuitism and Arminianism.

fusions, from foreign parts, foreign centuries and places, do eclipse and bewilder the poor soul of man! *Weh dir, dass Du ein Enkel bist!* Woe to thee, that thou art the grandson of so many grandfathers that were—not wise! Dead rubbish is piled over thee to the zenith.

A happy issue to this Parliament becomes as good as impossible. The Right Revd. Father in Christ, Dr. Neile, the Right Revd. Father, Dr. Laud, the king's spiritual councillors and right-hand men, are named as prime disturbers of this Church and Kingdom; the Tonnage and Poundage Bill is not passed; only bottomless questions, about the king's right to sue and seize for it without a Bill, are stirred;—filling the nation with confusion. 'Pass me my Bill! if I need a Bill, 'pass it!' cries the king, with flaming eyes, studying to be mild. 'Deign to understand, O anointed Majesty, that your 'Majesty does verily need a Bill!' urge the Commons in a low tone, low but deep. Matters grow worse and worse. Dawes and Carmarthen, leviers of the Customs, have been questioned; they have the king's warrant, the king vindicates them. Richard Chambers feels that he is worse screwed than in Turkey. Rolle, the Hon. Member, has been served with a *subpœna*. Doctor Beard is coming up from Huntingdon to testify of flat Popery; Burgess, the Bailiff, has run, it is supposed, for Ipswich, and the Serjeant is after him: he has been heard to say, I have been among a company of Parliamentary hell-hounds and Puritans; thank God, I am out!— There has been terrible examining: of Popish Colleges in Clerkenwell, of reprinting the Petition of Right, of seizing Hon. Mr. Rolle's goods, of serving Mr. Rolle with a *subpœna*: from the Attorney General to Burgess the Bailiff, no man could think himself safe.

But, in fine, as we say, the Customs officers, cross-question them as we may, reply only: That they seized these goods for such duties as were due in the time of King James; that his Majesty sent for them on Sunday last, and bade them make no other answer. Learned Selden, therefore, with a shrill voice (it was on Thursday 19th February, next week after Mr. Cromwell's 'flat Popery') cried: 'If there be any near 'the King that mispresent our actions, let the curse light on 'them, not on us! and believe it, it is high time to vindicate 'ourselves in this case, else it is vain for us to sit here.'[1] The learned Selden is getting shrill. The House, fiery Sir John Eliot for its spokesman, [declares] that it ought to be so; that Mr. Rolle ought to have privilege in this case.[2] Put that question. Speaker Finch says, 'he dare not put that 'question, he is otherwise commanded by the king!'[3] Learned Mr. Selden is thereupon heard yet shriller: 'Dare you not, 'Mr. Speaker; dare you not put this question when we com-'mand you? What is a Speaker that *dare* not put our 'questions? We may sit still and look at one another; busi-'ness is at an end. Other Speakers in other cases may say 'they have the king's command! Sir, *we* sit here by command 'of the king under the Great Seal of England; and you, by 'his Majesty, sitting in his royal chair before both Houses, are 'appointed to be our Speaker. Do your office!'[4] The Speaker dare not: other Hon. Members objurgatively bid, with higher and higher vehemence; he weeps, he dare not, resolutely will not. What is to be done? The House adjourns 'in some heat' till the day after tomorrow, that we may consider and see. Till Wednesday, the day after tomorrow; and on Wednesday the king, finding the House and all things still in some heat, thinks it will be better if they adjourn till Monday next, and try whether they can cool a little. Monday, 2nd of March is the winding up of an epoch in the Parliamentary History of England; and a scene which the readers of these pages shall

---

[1] Rushworth, i. 658.   [2] *Commons Journals*, i. 932.
[3] Rushworth, i. 660.
[4] Forster (*Life of Eliot*, ii. 438 *n*) says, 'Even Rushworth, misled by the passionate speeches spoken in this debate' of 19th February, 'has transferred to it also a portion of the proceedings which belong to the 2nd of March. It was not until the latter day that the speeches of Eliot and Selden, there misplaced, were delivered.'

contemplate for a moment. With faithful industry, refusing to be seized with locked-jaw, we fish out the details from Rushworth and Law-indictments—slumberous lakes of Dryasdust—and present them dimly visible to men.

Monday, 2nd March 1628-9.—The public emotion has not in the least calmed itself; the Parliament is hot as ever, smoking towards flame. The whisper goes round: his Majesty has decided to dissolve this Parliament straightway, such is his Majesty's resolution. This Monday we are to be adjourned again, then straightway dissolved. The Royal Proclamation is already drawn.[1] Our Speaker will never put that question of Mr. Rolle's privilege,—put any question more. Speakers of Parliament shall not ' dare' to put questions! Tonnage and Poundage will be levied without Bill; Neile and Laud will go on with Arminian rubrics; Treasurer Weston screwing men and merchants worse than the Turks do: are the Laws of God and Man about to be violated with impunity in this England? Ye men and Hon. Members that stand in the gap, it rests now with you! Of you now, as they do of us all, in a more than usually emphatic way, the past generations of England and the future alike ask: ' Will you trembling steal from your post? Will you not ' trembling, stand by it?' 'We will stand by it,' answers Eliot, answer hot Denzil Holles, hot William Strode from the west, Walter Long and others. Monday morning comes: let us enter this far-distant House of Commons, dim-visible, authentic across the extinct centuries, and see.

Speaker Finch, though he is on the wrong side, is a man one could pity this Monday morning; alas! whom could one *not* pity? They have arrived at the rending point; in this living social frame of England, fibre is to be torn from fibre: —not without pain. Speaker Finch's face, I think, is distressed with many cares. Hot Denzil Holles is seated on his

[1] Rushworth, i. 661.

right hand, and Walter Long[1] on his left, this morning:
there they have taken place, there, above his Majesty's official
servants, who sit on the lower stage in front. For what end?
Denzil's face, too, is loaded with a certain gloom. What face
is not so loaded? Mr. Hampden's lips are shut, his clear
eyes wide open. Mr. Oliver Cromwell looks mere anxiety and
gloom, as if some Last Day were arrived.

First business, Order of the Day, is that we put that
question concerning Mr. Rolle. 'That question, that ques-
' tion, put that question!' Mr. Speaker answers on the
contrary that he has a message from his Majesty to adjourn
this house till the 10th instant. 'That question, put that
' question!' cries the body of the House, in sorrow, in anger,
in a whirl of manifold emotions. Speaker cannot, Speaker
dare not ;—' Put it, the question, put it !' Eliot is offering
to speak; offering, and again offering :—Speaker, grieved to
say he must withdraw then, rises to his feet for that purpose: 'What ho, Mr. Speaker!' Denzil Holles, Walter
Long, the resolute Hon. gentlemen, are upon him, each by
a shoulder : 'By the Eternal God, you shall not go, Mr.
' Speaker! you shall sit there till the House give you leave !'
' Shame!' cries Hayman; 'you are a tool for tyranny!
' Hold him down!' Such a scene was never seen in any
House of Commons. They hold the Speaker down :—the
House all piping like the whirlwind. Hear Eliot now.

Eliot says :[2] ' We have prepared a short declaration of our
' intentions which I hope will agree with the honour of the
' House and the justice of the King'; 'and with that he
' threw down a paper into the floor of the said House'; saying,
' Mr. Speaker, I desire it may be read!' Speaker starts up
again ; is fairly out of his chair : ' What ho !' Valentine and
Holles drag him in again. Hold him down ! ' I desire that
' paper may be read.' ' No,' cry some ; ' Oh,' cry all ; ' read,
' read,' very many. House much troubled. Mr. Coryton
' strikes ' Mr. Winterton ; good Heavens ! Official persons

---

[1] Or Benjamin Valentine, say some.   [2] Rushworth, i. 667.

and such like want to go out: Sir Miles Hobart, 'of his own
'hand,' locks the door, puts the key in his pocket. Read!
Read! House much troubled. Strode says openly: 'Shall
'we be scattered like sheep, and a scorn put upon us in
'print?' 'Sir, I move that this paper be read: stand up,
'you that would have it read!'—Many stand up:—does not
Mr. Hampden, does not Mr. Oliver Cromwell?—Still the
paper lies unread. Mr. Selden: 'Must the Clerk read that
'paper.' Clerk does not read; how can a clerk, his Speaker
being speechless? 'Keep the door shut, hold him down!'
Since the paper cannot be read, Eliot will take the liberty
to speak the substance thereof. It is: That Neile and Laud
are disturbers of the church of England; that many of his
Majesty's Privy Council are going on wrong courses; that
Treasurer Weston walks in the Duke's footsteps; let us
accuse Treasurer Weston; let the Commons of England
declare as capital enemies to the King and Kingdom all that
will persuade the King to take Tonnage and Poundage
without grant of Parliament, and that, if any merchants shall
willingly pay these duties without consent of Parliament,
they shall be declared accessaries to the rest.—That will have
an effect, whatever become of it: 'no man was ever blasted
'in this House, but a curse fell on him!'—Speaker shudders
in his chair; he is chained there like Prometheus.[1]—Yes! if
he levy Tonnage and Poundage without a Bill, it may be the
worse for him. Walter Long says: 'If any man shall give
'away my liberty and inheritance (I speak of the merchants)
'I note him for a capital enemy of the Kingdom.' So the
House pipes like the whirlwind; articulate, inarticulate; and
Holles constraining the Speaker to sit, is redacting something,
putting it in pen-and-ink.

Hark! a knocking at the door! 'Who knocks?' 'His
'Majesty desires the Serjeant to attend him.' 'Silence!' 'His
'Majesty desires the Serjeant, Edward Grimston, the Serjeant!'
'Alas, the door is locked, and the key gone: I can't get out!'

[1] Rushworth, i. 669.

CHARLES'S THIRD PARLIAMENT

The messenger returns to Whitehall with that strange tidings. 'Be quick, Holles!' Holles is quick; Holles is ready: but hark! Here is another knock. Usher of the Lords' House and Black Rod, James Maxwell, by his Majesty's command. 'House locked, key lost, can't get in':—Holles, standing by the Speaker, since the Speaker is speechless, will himself, in this very exceptional case, crave leave to put the following three Resolutions, of which the House will signify its sense, say Ay, say No:—the Ayes have it: there is nothing else but Ayes. Three Resolutions which the most fastidious modern reader shall not get off without reading. No! all men, to the latest posterity, who hope to be governed by realities, in place of accredited false formulas; by true living Gospels, instead of dead cobwebs and 'four surplices at All-'hallowtide,' shall read these three Resolutions, and with thankfulness say Ay!

1. 'Whosoever shall bring in innovation in religion, or by 'favour seek to extend or introduce Popery or Arminianism, 'or other opinion disagreeing from the true and orthodox 'church, shall be reputed a capital enemy to this kingdom and 'commonwealth.'——Ay! four hundred ayes.—Twenty-seven million ayes!

2. 'Whosoever shall counsel or advise the taking or levy-'ing of the Subsidies of Tonnage and Poundage, not being 'granted by Parliament, or shall be an actor or instrument 'therein, shall be likewise reputed an innovator in the Govern-'ment, and capital enemy to the kingdom and commonwealth.' ——Ay, ayes, as above!

3. 'If any merchant or other person whatsoever shall 'voluntarily yield or pay the said Subsidies of Tonnage and 'Poundage, not being granted by Parliament, he shall like-'wise be reputed a betrayer of the liberty of England, and 'an enemy to the same.'

Ay! Twenty-seven million ayes, or three hundred million, from Europe, America, and the Colonies!

And now, having passed these Resolutions, vanish! Miles Hobart produces his key; Speaker is released; House of Commons disperses. King's Guard coming down with sledge-hammers, finds the door wide open; House of Commons gone, vanished into infinite night.—On March 2nd their Journal has no entry but that they were adjourned to the 10th March; the tenth has no entry at all, but stars. There was no House of Commons, then, on the 10th. The King speaks his Dissolution that day to the Lords,—no Commons there,—and calls the Commons 'vipers.' It is the last Parliament for eleven years.

CHAPTER VIII

RELIGIOUS ARISTOCRACY IN THE SEVENTEENTH CENTURY

How the Country Gentlemen had Puritan Chaplains, Tutors, instructing their households in the way of heavenly Truth; how noble dames and high lords listened to the voice of Gospel Doctrine, and had real 'Spiritual advisers' as a lamp to their path; and all England got impregnated with the wisdom preached abroad in Judea long ago;—these facts, now fallen into oblivion with us, might give rise to reflexions. Pitched fights in Theology, lasting sometimes for a couple of days, were common in noble houses. James, Primate of Ireland, Lecturer for the present, in Covent Garden, is a main hand at such operations. He strikes your Jesuit on the hollow of the body like a real artist; knocks the wind out of him one good time for all; the Jesuit, with a gasp, says: 'I 'am well punished for my presumption in arguing with such 'a man.' Beautiful souls, oftenest of the female sex, look on with more than curiosity, reward the victor with glances that mean mitres. Ought not he to have a mitre, and crosier, or shepherd's crook, who can save his flock from the wolves · who can lead souls safe, and land them in heaven? Several high females of the Buckingham kindred were troubled with tendencies to Popery; some of them were healed by pitched fights, others would not be saved, but heeled evermore, and fairly canted at last into the lap of the Man of Sin. And many a gracious Lady Rich, and gracious Lady Poor de la Poor,. —beautiful Appearances that graced the current of this world's history for a season,—gracious high dames not a few;—who would not try to save such souls, if it lay in him! Father Laud, for the Championship of England, had a three days' wrestle with Fisher, the Jesuit; and beat him into jelly, I would hope. Nay, the controversy, once world-celebrated, is in print; but no man henceforth to the end of the world can read it. Open it;—the print is clear, but there lurks in it mere torpidity. Guy Faux has ceased to be a Devil, has become a guy; rolls softly through the New Cut over the powdered ashes of Dragon's teeth and old dust of extinct Lions; begs merely for a few halfpence to buy beer.—

Puritan Chaplains and souls' Instructors have now changed themselves into Newspaper Leading Articles, dilettante Art and Artists, into George-Sand-Balzac Novels, and I know not what: the soul, as I apprehend, in this modern England, has learnt the way of dispensing with instruction, or taking that as it pleases to come; as Welsh Ponies do their corn,—when they can get it. 'Intellect once divorced from rank,' says my dark friend, 'signifies that rank is preparing for annihila- 'tion; that much is verging towards chaos!'—The last genuine relation between the two that has been seen in England, was this now forgotten one, of an earnest religious aristocracy to earnest Puritan Chaplains in the seventeenth Century. In the next, stern Samuel, with a stroke like Thor's, had to smite Patronage on the crown. Intellect stalks solitary, like an Angel of Destruction, through the world;—Rank, a beautiful idiot, rolls placidly towards its doom.

CHAPTER IX

NICHOLAS FERRAR—THE NUNNERY OF LITTLE GIDDING[1]

ONE night, about the time when King James was progressing southward to take possession of his crown, stirring all England into incontrollable confluences, and giving a dissolving view to the young grey eyes at Hinchinbrook, a certain other infantine character, in the upper room of a merchant's house in the City of London, was busied praying at great length, and with the intensest devotion. Nicholas Ferrar was the name of this young person; a creature religious by nature and habit; and carried away on this occasion into altogether extraordinary heights. He prayed the whole night, it would seem, with ever increasing fervour; felt himself lifted up, as some of the Catholic Saints have been known to do; had a foretaste of heaven; had a presentiment, such as a young heart in its preternatural expansion was capable of, that he ought to devote himself, soul and body and endeavour, to the special service of the Highest, in this vale of temptations and tears. This night, in Nicholas Ferrar's history, has, amid the general dark oblivion all round it, become clear to me.

Much afterwards is dark and dim; the merchant and his fortunes went the common course; in the path of Nicholas, too, there had occurred the inevitable chances and changes. His father had died, his mother still lived; he himself, grown now to be a man, unable to execute his childlike presentiment as yet; had been at Cambridge; had travelled, for instruction withal; had got as far as Rome, looked with wonder on the face of Antichrist himself, the Holy Father so-called;—whether Antichrist or not, Nicholas could not

[1] There is a brief account of the Nunnery of Little Gidding in Carlyle's *Cromwell*, i. 73-4.

say; but in any case the sight was certainly wonderful enough. Convents and ancient Papal practices had passed before the eyes of Nicholas; awakening deep questions in his heart. The way to get to an eternal Heaven? Yes, that is the question. By what road shalt thou travel, O my soul? Surely the steepest road or the sternest, through Gethsemane fields, eremite Thebaids, through flaming death-portals and the abysses of creation,—any road in such case were easy! To Nicholas this world was all a dramatic shadow, infinitely important as symbolising heavenly higher worlds, not important otherwise. The money lucre, traffic and poor profit-and-loss of this world grew yearly more insignificant to Nicholas; and the question: Which way leads to the interior Sea of Light through these phenomena? growing ever more intense, childlike presentiments re-awaken on you in the pressure of serious manly affairs.

Nicholas returns to England, tries employment under the Virginia Company, becomes Member of Parliament (1624), soon retires from public life, sad, silent, unserene of aspect, revolving in him many thoughts. His mother living, a pious clear old lady; he has a brother pious, a sister or sisters pious; the question with them all is: Which way, O ye kind Heavens, which way?

The traffic of the elder Ferrars, all winded up, yields reasonable sufficiency of money; traffic protracted to never such lengths, can do no more. Not traffic henceforth; henceforth our childlike presentiment how to be realised? Alas, how? For the world, with its rolling wains and loud tumult, here in London City, is importunate and soul-distracting. In the Eastern mosses of Huntingdonshire, comes offering for sale, the decent Manorhouse of Gidding Parva; Little Gidding Manor, with due fields and competent rentals:—Church, Manorhouse, and solitary lands of Little Gidding all our own; —why not? The Ferrars, clubbing stock, purchase this Little Gidding establishment, remove thither, bag and baggage, man and maid, and mother and mother's child of them,—some twenty souls in all, waving the world and its traffic a long adieu.[1]

And so there establishes itself, amid the prose realities of that time, one of the strangest poetico-devotional facts, such as only the earlier heroic times, under quite other circumstances, were used to; figuring now upon us almost as a dream. For Nicholas has been ordained Deacon; he is not head of the house only, but Pontiff of it; and the house is wholly as a Convent or Priory, there for devotion alone. Night and day in the little parish Church or Manor Chapel, the ritual goes on without sleep or slumber: at all hours of the dark or daylight, you can say to yourself some portion of the Prayer Book is getting itself executed; the men and women divided into relays (like ship-watches), relieve one another by turns, and the praying and chanting slumbers not nor sleeps. Is not that strange enough in a country where all Abbeys are voted down, and Hinchinbrook Convent has become the dwellingplace of the Golden Knight? Cursory readers have heard of it in Isaac Walton and others, not without uncertainty, astonishment. But there is no doubt of it. Cursory readers, if they please to take a country excursion with a friend of ours, extant in those times, named 'Mr. G.,'—shall see it with eyes;—with G.'s eyes, almost as good as their own. Painful Thomas Hearne has been so good as print the narrative of Mr. G.;—stick it into strange neighbourhood, as is his wont; from which it is still extricable and extractable.

Who 'Mr. G.' was?[2] The gods and painful Thomas Hearne are as good as silent. A Gray's Inn Lawyer, says Thomas Hearne; . . . a vanished name and man. A clear man nevertheless, of solid legal knowledge, business habits,

[1] Ferrar's mother had bought Little Gidding some time before this; and Nicholas joined her there in 1625, as later accounts show.

[2] Hearne calls him Mr. Lenton. The Narrative is in the form of a Letter from Lenton to Sir Thomas Hedly. See Thomæ Caii *Vindiciæ Antiquitatis Academiæ Oxoniensis* (1730), ii. 702-94.

courteous manners, and (wonderful wonder!) of solid piety; vanished all but the soul of him, which still lives, shining clear as a light-beam in this dark place:—whom in these strange circumstances we accompany somewhat as we might a spirit. He has been on Circuit business at Huntingdon or elsewhere, this worthy Mr. G. :—hearing much, as he has long and often done, of this Little Gidding institution, reflecting much on it; and so determined, the Circuit business being over, to take horse and see it for himself. Vanished rider, vanished horse; wilt thou not accompany him into these lone moors, across those vanished centuries sunk so long in Hades? Swift, then, spur apace, good G.; meritorious vanished man!

A pleasant dewy morning, Mr. G. The sun, long since rolled together out of Chaos, has been trying his beams here, he and human industry busy for a while, have made improvements. These waving expanses have got clothed with sward and tilth tillage; much has been built, has been drained, fenced, ploughed; quagmires themselves have grown firm and green; heath of the wold has given place to grass and grain. Brick huts and houses, framed in oak,—many a smokepillar redolent of life and social breakfast, rises over those once solitary regions. Houses, nay, Churches, pointing towards heaven itself. Kimbolton Castle lies grey on that hand; Peterborough with its Spires on this. The mud-demons have been wonderfully subdued. Birds singing clear from many an old trimmed copse and hedge-row; heavy plough-men tramping steadily a-field, plough-men, nay, rosy milk-maids, merry brats of children, clean coifed grandmothers, have been realised; and the dewy vaulted element of blue and Heaven's blessed sun bends not unkindly over all. A tolerably pleasant morning, I think, Mr. G., on the whole, a successful thing this Earth?—Mr. G. responds no syllable, sunk in his own reflections; silent till he himself see good. Here, however, is Little Gidding itself!—A handsome, modest, Manorhouse, amid tufted trees, trimmed gardens. Says Mr G.:

'I came thither after ten, and found a fair house, fairly seated, to which I passed through a fine grove and sweet walks, latticed and gardened on both sides. . . . A man-servant brought me into a fair spacious parlour; whither, soon after, came the old gentleman's second Sonne (Nicholas), a bachelor of a plain presence, but of able speech and parts: who, after I had, as well as in such case I could, deprecated any ill conceit of me, for so undutiful and bold a visit, entertained me very civilly, and with humility: yet said that I was the first that had ever come to them in that kind. . . . After deprecations and some compliments, he said I should see his Mother, if I pleased. I, shewing my desire, he went up into a chamber, and presently returned with these; namely, his Mother, a tall straight, clear-complexioned grave matron of eighty years of age; his elder Brother married (but whether a widower I asked not), a short black-complexioned man, his Apparell and Haire so fashioned as made him shew Priestlike; and his Sister married to one Mr. Cooles, by whom she hath fourteen or fifteen children; all which are in the house, which I saw not yet; and of these, and of two or three Maidservants, the family consists. I saluted the Mother and Daughter, not like Nuns, but as we used to salute other Women. And after we were all set circular-wise, and my deprecations renewed, to the other three, I desired that, to their favour of entertaining of me they would add the giving of me a free liberty to speak ingenuously, what I conceived of anything I should see or have heard of, without any distaste to them. Which being granted, I first told them what I had heard of the Nuns of Gidding; of the watching and praying all night, of their Canonical Houres, of their Crosses on the outside and inside of their Chapell; of an Altar there richly decked with Plate, Tapestry and Tapers; of their adorations and geniculations at their entering therein, which, I objected, might savour of superstition and Popery. Here the younger Sonne, the mouth for them all, cut me off, and to this last answered, First, with a protestation, that he did as verily believe the Pope to be Antichrist as any article of his Faith. Wherewith I was satisfied and silenced touching that point. For the Nunnery, he said: That the name of Nuns was odious, but the truth from whence that untrue report might arise was, that two of his Nieces had lived, one thirty, the other thirty-two years virgins, and so resolved to continue (as he hoped they would) the better to give themselves to fasting and prayer; but had made no Vowes. For their Canonical Houres, he said they usually prayed six times a day, twice a day publicly in the Chapell, and four times privately in their house. . . . I said if they spent so much time in praying, they would leave little for preaching or for their weekly callings. For the one I vouched the Text, "He that turneth away his ear from hearing the Law," etc. For the other, "Six days," etc. To

CHAP. IX.] NICHOLAS FERRAR

the one he answered: That a neighbour Minister, of another Parish, came on Sunday mornings and preached in their Chapell, and sometimes they went to his Parish. To the other: That their calling was to serve God; which he took to be the best. I replied that for men in health, and of active bodies and parts, it were a tempting of God to quit our callings, and wholly to betake ourselves to Fasting, Prayer and a contemplative Life, which by some is thought to be no better than a specious kind of idleness. . . . He rejoined: That they had found diverse perplexities, distractions and almost utter ruine in their callings. But if others knew what comfort and content God had ministered unto them since their sequestration, and with what incredible improvement of their livelyhood, it might encourage others to the like course. I said that such an imitation [or innovation] might be of dangerous consequence, and that if any, in good case before, should fall into Poverty, few afterwards would follow the example.

'For their Nightwatchings, and their rising at four o'clock in the morning,—which I thought was too much for one of four score years, and for children; to the one he said: It was not much, since they always went to bed at seven of the clock in the evening. For the other, he confessed there were every night two, *alternatim*, continued all night in their devotions, that went not to bed until the rest arose. For the Crosses, he made me the usuall answer:—That they were not ashamed of that Badge of Christian profession, which the first Propugners of the faith bore in their banners, and which we in our Churche Discipline retain to this day. For their Chapell, that it was now near Chapell-time (for eleven is the houre in the forenoon) and that I might, if I pleased accompany them thither, and so satisfy myself best of what I had heard concerning that. . . . In the meantime I told them I perceived all was not true I had heard of the place; for I could see no such Inscription on the frontispiece of the House, containing a kind of Invitation of such as were willing to learn of them or would teach them better. . . . He barring me from further compliments said, The ground of that Report hung over my head, we sitting by the chimney. On the chimney piece was a MS. Tablature; which, after I had read, I craved leave to beg a copy thereof . . . which he forthwith took down, and commanded to be presently transcribed and given me. . . . The words of the protestation are as followeth:

'"𝕴. 𝕳. 𝕾.

| He that by reproofe of our errors and remembrance of that which is more perfect, seeks to make us better, is wellcome as an Angel of God, | AND | He that by a cheerful participation and approbation of that which is good, confirms us in the same, is Wellcome as a Xian Friend. |

But

He that any ways goes about to divert or disturb us, in that which is and ought to be amongst Xians, though it be not usuall in the world, is a Burthen while he stays, and shall beare his judgement, whosoever he be.	AND	He that faults us, in absence, for that which in presence he made shew to approve of, shall by a double guilt, of Flattery and Slander, violate the bonds of Friendship and Christianity.

Mary Ferrar, Widowe,
Mother of this Family,
aged about Four score yeares,
that bids adieu to all Fears and Hopes of this world,
and only desires to serve God."

'... But we passed from this towards the Chapell, being about forty paces from the house. Yet staid a little (as with a parenthesis) by a glass of sack, sugarcake and a fine napkin, brought by a mannerly maid. ... At the entering [of the Chapell] he [N. Ferrar] made a low abeysance, few paces further, a lower; coming to the Half-pace, which was at the East end, where the Table stood, he bowed to the ground, if not prostrated himself; then went up into a fair large reading-place (a preaching place being, of the same proportion, right over against it). The Mother with all her Traine (which were her Daughter and Daughter's Daughters, had a faire Island Seat. He placed me above, upon the Half-pace, with two faire longe window cushions of green velvet before me. ... The Daughter's four Sonnes knelt all the while at the edge of the Half-pace: all in black gownes, and they went to church in round Monmouth-caps (as my man said, for I looked not back),—the rest all in black, save one of the Daughter's Daughters, who was in a Fryer's grey gowne. We being thus placed, the Deacon (for so I must now call him)[1] with a very loud and distinct voice began with the Litany, read divers prayers and collects, in the book of Common prayer, and Athanasius his creed, and concluded with the "*Peace of God,*" etc. All ended, the Mother and all her company attended my coming down; but her sonne Deacon told her I would stay a while to view the Chapell. So with all their civil salutations towards me (which I returned them afar off, and durst come no nearer, lest I should have lit upon one of the Virgins, not knowing whether they would have taken a kiss in good part or no), they departed home.' [Here follows an account of the Chapel, its decorations, etc., with questions and answers thereon.]

'... It being now twelve o'clock we ended our discourse, and I called for my horses, hoping that hereupon he would have invited me to stay dinner,—not that I cared for meat ... but that I might have gained more time to have seen and observed more of their fashions, and whether the virgins and younger sort would have mingled with us, with

---

[1] Nicholas had received Deacon's orders from Laud.

divers other things that a Dinner-time would have best ministered matter for. But instead of making me stay, he helped me in calling for my Horses,—accompanying me even to my stirrup. And so, I, not returning to the House, as we friends met, so we parted.

'. . . They are extraordinarily well reported of by their poor neighbours: that they are very liberal to the poor, at great cost in preparing physic and surgery for the sick and sore, whom they also visit often; and that some sixty or eighty poore people they task with catechisticall questions, which when they come and make answer to, they are rewarded with Money and their Dinner. . . . I find them full of humanity and liberality, and others speak as much of their charity, which I also verily believe, and therefore am far from censuring them, of whom I think much better than of myself. . . .'

Mr. G. thought, we see, they might perhaps invite him to stay to dinner; but they did not;—he rides forth at the gate again, bowed out by Nicholas Ferrar; and becomes, in soul as in body, to all persons henceforth, a vanished man.

Nicholas Ferrar spent much of his odd time in binding Church Books, in illuminating MSS., in writing Polyglot Bibles, making Commentaries, etc. :—a somewhat melancholy way of living, one would think. Alas, to penetrate into that Heaven's-splendour, and live there by any method, is not easy: and many have to stop by the way, involved in briars and intricacies, and say to themselves: 'Is not *this* it? I can 'no further; this shall be it.' The prayer-relays work steady, and for nine or ten years henceforth, at any hour from noon to midnight, and midnight round to noon again, you can say to yourself: There rises a chaunt or prayer from Gidding Parva now. That, after its kind, is a perpetual platoon-firing of devotional musketry with the Tower stamp or Lambeth stamp,—calculated, you would say, to effect a breach at last, and take heaven by storm? O Nicholas, my somewhat sombre gentleman!—I respect all earnest souls, and mourn withal to see under what imaginations, hearsays, nightmare bewilderments, pressures of the Time-element piled high on us as the zenith, the soul of man has to live, and comfort itself as it can.

CHAPTER X

DR. LEIGHTON

[1630]

AMONG the men of that generation Dr. Leighton may in one point pass for a superlative: so far as I know he is of all the then extant British subjects the ugliest,—if there be truth in brush or graver, if Granger and Print-collectors have not entirely deceived us. A monstrous pyramidal head evidently full of confused harsh logic, toil, sorrow and much other confusion, wrinkly brows arched up partly in wonder partly in private triumph over many things, most extensive cheeks, fat, yet flaccid, puckered, corrugated, flowing down like a flood of corrugation, wherein the mouth is a mere corrugated eddy, frowned over by an amorphous bulwark of nose,—the whole, you would say, *supported* by the neck-dress, by the doublet collar, and frankly resting on it, surmounted by deluges of tangled tattery hair: such is the alarming physiognomy of Dr. Leighton, medical gentleman travelling southward from the city of Aberdeen[1] (?) with Wife and Family in wagons, sea-craft, or such conveyance as the time afforded, with intent to settle in his Profession here in London. Doubt it not, this Doctor had thoughts in him, purposes very serious, cares of eating and of other sorts. Poor Doctor, how he toilsomely plodded about, seeking lodgings here, squatting himself into some attainable cranny, and assiduously hoping against hope, set himself to obtain practice by patience, valour, strong all-forgotten energy. Good Heavens, it is all a history unrecorded, a history ever re-enacted to these days; a painful valiant history such as oblivion swallows yearly by the million, and nothing more

---

[1] Or more likely from Edinburgh, in the University of which town he had received his education. He is said to have sprung from an ancient family possessing a 'seat near Montrose.'—*Dictionary of National Biography.*

said. How many already swallowed, as Dr. Leighton, like snow-flakes on the sea. O, Oblivion, thou art deep and greedy; but Life, thou too art ever young and unsubduable! No man can expect to be rewarded by rounds of applause for every manful thing he does. Certainly not. And if he cannot content himself with either the gods for spectators, or no spectators, he will never play well I think. Empty benches are perhaps the best, and an audience frankly cat-calling, not the worst. Cat-calling, I say, for their rounds of applause when such do come have often proved the ugliest thing they had to give to a man. O Doctor, heal thou a little sickness; abolish a little misery in this God's Earth, and call thyself blessed in that thou canst do aught Godlike, —which alone *is* truly blessed and manlike! Thou art not come hither asking this poor blockhead of a world to do thee favours, pay thee due wages; thou art come, with or even without wages, to do the poor blockhead of a world favours. Thou wilt say to it, keep thy favours, hapless blockhead, give them to this quack, and the other, these legions of quacks in high places and in low. I have work in me, help in me for a poor bewildered blockhead such as thou art now grown,— and it is not with thee that I will chaffer about wages. Go *thy* way, I have *my* way to go! Enough: this Doctor finds, what is a real satisfaction, that he has never yet died of hunger, that he has healed or tried to heal a little sickness, burnt up a little sin and misery from man; and so, laying both ends of his lot together, that he ought to go on in a moderately hopeful frame of mind.

Courage, Dr. Leighton, and arch thy brows in private triumph over several things. A Greater than thou in far lower abasement than thine said once, Fear not the world. Be of good cheer; I have overcome the world,—I, the Nazareth Peasant, with a knit wool sack for my apparel, owner only, under the wide sky, of my own soul and body and this, I have overcome it. And do we not justly worship such a one, with love ineffable draw near to him, and in such poor dialect as we can, say, Thou art Godlike, thou art God! All brave men have to overcome the world; are born kings of the world, and never rest till they overcome it.

Dr. Leighton's old brown Book[1] is still found on the shelves of Museum libraries, but will never more be read by any mortal. Living mortal glancing into it here and there, falls chilled as with the damp of funeral aisles; says mournfully, It is dead—dead; and till the last day, if even then, will never live again. Most melancholy, dim, with mouldered margins, worm-eaten, its pages, letter-press, all so dim soot-brown. Alas, and the meaning of it not a whit more living, all soiled soot-brown, illegible as the letter-press. And we forget that it was ever otherwise; it was once new, clean-margined, bright white paper, bright black ink,—Book and Book's purport wholly new, comfortable to behold. Leighton's Book was eagerly purchased over counters, eagerly read in parlours, the very odour of the paper still new, new the odour of the doctrines and discoursing, wholly a new invigorating thing, redolent of comfort, instruction, hope to the mind of man! For in two centuries paper waxes old, and much that stands on paper. O ancient Pamphlets, soot-brown, mournfully mouldering Golgotha of human thoughts and efforts! Yet the thoughts did once live, and work, like the Thinkers of them. And only thoughts that go down to the centre continue long working, of which sort there are naturally few. Dr. Leighton's Babylonian Beast, etc., struggling to point out the difference between Fact and Semblance, in a superficial way, were not of this number.

[1] 'An Appeal to the Parliament, or Zion's Plea against the Prelacie'; etc. The book had been printed at Utrecht, in 1628, and copies sent to England while Charles's Third Parliament was still sitting. Leighton had gone to Holland to be pastor of a church,—the English College of Physicians having objected to his practising medicine further in London,—his qualification being only a Leyden M.D. Degree. He was ordained (March, 1629), and inducted into the charge of an English Church in Utrecht; returned to London in the autumn of that year, having, it would seem, received a call to some church in the city, and was seized in February following, cast into Newgate, tried in June in the Star-chamber, and sentenced as stated, *infra*, p. 246.

Enough, if the men of that century or year read Leighton, rejoiced in the redolence of new paper and what other novelty there might be; men of other centuries or years must look out for themselves.

Swiftly however a new scene opens on me. Scene of the Star-chamber Court,—one of the lion's-dens in that menagerie of Westminster Hall, whither by the stern keepers of the place so many men, Daniels and others, have been cast. They say it arose in Elizabeth's time; . . . small matter with whom it originated, my wish is once to see it vanish and cease. Neither have I learned in what room it sat,—one hopes the room is long since burnt, and no ashes of it remaining recognisable. What I do see is a suitable human apartment, a room of good dimensions, of solid carpentry, with raised bench, with indistinct ushers, macers, apparitors, indistinct to the eye, and judges of grave aspect also very indistinct for most part,—if it be not one little man in lawn sleeves, in three-cornered hat, with wrinkly, short face, with a look of what one might call arrogant sorrow of a sort, reflexion of a sort, and assiduity and ingenuity which in this world has had many crosses, but doubts not to triumph yet as it deserves to do. It is he they call William Laud [soon to be] Archbishop of Canterbury; sometimes named in a vein of pleasant wit his Little Grace,[1] not on account of his little *stature* alone. His Little Grace has arched brows, horseshoe mouth, but

---

[1] Laud's small bodily stature seems to have been the source of many a jest in those days. To Archie Armstrong, the king's Fool, who like many others bore no goodwill to Laud, is attributed this *double entendre* : ' All praise to God and little *laud* to the Devil!' Archie's last joke at Court was made too at Laud's expense and bore bitter fruit. When Laud's attempt to press the new Service-book and Canons into use in the Kirk had resulted in an almost universal signing of the Covenant, and the unwelcome news of this had just arrived at Court (in 1638), Armstrong meeting Laud on his way to the Council called out to him, ' Whae's fool noo?' Laud was 'little' enough to take the matter so much to heart that he had the poor Fool brought before the Council and sentenced to have his coat pulled over his ears and to be at once dismissed from the king's service.

brows arched for another than Leighton's reason. On
the whole, what a contrast, that small, short, wrinkly face
on the bench, and this huge pyramidal one on the floor.
The debate I do not give; why should I if I could? ...
This only transpired that Leighton in his Book called the
Prelates by hard names, 'affirming that they did corrupt the
'king,' that he dared to call her sacred Majesty and royal
Consort, as being of the Popish religion, 'a daughter of
'Heth,' and to pray for her conversion; that in fact he was a
Scottish man without the caution characteristic of that
country, a man resigned to God and not to the enemies of
God, intemperate of speech, and also very unfortunate. ...
The judges were of one voice, each endeavouring to outbid
the other, regretting only that he was not tried for treason,
that they might have taught him what a gallows was. As it
is, he shall learn what pillory, prison and the branding-iron
are. Only first, as he is an ordained clergyman, and we would
not for worlds do a shadow of dishonour to the Church, let
him be taken across to Lambeth to the High Commission
Court, and there be degraded. The Bishop of London, or
the Commission acting with him, will not be loath to degrade
him! Dr. Laud, with his eyes, if you look at him there on
the bench, answers emphatically, No. Once well degraded at
Lambeth, let him be locked up in the Fleet Prison, let him
on the 10th of next November be brought into Palace Yard,
whipped, set in our pillory there, have one ear cut off, one
nostril slit, one cheek stamped with hot-iron letters, S.S.,
'Sower of sedition': that will do for one day.—Ye Judges
that sit in place of God, does this man deserve such slitting,
such branding and butchery? Is this actually the ugliest
scoundrel you can find in England, in this month of November
1630, that you mangle him in this manner?—On a day following, says the Court, let him be carted to the pillory at Cheapside, and there after a second flogging, have his second ear
cut off, his second nostril slit, his second cheek burned S.S.:
that will do for a second day. Then,—why then, fine him

10,000*l.* and pack him up in the Fleet Prison for life. Most potent, grave and reverend Signiors, who sit there by appointment in the place of God above, punishing the ugliest of His enemies here below,—have you properly riddled [sifted] the general scoundrelism of England, and made out that this man is actually the chief sample? You do actually slit his flesh here with cold iron and hot; there is no uncertainty as to that. Rhadamanthus? But Rhadamanthus is always sure. Good Heavens, if this man were *not* the chief scoundrel? And what do you mean by answering to God? This man means a thing by it, and I mean a thing by it, a very fact: precisely such a fact as you mean by answering to Charles Rex this afternoon in Whitehall. Will the royal eyes look beneficently on you, will they look daggers and dismissals? One or the other, I suppose. Good God, and what will the divine eyes do with you?

Poor Leighton, the day before the execution of his sentence, sat meditative in the Fleet prison, revolving many things in his troubled soul. Many friends call to comfort him; texts of Scripture are rife. In the dusk of the evening there called two friends of an indistinct colour, Mr. Livingston and Mr. Anderson, both unknown to me, both Scotch I should judge, and of pious cautious mind. In the dusk of the evening Livingston put off his cloak, hat and breeches, all of a grey colour. Anderson put off his doublet; all put off and miscellaneously put on, and become of an indistinct, irrecognisable grey hue; and all three as friends of Dr. Leighton, walked out into the foggy element, leaving the prison cell empty, and jailors to whistle for Dr. Leighton. Hereupon there is issued a ' Hue and cry': he hath a yellowish beard, a high brow, and is between forty and fifty.[1]

Is there any reader now alive or likely ever to live, that does not wish poor Dr. Alexander Leighton may get off? O Sandy Leighton, my poor Sandy, wert thou up among the hills of Braemar again, within smell of the peat-reek, among

[1] Rushworth, ii. 57.

the free rocks and forests, the pouring floods and linns,—thou mightst skulk and double there among thy own kith and kin,— for here meseems there is small mercy going. Ah me, one has friends there, perhaps a poor old Scotch mother still there that will weep,—Doctor, I shall fall into tears if I go on. The Doctor had only got into Bedfordshire, when he was overtaken: had to suffer his bloody sentence, part first on Friday, November 16th, and then part second, that day week,—as Dr. Laud, the zealous little individual, has jotted down in his Diary, with surgical minuteness, being indeed a kind of spiritual surgeon. A St. John Long of the English Nation, who will burn the sins of it out by actual cautery and make it worthy of God's favour.[1]

CHAPTER XI

ATTORNEY GENERAL NOY

[1631-4]

SHIPMONEY WRIT

IN the year 1631[2] Noy was made Attorney General. A 'morose man' says Clarendon, one of those surly Law-pedants, acute spirits of human intelligence cased in the hide of rhinoceros; kind of men extinct now. Used to get a pie from his mother at Christmas, ate the contents of the pie, but kept the crust and lid, the 'coffin of the pie,' as they then called it: this coffin of the pie used to serve for long months afterwards as a general waste-box for the papers of the learned Mr. Noy, Letters, law-briefs, wash-bills, a waste miscellany of learned and unlearned scriptatory matter found refuge here,—

---

[1] After this barbarity Leighton was taken back to the Fleet prison and kept a prisoner there till released by the Long Parliament in 1640. In 1642 he was made keeper of Lambeth House, which was then converted into a State prison. He survived until 1649. His second son, Robert, became the celebrated Archbishop Leighton. It is now said that the entry in Laud's Diary, above referred to, is a forgery.   [2] Wood, *Athenæ*, ii. 581.

CHAP. XI.] ATTORNEY GENERAL NOY 249

happy that there was any refuge. So say the old Pamphlets, grinning in their broad manner. Think of this, what a Law Chamber does this learned coffin of a pie presuppose! When the weather grew hot it is presumable the pastry, even to a Noy's olfactory nerves, became unsupportable. When the weather grew hot the pie coffin would descend to the dogs,—to be rejected even of the dogs; and the learned gentleman's papers would fly refugeless, like Sibylline leaves. William Noy: *I moyl in Law*.[1] Human nature at this date has little conception of such an existence. By what alchemy was a soul of man ever fascinated to the study of English law? It is inconceivable. This man has long ago no need of money, no benefit from money; look at the coffin of his Christmas pie used as Drawing-room chiffonnier.

In 1628 Noy was a patriot Member of Parliament, as Wentworth, too, was. But Wentworth is gained to the Court; now they decide also on gaining Noy. The King sent for him, says Weldon;[2] said he meant him for Attorney. 'Attorney? Humph!' said Noy; and went his way again without so much as thanking the king. Nevertheless it was as seed sown, this word of his Majesty's. That Rhinoceros Noy could be fitted with Court housings, served with gilt oats, be curried into Courtly glossiness of skin and have the honour to draw his Majesty on public occasions,—the thought was new; the thought gradually became seductive, became charming. In 1631 Noy is Attorney General. All his stupendous Law learning turns now to the king's side, he digs and pumps up from the abysmal reservoirs of Law such precedents as were never dreamed of before, pumps and pumps till his Law ditch-water submerges this Nation as Noah's Flood did the world.[3]

Of Attorney Noy's new taxes, benevolences, monopolies and oppressions of the subject, it were long to speak; he was the hatefullest of all men to us; not only unjust but decreeing injustice by a law. We mention two only: the first his

[1] An anagram on Noy's name.   [2] Cited in Wood, ii. 582.
[3] Weldon, cited in Wood, ii. 583.

monopoly of Soap. The King by Attorney Noy's advice[1] decides to become the great Soap-boiler of his people,—leases out the monopoly of making monopoly Soap to certain parties for a consideration. Potashes and oleaginous substances exist for you in vain; you shall not make soap but in the king's way and by the king's permission. The Attorney will try you at Law; fine you in 500*l.*, in 1000*l.*, in 1500*l.* apiece.[2] Eloquent, to endless lengths, in their dim way, are the old Pamphlets on this crying grievance of Soap: eloquent, doubtless, too, were the living housewives and inhabitants of England. For Soap is not only dear, it is bad, not lavatory but excoriating, and leaving the foulness, burns the skin. Who can live without soap? And good soap,—you cannot get it for money; it is hardly to be had. Your Majesty, must the human subject testify its loyalty by going in foul linen! Are grease-spots a sign of being well affected? I have heard of no monopoly more grievous to the universal human mind; the old Pamphlets in their dim eloquence are almost heart-affecting. Pepper, too, is put under monopoly; pepper, tobacco, etc.; what is there that is not put under monopoly? We speak only of Attorney Noy's second grand feat, his grandest and most famous, that of Ship-money.

In secret the Attorney being consulted studies long, pumps up from the Stygian well of old forgotten law, this right or practice that the old kings had of commanding ships from the Maritime Towns; draws out a writ to that effect: the greatest feat of Attorney Noy and the last. Before the writ got published, the Attorney was lying down deep under Roe and Doe in his grave, safe with Empson and Dudley, with extinct extortioners, no more to decree injustice by a law. The vintners drank carouses;[3] and a published account of the Dissection of Attorney Noy testifies, that 'his heart was made of

---

[1] '*Was* it by Noy's advice,' Carlyle has inserted in the MS. here.—I have not found a distinct answer to the question; but as Noy was Attorney-general he must at least have approved of the scheme, if he did not actually originate it.

[2] Rushworth, ii. 253. [3] Wood, ii. 564.

'old parchment proclamations, his brain was gone entirely to
'dust, and in his belly was found a barrel of bad soap.'
Frightful! And the Attorney leaves all [or nearly all] to his
son Edward, '*reliqua omnia*, etc., and the rest of my lands,
'goods, etc., I leave to my son Edward Noy, whom I make my
'executor, to be consumed and scattered about, *nec de eo melius
'speravi*, as I have always expected of him.' Which indeed
proved true; for within two years, the Attorney's son, busy
as his father had anticipated, in running through his fortune,
was himself run through in a duel: and the Attorney's big
Babylon that he had builded, vanished all like a parchment
castle, and was not. The vintners drank and the commonalty
caroused: but had they known what was coming! The
Attorney's last posthumous feat excelled all that he had done
while living. Here are some memorial verses which a patient
reader may peruse with what admiration he can :

> '*Noy's* flood is gone,
> The *Banks* appear ;
> *Heath* is shorn down,
> And *Finch* sings there.'[1]

Is it not beautiful? It means that Noy died on the 9th
of August, 1634; that Banks succeeded as Attorney General;
that Lord Chief Justice, Sir Robert Heath, was removed with
disgrace from the Common Pleas,[2] and in his room appeared
on 16th October Sir John Finch, the Speaker whom the
Commons held down in his chair, and was Queen's Attorney,
but was not understood to know anything of Law;[3] gowned
men inquired eagerly of one another, What can the meaning of this latter thing be? Not long. The riddle was
propounded on the 16th, and in four days, on the 20th
October, 1634,[4] it was solved—by promulgation of the Ship-
money Writ. The City of London petitioned against it;
but the City had to submit.

[1] Wood, ii. 584.   [2] Rushworth, ii. 253.
[3] Clarendon.   [4] Rushworth, ii. 259.

CHAPTER XII

A SCOTCH CORONATION
[1633]

So many things are hidden in that dead abyss of Past Time; only here and there a glimpse of actuality recoverable from the devouring night. And of these few the meaning and meanings are so hard to seize! For so it stands in this dark Life of ours. The figure of the actuality you may see; but the spirit of it? How it arose, as all does arise, from the unfathomable Deeps, old as the morning of Days, and tends onwards to this present day and still onwards to the ultimatum, so unknown, yet so indubitable, sure as very death, when the Last of the Days shall have become dark, and Human History have ended, and there shall be no other Day? This to the eye of Supreme Intelligence is clear; to God's eye, but to no man's and no angel's? And yet, did it not in very truth lie intelligible, had there *been* an Intelligence sufficient in the work of every man! Unconsciously the poorest mortal, in all acts and trivialities by which he consciously means so little, has a meaning deep as the primeval Death-kingdoms; and decipherable only by the All-knowing God. For the poorest mortal was present in embryo at the Creation, and will in essence be present at the Consummation. Of the unconscious meaning we can spell the pitifullest fraction: but in these past times even the conscious meaning, what the actors thought, what of their miraculous life the actors of personages had shaped into some articulation that they called thought, and gave utterance to in some futility of speech,—this, even this, has mostly perished. How can history be known? It is all a prophetic Sibylline Book; palimpsest, inextricable; over which hangs darkness and a kind of sacred horror.[1] We must catch a

---

[1] '*Not* so.' T. C.'s note on the MS. here.

CHAP. XII.] A SCOTCH CORONATION 253

glimpse where we can; we must read some fraction of the meaning of it as we can.

On Saturday 15th June, 1633, by a singular chain of accidents, I obtain some view of the ancient city of Edinburgh; and discern a few things there in a quite visual manner, several of which it would gratify me to understand completely. But sure enough the June sun shines on that old Edinburgh, clear as it does on the new and newest; and men are alive and things verily extant there,—and even a state of excitation is discoverable among them. Curious to see. Westward on its sheer blue rock towers up the Castle of Edinburgh, and slopes down eastward to the Palace of Holyrood; old Edinburgh Town, a sloping high-street and many steep side lanes, covers like some wrought tissue of stone and mortar, like some strong rhinoceros skin of stone and mortar, with many a gnarled embossment, church steeple, chimney-head, Tolbooth, and other ornament or indispensability, back and ribs of that same eastward slope,—after all not so unlike some crowned couchant animal, of which the Castle were crown, and the life-breath those far-spread smoke-clouds and vapour-clouds rising up there for the last thousand years or so. At the distance of two hundred years or more this thing I see. Rhinoceros Edinburgh lies in the mud: southward a marshy lake or South Loch, now about to be drained; northward a marshy lake or North Loch, which will not be drained for the next one hundred and thirty years.

Faring westward from Dalkeith comes a cavalcade somewhat notable: a many-footed tramp of stately horses, a waving grove of plumes, scarfs, cloaks, embroideries; it is the choicest cavalcade that could be got up in these Northern parts; and in it ride Church and State, Charles Rex namely and William Laud, Archbishop, who in ordinary papers signs himself 'Wil. Cant.'[1] Other figures I could particularise, but

[1] Laud, now Bishop of London, became (on the death of Abbot) Archbishop of Canterbury, 6th August 1633, immediately after his arrival home from this visit to Scotland. Although he was not nominally Archbishop of Canterbury at

of what avail were it? James, Marquis of Hamilton, home from the German Wars, is there, and the Earls of Northumberland, Arundel, Pembroke, Southampton, and Holland, and many other persons of quality.[1] They have lodged all night in the House or Palace of Dalkeith, which, within the memory of old men, James, Earl of Morton, built,—prior to losing that strong cunning head of his for privity to Darnley's murder, for accumulated enemies, accumulated hatreds and other causes. His Majesty on Progress travels with a large retinue, harbingers, heralds, etc., and in one word no fewer than two-and-forty scourers and bottle-washers. Two-and-forty human souls spend their days in scouring dishes for his Majesty to eat from; what must the other higher items be! Proclamations have been published to keep down the markets on his passage, lest, like the locust swarm, he might create famine of horses' meat and men's meat. I could tell thee where he lodged each night, how the Lord of Newcastle, at Welbeck, laid out on one dinner for him the matter of 1000*l*., equal to, perhaps, 3000*l*. or 4000*l*. now. How he was wetted at York, and the Archbishop 'Wil. Cant.,' Primate of England, was witty.[2] How already in Huntingdonshire, he had called at Little Gidding, and collationed there with Mrs. Mary Ferrar and her noteworthy Protestant Monks and Nuns.[3] All this I could tell thee, and more; but it would be dull, dreary; and indeed a crime in me to do it. Solely, at utmost Berwick-upon-Tweed I noted the elegant Recorder, Mr. Thomas Widdrington, in a style sublime and beautiful haranguing him; how the ancient decayed Town, lying like a decayed warhound in time of peace, disconsolate between its hills, grew young to see the face of Majesty; and this year,

---

the time of this Scottish visit, he had long performed practically all the duties of Primate.—'Wil. Cant.' is of course an abbreviation of *Wilhelmus Cantuariensis*.
[1] Kennet, iii. 69.
[2] 'May 24th. The King was to enter into York in State. The day was extreme windy and rainy, that he could not all day long. I called it "York Friday."'—*Laud's Diary*.
[3] See *ante*, p. 234; and Carlyle's *Cromwell*, i. 73.

1633, would be for all ages a miraculous Plato's year:—whereupon Mr. Thomas kneels at Majesty's bidding, and after due slap of sword is bid 'rise Sir Thomas Widdrington, 'Knight.' A knight really worshipful enough, of learned middle-aged face, in decent Vandyk beard, white collar and black gown; for he is of Gray's Inn, and Recorder here. One of those famed Border Widdringtons,—posterity, like enough, of the Chevy-Chase Widdrington who fought upon his stumps. Understand next that close on Berwick, at the place they call the Bound-road, or limit of the Kingdoms, the Scotch chivalry waited in gala-dress, carrying their estates on their back. And then understand further,——— But no, thou unhappy reader, I will not strain thy patience till it crack. Widdrington speeches, ceremonial upholstery and blaring of trumpets, and indeed all large bulks in the inside of which is small or no reality, have in these latter days grown wearisome even to blockheads, and have to me ceased to be wearisome, and become something more. Noise with no meaning in it, bulk with no substance in it: is there, in truth, if one will consider it, a more sinful, I might call it insolent, blasphemous phenomenon easily discoverable at present? Truce, therefore, to the antecedencies of this same Royal Progress,—sufficient that thou seest the Progress itself; and sufficient for the day is the evil thereof.—Ambling along by the South-western roots of Arthur's Seat; through the green June country towards Edinburgh, tower-crowned, blue-cloaked,—whither, as extreme, compressed agitation is reigning there, may not we as well run and announce that at last the King *is* coming?

At the West Port of Edinburgh there is no entrance except one overleap the wall,—which indeed for the genius of History, is easy. But the huge planked gate we find is shut there; and within it,—ay, within, do but look! Solemn, on each side of the way, three firm ranges of wooden seats, whereon sit, in awful expectancy, clad in velvet, clad in satin silkgowns, Mr. Archibald Clark (?), Lord Provost of the City, with his Bailies, with his Councillors, in full complement; names entirely unwritten, if not in the universal Doom-book, figures that were and are not,—waiting what will betide. O Mr. Archibald, brother shadow of the seed of Adam, whom I never saw before, and hope never to see again, what an hour is this! The King is coming; thou hast a speech to make, multiplex ceremonies to do, and see well done, today. Thou sittest there, thy shadow Bailies, Councillors, all round thee; that blue Castle rock and battlements frowning over thee; and shortly thou shalt make a speech and genuflexions, thou hapless, happy civic functionary, here at the West Port; all Edinburgh looking on, and Scotland, and three kingdoms;— and thou waitest for the shadow of the King's Majesty! The Heavens send thee well through it, say I; for the moment is great. Mr. Archibald sits with thick-drawn breath, and all mortals draw their breath thick. I mark however, that the middle street is sanded smooth, the sides railed-in with wooden fences, with due Town-guards and Lochaber-axes, to debar the profane vulgar. O, ye vulgar, whom I see as with eyes, yet know no face of! bone of my bone, you and your fathers, who are my fathers, all unknown to me from the beginning of days! A fair good-morning, nevertheless! Sturdy Scotch figures in breeches, beautiful Scotch figures in petticoats;— honest men and bonny lasses,—there ye are. And those heads are full of thought, and those hearts, of joy and sorrow,—and it has all finished, where is it? All gone silent, an inarticulate hum as of the big Ocean moan of old Eternity. A fair good-morrow to you,—with thoughts for which there are no words!

Thirteen score of volunteer guards-royal, the handsomest youths in Edinburgh, wait somewhere, I think, in the Grassmarket, all in white satin doublets, black velvet breeches, white silk stockings, beautiful in pyet plumage: of these I reck not specially. Alas, all plumage is soon shed, swept bare;—all plumage is stript, I say,—cloth-plumage, flesh-plumage,—the very bones and dust are stript to nothing,—and all souls are bare,—Queen of England and Janet Geddes, maid-servant, all one. O Janet, thou in thy long-eared mutch (which the Germans still call *Mütze* and we mob-cap), in thy humble linsey-wolsey woman's dress, what doest thou today? Busy, belike, with broth-pot and dinner-stuff, like a hardworking servant, hoping only to catch some glimpse of Majesty hastily, from a front window? At this day, among the 753 portraits that there are of Charles Rex, I could wish there had been one of Jenny Geddes! Dimly I have seen her, poor woman, in deep closes [lanes], in high garrets; scouring, sweeping, as a poor servant-wench; reading her old Bible by a candle-end when all the house lay quiet; closing the day of drudgery with prayer to the Highest God. Authentic prayer, my friend, which is not so common a thing. Her grandfather, I doubt not, heard Knox preach; and to Jenny also a great Gospel has come. Gospel,—what Gospel ever equalled it? That in poor and poorest Jenny, too, under her coarse mutch, under her dusty coarse gown, there dwells an Eternity; strangely imprisoned so, a gleam of God Himself? Believe it, Jenny; believe it as thou canst; for it is true, and was, and forever will be; and in comparison there is no truth worth believing at all! Hardworking Jenny has exchanged glances with various handsome lads of the neighbourhood, but yet made no wedding. She seems to me, quiet as she is, of quick, deep temper: perhaps infirm of temper. Other scandals, reported by the crew of dragons, I have read, and then found reason to consider lies. Scrub away, poor Jenny; this day thou mayest see the King as he passes,—and shalt not fail another day, to do the King an errand, send the King a message of its sort, unlikely as that looks at present.[1]

Strolling along these holiday streets of Edinburgh, a number of questions suggest themselves. Some answerable, too many of them unanswerable. For, see, not only at the West Port, where Mr. Archibald Clark with his Bailie retinue sits,

---

[1] See the chapter on 'Jenny Geddes,' *infra*, p. 299.

thick-breathing; but here, at the West Bow, an inner closed gate, at the head of that tortuous street, stand orators, nay, I think stand Allegories, judging by their personations;—and then again, as we emerge into the High-street, what are these in sky-blue cloaks and plumes, various as the rainbow, as sky messengers newly alighted to congratulate the king's Majesty? The old Tolbooth and all St. Giles's Cathedral never looked so brave. In the bowels of the High Cross fountain there circulates, impatiently demanding egress, a lake of Claret. Judge if this decoration is a popular one! And a little farther on, at the public Weigh-house,—what the Scotch call Tron, not yet a Church, but a public Weigh-house,—see, the blunt edifice, by plaster, planks, draperies and upholstery, is changed to an Olympus, on which hover—the Nine Muses of Antiquity, and much else! These too, are to congratulate the King's Majesty; in verses as melodious as possible, apprise him that he is King by 108 descents, counting from the First Fergus, and prophesy that 108 or more shall descend from him in like manner. Of a new set of Allegories at the Nether Bow or lowest gate, of all that is going forward in the interior of Holyrood, and chapels with tapestry, bed-hangings, and furnishings, etc., and the cooking and furbishing that goes and has gone on there, my patience fails me to speak. For, on the whole, what is it but a scenic phantasm, rather helplessly adumbrative of somewhat, not of much? Adumbrative, as indeed all ceremony is, of men's worship for heroes or even for the cloaks of heroes; but, alas, in how helpless a manner! For in truth, O reader, the cloak of a hero cannot by any industry of man be worshipped at all; and at intervals the dreadfullest contradictions ensue from attempting and pretending to worship it. Good Heavens! it is like a veritable bolt of Heaven striking through a resinous torch and pasteboard thunder-apparatus at Drury Lane: the lamentablest accident; which, nevertheless always at intervals occurs. For when a Noah's Deluge by Law of Nature is due, there is no remedy in May-games, in careless dalliances, in marrying and giving in

A SCOTCH CORONATION

marriage: either thou wilt with faith and true labour build an Ark, or the floods due by Law of Nature will wash thee out of the way. For which reason, when thou seest clothworship going on, quit it, I advise thee: it is not safe, it is far from safe.

An historical secret that will interest,—this pageantry has all been got up by Mr. William Drummond of Hawthornden, a gentleman of much genius who lives 'vacant for the Muses,' as he calls it, out at Hawthornden. By him and by fit upholsterers has all this pageantry been got up.[1]

This then, is what Mr. Drummond could contrive to make of it, this miscellany of skyblue Muses, on their Tron Olympus, begirt with Scotch Lochaber axes, authentic Mr. Clark and the astonishing etceteras that we see? Drummond

---

[1] Jamesone, a portrait painter, had come up from Aberdeen to superintend the scenic part of this Coronation pageant. Drummond, in consultation with Jamesone, wrote the Speeches in ornate prose and the Poems in still more ornate poetry. These may now be read in Drummond's Works, under the title of 'The Entertainment of the High and Mighty Monarch Charles, King of Great Britain, France and Ireland, into his ancient and royal City of Edinburgh.'—These are:

In Prose,

'A Speech intended to be spoken at the West Gate,' beginning, 'If nature could suffer rocks to move and abandon their natural places, this town,' etc.—offering 'hecatombs of happy desires,' etc.

And *in Verse*:—'Speech of Caledonia, representing the kingdom:' followed by a 'Horoscopal Pageant by the Planets,'—opened by Endymion 'apparelled like a shepherd, in long coat of crimson velvet . . had a wreath of flowers on his head, his haire was curled and long, and in his hand he bare a sheep-hook; on his legs were buskins of gilt leather.' After his address come Speeches from Saturn, Jove, Mars, the Sun, Venus, Mercury and the Moon: which last, after praising 'the fair Queen and her Golden Maids,' prophesies to the King:—

> 'Beneath thee reign Discord (fell mischief's forge,
> The bane of people, state and kingdom's scourge),
> Pale Envy (with the cockatrice's eye,
> Which seeing kills, but seen doth forthwith die):
> Malice, Deceit, Rebellion, Impudence,
> Beyond the Garaments shall pack them hence,
> With every monster that thy glory hates:
> Thus Heavens decree, so have ordained the Fates.'

These delivered, Endymion perorates with a flourish; concluding thus: 'All shall observe and serve this blessed King.'

meditating in his elegant melodious mind the God's-fact as it stands between this Scottish Nation and its Charles Rex, found nothing so adumbrative of it as even this, this puffy monstrosity, rich in silk velvet and such like, but in all else most poor. Not beautiful, not true, significant of little; comparable to the huge puff-breeches of the time, and within them no limbs; at which the human mind two centuries removed stands stupent,—not condemnatory, no. And Mr. Drummond was a genius? I expect his singing will differ a little from that of the old Iliad Homerides,—merging direct with fiery veracity towards the fact, melting into music by the very truth and fire of it. Alas, yes, from the Greek Homerides, from the Norse Skalds, from the English or Scotch ballad-singer, from all men that ever at any time sang truly. The true singer hurries direct—towards the fact, intent on that alone, melts into music by the very fire of his veracity. Drummond's genius one would say is that of an accomplished Upholsterer rather.[1] Different from Homer's—as a pair of the costliest slashed puff-breeches, stuffed broader than a bushel with nothing in them, may differ from a pair of Grecian Hippolytus' limbs with nothing superfluous on them. But good Mr. Drummond is a type of his age. His monstrous unveracious puff-breeches ovation is the emblem of so much other unveracity. Mr. Drummond, had I been there, I had bowed almost silently to this King's Majesty, and thought within myself, O King's Majesty, I know not, the Scottish Nation knows not, what thou art,—half phantasm, half reality; God only knows. The Scottish Nation bends its head respectfully in the meanwhile, will cheerfully find thee victual and lodging of its best for the time being. What a pity there were *any* pageant and ceremony not full of meaning! They are all false, and they cannot all, like the Lord Major's coach, be safely trusted to the children to see

---

[1] In later years, especially after reading Professor Masson's 'Drummond of Hawthornden,' Carlyle formed a higher estimate of Drummond's genius than he has expressed here.

that they are false. Pity that there should be any *grimace*: a gesture that means nothing is an unveracity which man should avoid. Thy very horse scorns it. The neigh of the horse is sincere, and his kick is sincere.

Pageants are of small moment to us: nevertheless we must look on this occasion how it stands with Mr. Archibald Clark at the West Port. The heart of the man beating thick with painful expectancy, his breathing fluttered into a series of sighs. Edinburgh waits, with Mr. Clark at its head, in painful expectance of the King's Majesty. Hark, see far overhead: the old Castle has heard his Majesty's trumpet, and answers from her metal throats, in thunder, in rolling smoke-clouds barred with long spears of fire. Fifty shots of their great ordnance: 'fore Heaven a very handsome salute. And there, aye there, Mr. Archibald; loud knock at this thy West Port door, Majesty knocking for entrance: thou must rise, bestir thee, for the hour is come!—Pageants are a thing valueless as dreams; records of Pageants are like the dream *of* a dream. Nevertheless, as this old Edinburgh Gate opens, flung back by old Edinburgh beefeaters, the Lord Provost kneeling, presents his oration, and the keys of the City in a silver bason, having first shaken into it a purse of a thousand gold coins; which Marquis Hamilton as Master of the Horse and Grand Chamberlain of Scotland, receives; and the King's Majesty listens, and Earth is attentive, and Heaven; the June sun looks down on it, and two centuries have fled since then; while all this goes on, I say, and the plumed cavalcade fares slowly through the Grassmarket, West Bow and along its upholstery orbit, looked on by a hundred thousand eyes, the light of which is gone two centuries ago,—I could like to institute a few general reflexions. A few passing glimpses even, were not without interest to us. For this Pageant, spite of all the velvet mantling, fustian oratory and other Drummond furbishment, has a reality in it, though a small one. There verily are certain two-legged animals without feathers under it. Strip it bare as thou wilt, these do result. These;

and whatsoever in themselves and in their mutual relation these may mean and be. Reader, it is withal a most abstruse, and if well seen into, a most astonishing reality; compared with which this Hawthornden upholstery and Nine sky-blue Muses, etc., are very paltry. Nay, did nine real old Muses, with a real Apollo, light here on the Tron Weigh-house, and Drummond fly home shrieking, even that were not more wonderful. These unfeathered bipeds, could I rightly say whence these came, whither they are bound, and whence they got this gear they have within them and upon them,— these laces, Genoa velvets, still more, these thoughts, beliefs, imaginations, expectations,—I were a Thrice Greatest and Mercurius to thee.

Observe, for example, him they call King's Majesty, Charles Rex, by one hundred and eight descents, who sits stately on his brown barb, footcloth of black embroidered velvet, bits golden, stirrups silvern, crupper and headstall glittering with gems of Ind,—is not that a proper man? What thinkest thou of him? Of the white taffeta cloak, of flat-brimmed Spanish hat and white plume, I say nothing: except that all is suitable to each; that it is a king's Majesty very handsomely done. The long deep-browed visage, shaded with love-locks, terminating in delicate moustaches and peaked beard, is not without elegance and an air of pride or royal superciliousness, shaded you would say with sorrow. There is in it a solemnity partly conscious that it ought not to be solemn—that it is not solid or really solemn, rests not on solidity or energy, depth, or inward faculty of any kind; but solely on the white taffeta cloak with etceteras. Wholly the great man except the soul of him,—like the Tragedy of Hamlet, the part of Hamlet left out by particular desire. To me it has a certain fatality of aspect. This man has not achieved greatness; he has been born great,—in gesture, decoration, place and bearing. His elegant thin hazel eyes seem very rapid and very deep, and turn up occasionally as if Heaven would make all good nevertheless. Pretension and ability seem far out of proportion. He is descended from some one he calls Fergus the First by 108 generations, and at some later point of the genealogy, from Elizabeth Muir of Rowallan, in Renfrewshire, whom some assert to have been an improper female. Falsely, I hope,—but indeed, what matters it? We have all some 108 descents, or more, counting from Adam, or even from Japheth, downwards, and at some step it is odds but some improper females and not very many proper males have intervened. From Elizabeth Muir, at all events, the Steward of Scotland, begotten by poor Robert Bruce, second of that name, did issue, and became king and took his Trade's name for surname, and had descendants and adventures, and so we have now royal Stewarts, who reign over both nations, by divine right, by diabolic wrong, or probably by a mixture of these two. Mixture somewhat difficult to disentangle.

Of Marquis Hamilton riding at the King's right hand, who has just received the bason, keys and gold coins, I ask thee, Whether he too has not something of fatal in the face of him? A man favoured by his Majesty, the old playmate and constant familiar of his Majesty, who has slept in his Majesty's bedroom, and yet has had misventures, and is like to have. Where, O Marquis, for example, are the 6000 men thou leddest to the relief of Protestant Germany and Gustavus, Lion of the North? Six thousand went, a fiery miscellany of British valour and adventure: wasted, yellow with disease, not many units return! Even death in Battle was refused them. They had to die inactive, mostly of famine and heartbreak, and Gustavus or Protestantism never saw the mark of their swords. Hoping to purchase a little glory, thou hast paid the money, thou hast *not* got the ware! Jacobus[1] Cunctator, I consider thee a very questionable

[1] *James*, third Marquis of Hamilton. He was created Duke of Hamilton in 1643. His last exploit was the leading of a Scottish army of 20,000 into England; he was defeated by Cromwell at Preston, taken at Uttoxeter; and, after escape and recapture, was condemned and executed in 1648.

general. Better to stay in green Clydesdale by the Falls of Corra, in that palace of thine. But the old Lady Mother is fond of glory, is fond of Protestantism; and on the whole a young Marquis is still a young king, and neither kings nor Marquises have yet reached the stage of Donothingism, *Rois Fainéans*, which is the penultimate stage. This young Marquis, if you saw him on foot or at Court, has the strangest, slouching, crouching, luridly bashful attitude and ways; something really sinister, and painful even, as Mr. Hyde assures me: alas, a deepfelt disproportion between place and power to fill it, between what you expect of yourself, and what you will ever perform; this is painful enough! this untempered by heroic humility, heroic self-suppression, self-killing, far too hard a process for the most, this is sinister enough! I pity this poor Marquis, a man of keen anxious feelings, keen attachments even, not unkindly, not unconscientious, were they not so dashed by egoist terrors which he cannot well help: there are thousands of worse men. See what a viperous glow in those otherwise frightened eyes of his, as of the viper and poor innocent frog. I do not like such eyes. The Cunctator's brows are already waxing heavy, in a few years more of such conspicuous misventures, futile seekings of glory, by paying his cash and not getting the ware, the corners of his mouth will palpably descend, and one shall find him a man of horse-shoe mouth and frog-viper eyes, a conspicuously sinister man. For the present in much sunshiny weather, close to the King's Majesty, cheered by the Scottish bason and gold, and genial sunshine, he rides in moderate comfort, hoping better things.

One glance, too, at him on whom all eyes are glancing, Thomas Howard, Lord Marshal, Earl of Arundel and Surrey, first nobleman of England, who rides in state here richly caparisoned, the cynosure of many eyes. A luminous, distinguished man, to us still recognisable though faintly. Processioning, at home and abroad, on embassies, solemn missions in foreign parts, the first nobleman in England;—

to us all this has grown most dim, small and as it were extinct. By how feeble, neglected a ray, does Thomas Earl of Arundel still glimmer visible to thee, O reader of the Nineteenth Century and me? Neglected in his garden in the Strand lie certain mutilated blocks of foreign-hewn stone: These, Thomas Earl of Arundel found lying for sale at Rome, on his foreign missions or travels; these, the price seeming reasonable, he purchased and brought home; some unknown Greek man (1500? years ago) had got them hewn, sculptured with dates of old-world deeds and epochs, in which state they long stood read by curious dark Greek eyes, then lay tumbled, devastated by the Turks, no black or grey eye heeding them, —except the salesman who persuaded Thomas Earl of Arundel to purchase them. Thomas purchased them, laid them in his garden in the Strand. They lie there neglected while Thomas rides the streets of Edinburgh with king Charles. But now in this present year [1843], these Parian hewn stones, — what of them escaped being set in grates by masons, rescued by the illustrious Selden,—stand in the door-way (?) of a College at Oxford, and are a Parian Chronicle, and fly abroad printed in Books, and are the Arundel Marbles, known to all mortals,—shedding some faint veritable ray into the otherwise Cimmerian night of early Time.[1] Such virtue was in English Thomas Howard's guineas well given—in the stroke of that Greek's Parian chisel judiciously laid on. Thanks to Thomas Howard, whom we name, that he purchased these marbles; but thanks also to that invisible but indubitable Greek who quarried and sculptured them, whom we cannot name. By this faint ray shed into the far night of Time, shall Thomas Howard be long memorable; when all else of him is forgotten. O money-capitalists, Earls, Dukes, persons of capital and

---

[1] The marbles of which the 'Parian Chronicle' is the most interesting item, were presented to the University of Oxford in 1677, by Henry Howard, grandson of the above Thomas Howard. The marbles are now, nearly all, deposited in the basement of the Ashmolean museum.

honour, striving to purchase a little glory, my advice were that you went to the right shop for it, that you did some actual thing, or fraction of a thing. Glory is purchasable if you want it; but the tailor, upholsterer, coachbuilder, etc., have it not to sell. Palaces, valets, and caparisons, the whole honour and splendour of this Thomas are clean gone; the mountains of venison and beef, the oceans of Burgundy and *vino secco*, sherries, sack, he poured through his thousand throats, to the admiration of contemporary flunkies, where *is* all that? By the few guineas he gave for the Arundel Marbles does Thomas Howard, like a farthing rushlight in a galaxy all tenebrific, assert some feeble honourable visibility. Glory? my right honourable friends, it is not by sumptuous expenditure and sumptuously consuming, that man, had he the throat of Bel's dragon,[1] can rise to the immortal gods. No! nor even by dressing Parliamentary cases, rising to the head of Ministries, and victoriously guiding the spigot of taxation, what we call the helm of Government. My right honourable friends, might the heavenly wisdoms illuminate you; for failing them, I think the Tartarean Fatalisms, are not far, which never fail to prove didactic though a little too late!—

Meanwhile I ask thee, good reader, hast thou seen many prettier youths than this young Earl of Montrose?[2] Mugdock, beyond the Forth Meadows, is unluckily a hungry house; but here it has sent forth a proper man. Cardinal de Retz, a judge in such matters, finds a resemblance here to the heroes of Plutarch. So do I too, as realities of the human kindred all resemble one another. If King of Scotland mean strongest or largest soul of Scotland, why were not this man King? Alas! such thought be far from us; from him how altogether far is it! For the Past exists too, some four or five year-

---

[1] See the story of 'Bel and the Dragon' in the *Apocrypha*.
[2] James Graham, the 'great Marquis,' born 1612. He deserted the Covenanters at the close of the Second Bishops' War, espoused the royal cause, and, after a glorious but ill-fated career, died on the gallows, May, 1650.

thousands deep;—not to be abolished, thank Heaven! And in all times and places, the Present cannot get existed except by adopting all that is true of that, and honestly growing out of that. Shambling Charles Stuart is king, and firm-footed, fire-souled James Graham aspires but to be an accepted implement of his. Accepted, how thrice happy were he. Alas, the poor youth's estate, squandered in France, too, and foreign travels, etc., lies mainly on his back, I doubt: and he has wild wishes within him, a wild deep soul, insatiable as fire and noble too and fierce and bright as that. I like that lion-lip of the young Earl, that massive aquiline face, that broad brow, and the eyes, in which I discern smoke enough. He rides sumptuously but unnoticed, King's Majesty would take no notice of him, wherein some say Marquis Hamilton, speaking of broken fortune, ambitious, vehement temper, did him no good. Pass on, my Lord Marquis; possibly we shall meet again.

Dr. William Laud, now Bishop of London, Privy Councillor to his Majesty, Member of the High Commission Court and Star Chamber, etc., rides too in that procession, gazes somewhat over the high edifices and street phenomena, trying to remember them again, after an absence of sixteen years. Yes, my Lord Bishop, those old stone houses are there, but in your Lordship's self many things have changed: your hair which was then black is now getting grizzled, and you are a man of sixty; the church, too, has changed, and the world. English Solomon who never loved you, is gone to his glory, old age and strong Greek wine having done their part. He grew at last so stiff, that when they set him on horseback, he would stick unaltered through a whole stag-hunt, merely demanding liquor, from time to time; and come in with the hat sunk a little into the hollow of his neck, but otherwise unaltered in position,[1] swearing Scotch oaths, and not in the

[1] James was not always so fortunate as that in his riding. It is on record that, as 'he was riding on horseback abroad' (after dinner on the day in which he had dissolved his Third Parliament, 6th January, 1621-2), 'his horse

worst humour. A right religious Sovereign he, and true father of the Church, whose loss would have been irreparable, —had we not here, by Heaven's blessing, got a new and better! What king James but meditated king Charles will do.

Alas, all changes, all grows, decays, and dies. We were then a poor subaltern of an underfoot chaplain, busy packing, in a subterranean way, Scotch General Assemblies, under the cold shade; and we have been since then a pretty way. Dean of Huntingdon, Bishop of St. Davids, Dean of Chapel Royal, etc., and are now third Bishop of the realm, within sight almost of being first,—for poor old Abbot cannot hold out long. And the church—what a reformation; which then we durst hardly dream of! Altars, in most places, built into the East wall, surrounded with a decent rail; the priest in dispensing the elements going through his genuflexions in many places with propriety. Chinese Mandarins, heathen Bonzes, Talapoins,[1] shall they surpass us in fitness of gesture? And they but Idolaters! By Heaven's blessing, we shall surpass them.

CHAPTER XIII

ENGLISH MEN AND WOMEN IN THE TIME OF PURITANISM

Is it not worth our while to look back for a moment at the last great expansion of England? We will look at Puritanism and the time of Oliver Cromwell. A time of darkness, straits; when the soul of England pent within old

stumbled and cast his Majestie into the New River, where the ice brake: he fell in, so that nothing but his boots were seene. Sir Richard Yong was next, who alighted, went into the water, and lifted him out. There came much water out of his mouth and bodie. His Majestie rode back to Theobalds, went into a warme bed, and, as we heare, is well, which God continue!' *Harleian MS.*, 389.

[1] Bonzes and Talapoins are Buddhist Priests and Monks.

CHAP. XIII.] ENGLISH MEN AND WOMEN 269

limits, could no longer live, felt that it must be delivered or die,—and with endless tribulation and confusion, did verily deliver itself, and get new freer limits to live in! What is in the Future we know not; but know well it will be of blood-relation to the Past. Wouldst thou know the coming grandchild, look in the portrait of his grandfather. The clothes will be different, how different: but the features, never doubt it, will have a resemblance.

Landor has written 'Imaginary Conversations'; but the *real* conversations were an entirely different matter. Much more is required for men's understanding one another than their speaking the same vocables of language. The Edinburgh man brought suddenly into a London circle feels himself, in spite of Newspapers, so much of an alien. The topics of his new neighbours are not his topics, they think too, in quite a different style about them: What the neighbours say to him, what he says to the neighbours, is alike in good measure unintelligible, conversation frustrate, speech that cannot be heard.

Fancy a figure from one of our extant soirées, suddenly carried back 200 years into the dark past, and set down face to face in a social evening party of Cromwell's time. Pause a little over this. No doubt at all our ancestors *had* evening parties; there in apartments swept, heated, lighted, cheery with the hum of human voices they do meet together; certain as if we saw it, there they are. Of stature, figure, structure bodily and spiritual, altogether like our own; nothing but the outer tailor's work dissimilar. Their faces in all lineaments are as ours: behold the English noses in their shapes and unshapes,—the due proportion of them tipt with carbuncular red: the surly square English faces, alas, sorrowfully truculent perhaps, sorrowfully thoughtful, loving, valiant, sorrowfully striving to be glad. For the basis of their life is earnestness; too apt, in such a world as this, to have itself made into sorrow, silent, mournful indignation and provocation, noble or ignoble spleen,—what you would call a radically sulky kind of people. In whom nevertheless lies laughter and floods of honest joy; the best and only good laughter,—as rainbows and all bright pictures shine best on a ground of black. Faces altogether such as ours; and figures, the broad-shouldered Herculean, the taper-limbed Apollo figure, and other varieties, not to speak of bow-legged, squat, with pot-bellies. Neither in spite of time can their curls, wimples and fantastic dresses and head-dresses hide from me that here are true daughters of Saxondom, bright as the May month, beautiful as the summer dawn. Behold them. The face a beautiful, improved, transfigured, female version of the male face, a thing really worth beholding. Truculent sorrow, where is it now? Become a noble dignity, sunny grace made lovelier by a shade. These are the daughters of England, the mothers of England. Beautiful enough for that matter. Complexion as of milk with a tinge of roses; shapes as of the wood-goddess with her nymphs;—and in those blue eyes, as quiet as they look, have I not seen festive radiances, lambent kindlings; brighter far than the glance of diamonds. It was the flash of their minds that had life, that was soul, and had come from Heaven. Properly the brightest of all weather gleams in this lower life. Alas! they go out so soon in dead darkness, and all that vision is away, away!

Such figures in their silks, in their cloth habiliments, bright-dyed enough, are veritably there, alive, and lights burning round them, and the modern figure entering with the truest wish to commune, what a stranger is he! Talk goes of my Lord Marshal and his Parian Chronicle that lies mouldering in Arundel House, by the Strand of Thames, and how the masons have broken part of it, and sacrilegiously set fire-grates with Marmora Arundeliana. Of Lambeth and his Grace, by some called his Little Grace, so overwhelmed with Star chamber and High Commission business,—Bastwick's ears to be cropt in Palaceyard; obscure sectaries getting loud everywhere; of King's right to Tonnage and Poundage without Parliament or not without; of Altars railed and fronting the East, or Communion Tables which are not Altars nor railed, and stand either East or West as it chances. Ah me, and of Grace, Predestination, Goodworks, Faith, and of the Five Arminian Points condemned at Dort. A dim hum of these things reaches our ears; but they are become unmomentous, undelightful,—unintelligible, like the jargoning of choughs and rooks!—We shall never get into that old soirée; neither let us lament that we cannot. And if in these circles one spoke a word of Parliamentary Reform Schedules, Sir Robert Peel and the prosperity of Trade? German Literature, Almack's Toleration, Railway miracle, or the Cause of Civil and Religious Liberty all over the world? Time was, but the time that was is not any more; has no more the right to be.

CHAPTER XIV

BASTWICK, BURTON, AND PRYNNE

[1637]

On the 30th of June, 1637, I see a crowd in old Palace Yard: Old London streaming thitherward through King Street, by boats at Lambeth ferry, through all streets and ferries, with various expressions of face, with thoughts—who can know their thoughts? Dim through the long vista of years, and all foreign, though domestic, nay, paternal, has the whole grown to me: men and women many thousands, in hoods, in long lappeted cap and gown, in steeple hat and Dutch-looking breeches,—of indistinct costume,—close packed together—stand gazing there; but the features I see are English, a sea of English faces,—a miscellaneous sea of English souls with such most indistinct miscellany of thoughts as the scene brings. My Fathers and my Mothers! For behold, the three prisoners come out, guarded by due tipstaves, by long-skirted persons in authority; mount aloft to their scaffold, into the general eye of day, of that day,—and of many days, onward even to this day and farther. Indistinct murmur, thrill of manifold fellow-feeling runs through that crowd. They were seditious men, these three, or they were not seditious but speakers for the rights of Englishmen? They shall lose their ears this day, be heavily fined and take farewell of liberty in jail till death: so much is certain. They are of a sort not usually seen on Pillories; Reverend Henry Burton, of Friday Street Chapel; William Prynne, Esq., of Lincoln's Inn, Barrister at Law, and John Bastwick, M.D. Burton was a Graduate of Oxford, had at one time been Tutor to the King, a man held in great estimation, and chargeable with no fault but a certain anti-Laudism which could not then, and cannot now, either in the matter or even in the manner of it, be regarded by the public as a crime very heinous, but as the reverse of one. W. Prynne whom we are accustomed to picture to ourselves as a dingy unwashed, contentious, writing-sansculotte, was far other in reality: a gentleman by birth and breeding and behaviour, a Graduate of Oxford; laborious conscientious Student of Law, a man of much learning which to his own generation was very far from looking crabbed and obsolete as it does to ours. John Bastwick, too, is a gentleman and scholar; has studied at Cambridge, learned medicine at Padua, and practised it at Colchester. These three persons disreputable to nobody, warmly esteemed and even venerated of many, appeared on this 30th June, 1637, on what might be called a new stage, and exhibited a very strange spectacle to England. They were conducted from prison to their scaffolds in Palace Yard; fixed in their pillories for two hours, as if they had been pickpockets: at the end of two hours the executioners with attendant surgeons, with braziers, branding irons, and due apparatus, stept forth and shore their ears off them, staunching their blood with the actual cautery of red-hot iron hissing in their flesh,—the people looking on, not with noise, with a silence which we find had grown 'pale.' All people might naturally ask themselves, Whitherward is all this; what will it end in? Bastwick's wife caught his ears in her lap, and kissed him without tears. Brave dame Bastwick, worthy to be a Mother of men![1] In Burton's case, who had preached all the time of the pillory-penance, they cut an artery, and the blood came leaping; his face grew pale, as all faces did; 'I am not hurt,' he cried. Prynne's ears, which had been sliced before but sewed on again, were now grubbed out beyond surgeon's help; the executioners rather sawed than cut him; Prynne said with emphasis: 'Cut me, tear me, burn me; I fear the fire of 'Hell, but none of you.' Burton when they carried him into a house in King Street, the execution being done, and laid him on a bed, was heard to say, the June temperature too being very high, 'This is too hot to last.' Words which circulated through the London multitude and through all England, with something of a prophetic application.—O, my brothers, my poor maltreated Bastwicks, Burtons, and Prynnes, never so rude of speech, so obsolete of dialect and logic, it is you withal whom I will honour. If no triple-hatted, shovel-hatted or other chimera do now oppress us, if the attempt to do it would raise England, Europe and America as one man and explode such mad chimera into limbo,—whom have we to thank!

This was the last and greatest of the High Commission and Star-Chamber performances in the way of slitting and branding. We may give it as the culminating point and apex of a large unrememberable mass of pilloryings, finings, and ignominious severities inflicted on Englishmen for scrupling

[1] 'But thus too the poor Scotch woman, John Brown the carrier's wife, at that cottage door in Clydesdale, bound up her shot husband's brains, and sitting down in silence, laid it on her lap, bidding her orphans not weep, but wait this stern blessed morning the farther will of God. And when the Claverhouse trooper asked tauntingly, " What think ye of your husband now?" she answered, " I thought always mickle of my husband, and I think more of him now than ever!"
—May it please your Grace, this seems to me better than altars in the East.'
From another Paper in this MS., headed ' Prynne and Bastwick.'

to become inane China-men, and worship God in the Laud manner by bowings and beckings towards the East, etc. 'Is 'the living God a buzzard idol,' asks Milton,[1] as with eyes flashing empyrean fire: Darest thou worship Him with grimaces, and Drury Lane gesticulations? I dare not, and must not, and will not! You shall! said little Laud, with his shrew voice elevated, and his red face still redder; and so the matter went on, and had grown 'too hot to last.'

CHAPTER XV

LAUD'S LIFE BY HEYLIN[2]

LAUD's Life has been described by Peter Heylin, D.D.; the man known usually in Presbyterian Polemics by the name of 'Lying Peter.' He is an alert, logical, metaphorical, most swift, ingenious man; alive every inch of him, Episcopal to the very finger-ends. This present writer has read the old dim folio, every word of it, with faithful industry, with truest wish to understand. A hope did dawn on him that he of all Adam's posterity would be the last that undertook such a trouble: some one of Adam's sons was fated to be the last; why not he? It had been too sad a task otherwise. For if the truth must be told, this unfortunate last reader found that properly he did not 'understand' it in the least, that though the thing lay plain, patent as the turnpike highway, no man would ever more understand it. For the mournful truth is, that the human brain in this stage of its progress, refuses any longer to concern itself with Peter Heylin. The result was, no increase of knowledge at all. Read him not, O reader of this nineteenth century, let no pedant persuade you to read him. Spectres and air-phantoms

---

[1] '... Who thought no better of the living God than of a buzzard idol.' *Eikonoklastes.*

[2] *Cyprianus Anglicus; or the History of the Life and Death of William Laud, Archbishop of Canterbury, by Peter Heylin* (London, 1668).

of altars in the East, half-paces, communion-rails, shovel-hatteries, and mummeries and genuflexions; I for one, O Peter, have forever lost the talent of taking any interest in them, this way or that. As good to say it free out. My sight strains itself looking at them; discerns them to be verily phantoms, air-woven, brain-woven; disowned by Nature, noxious to health and life,—dreary as an aged cobweb full of dust and dead flies. Peter, my friend, it is enough to sit two centuries as an incubus upon the human soul; thou wouldst not continue it into the third century? Thou art requested in terms of civility to disappear. Incubuses have one duty to do: withdraw. Were Peter's Book well burnt and not a copy of it left, this therefore were the balance of accounts: human knowledge where it was, and two weeks of time and misery saved to many men. On these terms, this last reader will not grudge having read.

In these present years, much to the wonder of the world, considerable phantasmagories of theoretic logic as to Church and State and their relation and subordination and coördination, figure, once again, like ghosts resuscitated from a past century, through the heads of certain English living men. Into such conflict of phantasmagories thou and I, O reader, have not the faintest purpose to enter. By Heaven's blessing we belong not to the seventeenth century; we are alive here, and have the honour of belonging to the nineteenth! What concerns us is to discern clearly across mitres, coifs, rochets, tithes and liturgies what is a Church and what is no Church at all. The Church is the messenger from the world of Eternity to men who live in this world of Time. What credible message she delivers in this visible Time-world as to our possessions, relations, prospects, in the unseen world which lies beyond Time; this for the while is the religion of men. How the *true* Church will relate itself to the practical State, this is ever the interesting question, the question of questions. How the *seeming* Church will do it, is, if she be no true one, a most unimportant question. Church and State are Theory and Practice. Church is our Theorem of the invisible Eternity, wherein all that we name world in our earthly dialects, all from royal mantles to tinkers' aprons, seems but as an emblematic shadow. Emblematic, I say; for thou wilt discern that the real Church of men does always transfigure itself in their temporal business. Of many a man that signs the Church credo *without* either smile or sigh, what were the *real* Thirty-nine Articles, could we, or even could he himself, poor stupid insincere man, contrive to get them out of him? One huge Note of Interrogation: Is there any unseen world? What is it? Some say there is? That were his Thirty-nine Articles—the homily from which we may likewise see dimly drawn, and, if not preached, daily cited. Man's soul is his stomach; thou son of man, have an eye to victual; in victual, from pudding up to praise, how rich is this earth! A Note of Interrogation: Others I have known whose Thirty-nine Articles were one huge zero.—It must be owned King Charles's Kingship, and Archbishop Laud's Archbishopship were extremely on a par.

Church: look, 1800 years ago, in the stable at Bethlehem, an infant laid in a manger! Look, and behold it; thou wilt thereby learn innumerable things. The admiration of all nobleness, divine worship of Godlike nobleness, how universal is it in the history of men.—But mankind, that singular entity mankind, is like the fertilest, fluidest, most wondrous element in which the strangest things crystallise themselves, spread out in the most astonishing growths. Bethlehem cradle was one thing in the year One, but all years since that,—1800 of them now, have been contributing new growth to it;—and see there it stands: the Church! Touching the earth with one small point, rising out therefrom, ever higher, ever broader, high as the heaven itself, broad till it overshadows the whole visible heaven and earth, and no star can be seen, except through *it*. Whatever the root and seedgrain were, thou dost not call all that enormous growth above ground nothing? Surely not; it is a very wondrous thing, nay, a great instructive and venerable thing. Were its root gone to nothing, sure enough *it* were still there. Alas, if its root do give way, and it lose hold of the firm earth, what, great as it is, can by any possibility become of it, except even this, that it sway itself slowly or fast, nod ever farther from the perpendicular, and sweeping the eternal heavens clear of its old brown foliage, come to the ground with much confused crashing and lie there a chaos of fragments, a mass of splinters, boughs and wreckage, out of which the poor inhabitants must make what they can! Do not forget your root, therefore, my brothers! I have comparatively a most small value for your biggest magic-tree when the root of it is gone.

Certainly among the characters I have fallen in with in history this William Laud has not been the least perplexing. Pyrrhuses, Pizarros that fight, kill and truculently cut their way to promotion in that manner, one can understand; mighty hunters who live to kill foxes, we have likewise seen; missioned Cooks, Columbuses who cannot rest till they have discovered continents; Spanish Soldier Poets writing Araucana Epics on leather; Tychos and Keplers searching out, in weary night watches, in bitter isolation and hardship and neglect of all men, the courses of the stars: but what this man means by cutting off men's ears, branding their cheeks S.S., and chaining them to posts under ground, and keeping the whole world in hot water, for the sake of getting his altars set in the East wall? Good Heavens, suppose the altar were set in the West wall, or in any or no wall, so that the living hearts of men would be turned towards the God of the altar! Their ears might then stick on their heads, one would say, and all go well and peaceably. But no; the Puritans, it appears, are turned but *too* intently towards the God of the altar; and that is no excuse for them with William Laud,—nay, as probably begetting an impatience with East-wall altars, and other Episcopal Upholstery, it is part of their offence. They are too religious; and a Christian soul's Arch-overseer has the strangest care laid upon him,—that of making his people *less* religious! The trouble this soul's Overseer has taken in promulgating the Book of Sports[1] and such like, with penalties and admonitions, is considerable in that direction. If the Divine Powers favour, the Earthly ones have done their part; and this people on the Sabbath day shall not indulge themselves in praying, but come out to sport and drink ale. And the man reads the same Bible still printed in this country, and is Archiepiscopus, Primate of all England. Stranger Primate of all England I have never in my life fallen in with. And it is a clean-brushed, cultivated man, well-read in the Fathers and Church history; a rational, at least much-reasoning, extremely logical man. He will prove it for thee by never-ending logic, and the most riveting arguments, if thou hast patience to listen. What he means, what he can possibly mean?

There have been many *Præsules* of England, Arch-overseers of Canterbury, and some of them through Wharton's *Anglia Sacra*, *Lives of Saints*, and such windows as I could discover or attain to, I have looked at with attention, affliction, admiration, generally with amazement: but this *Præsul* of England amazes me more than all, afflicts me more than all. Eadmer's Life of Anselm in the rough Norman days, one can still survey with interest; his old Anselm one can still discern to be a living man, a kind of hero, and reverently salute him as a sublime though simple old Father, through the dim eight centuries that intervene; but this new *Præsul*, distant but two centuries, did he ever breathe, and step about on black leather? Already poor William Laud is too inconceivable. Not among the heroes of this world . . . is he to be ranked. Human scepticism will not go the length of disbelieving that he lived; and yet alas, in what way; how could a human figure,

---

[1] King James's 'Book of Sports' (see *ante*, p. 138) was reissued by Charles and Laud in 1633.

with warm red blood in him consent to live in that manner? It is, and continues, very difficult to say! Future ages, if they do not, as is likelier, totally forget ' W. Cant.,' will range him under the category of Incredibilities. Not again in the dead strata which lie under men's feet, will such a fossil be dug up. The wonderful wonder of wonders, were it not even this, A zealous Chief Priest, at once persecutor and martyr,[1] who has no discoverable religion of his own?

Or why not leave Laud very much on his own basis? Let the dead bury their dead. Laud is little to me. Yet as the straggling bramble which you find suspended by many a prickly hook to the noble oak tree, to the fruitful fig, so high and protrusive is the bramble you are obliged to notice it.—The present is like boundless steam or gas; boundless, filling the Earth and the Solar System: wait a little, it will from gaseousness become liquid, become dried and solid, sink into the quiet thickness of a film. Large epochs lie in one rockstratum of that deep mass that lies piled up from the centre of Beginning. Under feet of the living lies as soil and as rocky substratum, the ashes of the dead. Organic remains, it is all organic residues, and was once alive and loud as you are. It lies now so quiet, growing mere corn for you, supporting your partridges, game-laws, and much else !—

How then shall we name this singular Wil. Cant.? Name him Arch *Præsul* of the so-called ' Nag's-head Church.' A Church evidently of the temporary kind, which could exist only in certain centuries, and in all other centuries will be sought for in vain.—In the times of Anselm and the Vatican, it was a life-and-death question, Shall Europe become wholly a Church, its Kings mere administrative deacons therein, the universal Sovereign of it sitting aloft at Rome, crowned in his three hats, a kind of human God? Or shall the Heathen

---

[1] Articles of impeachment against Laud for having attempted to subvert religion and the fundamental laws of the realm, were unanimously voted by the House of Commons in Feb., 1640-1. He was soon afterwards sent to the Tower, and beheaded on Tower Hill, 10th January, 1644-5.

secular element of it, withal, not be suppressed; since it too was made of God? Psalms and Litanies being everywhere chaunted to the utmost perfection, there will remain yet innumerable things to do,—cotton to be spun in Lancashire, for instance, grain to grow in the Lothians, and much else! Everywhere cities are to be built, swamps to be drained, and wastes to be irrigated, savage tribes and places to be drilled and tilled, whole continents to become green, fruitful with life and traffic. The Heathen element, as you call it, ought withal to assert itself, and will. Jesus of Nazareth and the life he led and the death he died, through which as a miraculous window the visions of martyrdom, heroism, divine depths of sorrow, of noble labour, and the unspeakable silent expanses of Eternity disclose themselves: he, the divinest of men, shall be the alone divine? The vision of Eternity, such vision hid from the outer eye, yet real and the only reality to the eye of the soul, shall it assert itself in man's life, and even alone assert itself? The vision of Eternity shall be all; and the vision of Time, except in reference to that, shall be nothing. My enlightened friends of this present supreme age, what shall I say to you? That essentially it is even so. That he who has no vision of Eternity will never get a hold of Time. Time is so constructed; that is the *fact* of the construction of this world; and no class of mortals who have not, through Nazareth or elsewhere, come to get heartily acquainted with such fact, perpetually familiar with it in all the outs and ins of their existence, have ever found this universe habitable long. I say they had to quit it soon and march,—as I conjecture, into chaos and that land of which Bedlam is the Mount Zion. The world turned out not to be made of mere eatables and drinkables, of Newspaper puffs, gilt carriages, flunkies; no, but of something other than these! . . .

CHAPTER XVI

LAUD'S REFORMATION

EARLY in the Seventeenth century, Dr. William Laud, this small man of great activity, had formed the wish, which, as dignities accumulated on him and occasion offered, became the purpose, to introduce a Reformation into England (Reformation is what Peter Heylin names it)—into England and her affairs. England has never since I first heard of it, been without need of a reformation; every man too is called to introduce his bit of reformation into his corner of this earth while he sojourns in it: that is properly the meaning of his appearance here. Let him by all means introduce his reformation; nay he will do it, and cannot help doing it; ugly clay will grow to square-moulded hard-burnt bricks, to perpendicular, rain-tight houses, in his hands; untanned skins of cattle to mud-proof elegant boots; brutal putrescent Poperies to rugged Lutheran Evangelisms;—according to the trade and opportunities of the man, let him by all means give us what reformation is in him. It is his contribution to the general funded capital of this God's Earth, and shall be welcome to us.

This small William Laud with the great activity, is now ever since the year 1633 Archbishop of Canterbury, Primate of all England, favourite chief counsellor of his Majesty Charles the First of the name, and feels himself in a situation to undertake reforms. In a position, and surely not without a call; for he is chief Spiritual Overseer of England, responsible more than another for the eternal welfare of the souls of England. Let him ascertain well what reformation he can make, and in Heaven's name proceed to make it. The Reformation introduced by this small Archbishop Laud brought along with it such a series of remarkable transactions and catastrophes, conspicuous to England and to all lands, as could not at that time have been anticipated by him. For in truth, if we consider it now with these modern eyes of ours, it claims to rank among the most singular reformations ever introduced into human affairs by any son of Adam; whereby singular results could not fail to follow from it.

Laud as by office and duty bound, turns naturally his first attention to the spiritual state of England,—the spiritual is clearly enough the parent of the practical in every phasis of it, the spiritual given, all is given. Well, wherein is the soul of England sick? What is wrong in the spiritual state of England? Much every way. Much,—the origin and condition of which would lead us into boundless developments.— The Spiritual is wrong, the Temporal is wrong; much has gone wrong; but shall if it please Heaven be rectified.

The candid human intellect if it study intensely for five years under constant danger of locked-jaw, will still in this nineteenth century detect a busy inquisitive original faculty in William Laud, but a faculty imprisoned deep as the world's centre in such element of world-wide obsolete delusions as renders it, when never so well detected, of no use to us except for scientific purposes. A fly, once so busy, imbedded in amber, which by much manipulating becomes translucent. The fly once so busy is now quite quiet, dead totally; the amber is—one knows not what.

A busy logical faculty, operating entirely on chimerical element of obsolete delusions, a vehement shrill-voiced character, confident in its own rectitude as the narrowest character may the soonest be. A man not without affections, though bred as a College Monk, with little room to develop them; of shrill tremulous partly feminine nature, capable of spasms, of most hysterical obstinacy, as female natures are. Prone to attach itself, if not from love, at least from the need of help, a most attaching creeper-plant, something of the bramble species in it. The bramble will prick you to the bone, while the oak to your handling is sleek; the bramble by its very prickers and climbing will train itself aloft and be found at the tops of the highest trees : you shall judge thereby if it was not a strong shrub that bramble ! Dr. William Laud has pricked a man or two that handled him, and he has clung withal to this and the other rising forest tree, to Bishop Williams and King James, to the Duke of Buckingham, to King Charles ; and his black berries such as they are now cluster the forest, like the noblest fruit that is to be found there. A conspicuous bramble, judged by some to be a shrub of proud strength. O Charles Rex ! the royal Cedar that has not the art and health to eject brambles from it, but carries brambles up along with it, as if prickers were strength and black berries a noble fruit—such royal Cedar is in no good way. The first proof of a king or a man is the question, What men does he esteem ; the man I choose will be the counterpart and complement of my own self ; what I loved in myself as a possession, and doubly loved as a wish and ideal which I longed to possess, but could not : the embodiment of this will be my loved one. Kings and Cedars that carry up brambles along with them are themselves bramblish.

In this way thinks Dr. William Laud (Wil. Cant., as he is now better called [1]) may England be reformed. All England ranked up into drill order ; bowing towards the East, becking, gesticulating, with W. Cant. for fugleman : in this way the drill exercise were perfect, and we were a happy people. Infatuated W. Cant. Wilt thou make the English into a nation of Chinese Mandarins, adequate merely to bow towards the East, and pay First Fruits ? The respectable English Nation, always alive hitherto, shall now wither itself into dead dry lath and wire, a nation of lath clothes-screens, and go jerking, sprawling and gesticulating as thou fuglest ! There will then be the wonderfullest uniformity ; at the turning of thy rotatory calabash, they shall all go like the keys and stops in one vast barrel organ ; and a thing that can be called music rise to Heaven. Thou infatuated mortal, dost thou think

[1] See *ante*, p. 253 *n*.

man's soul is a Dutch toy made of four sticks to be twitched hither and thither? Darest thou, unspeakable clothes-screen, approach the Unnameable, Fountain of Splendour and of Terror, with such fugle movements? Dost thou think the living God is a buzzard Idol, whom it is safe to mimic and gesture with, and worship by beckings towards the East? Thou—a pale grey faded ghost in fact, fast vanishing from us into eternal dusk and death, forever forgotten by men, and shalt from me have no hard words.

Dr. Laud's Reformation, it must at the same time be admitted, is one of the most surprising ever presented to the mind of man. To Dr. Laud's mind it had presented itself, that is a fact, of which, incredible as it seems, History bears the unquestionablest testimony. How doubt it? Prynne's ears are off, twice slit publicly away, the second time down to the very stumps. Prynne can have no doubt of it. Dr. Leighton's large unhappy nose is slit, Mr.[1] ——— walks in the Gatehouse with a collar round his neck. Some hundred processes in Star-chamber, High Commission Court and elsewhere, and most Parishes in England set to jangling, law-suiting, and recriminating: these do bear witness that to Dr. Laud's mind it was not sport but stern earnest. To this fact we must anchor ourselves if we would fish for some shadow of meaning in the existence of Dr. W. Laud: That he had a Reformation in view and was willing to slit men's noses, slice off men's ears, and front the jangle and contradiction of all England for the sake of the same.

To Dr. Laud, much pondering the matter from his early years, it has grown clearer and clearer that the Spiritual condition of England is wrong, that hence nothing else can be right. The Spiritual condition is wrong; in other words, the Church Devotion has fallen into a most imperfect condition, and is falling ever lower. The minds of men not turned towards God their Maker? Why, at least their bodies are not turned towards the East when they partake of the elements

[1] Name omitted in the MS.

on Sunday. Certain persons called of the Church of England preach in imperfect Surplices, linen cloaks, or in no Surplice or linen cloak at all. P. P. Clerk of this Parish has in too many instances altogether neglected to iron the Surplice and lay it in lavender. Priests are not select in their tailoring as they ought to be, nor obedient to the rubric. How are the Communion elements desecrated: the bread cut with a knife not solemnly set apart, knife which perhaps in the next instant will have to cut mutton or spread butter. Good Heavens! It is horrible. And the Chancel of Churches is a place in scandalous neglect: have I not seen dogs, stray dogs, in sermon time rambling in the sacred precinct as if God Almighty were not particularly There any more than He is Here! What are we to think?

For the truth must be confessed, there is a generation of men, affecting to strive after personal communion with God, who undervalue all those things, nay, despise them. Puritans; a disobedient generation, of sour, gloomy aspect, irreverent of the tailoring of priests,—to whom the highest lustre of it, even the crown itself if on an addle-head, is little other than a miserable piece of gilt tin!——O Dr. Laud, it is impossible for posterity anchored never so stedfastly to that historical fact of thine, and fishing never so desperately for some meaning in thee, to comprehend a Dr. William of the seventeenth century even from afar. Thou art and remainest a ghost to us, my thrice reverend friend, a personage chimerical, inconceivable, and as it were impossible. No posterity never so distant, will ever again comprehend thy soul's travail in this world,—nor perhaps in any other. Thou wert a fact, alas, a most fatal tragic fact, and now thou art become an historical cobweb, and our lazy imaginations pronounce thee impossible.—Charity will perhaps demand that one be brief with thee.

By Heaven's blessing Dr. Laud will reform this. 'All 'who want canonical cloaks, commonly called priest's cloaks, 'shall provide themselves before Allhallowtide next, on pain 'of Ecclesiastical censure.'[1] All ye that labor and are heavy-laden come unto me and I will—order you to buy Canonical cloaks.

There will then be the wonderfullest uniformity! From the East to the West the united English people, ducking, becking,[2] going through their devotional drill exercise, under their respective drill-serjeants, one great General at Lambeth in the centre of them, a sight which cannot but be gratifying to Heaven.

In fact Dr. Laud's ideas of religion are peculiar. Whatsoever people ranks itself in line and goes through the specified parade-movements, has a religion; whatsoever people does not, has none.

. . . The reader of our time will perhaps gain a glimpse into W. Laud if he take this discernible fact along with him, That Laud meant by worshipping, not the turning of one man's heart towards God, or the turning of many or of all men's hearts so, but first and foremost a turning of faces towards the altar at the East, done simultaneously by many men, with a certain decorous symmetry, of the military sort. This, thought his Grace, will be the method, if method there is, of getting all hearts turned towards God, that they turn first in a symmetrical drill-serjeant way towards God's altar built into the Eastern wall. Sharp serjeantry and drilling must civilise these awkward squadrons into symmetry, simultaneity. 'Worship is a social act.' 'When two or three 'are gathered together.' In all which is there not something of truth: simultaneous worship is desirable,—if it can be had. Lay the dim embers together, they will glow into white fire. And yet, may it please your Grace, I have known worship transacted well by solitary men too. Nay, the best worship ever heard of: Elijah the Tishbite's for example,

---

[1] 'A rescript 11th August 1634; addressed by Sir N. Brent, Laud's man, to the diocese of Lincoln. Kennet, iii. 73.' T. C.'s Note.

[2] Becking (for bowing) is a word frequently used by the Puritan writers of the 17th century.

when the ravens fed him; and His who was carried of the Spirit to be tempted forty days in the wilderness,—far from all human episcopal help and drill, alone with God and His own sore struggling nigh sinking soul. Consider it, your Grace, to have the heart of a man, by what means soever, so kindled from Heaven that its earthly dross be consumed, is the meaning of all worship. The heart of one man so kindled is more venerable to me than all the St. Peter's High Masses, than all the most perfect devotional drill serjeantry of Lambeth or elsewhere. Your Grace forgets. If the heart have not some kindling in it, the great want will be fire to kindle it. The embers being not dim, but black, dead, what steads it on what grate you gather them? They are dead, black; all grates, all bellows and bellows-blowers are vain, and the proffer of them in such circumstances a sorrowful mockery to me. In fine will your Grace please to inform me where Jonah, when sunk in the whale's belly, found his prayer-book?

Dr. Laud was in Scotland in 1617, and again in 1633; but in Scotland he could find no religion. Their religion, he says, I could see none they had! Their churches are little better than barns or dove-cotes; in their worship no fixed order, all left to option. What religion had they? If they had a religion where or what was it?—Really, your Grace, it might be hard to say. But could not you perhaps give them one, the unfortunates? The Dr. has his own thoughts that way; time will try.

How much has grown indifferent to us in all that, valueless as the dust of worn-out clothes. The laystall is the place for it, let no man reprint it again, present it to be read again, let it lie in the laystall to be mingled gradually as freshening manure upon the general soil of human things. There are dead shell-fish which have pearls in them; yes—and there are others which have no pearls, but mere hydro-carburetted gases to fatten the soil as manure. Indifferent,—unspeakably indifferent to me, is the controversy with Fisher the Jesuit, masterly as it was. What have I to do with Fisher the Jesuit? He is indifferent to me, as the temple of Upsala; his arguments as the seventy horses' heads stuck up there, gone all to nothingness now. O Fisher the Jesuit, once for all I do not believe thee; not a jot of fact has turned out for me in all that hypothesis of thine: it is not true, Fisher; begone, and let me have done with it and thee. Can I dwell forever in the old spectral night with its vampires and foolish hobgoblins, because there are shovel hats there? With a sacred joy I hail the eastern morning—anthem once again of God's eternal daylight, and request and even command all Fishers with their trumperies to get behind me.—Something eternal in Puritanism, nothing but temporary in Laud. One grows yet in part; the other has gone wholly to the laystall, nothing but an inheritance in Puseyism to pick up again, and plant it again.

CHAPTER XVII

THE COLCHESTER PROPHETS

[1638-41]

WHAT Hampden, Cromwell, and other educated men may be thinking, I know not; but what a cloud of bodeful meditation, earnest as death, is spread over England in these dark days, many symptoms teach us to know. The melancholic English character, in such a turbid twilight of things, intensely gazing on its Bible as the one sure transcript of God's purposes and ways with man, comes to very strange conclusions. For it is a melancholic character of endless seriousness, carrying gravity even into its cockfighting, and by these Reformation controversies has stirred up the lowest lees of it, made it very serious indeed.

For example, in Colchester Town in Essex County, on its green height, girt by the kind embrace of the river Colne; assiduous in a certain lane of that city, I have for some time had my eye upon a weaver, nay, upon two weavers. Richard Farnham, that is the chief one; let us in these days, while the Scotch Assembly is sitting, cast a glance into Colchester; and look, for by miracle we can still do so, we with our modern eyes, into the dingy shop and ancient earnest existence. of Richard Farnham. Methinks his establishment is somewhat dingy, redolent of suds, weaver's batter and Gallipoli oil, —for Richard, I conceive, works Colchester serges, hanks and sporls, which with their reels and reel-bobbins are scattered confusedly around. And Richard with sallow, unshaven face, unkempt hair or greasy nightcap, plies the shuttle with a multitudinous, monotonous jangle adding thread to thread. O Richard, Richard, and it is thou in very deed, no dream of any Fabulist's or Novelist's brain; but a production of the Universe's brain, a very fact, there jangling its daily yards of serge cloth in a certain lane of Colchester in the year 1638?

Many persons I find are in the habit of visiting Richard, to ask most serious questions of him, for his fame as a knower of Scriptures has spread out of his lane into the main streets, nay, into adjoining parishes. The wrestlings of Richard have been deep as those of a Luther or an Augustine; down to the depths of being has this poor soul been forced to dive and bring up tidings. This and the other worn soul, ready to perish, has he comforted, given guidance to,—for he knows the pathways, and the impassables; he has been there, he. To many has Richard Farnham been a comfort, but to none so much as to a brother weaver, John Bull, whom he often consorts with, whom in these days he has raised from darkness into the most surprising light of wisdom or delirium, —or of both in one; or quasi-light, one part of Heaven, nine parts of Bedlam. Richard Farnham and John Bull, the two individuals weaving serge two centuries ago in the Town of Colchester, will deserve a moment's notice from us.

Many persons visit Richard; question him as men do an oracle; but he answers not alike to all. Is your questioning a mere profane curiosity, Richard swiftly by a counter ques-

T

tion or two detects you; takes up his shuttle again, and dumb, with a shake of the head, recommences his weaving. On the other hand, do your answers please, and seem to indicate to Richard that you have an awakened soul capable to apprehend divine truth, the shuttle pauses; there come hints, come utterances, frequent words exciting meditation enough, compelling you to new visits and ever new. Of his ideas about the Holy Ghost, perseverance and the sin against the Holy Ghost, I say little. 'Have you not read Revela-
'tions 11th and 12th? Few read with understanding. Woe
' to the land that is sunk in idolatries, in falsities, in whore-
' doms with the Scarlet woman. Darkness rests over it.
' Destruction draws nigh to it. And yet, observe, are there
' not Two Witnesses spoken of? Have you not read Hosea?
' How the grim Hebrew soul darkened down almost to despair
' and death by the wickedness of a world following falsities
' and blasphemous fatuities of speech and act, certain of the
' wrath of the Most High, blazes by fits into supernal glare of
' brilliancy, sees shapes, prefigurements, admonitory messengers,
' pillars of fire? The darker your gloom of earnestness, the
' more supernal your illumination,—through the portals of
' Death shall issue Angels whose face is as the Sun. Few read
' with understanding.' We oftenest cannot read at all in these wretched dilettante days. Richard has read; in Richard's soul there are sorrows like that of Hosea, Isaiah, and Ezekiel, as deep as any man's; no terriblest glare in their rapt phantasy but awakens due glare and shadow in the phantasy of Richard,—a soul of man is like the souls of all other men; and everywhere in Nature deep calls unto deep. The wickedness of England, the billet-moneys, the martial laws, injustices in high places, the backslidings, unbeliefs, perversities, the rejected Gospel, the vain mummery of Altars in the East and four surplices at Allhallowtide, have sunk down on Richard; made him dark as a very Hebrew, kindling here and there with supernal glare of brightness intolerable to the Colchester eye.—O reader, thou with the utmost stretch and

CHAP. XVII.] THE COLCHESTER PROPHETS 291

dead-lift endeavour of all thy artistic faculties (bless the mark!), and imaginative faculties, and all the half-dead dilettante faculties thou hast, wilt never know what a splendour of highest Heaven mixed with the gloom of lowest Bedlam is in the soul of that poor weaver. But let us not be profane, let the divine temple of a human soul, even a poor Colchester weaver's, be still a kind of temple. Richard has no mind to write Epics, which is apt to be a low trade compared with acting them; he has no artistic faculty but that of making serges. He sits there, asking of men, whether they do not know the Two Witnesses, the Two Olive Branches, etc., whether these death-deeps of the Hebrew soul call not with something of a divine voice to all English souls.
——He that lives in this dead generation when Reform means more victual to eat with less work to do, and all soul of man is, as near perhaps as can be, sunk into a stomach of man; he that lives in this generation, and is not only with it but of it, will never know, nor in the remotest manner conceive, what passed in England in that living and heroic one. What brotherhood have we with inspired Hebrews? To catch the attitude of them for artistic purposes in Drury Lane and elsewhere. Like some brutish Roman populace holding up their thumbs when the gladiator died, and saying, 'How well 'he does it!' A miserable rabble; doomed either to new veracity of conduct or to swift destruction. Do we not sit round the blaze of old Heroisms, as apes do round a fire in the wood; chattering, 'Aha, it is warm and good!'—and have not the gift or possibility, any ape of them, to add a new stick to the fire, but sit till it has all gone out, and the very ashes are cold, and they chatter to themselves, 'Hoohoo, how warm it *was*!'

But as for this poor Richard Farnham, I find that for long years the mystery has been deepening in him; which on repeated visits, if you are found worthy, Richard cautiously discloses, to the astonishment of all hearers. The Two Witnesses, it would clearly appear, are these two Colchester weavers, Richard Farnham and John Bull! Even they. These are the two Anointed ones,—purified in great suffering; they are also called Olive trees, and Candlesticks, in figurative language. Bull and Richard Farnham, these are the two. They prophesy on earth very wondrous things, out of their mouth proceeds fire; for a certain length of time they can turn the waters into blood; can smite the earth with what plagues they will, and have power, for one thing, to shut the heavens that it rain not for 1260 days. What will become of the agriculture in Essex? Sayest thou, O Richard! The obscure public listens with upturned eyes.

Yes, continues Richard; and it is withal a fearful preeminency, not to be courted by the natural man. For when they have finished their testimony in the world, this Bull and Farnham, the Beast that ascends out of the Bottomless Pit is to kill them outright, and they are to lie dead in Jerusalem for three days and a half: and the nations will not suffer their dead bodies to be buried. If there is truth in Scripture, says Richard, these things I think must be so. But they are 'things of a high nature.' For after three days and a half, the spirit of life is to return to Bull and Farnham, and, to the amazement of all their enemies, they are to stand on their feet there in Jerusalem again, and Farnham is to be king on David's throne and Bull priest in Aaron's seat; and they are to reign forever.—In my experience of prophecy I have heard nothing stranger And persons of good gifts, very knowing in the Scriptures, give credit to Richard,—for there looks out of his sallow visage and glaring eyes a belief which you cannot disbelieve. Neither is he mad; he sits there composedly weaving serge at sevenpence a day, waits patiently, not in haste to encounter these glories and these terrors till the time come. O Richard, Richard,—in what ambient element of Bœotian fog and Egyptian murk and stupidity unconquerable by the gods does poor human nature walk abroad in this world!

A questionable incident however here emerges in Richard's

history; an incident at which the profane world cannot fail to cavil; by which it is like the catastrophe will be precipitated. Richard, a prophetic bachelor hitherto, is not made of brass; no, and all fires, it is said, are of kin to one another. One of Richard's chief disciples, the knowingest in the Scriptures of them all, is of the female sex,—her husband at sea; one Haddenton, gone far enough, 'to the Indies,' or I know not where. Richard, driven by strange impulses prophetic and other, is whirled in the strangest chaos, clutches with avidity at this fact, that he ought to 'marry a wife of whore-' doms,' as the prophet Hosea did?[1] Very probable. He marries Mrs. Haddenton, her husband far off in the Indies; this is the wife wanted: she, a religious professor, knowing in the Scriptures, of good life and gifts, is contented to be that same peculiar kind of wife for Richard, whom I think she probably loves and indeed worships. Greater scandal has not happened in my time. But it lies in nature. Who could refuse a celestial for a husband, even though he were a weaver of serge? As we are now approaching the Doctors Commons and the Abyss of everlasting Night, and hear in the distance Bedlam and the grinding of the Treadmill, we may as well quit Richard for the present? One little prophetic rushlight shedding a faint ray over many things. An England reading its Bible as Richard Farnham did, how can such an England be obedient to the fugle motions of a W. Laud?

Farnham and Bull have ceased to weave in Colchester, we know not by what stages, whether voluntarily sallying forth to prophesy, or compulsorily haled forth by Sheriff's officers to go to judgment; but their shuttles have ceased to vibrate, the multitudinous jangle of their serge-looms is heard no more. Compulsory Sheriff's officers, I believe, have haled them both to prison. Haddenton has returned from sea, has claimed his wife: there are charges of Bigamy, charges of Blasphemy; in brief, Farnham is in New Bridewell Prison,

[1] See Hosea i. 2.

Bull in Old Bridewell in the City of London. 'Colchester Jack' (Haddenton), claimed legally to have his wife again; legally had her restored to him after solemn trial. She is not to be hanged for Bigamy, being to appearance a good, deluded woman. She is reprieved, given back to Haddenton; —and there ensued passages between them in the New Bridewell Prison which a refined history had rather not report. For she was a wife of aberrations, appointed so to be. Nor, in brief, can the law ultimately avail to restore to Jack of Colchester his wife of aberrations; these three, Richard Farnham, the Prophet Hosea, and her own female will, all conspiring to the contrary. So Jack having set sail again for the Indies, she is Richard's once more; for it was written in Hosea, she should 'abide for him many days,'—as in the New Bridewell Prison, under the thraldom of Haddenton and the Sheriff's officers, she has now done. A scandal to religion, much to be deplored! But as I said the Prophets themselves are in prison, their prophecies and bigamies having given offence; and safe under lock and key, let them get to Jerusalem as they can.

And now in these sad winter days, they have fallen sick, as many do of a grievous sickness which is killing many, and the humane officials permit them to go out occasionally, and at the house of Mr. Custin, Rosemary Lane, I have often seen them interpreting the Scriptures to one another. With Custin and Mrs. Custin and other believers, especially a Mrs. Ticknall, a carpenter's wife in Wapping, a creditable woman skilled in spiritual things.—O reader, thou canst not laugh at this thing, thou art ready to weep at it,—under such nightmare obstructions struggles the agonised soul of man, climbing the slippery precipices, stumbling at every step, if haply he may reach the sacred mountain-tops, and bathe in the everlasting dawn.—Custin dies, the women weeping over him, bidding him keep the faith. In this dim house in Rosemary Lane January 8th, 1641-2, lies another ready to die, lie two others, the Prophets themselves. Farnham's hour is first; Bull, from an adjoining truckle-bed, calls on him to hold fast, to trample the Devil and his terrors under foot, and ford steadily the devouring death-stream with his eye on the other shore. Farnham is dead, in ten days more Bull also dies and is buried, steadfast to the last. And now there remains but Mrs. Custin, Mrs. Ticknall from Wapping, and the wife of aberrations, with a future as obscure as three good women ever had.

For they consider that the Two Prophets do indeed, as the Scriptures must be fulfilled, seem to lie dead, having been three days in the belly of the earth; but that according to other Scriptures they are not dead but living, and gone on a far voyage, far beyond Haddenton of Colchester,—gone in vessels of bulrushes to convert the Ten Tribes, wherever they may be. Beyond the gates of Æthiopia and the chambers of the morning! They are to come back from the rising of the sun, these Two Prophets, and then, mark it ye proud ones of this world, they shall tread on Princes as mortar, as the potter treads clay having perfect command of it. What then will become of King Charles, Mr. Hyde, and Sir John Culpepper? And Archbishop Pashur?[1] Pashur girt-with-trembling, and his surplice, will have a poor outlook! If there be truth in Scripture, say these three women, this is true. Did an intelligent Christian ever hear the like? I grieve to add that these are understanding women, women of fine parts for knowledge in the Scripture, of seemingly devout ways, even the wife of aberrations has the air of a pious person who has obeyed prophecies merely. But words and arguments are vain; vain even that you offer to dig into the graves of these Prophets and show their very bodies still there, not gone to the gates of Æthiopia in vessels of bulrushes; but there: ' Of course they will seem to be there,' the women answer; ' to your carnal unbelieving eyes they will be there;

---

[1] Pashur, *i.e.* Laud. 'Then said Jeremiah unto him, the Lord hath not called thy name Pashur, but Magor-missabib.' Jeremiah xx. 3. Magor-missabib = Girt-with-trembling; literally ' Fear-round-about.'

'it is the penalty of your unbelief. This wicked and adulterous 'generation seeketh a sign,—to them no sign will be given; 'to such as them how can or could any sign be given: leave 'us alone here, ye profane!' Adieu, my ancient sisters; adieu then, since it must be so: I part from you with thoughts for which the English and other modern languages have at present no word. May ye reach the sacred mountain-tops whither we too and all that tend any whither are painfully tending and climbing.—O Heavens, ye much endeavouring, much enduring, ye shall reach them to bathe a sick soiled existence, and wash it clean from all its darkness!

CHAPTER XVIII

LOOM OF TIME

(OCCUPATION OF THE ENGLISH GENTRY)

How do the English gentry employ themselves in this age? They ride abroad with hawks and hounds, speculate on the flying of their hawks, on their hounds; pay visits with high ceremony; at the very least they can fight cocks. They read a good deal, especially in divinity, Sidney's *Arcadia,* and high-stilting Romances, if not Shakspeare's glowing Histories, yet Spenser's frosty Allegory, with Davila's Civil Wars [of France],[1] Holinshed and the great historical compositions, not to speak of Acts of Parliament, Spelman, etc., up to Ployden and Fortescue *De Laudibus* [*Legum Angliæ*]. Not once to mention what is the staple article of all serious men, immensities of Sermons, Bishops' Charges, Chilling-

[1] Henri-Catherin Davila, son of Antoine Davila, a member of an extensive Spanish family. Antoine came into France in 1572, and was befriended by Henri III. and Catherine de Médicis. In acknowledgment of their kindness he called his second son Henri-Catherin Davila. Henri-Catherin was born near Padua in 1576. His great work, *The Civil Wars of France,* was first published at Venice, 1630, in 15 volumes 4°. It was translated from Italian into French, and published at Paris in 1642; and an English translation of a large part of it appeared at London in 1647. *Biographie Universelle.*

worth's *Religion of Protestants, a safe Way to Salvation.*
Especially Divinity: frightful Dutch Divinity of Vorstius,
Anti-Vorstius, the Synod of Dort, Five Points, and one
knows not what or whose; for it was matter of eternal
moment in those days. King James was heard to thank
God that the Prince could manage a dispute in Theology
with the learnedest clerk of them, so thoroughly grounded
was he. Cockfighting, gambling, duelling, loving and hating;
—the daily household epochs, three hungers and three satis-
fyings daily: that, at all times, is a resource for human
nature. Alas, at bottom, what would become of human
nature without that? Our mean wants and the necessity
of satisfying them: they are as ballast for the soul of man,—
the soul of man without these would soar and sail away very
soon into the inane. Acorns fall, oak trees are felled; men
bake fresh bricks, hew ashlar stone; and huts and manorhouses, bright in their first colours, dot the green face of the
world. The Tron Kirk of Edinburgh is getting built since
his Majesty was there, is shooting out its white steeple
higher and higher into the sky this very year.[1]

It is the enormous Tissue of Existence never yet broken,
whereof we, too, are threads; which is working itself then as
now, with low-voiced, jarring tumult, wide as our dwellingplace, the Universe, through that unimaginable and yet
indubitable, miraculous, enormous Loom of Time. The Loom
of Time,—it is no flourish of speech, strange to say, it is
a fact very imperfectly so spoken. Wide also as the Universe
is this Loom, higher than the Stars, deeper than the Abysses.
O, cultivated reader, hast thou ever contemplated in thy soul
the thing called Time, and yet sayest thou the age of Miracles
has ceased?[2]

---

[1] The building of the Tron Kirk was begun about 1637, but, for want of money, proceeded so slowly that the kirk was not ready for occupation till 1647, and was not completed till 1663. — See R. H. Stevenson's *Chronicles of Edinburgh*, p. 293.

[2] *Cf. Sartor Resartus*, Book iii. cap. viii.

CHAPTER XIX

PATIENCE AND HOPE

[1637]

THE Shipmoney has been solemnly argued, and Hampden's cause is lost.[1] By monopolies, forced loans, fiscal extortions, we are punished in our purse; by scourgings, slit noses, cutting off of ears, in our persons and consciences: what is an Englishman coming to? Would we fly to New England for shelter in the wildernesses beyond the ocean, even this is not permitted us: Saybrook is building itself in Connecticut; but the Lords Saye and Brook shall not be permitted to go thither. Eight ships lie embargoed in the Thames; the Puritan Emigrants forbidden to depart; ye shall remain here, ye Puritan insubordinates; we want your ears on our pillories here.—And the dull people endures it all; this people sunk under *mumpsimus* and *sumpsimus* in dreary enchantment seems incapable to help itself, seems ready to endure all things. Do not God's Gospel ministers lie dark in dungeons; Mr.[2] —— with a collar round his neck? God's Gospel silenced and blasphemously trodden down at altars in the East, hateful chimeras in their copes and tippets are becking and gesticulating as if the living God were a mimetic mummery and conventionality and man were an Imitation and Hearsay and had no soul in him but an ape's. And the people resist not; since they held down the Speaker, nothing emphatic has been done by them. Fiery Eliot lies dead and cold, Strode reads his Bible, rugged Pym his Bible and briefs, etc., etc. We shall grow all, I think, into a Nation of mimes and Chinese automatons; living quietly with a witness,—standing quietly as the wooden Chinese tumblers

---
[1] See *Letters and Speeches*, i. 98.
[2] Name omitted in the MS. See *ante*, p. 284.

with lead in the bottom of them do, and all beck and bow when the little red-faced Grace of Lambeth pulls the check string. No, Mr. Oliver; speak not so. This people's patience is among its noblest qualities, in respect for the constable's baton it is easy to be deficient, not easy to exceed. Patience, patience, till you can no more. Time with its births and deaths is rolling on. Help in this universe comes often one knows not whence; this universe, to the just man, is in all fibres of it, feracious of help. The just man's cause is the universe's own cause; what the universe always through all its entanglements and superficial perplexities means, has meant, and will mean: ever amid all the thousandfold eddies and back currents which bewilder eye and soul, this is the grand interior tide-stream and world-deep tendency which must and will succeed.—Look up to the highest as thou dost and study to be of good cheer. 'I to the Hills will lift mine 'eyes, from whence doth come mine aid.'

To the Hills indeed ;—and look what is this that is befalling in the remote North Country in these days? History will hasten thither.

CHAPTER XX

'JENNY GEDDES'

[1637]

PURITANISM throughout the English lands lies crushed down, driven into silence, and, it is thought, into annihilation. Parishes of respectability have their altars at the East, their Four Surplices at Allhallowtide, and hope they have embraced Dr. Laud's Reformation, and terminated Dr. Luther's. So far as officiality can go, the disobedient spirit of Puritanism is abolished.

Nevertheless there are things that cannot be annihilated, let respectable officiality do its best and worst. Whatsoever holds of the Eternal in man, addressing itself to the eternal sense of justice, conscience, implanted in us by the Maker, it is born anew with every new man into this world, and can never be suppressed. The more you press and compress attempting to suppress it, the more fiercely will it recoil against you one day, with heavy compound interest for all it has suffered. Especially if it have suffered quietly;— dread these quiet sufferers, there is a strength in them beyond what they themselves know! Dr. Laud, with his rubrics, formulas, and Four Surplices at Allhallowtide, is playing a heavier game than he wots of.

For example it is now some half century that the Scottish people have had to suffer the saddest obstructions: their beloved National Church, founded we may well say in the travail of their souls, and the true emblem to them of God's presence in this Earth, has for half a century been obstructed, and at times threatened with suffocation under the nightmare of foreign Prelacy. The naked vigour of Knox and his heroism, which prefers the humblest real coat to wearing one of cobwebs, shall now be covered up and decorated with rubrics, formalities, and Four Surplices at Allhallowtide, what the spirit of Knox feels to be unveracities, and will once for all have no trade with, betide what may. For long a baleful death-shadow has hung over the Scotch Church; true Assemblies prohibited, exploded canonicals permitted,— Episcopacy, in its rochets, tippets, and rotten rags of an extinct Popery, abhorred by Heaven and Earth, actually walking abroad in the country. O Dr. Laud, it is cruel, if thou knew it; but thou wilt never know! These men, in such poor rude way as they can, protest against deliriums and delusions; they say, Our life is true and not a lie, an eternal fact, no shadow or tradition, but a God's fact:—dare we pretend to believe manifest incredibility, to serve the living God with things sacrificed to dumb wooden Idols? We dare not, we dare not; and, as God is our witness, we will not! Doctor, there is not a holier feeling in the soul of man than this same, nor a more benign one for the world: properly it is the light of the world, found here and there in a human heart; it is the sacred element which keeps this world from becoming all one horrid charnel-house. Doctor, you had better let these feelings alone. Observe too, how quiet the people is; this half century it has generally held its peace, leaving it for most part, as Hampden says, to the Almighty. The Scottish Church is under a fatal cloud. King James's Prelates, like winged rocheted harpies, hovering to devour it; they have not devoured it, God's Gospel is still preached among us; and the faithful man can save his soul alive; let us trust in God for this cause of His. To God we may complain in prayer; against supreme royalty and sovereign powers that be, what man can rebel? No quieter people, more reverent towards the Highest King in heaven, or towards its lower kings on earth, exists anywhere.

Dr. Laud has been in Scotland twice over; he drove with unheard-of peril to himself and coach to various districts of the country, inaccessible except to zeal, looked with his own eyes on the nakedness of the land and its religion. Religion? he says, I could find no religion. Their Churches were little handsomer than barns; their worship no worship, mere unmethodic confusion, according to the notions of particular men. Any particular man rose up, prayed, without book, whatever lay in him. Drill exercise, done in a more slovenly way, I will thank any man to show me in this world. When a Right Reverend Father in God gives the word to a Nation, 'Shoulder arms,' and the Nation does not do it, but one person stands at 'attention,' another stands 'at ease,' another 'draws ramrod,' and some even 'present,' threatening to fire, —what kind of manœuvring is that! I put the question, Is that people and its devotional Drill exercise in a good way? What fatal dim owls of Minerva do perch themselves with authority in a Nation's Holiest of Holies, from time to time, and scratch and hoot there, 'Too-whit Too-whoo, No worship 'Hoo,' till—till people's patience with them is exhausted!

Dr. Laud in 1617 as king James's Chaplain, and still more when he went with Charles to his Coronation in 1633, failed not of one thing, to regulate the Chapel-royal according to the true model. Heathen Scots without any religion, if they stept down to Holyrood might have the satisfaction to see religion. Here you observe due Altars in the East, the Four Surplices just lifted out of lavender foldings, an honour to the laundress, men bowing at the name of Jesus, bowing at many things, response, re-response, and Collect of the day, men answering like clock-work to the fugle motion, so that when you say, 'Ground arms,' they make one simultaneous rattle of it, and the manœuvre is perfect. Ye unhappy Scots without religion, does it not charm you at all? The unhappy Scots look on with vinegar aspect and closed lips, on their grim countenances no sign of charming is yet legible.

And yet good example is contagious and persuades the hardest hearts. Dr. Laud thinks clearly this fifty years' expectancy should become fruition,—and real Scotch Bishops, which are as yet little better than Ghosts, should take shape and substance. King Charles, sensible, by instinct and conviction, of this truth, 'No Bishop no King,' is easily persuadable. The real Liturgy shall be introduced into all churches, the Prayer-book printed, and not without due, gradual, oft-repeated admonition impressed into all parts of Scotland on a given day. What good is it to trample down Puritanism in England, if a whole Scotch Nation is allowed to practise it?

Nay, it would appear King Charles is about endeavouring to recover the Church lands; at least taking steps that way. In the disastrous times of Knox, a hungry nobility, with the promptitude of cormorants, swallowed the Church property, as it were in one day, and poor Knox when he demanded it back to make Schools with it, build Churches with it, teach and spiritually edify and enlighten the people with it, found that it had become a devout imagination. To his sorrow, to the sorrow of many men since that. It will require a new pious thousand years to accumulate the like for spiritual uses, and as yet in these two centuries the process has not begun.

It was a step of extreme delicacy this demanding back the Church-lands, or seeming even afar off to demand them back. Possession for two generations is something in this mutable world; all men when you touch them in the purse are likely to be sensitive. These old National Church properties, had they been demanded back for a Church which was never so National, rooted in the hearts of the whole Nation, would not have come softly back; now that the better part of a century had fixed them in their new places, with their new holders, not without a violent series of wrenchings, backed by the sacred determination of the whole people, could that spoil have been regained. But to demand them back for a Church which was not National at all, which was disliked and fast growing detested by the nation, and in broad Scotland had no hearty partisan, that one can see, but Dr. Laud and our royal self? King Charles is thought to be looking this way; and surely this is not the way to facilitate the getting in of his Service-book.

Galvanic Dryasdust, generally very offensive, becomes as it were intolerable when he gets to treat of any matter that has a soul. Being himself galvanic merely, he cannot believe that there will be, is, or ever was, in man or his affairs any soul,—any vital element whatever, except the galvanic irritability, Greediness of Gain. This, according to Dryasdust, is sufficient in common cases; in uncommon cases, Protestant Reformations and such like, he superadds some *quantum suff.*[1] of delirium, calling it enthusiasm, the passions, or such like; and considers the phenomenon explained in that way. Cost what it may, he will not, and cannot, admit any soul. When a Luther rises Godlike to defy the powers of Earth and the whole created Universe in behalf of God's truth once more, the purblind Dryasdust sees in it some shopkeeper grudge of a grey monk against a black one.

[1] *Quantum sufficit*, a sufficiency, enough for the purpose.

When Protestant Reformations take place, it is chess-moves of Diplomacy, it is hungry barons greedy of Church spoil: look at Germany, look at Scotland, in the pages of Dryasdust. Nations when they flame up with fire once more as if from the centre of the world, are to Dryasdust nothing but heaps of flagrant madness, meaning at bottom, so far as there is any meaning left, to fill their pockets or stomachs. In all which, O reader, if thou reflect on it, is there not something infinitely fatal not to say nefarious, and if it were not pitiable, detestable? Blasphemy is the name it ought to go by. You can't sue Dryasdust in any court of law; yet who is there that has injured you as he? Elymas, the base sorcerer, who perverted men's hearts and minds from God's Gospel, God's splendour struck him blind: was it not a merited punishment? Dryasdust was punishable in those days. But indeed the Apes by the Dead Sea, they still chatter without any soul, having disbelieved in souls,—that is a punishment which in no time can be abrogated. Thank God for it, and mark it, and shudder at it. My readers and I will not believe that German Reformations, Scottish Reformations, Scottish Presbyterianisms, French Revolutions, ever did or can proceed from the hungry avidities or despicable penny wisdoms of Jack and Will, Dick and Tom. Such slaves are there present in all Heroisms, as ashes in all fires, but the ashes are not the fire.

Poor old Edinburgh, it lies there on its hill-face between its Castle and Holyrood, extremely dim to us at this two-centuries' distance; and yet the indisputable fact of it burns for us with a strange illuminativeness; small but unquenchable as the light of stars. Indisputably enough, old Edinburgh is there; poor old Scotland wholly, my old respected Mother! Smoke cloud hangs over old Edinburgh,—for, ever since Æneas Sylvius's[1] time and earlier, the people have had the art, very strange to Æneas, of burning a certain sort

---

[1] Æneas Sylvius was born in 1405; sent on a mission to Scotland, etc., in 1432; and became Pope Pius II. in 1458.

of black stones, and Edinburgh with its chimneys is called 'Auld Reekie' by the country people. Smoke-cloud very visible to the imagination: who knows what they are doing under it! Dryasdust with his thousand Tomes is dumb as the Bass Rock, nay, dumber, his Tomes are as the cackle of the thousand flocks of geese that inhabit there, and with deafening noise tell us nothing. The mirror of the Firth with its Inchkeiths, Inchcolms and silent isles, gleams beautiful on us; old Edinburgh rises yonder climbing aloft to its Castle precipice; from the rocks of Pettycur where the Third Alexander broke his neck, from all the Fife heights, from far and wide on every hand, you can see the sky windows of it glitter in the sun, a city set on a hill. But what are they doing there; what are they thinking, saying, meaning there? O Dryasdust!—The gallows stands on the Borough Muir; visible, one sign of civilisation; and men do plough and reap, and weave cloth and felt bonnets, otherwise they could not live. There are about a million of them, as I guess, actually living in this land; notable in several respects to mankind.

They have a broad Norse speech these people; full of picturesqueness, humour, emphasis, sly, deep meaning. A broad rugged Norse character, equal to other audacities than pirating and sea-kingship; and for the last 1000 years, in spite of Dryasdust's goose-babble, have not been idle. They have tamed the wild bisons into peaceable herds of black-cattle; the wolves are all dead long since; the shaggy forests felled; fields, now green, now red, lie beautiful in the sunshine; huts and stone-and-mortar houses spot for ages this once desert land. Gentle and simple are there, hunters with Lincoln coats and hawk on fist, and flat-soled hodden-grey ploughmen and herdsmen. They have made kings this people, and clothed them long since in bright-dyed silk or velvet with pearls and plumages, with gold and constitutional privileges and adornments. Kings? Nay, they have made Priests of various kinds, and know how to reverence them, and actually worship with them. For they are of deep heart; equal to still deeper than Norse Mythologies, and the gilt Temple of Upsala has for a thousand years lain quite behind them and beneath them. The Nation that can produce a Knox and listen to him is worth something! They have made actual Priests, and will even get Highpriests,—though after long circuits I think, and in quite other guise than the Laud simulacra who are not worth naming here. This is the people of Scotland, and Edinburgh is the capital of it; whom this little red-faced man with the querulous voice, small chin and horse-shoe mouth, with the black triangle and white tippets on him, has come to favour with a religion. He, in his black triangle and Four Surplices at Allhallowtide, will do it,—if so please Heaven.

Who knows, or will ever know, what the Edinburgh population were saying while the printing of Laud's Service Book went on? For long it threatened; the Scotch simulacra (of Bishops) were themselves very shy of it, but the little red-faced man whose motto is 'thorough,' drove it on. And so, after various postponements, now on Sunday the 23rd day of July, 1637, the feat is to be done; Edinburgh after generations of abeyance shall again see a day of religion.

'The times are noisy,' says Goethe, 'and again the times 'sink dumb!' How dumb is all this Edinburgh, are the million and odd articulate-speaking voices and hearts of Scotland of that year 1637! Their speech and speculation has all condensed itself, as is usual, has sunk undistinguished into the great Bog of Lindsey. He were a Shakspeare and more that could give us, in due miniature, any emblem of the speech and thought of Scotland during that year. No Shakspeare was there; only Dryasdust was there; and it is now grown silent enough. The boding of fifty years is now to realise itself, the thing, that we greatly feared has come upon us. The heart of this Scotland pauses aghast. A land purged of Idolatry shall again become Idolatrous?—Really, O modern reader, it is worth taking thought of. Idolatry, which means use of symbols that are no longer symbolic, is it not, in the Church and out of the Church, verily the heaviest human calamity? In the Church, and out of the Church, for all human life is either a worship or it is a chimera, Idolatry may be defined as the topstone of human miseries and degradations; it is the public apotheosis and solemn sanctioning of human unveracity, whereby all misery and degradation physical and spiritual, temporal and eternal, first becomes rightly possible; the deliverance from it rightly impossible. Admit honestly that you are naked, there is some chance that by industry and energy you may acquire a coat; clothe yourself in cobwebs, and say with your teeth rattling, How comfortable am I, there is no chance of ever being clothed, there is no wish for or belief in the possibility of ever being better clothed. Men say with the drop at their nose, and teeth playing castanets (as you may hear them anywhere in these sad days), How comfortable are we!

With Jenny Geddes it has fared as with Pompey and others: there remains the shadow of her name. As Hercules represents whole generations of Heraclides and their work; as Marat in our compressive imagination did all the Reign of Terror;[1] so Jenny is the rascal multitude, by whom this transaction in the High Church was done. Her name is not mentioned for twenty-five or thirty years afterwards in any book; nevertheless it remains lively to this day in the mouth of Scottish tradition, and a Poet Burns in such mocking apotheosis as is permitted us in these poor days, calls his mare Jenny Geddes. Good Jenny, I delight to fancy her as a pious humble woman, to whom, as in that greatest Gospel is the rule, the Highest had come down. In her kerchief or simple snood, in her checkered plaid and poor stuff-gown she is infinitely respectable to me; reads that Bible which she has in her hand, a poor bound Bible with brass clasps, and

[1] See Carlyle's *French Revolution*, iii. 256.

sits upon a folding stool. It is the belief of Jenny that God's grace is in store for her, or God's eternal judgment, according as she behave well or behave ill: respectable Jenny!

Dim through the pages of Dryasdust we notice conclaves of Scottish Puritans, dignitaries, nobles, honourable women, taking earnest counsel on the matter; meeting for conference in Edinburgh and elsewhere. The old Duchess of Hamilton, says Dryasdust, rode about with a pair of pistols in her saddle. Like enough; with pistols in her saddle, and a variety of thoughts in her mind. Dim, owlish Dryasdust, as is his way in such cases, imputes the whole phenomenon to those conclaves: it was all a wooden puppet-play, constructed and contrived by these higher personages, the wires all fitted on, the figures all whittled and dressed, the program all schemed out;—and then some Duchess of Hamilton pulled the master-wire, and a dramatic representation was given. Disastrous Dryasdust, is human life dead, then? Art thou entirely an owl and tenebrific ray of darkness, then?—Enough, the 23rd morning of July, 1637 has risen over Edinburgh city; a silent Sabbath morning, not to be a silent day and evening; the dissatisfaction of long years will perhaps give itself voice today. But the Bailies and Officialities are getting towards St. Giles's Church,[1] and many mortals with speculation in their eyes; right reverend Sydserf[2] is there, and Dean Hanna, etc., all in due rochets and pontificals; the miscellaneous audience sits waiting, nothing heard but here and there the creaking of some belated foot, slight coughing of some weak throat, and generally in all pauses, an irregular chorus of sighs. Dismal enough. They are going to worship here it would seem?

See, the Dean enters, a man irrecognisable to us at the distance of 200 years, recognisable only as an aggregate of

[1] Edinburgh had been lately made a separate diocese, and St. Giles's its Cathedral Church,—Lindsay being now the Bishop, and Hanna the Dean.
[2] Sydserf, Bishop of Galloway, since 1635.

tippets and rochet, with a Laud's Prayer Book in its hand. At sight of Dean Hanna in this guise, imagination hears a strange rustle in the St. Giles's audience; sees Jenny Geddes's lips compress themselves, her nose become more aquiline; and the general rustle as our Dean mounts the reading-desk sink into silence as of death. One can fancy the Dean's heart palpitating somewhat. Opening the Prayer Book he breaks the silence.—Hm—hm—hum! ever louder hums the audience, each taking courage and example from the other, the hum mounting in rapid geometric progression, till it breaks out into interjections, castings-in, as we call them, of a most emphatic sort. Some do make responses; inserted probably by Sydserf or Lindsay, as 'clackers' are in the first night of a play. Hired 'clackers' if so be they may save the play from being damned. Hired clackers,—or any not uncharitable soul to reinforce a poor Clerk in these circumstances? Service cannot be heard; the Dean growing redder and redder in the face, reads on; inaudible for hums, for growls, for open obstreperous anger of all men. Jenny Geddes (it appears from Dryasdust) has risen to her feet, many persons have risen. A hired clacker, close at Jenny's back endeavouring to make the response, her righteous soul able to stand it no longer, she flames into sheer wrath and articulation with tongue and palm; and exclaimed, says Dryasdust, smiting the young man heartily on alternate temples, 'Thou foul thief, wilt thou sing a Mass 'at my lug?' What a shrill sharp arrow of the soul! We have had long battles with the Mass; black nightmares of the Devil like to choke us into Death eternal; and they are gone and going, and we are awake to God's eternal sunlight, and the Devil's nightmare is to return? All women, all men and children feel with Jenny. The tumult rises tenfold. 'Out, 'away, off, off!'—So that Lindsay in regular pontificals is obliged himself to mount into the Pulpit. Poseidon in the tempest raises his serene head, to calm all billows. 'Let us 'read the Collect of the day.' 'Collect? Collect?' cry many. 'Let us read'—reiterates he. 'Deil colick the wame o' thee!'

cries Jenny, all clear flaming, regardless of the Devil and his angels; and hurls her stool at the Bishop's head. The Bishop ducking adroitly avoids the missile. But now, as when a light-spark falls on fire-damp, it is all one flame, this smoking element of madness and sheer riot; and stools, walking-sticks, whatsoever missile and vociferation can be snatched, fly converging towards one point,—which no Bishop, unless he be a cast-metal one from Birmingham, can pretend to stand. Official Bailies with their beefeaters rush down distracted, conjure with outspread hands, menace, push, they and their beefeaters, who I hope have Lochaber axes, or at least good truncheons,—gradually with confused effort drive out the rascal multitude, leaving only the hired clackers or charitable men bent to reinforce a weak clerical. The rascal multitude patter on the windows, vociferate, shriek and howl: the Collect of the day cannot too soon terminate; I wish even we had the Bishop well home.

Imaginative readers can conceive the rest. How the riot spread over Edinburgh, over broad Scotland at large; the element, getting ready for years, being all so inflammable; no man, or hardly any man except Lindsay and his clackers, having any real desire to suppress it. How pious lairds and lords and clergy, many a pious Scottish man, flocked in from all sides to Edinburgh, if only to hear the news,—and did hear several things, and did see this one thing. What a multitude they are, what a temper they are of!

Jenny is a Deborah in Israel.—

CHAPTER XXI

DISCOVERY OF THE THURLOE PAPERS—TRADITION

THE learned Mr. Thomlinson of No. 13 Lincoln's Inn had gone to the country for the Long Vacation, and given up his rooms to a certain Clergyman of uncertain pursuits, name not known, pursuits not known, whose time it would seem hung heavy on his hands. This Clergyman, then, having no resource in looking out of the window or the like, took to poking about the carpentry and by-nooks of his apartment, tapping on wainscots, garret ceilings and such like, reflecting in an idle manner on the unknown series of wigs and gowns and learned human creatures that had tenanted this temporary domicile of his. Nothing can be figured more miserable; yet it proved not altogether so. Tapping miserably on wainscots, garret ceilings, this melancholy young Clergyman came upon a secret ceiling of his garret, came upon a hidden box or package stuffed aside there, with an immensity of papers in it. One thing was clear, they were letters of the seventeenth century; and at last another thing became clear, that Chancellor Somers, the patriotic collector, would give a consideration for them. With Chancellor Somers, very busy otherwise, they turned to little account; nor with others into whose hands they fell. By and by Mr. Birch, however, subsequently of the British Museum, putting on his historic spectacles, easily discovered that here was a correspondence of the seventeenth century, abounding in the highest historic names, and turning up his Dryasdust repositories, easily remembered that a certain John Thurloe, Government Secretary, in his latter days resided here;—discovered therefore that this was Thurloe's secret hoard of official correspondence; which, unwilling to lose it, yet in evil times afraid to keep it, the good man had buried there in that box in the wall, and now after about a hundred years, it had unexpectedly come to light. Mr. Birch with enlivened hope, with alacrity, with persevering industry, proceeded to copy, decipher, arrange and commit to the press, that mass of dead letters; and so in seven folio volumes we have to this day a Thurloe Correspondence which he that runs, and is not afraid of locked-jaw, may to all lengths read.

Life being short and Art long, few or rather none, have ever read this Book, but all of us pry into it on occasion. Historic Art gratefully skims through it on a voyage of discovery, hangs with outspread pinions for moments in the strange twilight, in the strange silence, of that wide-spread City of the Dead, descrying what it can,—little of moment for most part. For in truth the region is most awful, of a leaden quality, a leaden colour, guarded by basilisks, inhabitated by ghosts; and the living visitor is in haste to return. We, at the very door of it, have snatched the following morsel:

[Here follow directions to copy Oliver Cromwell's Letter of the 13th October, 1638, to his beloved Cousin, Mrs. St. John. It stands in the *Letters and Speeches*, as Cromwell's Second Letter (i. 100).]

Much remains obscure, lost beyond recovery. Alas, and the very spirit of the writing, how it is lost too; and the abstract words become meaningless to us; as are the proper names. . . . The appellations and ideas, we say, are not less obliterated than the proper names and persons. Who knows what to make of dwelling in Meshec, which signifies *Prolonging*, or in Kedar, which signifies *Blackness*? How could a man supposed to be of vigorous sense write down such imbecilities, or what did he mean by them? Dryasdust is terribly at a loss; the living intellectual circles wait with blank eagerness, some word of explanation from him, and he as good as feels that he has none to give.—'Cant, Hypocrisy'; the intellectual circles have rejected these;—well then, 'Enthusiasm, Fanatic-'ism, some form of the grand element of cloudiness?' 'Yes,' with a kind of nasal interjectional 'Hm—hm,' as if still all were not right. But they are found to rest satisfied with this: The square-jawed, rugged-looking individual, with massive nose, with keen grey eyes, and wart above the right eyebrow, was partly in a distracted condition. If it should ever by chance, as there is passing need otherwise, be disclosed to the intellectual circles that they have souls to be saved, then the last hypothesis of Dryasdust will go like the rest, I think ; then woe in general to Dryasdust: his hypotheses and foul Hecate eclipses will fleet away with ignominious drumming in the rear of them; the very street urchins approvingly looking on; and a most poisonous eclipse be lifted from the whole Past, the whole Present and Future time! O Dryasdust! Expediency, Windbag and Co. will march, the gates of native Chaos yawning for them, and the public thoroughfares will be clearer for a while. Consider, O intelligent reader, if by beneficent chance thou knewest that there was in verity after Death a Judgment and Eternity, that all the Earth and its business were but the Flame Image of a great God, his throne dark with excess of light, and Hell pain or Heavenly joy were forever in few years sure for thee. Thou wouldst fly to the mountains to cover thee, to Christ, to whosoever brought a hope of salvation for thee. Thy life were then a perpetual sacred prophecy, or, through the obstructions of the terrene element, a perpetual effort to be such. Prayers, tears, never-ending efforts, the sacrifice of very life, all this were a light thing for thee. Thou too, and all thy life and business, like the Earth thy mother, wert a kind of flame-image through which, now in bursts of clear splendour, now in fuliginosity and splendour overclouded, the presence of a God did verily look. Thou too wouldst write passionately for Dr. Wells to Mr. Story at the Sign of the Dog.[1] But thinkest thou this depends on Dr. Wells or Mr. Story, on any printed Book, Hebrew or other, or on any man or body of men, Hebrew, or other? That Dr. Wells or Mr. Story can make it or unmake it? My friend, when Dr Wells and Mr. Story and all that was in the brain or memory of either of them shall have vanished like dreams never to be in any human memory more, this thing in its essentiality wil. remain true.

Here however, there are two courses that open themselves for the human species, leading to the notablest divarication, with the results of which History is full. The poor human genius is wrapt in traditions inwards to the very soul of it, and never comes out except wrapt in clothings, what it well calls habits. Did not Adam of Bremen see a gilt Temple at Upsala totally different from St. Catherine's

[1] See Letter I., *Cromwell*, i. 90.

Church; with festooned gilt chains round it, and horses' heads set high on perches, some seventy in various stages of decomposition? The modes of Divinity are properly endless among men: but they reduce themselves mainly into these two.[1]

Under the green Earth, so flowery, cheery, shone on by the sun, lie dismal deeps, dwelling-places of we know not what mis-shapen gnomes, Rushworths, Dugdales, Rymers, dark kingdoms of the vanished Dead. He that would investigate the Past must be prepared for encountering things unpleasant, things dreary, nay, ghastly. The Past is the dwelling of the Dead; the pale kingdoms of Dis and the Dii Manes. Ulysses did not descend to the Dwellings of the Departed without struggles and sacrifices; nor when there did he find the region cheerful. Achilles, Prince of Heroes, is right mournful as a Shade: 'Do not extenuate Death to me, illustrious Ulysses: 'I would wish, as a field-labourer to drudge for another man, 'though a mean one, to whom there were small substance, 'rather than be king of all the vanished Dead.'[2] How faithfully this old Greek notion of Achilles in Elysium represents his condition in the human memory,—his relation to the living Biographer! He is vanished, or nearly so, a thin, melancholy shade. Speak of the meanest day-drudge who is yet alive and visible to me; speak not of the Dead, for I behold them not.—It is like thou beholdest them not! The Club Anecdotes of a Jabesh Windbag, how much more interesting to us than all that the Philosopher and Poet can say or sing of an Oliver Cromwell!

TRADITION

Tradition, too, is to be commended; in Tradition, too, is something of divine. Tradition is the beatified bodily form of all that once was; of what our Fathers from immemorial time have tried and found worthy. It begins beyond record

---

[1] *i.e.* Paganism and Christianity.   [2] *Odyssey*, xi. 487-91.

or memory; it too, so to speak, begins in Eternity. To the first men, they that with fresh virgin eyes looked forth into a Universe on which as yet no thought or sight had tried itself, all was new and nameless, was wonderful, unnameable, was godlike or God; the first stratum of Tradition is the life of these First Men; Tradition begins with the beginning of Time, it abuts on Eternity, is as a thing shed forth by the Eternal. Thou shalt worship Tradition too; thou dost well to recognise a divineness in the Past. If Human History is the grand universal Bible, whereof almost all other Bibles are but synoptical tables, illustrative picture-books, then I reckon that what has hung suspended in the general human memory will be well worth gathering. Nay, worthy or not, it has to be gathered. We are born into a shaped world, not into a world which is yet to shape. What went before is a fact not less inexorable than what will follow. How the world is shaped and how farther it is shapable,—these are in a manner the two sole questions for a man.

Tradition is as the life-element, the circumambient air. We unconsciously live by it; the rabidest Radical is penetrated by Tradition to the innermost fibre of him, at all moments of his existence, even when he is loudest in denouncing and gainsaying it. His denunciation of Tradition is itself in how many ways traditionary! He demands Electoral Suffrage, Free Parliaments, Ballot-box, etc.; him too the wisdom of his ancestors taught that. Tradition? Does he not speak English, a kind of English? That of itself, if he reflect on it, is as the azure element that towered up boundless over Phosphoros, filling immensity for him, and fixed him down as with the weight of mountains under perpetual chains, perpetual beneficent leading-strings as we may call them withal. Imprisoning weight as of mountains reaching to the zenith, says one;—beneficent roofing, household accommodation and security, says another.

Poor Zacharias Werner, in a rhapsody not intrinsically of much meaning, gives this account of the emblematic individual, Phosphoros, the Light-bringer, meaning evidently by him the soul of man, or perhaps, as some now speak, the soul of mankind:

> 'And when the Lord saw Phosphoros his pride,
>   Being wroth thereat, he cast him forth,
> And shut him in a prison callèd LIFE;
> And gave him for a garment earth and water,
>   And bound him straitly in four Azure Chains,
> And pour'd for him the bitter cup of Fire.' [1]

. . . .

This rhapsodic imagery has truly a resemblance to the fate of Man under Tradition.

The air in small portions is transparent, of no colour or noticeability; but take it in totality as an atmosphere, it is azure, beautiful, almost divine-looking, and encircles us everywhere with a Dome which we well name Heaven. Infinitude does so in all senses, in all cases. Tradition is properly the Totality of the memorable acts and thoughts of all mankind. We are alive because we have an atmosphere round us; we are socially alive (we are in so many senses spiritually alive) because we have, and have long had, brothers round us, and the memory of *their* relations to the Universe. This, too, is an atmosphere; builds an azure heavenly world round our terrestrial one.

The laws of spiritual as of physical optics act here too! Masses of the Past get compressed by distance, compressed and transfigured to sapphire colour; and one highest peak becomes the name of a wide district. From the Greek Homeric Songs, to Longobard Paul Deacon, there rhymes itself a kind of order out of past human things; and arid History becomes a rhythmic Mythus. Hercules prints his name on long centuries of Herculean work and enterprise. Past events are deified. Does not every people, looking at its language, consider that the first Grammarian was God,

---

[1] For the remainder of this, the Legend of the Old Man of Carmel, see Carlyle's Essay on Werner, *Miscellanies*, i. 128 *et seqq.*

the Maker? The Lawgivers of most nations, including our own, if we go out of Westminster Hall into Westminster Abbey, are esteemed still very clearly to be gods.

CHAPTER XXII

HAMPDEN AND LAUD—REALITIES AND PHANTASMS

How many voiceless men ride busily with hawk and hounds, sit studious, sit bibulous, refectory and requiescent within doors, fare busily on highways and fieldworks, on their several errands, smite upon the anvil and malleable hot iron in their rustic smithies, ride fruitlessly abroad with idle hawk upon their fist, and hounds and valets following them, at this same hour. All voiceless now, at that hour all loud and celebrated. Oblivion come to the aid of memory! How can we remember you all? In this city where I write in my garden, are some 1,800,000 human souls, to every soul of whom do not the heavens vault themselves into an arch with its crown right over *his* head, as if *he* were the most important man, to produce whom all things had hitherto been tending? There is no remembering of you all! I will beg some 999,999,999 of you to let your selves be forgotten peaceably that the unit may find room for himself. Alas, in the human memory as on the stage of Life, one set is ever crushing out another, and Godlike silence and evanition into serene azure is sooner or later the lot of all men and all gods.

Black walls of oblivion, like dark cloud coulisses must bound our small illuminated theatre. Wherefore History, though with reluctance, will be silent.

Amid the valleys where the Ouse languidly like an aristocratic river, collects its brooks, folded up among the green valleys, sheltered by the Buckingham beeches, is the Hampden Manorhouse and Church, the mansion of John Hampden; is John Hampden himself, a man of grave but cheerful affable ways, as I judge by the look of him, not without Teutonic fire in his heart, but deep hidden, whom it were delightful to look in upon, did time permit! Authentically, sure as I am now here, he is then there, riding abroad to look up his tenants, to visit some neighbour, or the green earth and azure beeches at least; sitting at home reading Davila on the Civil Wars,[1] reading Chillingworth and Dutch Divinity,—looking earnestly into an ocean that his eyesight cannot bound, which is indeed bottomless, deep, which the sharpest human eyesight only seems to itself to reach the bottom of. In the bottomless ocean there does ever appear to be a bottom; where the light fails and the eye can reach no farther, there the eye rests contented as on the primeval basis, there is the bottom so-reckoned · it is the law of optics for men here below. Mr. Hampden's eye reaches down farther than most, discerns as the deepest primeval fact, that in the heart of this world a God dwells verily, that man, poor imprisoned creature does of a felt truth reach up to Heaven and down to Hell, that the question how he demeans himself in this poor life, is actually of infinite moment to him. There, intrinsically, is the bottom for John Hampden,—as it is indeed for me, and for the clear-sighted reader. Hast thou heard of any deeper depth yet reached by telescope or otherwise? I have heard of extremely shallow depths trumpeted abroad, as the wonderful wonder and real bottom found at last, in these enlightened days: how there dwelt no God but a mere steam-engine and clock-mechanism in the heart of this world, and man's real duty was but to find due Jamaica treacle for himself, a finite duty, not infinite, with other most mournful matter, which, for the credit of the house, I will not enlarge upon. Such extremely shallow depths have I been vociferously invited to contemplate in these days,—but a deeper than this of Hampden's no man ever saw,—nor will see, I imagine. Two things strike me

---

[1] 'Hampden was,' says Sir Philip Warwick, 'very well read in History; and I remember the first time I ever saw that of Davila of the Civil Wars of France, it was lent me under the title of " Mr. Hampden's *Vade Mecum*."'

dumb, even as they did Herr Kant of Königsberg, as they did John Hampden of that Ilk, as they have done all men that had an open eye and soul, since soul and eye did first open on this world: Two things strike me dumb, the Starry Firmament, and the Law of Duty in man. Infinities both. Do they set thee talking?

But now suppose an earnest Mr. Hampden searching with his whole soul into those beautiful and divine depths had heard it confidently affirmed by all credible persons, and never dreamt of doubting it, That God the Eternal Lawgiver did once break the silence of Eternities, and speak; that here in this Hebrew and Greek Book was his authentic voice, here and not elsewhere at all? That as you learned His law here and did it, or neglected to learn and do it, Eternity of Blessedness, or endless Night of Misery, awaits you for evermore. That all this were a truth, true as sunrise and sunset, terrible as Death and Judgment. Certainly it were a fact of some importance, this, to Mr. Hampden. Certainly the impatience of Mr. Hampden with Vatican Popes, and Lambeth Pontiffs, and Phantasms with Four Surplices at Allhallowtide, were considerable. Ye audacious Phantasms in Four Surplices at Allhallowtide, what is all this? How dare you parade yourselves in such Guy Faux mummeries before the Eternal God! and address Him in set words that mean almost nothing for you! Are you sure of your way here? Has God commanded saying, This is pleasing to me; or was it only Dr. Laud that commanded?—Mr. Hampden, we had better not articulate ourselves farther on these subjects; but study to possess our souls in patience, or at any rate in silence. Mr. Hampden, the noble speaker, has a talent of silence too. Like his people, Mr. Hampden is of silent nature; prepared in so imperfect a world to put up with many things. Much is uncertain. Much is wrong; but all will be manifest; all will be perfect, and no grievance more forever, very soon.

And the Phantasms on their side have not the slightest misgiving about it. They answer: Good Mr. Hampden, we are not entirely Phantasms; we are partly human too after a sort! It was in this way that the earliest Fathers from beyond human memory taught us, and in the Book itself is said, Do all things decently and in order; this is the order, we fancy; this is what the earliest Fathers, etc. We rest on Tradition, ring after ring round our horizon, the outer ring of which lies seemingly in contact with God himself and Eternity,—seemingly as the vapours over Paddington heights and the hills of Norwood lie in contact with the stars and are part and parcel of the firmament. Infinite star-firmament, law of human duty, direct voice of God, opened human soul: we know nothing of all that; our own souls, it appears, must be shut to us, suspect to us,—though we received a University education. We never saw any opened human soul, heard within us or without us any direct voice of God,—heard only the direct voices of the spectral Archbishops, saw with such eyes as we had the eternal firmament rest firmly on Paddington and the heights of Norwood and Dulwich! And so they provide their Four Surplices at Allhallowtide with ruffled temper, chaunt ancient metre, and go on nothing doubting.

Good Heavens, when I look at these two classes of men, the Phantasms partly human after a sort, with their temper getting ruffled, and the Realities with their patience getting exhausted,—I could fancy collisions coming to pass between them. And what a business will it be, getting at the considerable heart of truth which consciously and unconsciously does lie in both, and having it presented in pure form. Due reverence for venerable human forms, due reverence for awful divine realities which transcend all forms: it will be centuries before we see these two made rightly one, and a wide glorious blessed life for us, instead of a narrow contentious and cursed one.

CHAPTER XXIII

WENTWORTH (STRAFFORD)

As a lake of discontent it[1] spreads and stagnates these eleven years over England, swamping all England more and more into a sour marsh of universal discontent, without hope, without aim. England is slow to revolt; that is the reason why England has been successful in revolting. This man[2] has no notion to revolt, what hope is there for a man? The King is strong, the King is given over to his Lauds, his haughty fierce Wentworths, his swoln Attorney Noys, their belly full of parchment, where for press of Law no Justice can find audience. One must be patient, one must be silent. God's true messengers shall be cast into dungeons, set on pillories, with branded cheeks and ignominious slashes, their true voice smothered by the hangman. We must fly far, to America, New England, crouch low and be silent; waiting God's good time. In the end, ah yes, full surely yes, in the end God's will shall be done, not Dr. Laud's.—And now if out of so much smoke there did arise fire, what a blaze, sudden as continents of dry heath, fierce as anthracite furnaces, would it probably be!—It is the crowning moment of a man's life when he does take up arms, in the name of God, against an evil destiny, resolved to better it or die. Crowning moment of a man's life and also of a Nation's. The nation that never yet did so is still in the pupil state, and wants for present and coming times the noblest consciousness of a nation.

Sir Thomas Wentworth of Wentworth Woodhouse, Yorkshire, Baron Wentworth, my Lord of Strafford that is to be,[3] was busy in the north of England at Council of the North, is busy still in Ireland, Tyranny's strong right-hand man. But the uninitiated reader, though the Strafford Papers have been

---

[1] The policy of Laud and Charles.   [2] Hampden.
[3] See *post*, p. 323 *n*.

printed these many years, will inquire vainly about that. They are enchanted Papers, those Strafford ones, shed a torpid influence, benumb into languor, into tetanus or sleep, all motion in the souls of men. O Radcliff, Heylin, Hacket, Rushworth, Nalson, Burton, Whitelock, Heath, and Vickers, why does posterity execrate you? Were ye not faithful in your day; and drove jocundly your waggon-loads of contemporary printed babble, jocundly shot it there, not calculating that it would be rubbish? Posterity did nothing for antiquity: posterity must take contentedly what antiquity was pleased to bequeath it: casket of gold grains precious in all markets, mountain heaps of gravel and indurated mud in size like the ruins of Babylon; no Pactolus[1] rolls metal alone, but metal and gravel mixed.

Wentworth, Strafford that is to be, a man of biliary, choleric temper, of fierce pride and energy, is busy in Ireland and England, and has long been. I knew him once as a Reformer; in those days when we were about to hold our Speaker down, he was among us, resolute as the rest; but when we actually held our Speaker down, when we had obtained our Petition of Right, he was not with us any more. He had gone away from us, gone over to the Four Surplices, to Whitehall and the gilt Formulas. Canst thou not conceive an honourable soul seduced? I have known such, more than one. The elevated soul seeks advancement, seeks to see itself an elevated soul;[2] the smile of kings, like radiance out of Heaven, says to them, 'Saul, Saul, why perse-'cutest thou me?' Sir John Savile,[3] long a pestilent eye-sore to thee, lo! my glance shall dissolve him from thy path; in no County meeting shall any Savile, or man of them, outshine

---

[1] A river of Lydia, famed for its golden sands.

[2] 'It is a chaste ambition if rightly placed, said Strafford at his Trial, to have as much power as may be, that there may be power to do the more good in the place where a man lives.' Rushworth, *Trial of Strafford*, 146.

[3] The office of Custos Rotulorum, in Yorkshire, was through Buckingham's influence taken from Wentworth and given to Sir John Savile in 1628; the writ for Wentworth's removal being handed to him as he sat in open Court presiding as Sheriff.

thee any more. It shall be so, it is so. Am not I good to thee; why persecutest thou me? Gratitude, sunburst of unexpected limitless hope and heavenly radiance, will have effect on the heart of man. Sir Thomas sees a new shorter course open to him; much that looked ugly under the winter twilight and shadow of intolerable old Savile, is grown beautiful when illuminated by such light from the king's throne. O my high struggling soul, see, by this way too, thou shalt get on high, be recognised by thyself and others for a high soul. Privilege of Parliament, Petition of Right, much that was ugly under the shadow of old Savile and cold obstruction, is now grown far less ugly under the summer sunlight. Privilege of Parliament, much may be rationally doubtful to the mind of man; but this that thou art President of the North,[1] and hast dissolved old Savile and all Yorkshire gainsayers from thy path, this is not doubtful, this is certain, a most blessed indisputable fact. Sir Thomas sees a new shorter course not doubtful but indisputable opening to him; sees gradually a new heaven and earth; all old things are passed away, behold all things are become new, even a shrill hysterical chimera in Four Surplices at Allhallowtide, even he, since his spasms pull my way, and he cheers me on to the top of my bent, is not unlovely to me.

Look not in the Strafford Papers, O reader, unless thy nerves be strong, thy necessities great. They are grown enchanted Papers, as we said; dim as Ghostland, and have a torpid quality, agreeable only to the soul of Dryasdust. We see Dr. Laud and Viscount Wentworth with much of the King's Majesty's business, the interests of Supreme Justice and Dr. Laud's and Viscount Wentworth's in this world; in a highly unsatisfactory manner;—and shall observe only that Wentworth, as well as Laud, is for '*Thorough*.'

Wentworth is a man of dark countenance, a stern down-

[1] Wentworth became President of the Council of the North, Dec. 1628; he was made Earl of Strafford and Lord Lieutenant of Ireland in January, 1640. His Trial and execution took place in the spring of 1641.

looking man, full of thoughts, energies,—of tender affections gone mostly to the shape of pride and sorrow, of rage sleeping in stern composure, kept strictly under lock and key: cross him not abruptly, he is a choleric man, and from under his dark brows flashes a look not pleasant to me. Poor Wentworth, his very nerves are all shattered, he lives in perpetual pain of body, such a force of soul has he to exert. He must bear an Atlas burden of Irish and other unreasons: from a whole chaos of angry babble he has to extract the word or two of meaning, and compress the rest into silence. A withered figure, scathed and parched as by internal and external fire. Noble enough; yes, and even beautiful and tragical; at all events, terrible enough. He reverences King Charles, which is extremely miraculous, yet partially to be comprehended; King Charles, and I think, no other creature under this sky. Nay, at bottom, King Charles is but his Talismanic Figure, his conjuration Formula with which he will conjure the world; he must not break or scratch that Figure, or where were he? At bottom does not even reverence King Charles; he looks into the grim sea of fate stretching dark into the Infinite and the Eternal, and himself alone there; and reverences in strange ways only that and what holds of that. A proud, mournful, scathed and withered man, with a prouder magazine of rage lying in him.

CHAPTER XXIV

THE SCOTS AT DUNSE LAW—PACIFICATION OF BERWICK, OR THE FIRST 'BISHOPS WAR'

[1639]

In the early summer days of 1639, there was seen at Dunse Law near Tweedmouth on the left bank, a notable thing: some 30,000 Scottish men all encamped on the conical Hill or Law, with tents, trenches, with pikes, muskets, Bible and

Psalm-books, and munitions of temporal and spiritual warfare,—advanced hither to their own Border, to petition his Majesty, in a most respectful but emphatic manner. Many lie there encamped; Nobility, Gentry, Clergy, Commonalty, each Earl or Lord with his tenants and dependants round him, a Colonel he, a hardy drilled regiment they; on every tent flies this bandrol, 'For Christ's Crown and Covenant,' and at evening and morning tide, as the drum rolls, there rises the voice of prayer and of psalms. Alexander Leslie of Balgony, a little crooked Fieldmarshal in big cocked hat, presides over it all, with supreme natural discretion, and military vigilance and experience; a man equal to all emergencies, whom years, hard German service, and example of Gustavus Adolphus, Lion of the North, have taught wisdom; who has looked in the face of Wallenstein before now, and rolled him back from Stralsund ineffectual after a siege of many months with all his big guns. Little Alexander in his big cocked hat, is thought to understand these matters. His Majesty looks at the phenomenon through his spy-glass on the other side of the river from Birks near Berwick, where his royal army lies encamped. Your Majesty, we are come out to petition, at the Borders of our poor country here, if your Majesty before invading us with sword, Service-book, and actual execution, would but hear our humble loyal desires! Men loyaller to your Majesty, breathe not under God's sun. We kiss the hem of your Majesty's cloak, and fling our hair under your Majesty's feet, and indeed are inclined to be flunkies, rather than rebels, but we dare not worship the living God with Drury Lane gesticulations, Prompter's Service-book, Chinese beckings to the East. Alas, we dare not and must not; and upon the whole we will not. We are here as your sacred Majesty sees, the representatives of a whole Nation, driven to petition at last with muskets in our hands. May it please your Majesty, reverse that Prompter's Service-book, we will not have it, we will be cut in pieces sooner!

To such height has the matter come in two years. Matters long compressed rapidly expand themselves when they do burst forth. On signal of Jenny Geddes's stool, the whole Scotch Nation rose,—not in violence and musketry; very far from that; their fire we hope lay deeper in them than that. By skilfullest management, guidance, wise, gentle as the dove, walking always by the old law, or gently stretching it so that it never broke, by petitions, legal protestings, by Convocation Tables, by National Covenant, Sacrament, and General Assembly, here we are, peasant and peer of us, man, woman and child of us, a whole Nation gone forth in the name of God to protest against this thing, and have the happiness to be represented by 30,000 armed men under Fieldmarshal Leslie here.— His Majesty looking close at it sees good to accept the Petition, or seems to accept it, *Soit droit fait*, and we all go home again, each in a whole skin for the present. Not a stroke was struck in this 'Bellum Episcopale.'[1] Earl Holland, he that built the extant Holland House, and lost his own head at last, poor man; he, as Master of the Horse in this royal army, did ride across in a warlike manner, towards Kelso as if he had meant something, but the steel beginning all to glitter on the hill sides as he came near, and Scotch trooper regiments to rendezvous themselves in a deliberate manner, his Lordship saw good to call Halt and ride back again, without blood drawn. The glittering steel masses followed him; not chased him, Heavens, no!—escorted him rather, as a guard of honour, and saw him safe over Berwick Bridge again. The truth is, this English army had not the slightest disposition to embark in butchery with these poor Scots on any such quarrel. They wished them well rather, said in their hearts very many of them, God speed you, poor Scotch people; and deliver us from the heat of the weather in Palace Yard[2] and elsewhere. You are in the van, the forlorn hope, we also seem to stand amongst you, in the rear of the same host. The management of the Scots in standing firmly on their guard, yet offering on the great and on the little every conciliation to their individual brethren of England,

---

[1] The 'First Bishops' War,' so called.   [2] See *ante*, p. 273.

is considered to have been of a very superior description. This was the Pacification of Berwick, not destined to hold long.

CHAPTER XXV

PUBLIC BURNING OF THE SCOTTISH DECLARATION

[1639-40]

ON [a day in][1] August 1639 at Cheapside the hangman is again busy with braziers and kindled coal fires, escorted by halberdiers and mounted or walking constables, presided over by long-gowned Sheriffs and official persons,—doing stern execution by fire, happily on Papers only: He is conflagrating publicly in this solemn manner, a printed Paper called Scots' Declaration;[2] sending up in flames and down as black powdery ashes, so many copies as he can procure of it; how many, I have nowhere learned. There rises the flame, crackling aloft, there fall the ashes, at Cheapside; emblematic of royal indignation;—the history of which transaction looks forward and looks backward. Backward it is as follows:

The Pacification of Berwick was drawn out fully on official paper, for anything I know, on sheepskin and vellum, but there were some subsidiary corollaries and annotations, which in the great hurry and anxiety it was only found possible to carry off by word of mouth. For example, his Majesty in the written Pacification could not well depart from the phrase 'Pretended 'Assembly,' as applied to the Glasgow General Assembly of the

[1] Blank left in the MS. for the day of the month, which was probably the 11th,—the day on which the Proclamation for burning the papers was issued by the King and Council.
[2] The Papers burnt were: 'The Scottish Exposition of the Treaty of Berwick, entitled "Some Conditions of his Majesty's Treaty with his subjects in Scotland, before the English Nobility, set down here for remembrance." To which is subjoined the Scottish Army's Declaration concerning their acceptance of the King's answer.'—*S. P. Dom.*, ccccxxvii. 14; Rushworth, iii. 965.
The order for burning these Papers was made at a meeting of the Council, 4th August, 1639.

year before, which the Scots believed and asserted one and all
of them by tongue and pen, and were there to assert by pike
and gun, and every organ of soul and body, to be a most true
irrefragable Assembly;—the Acts of which his Majesty indeed,
as the basis of the whole Pacification, had consented to accept
and substantiate by a new Parliament and a new Assembly to
which there should no objection lie. Why did he not then
retract the phrase 'Pretended'? Well, perhaps it had been
better. Our haste is great, our anxiety to get the matter done.
Two hungry armies lying within wind of one another, hovering
and parading round one another: judge if this is a time to
spend hours, any hour of which may produce explosion, on
mere points of form: but his Majesty's temper, none of the
sweetest, had been sorely tried in regard to essential points;
why fret him and get into new discusssions about points seemingly more of form than substance? You know what his
Majesty meant; his Majesty with his royal lips in our hearing
gives assurance that he means it so. The Scotch Commis-
sioners, as anxious as the English to have done, accept the
word-of-mouth assurances, leaving the writing as it is, report
in their own camp, redact and publicly sign the word-of-mouth
assurances as expository of the Treaty;—and so with mutual
civilities, public dinners, speeches, prayers and great waving
of caps and friendly gesticulations, retire Northward, their
brethren of England retiring Southward, as from a business of
powder magazine and lit matches,—a business that could not
end too soon. And so the new Scotch Assembly have met,
and the new Scotch Parliament, and have done or are doing
what was consented on, and the word-of-mouth assurances
put to paper on Dunse Law in the year 1639, are put to
print in Edinburgh; these with the needful developments
are put to print, and come forth as the Scotch Declaration;
—which his Majesty, revolving in his altered soul the past and
the present phases of things, is now getting burnt by the
Hangman at Cheapside. That is his Majesty's resolution
touching those same word-of-mouth assurances, touching this

version of them: hateful they and all versions and reminiscences and accidents and qualities of them, worthy of the Hangman alone. For his Majesty has now got other game afoot than those word-of-mouth assurances, or any version of them true or untrue. He has got Strafford over from Ireland, prospect of Irish subsidies, Clergy subsidies, benevolences, and an English army: War and *væ victis* to the treasonous Scots rebels. We will summon a new Parliament for the fourth time,—an English Parliament,—we will ask them for supply against Scotch rebels: if they refuse, your Majesty is absolved before God and man, and must have recourse to other methods. Your Majesty has an Irish army to control that country,— 'that country,' or was it 'this country'? Sir Henry Vane the Elder's recollections are uncertain, nor could the world ever yet entirely decide.[1] Backward such is the history of that transaction of the Hangman at Cheapside.

Forward, it issues in what the following Chapters will show.

CHAPTER XXVI

MEETING OF OLIVER ST. JOHN AND EDWARD HYDE[2]

[1640]

THESE two Barristers happen to meet one another in Westminster Hall on 5th May, 1640. Hyde is a firm-built, eupeptic Barrister, whose usual air is florid-hopeful still; a massive man; unknown depths of impetuosity kept down under mountain rock-strata of discretion, which yearly pile themselves higher and higher and are already very high for his years. The other is a slouching, lean, long man, seems

[1] 'The Earl of Clare and others debated with Vane (the elder Vane) sharply, What "*this* kingdom" did mean; England or only perhaps Scotland? Maynard quickly silenced him: "Do you ask, my Lord, if this kingdom be this kingdom or not?"'—Baillie (cited by Carlyle, *Miscellanies*, vi. 60).

[2] Edward Hyde was created Earl of Clarendon in 1661.

of atrabiliar humour, deep-eyed, internal fire enough, but burning as in a reverberatory furnace, under thick iron covers, only gleams of it shining through in crevices, rather questionable-looking. The man is of immense legal toughness and talent; gained immortal or quasi-immortal law laurels the year before last pleading for Mr. Hampden in the Ship-money case. The two Barristers as they meet in Westminster Hall this day, seem to have changed characters: the florid, hopeful Barrister looks sad; the gloomy lean Barrister looks joyous, the dark-lantern visage of St. John shines almost like a light-lantern. 'How now?' says Barrister Hyde. 'You do not seem 'sorry that his Majesty has dissolved us all, and rashly smitten 'his good Parliament[1] in pieces today?'—'Yes, our good Par-'liament, as you call it, could never have done the business. 'We shall get a better Parliament before long. Things are in 'the wind that will bring a really good Parliament. We must. 'be worse before we can be better and well.'—For his Majesty has this day dissolved his Parliament, in a very short style he asked them for supply against Scotch rebels, that he might first chastise rebels, and then redress all manner of grievances that it had entered into the heart of man to conceive. The Parliament after due hemming and hawing, signified that it would prefer the other method,—grievances redressed first, or at least grievances and supply going *pari passu*. Are you serious, are you inflexible? asked his Majesty, in the official dialect, yet with haste, haste indorsed on all his questions. The Parliament with much hemming and hawing managed to grunt out decisively, We are serious, we are inflexible. Then disappear, hastily answered his Majesty.—

And so the Barristers, Ex-members, meet in Westminster Hall, as above said; and all Ex-members are busily packing up their goods to be gone from Town again; and Mr. Oliver Cromwell, Ex-member for Cambridge, is packing up, and intending for Ely and stock-farming in these Fen regions, and will probably take Cambridge by the way, and render some account of

[1] The Short Parliament, which met on the 13th of April 1640.

his stewardship to the Freeholders and corporation there. And his Majesty is now intent on raising supply by other ways, which in the course of that summer he does, by private subscription, by clergy benevolence, by every devisable method. Not in the successfullest way. Official men indeed subscribe. Strafford dashes down his name for 20,000*l.* at one stroke, the decisive Strafford. His Grace of Canterbury keeps his convocation sitting, passing canons, an Etcetera Oath,[1] much noised of then; granting clergy subsidies. Walter Montague and Kenelm Digby urge the Papists to come forward in a body, now or never, in his Majesty's extreme need; Scotch rebels hanging on him and refractory English Puritans hanging back from him. Down with your dust now! Alas, it comes to little. The City of London, requested to favour Majesty with the loan of 100,000*l.*, grimaces in the painfullest way, and at length answers, 'Cannot, your Majesty'! We have not the sum convenient, just at this juncture. Whereby the Commission of Array and Second *Bellum Episcopale* cannot have a fair chance, I should doubt, War and no sinews of war. For all England is as the City of London; answers in every way, 'Cannot, your Majesty';—our hearts are in no way set to this second Episcopal War; they are set totally against it, your Majesty. Why should we shoot the poor Anti-episcopal Scots for the little shrill Archbishop's sake? It were sheer suicide; shooting our own forlorn hope. We wish the Scots right well in this business. Distressed to say we have not the sum; we have not any sum or thing in the shape of help convenient just at this juncture! The apprentices of London, what we should now call the City Shopmen and such like, five hundred of them, not without firearms, roll down in tumultuous assemblage to Lambeth, grimly inquiring after Laud, his

[1] An Oath imposed by the Canons of 1640: 'I,' A. B., 'do swear that . . . I will never give my consent to alter the government of this Church by Archbishops, Bishops, Deans, and Archdeacons, etc.' 'A prodigious, bottomless and unlimited Oath,' as a writer of that period calls it. The people protested vigorously against being required to swear to an etc., hence the name of the Oath. It is printed in Rushworth, iii. 1186.

little Grace.[1] His little Grace, the red face growing piebald with fear, barricades his palace, ducks off to Whitehall, to Croydon, to various successive places, and becomes a Chief Priest eclipsed, or Archbishop girt-with-trembling.[2] The apprentices ransack his Lambeth, smash all glass in pieces, disappointed of their Archbishop, and one of them gets hanged, drawn and quartered for it,—his head and limbs blacken aloft on London Bridge for a sign.[3] Not satisfactory to the apprentice mind; unsatisfactory, though compescent for the hour.—And the straggling army marches towards the rendezvous at Selby, at York, or Newcastle, with few muskets or munitions in it, and such a temper as I have rarely seen. Vociferous against Bishops and their chimerical Mandarin fugle-work, now like to issue in cloven crowns; decided not to be officered by Popish rascals; 'you are a 'Papist; you shall not lead us, that's flat!' Poor thickheaded, heavy-handed, hobnailed men, hauled from the workshop and furrow-field, set marching on such an errand; they aggravate one another all day through the weary march: Popish ceremonies, surplices at Allhallowtide, pampered High Priests riding prosperous, and godly Mr. Burtons set in the pillory to have their ears sawed off; and we marching here in the dusty weather, in the broiling sun, and not a cup of beer rightly allowed us; for the beer is ineffectual,—and we have never seen the colour of money, for they seem to have no money

---

[1] On 11th May 1640.   [2] See *ante*, p. 295 *n*.
[3] The name of this unfortunate man was, I believe, John Archer. He was a glover by trade, and had been acting as drummer to the rioters; was captured and put to the rack that he might disclose the names of the more important instigators or ringleaders of the attack on the Archbishop's Palace. He maintained silence; and in a day or two was hanged, drawn and quartered. Archer's case is notable as being the last instance of Torture in England. More than eleven years before, when Felton was tried, the Judges had unanimously declared that Torture was altogether illegal; Charles, however, by royal prerogative since the law would not serve him, ordered the rack for poor Archer. The warrant, 'Given under our signet, at our Court at Whitehall, 21st May, 1640,' still exists in the State Paper Office. See Masson's *Life of Milton*, ii. 133-4.

and no credit! 'Steady men!' cries the marching Lieutenant. 'Steady?' answer they under breath and sometimes above breath, with huge universal growl, recovering their few available muskets, bursting out into sheer mutiny. 'Several of 'their Officers were shot by them during the march'; the reader can expand that little sentence; and this, 'They broke into 'Churches tricked out according to the Laud fashion, tore away 'the Altar-rails and other newfangled tackle,' kick them down and I daresay with curses, and reduce matters to the old footing. Puritan painful ministers had reverent salutation from them; Anti-puritan found it convenient to become rapidly absent. Such detached cloud streaks of military force are wandering from all sides of England towards Selby and the Northern parts;—likely when combined to make a formidable army indeed! They have no money, few muskets, the arms are not yet come up, men are only carting them from Hull, and conveyances are scarce owing to want of money: what thing have they? The Earl of Strafford—yes, he is a thing; but he is not all things. Where was the Earl of Strafford's wisdom when he embarked himself, life and fortune, on such an incoherent, explosive, self-divulsive flotilla as this same? I cannot esteem him wise, I esteem him rash and desperate, if he think to face Scotch Puritanism, the practical Fieldmarshal of Stralsund, solemn Covenant, and dear Sandy's[1] troops with such an apparatus as this. He will do it, he says; yes, by the help of God, and that Irish army, Papists mostly. He is sick but unwearied, hopes against hope. Had all men been Straffords; —yes, but there is only one Strafford. Flaming fire cannot kindle brick-dust, but must itself die amid the rubbish. What kind of army this was, full of mutiny, without arms, munitions or money, Lord Conway the practical general knows best; as readers may still see in his narrative; an army full of mutiny, empty of money, discipline, arms and goodwill.

[1] Sir Alexander Hamilton's.

CHAPTER XXVII

A SCOTCH ARMY ENTERS ENGLAND—THE SECOND 'BISHOPS' WAR'

[1640]

A Scotch army marching with pike and musket, sonorous with the voice of psalms and the noise of fifes and drums; 'a 'travelling Presbytery' goes with it, the regimental chaplains make a Presbytery. It has waded solemnly across the Tweed at Dunse, Montrose marching with decisive splash solitary in the van; and day sets on Norham's castled steep somewhat otherwise than it did in Marmion's journey six score years before. This Scotch army, Officers and all, in blue-bonnets, of the Kilmarnock species as I take it, with a cockade of Covenant ribbons at the ear;—men had called them in derision bluecaps; and they, with their very Colonels, Earls, Peers, Dignitaries most of them, mounting the derided head-gear, had symbolically answered, 'Yes, our caps are very evidently blue; '—have you any objection?' 'None I, for my share.' To have seen this army either in hats or caps,—to have seen the Montrose head with its stern still eyes, with its haughty closeshut lips and look of sorrow and valour, the face of one of Plutarch's heroes, as a good judge[1] called him; to have seen this face, I say, in blue-bonnet and cockade as he stept with decisive splash across the Tweed, would have given me real pleasure,—in whatever bonnet it had been;—and the reader can advise me whether mocking of it, except in a very taciturn way, is like to turn out well.

On the 28th of August, accordingly, we find the little crooked Fieldmarshal Leslie, having now fairly crossed Southward with his blue-caps, committees, leather and iron guns and

[1] Cardinal de Retz. See *ante*, p. 266.

CH. XXVII.] SCOTCH ARMY ENTERS ENGLAND 335

other apparatus, paying his way in the handsomest manner, and emitting Proclamations of the most brotherly and consolatory character, decides that he will wade the Tyne at Newburn, the first ford above Newcastle, being desirous once more 'to 'present a petition to his Majesty.' A petition backed by Twenty Thousand armed men and a practical Fieldmarshal with artillery and Committees of Estate. Alas, yes, fewer men might carry the petition, but a malignant faction round his Majesty would not permit it a hearing. His Majesty, in sight of the 20,000, will perhaps hear it. We crave leave of my Lord General here at Newburn, to pass peaceably and try. 'Three hundred of you may pass with the petition, answers Conway; 'more I cannot suffer to pass. I must stand to my 'field-works and my guns in case of more.'—'Alas!' answers the practical Fieldmarshal, who however has already over night been busy at his own great guns withal. There are nine of them, I think, rightly planted, manned, masked with bushes on the brae-side, and Sir Alexander Hamilton, whom we call dear Sandy, waiting but a signal. Who could expect other, this long while? Gloomy Rushworth[1] is on the height behind Conway's batteries, out of gun range, with ass-skin and black-lead ready; he has come North into his own country, that he might take all this in characters. Thanks, my gloomy friend; look then, and let us look.

To the eyes of Rushworth[2] there emerges first from the indistinct mass, a Scotch horseman with black plumes, prancing exploratory on the farther side of the river, Rushworth knows not distinctly why. See, there rapidly deploy themselves three hundred other horsemen, ride deliberately into the stream, deliberately advance with drawn sabres towards Conway's battery; Conway's battery fires, the horse skip deftly to the right, still to the right, and rather backwards. . . .

---

[1] 'A man,' says Carlyle, elsewhere, 'of simple aspect, yet assiduous, whose gloomy look is not that of moroseness or ferocity, but merely that of severe industry feeling conscious how severe it is,'
[2] *Collections*, ii. 1237.

[The remainder of this Paper is lost. It was probably extracted from the rest of the ms. to be used in *The Letters and Speeches of Oliver Cromwell*. In the Chapter entitled 'Two Years' (Library Edition, i. 106) there is a short account of this 'Battle of Newburn,' as it is sometimes called, and of the events which rapidly followed it. It appears that the Scottish Officer mentioned above had come down to the river merely to water his horse, suspecting no danger, the men of both armies being on good terms with each other. An English soldier, provoked by the leisurely manner of the Scot, who was gazing at the English trenches while his horse drank from the river, suddenly raised his musket and fired: the Officer dropt from his saddle, wounded. Thereupon the battle began. The crackle of musketry was soon followed by the roar of cannon. The Scottish artillery from the hillside and even from Newburn Church steeple played down upon the English trenches with such effect that their first trench was soon vacated. As soon as the tide would permit, Leslie ordered the three hundred horsemen, above mentioned, to cross the Tyne,—the Scottish cannon meanwhile directing their fire on the English second trench. This, too, was soon abandoned. The three hundred got safely over, followed by others and again by others. Before the Scotch army had all crossed the river the English, vho made only a half-hearted resistance, turned and fled. Their loss was sixty killed and 'some prisoners'; the Scotch loss was some ten or twelve killed. The Scots took possession of Newcastle next day; and gradually of all Northumberland and Durham, and remained in various towns and villages for about a year, on an allowance from England of 850*l.* a day; and were very welcome to the English Puritans. A peace was patched up at Ripon, and Charles, after vainly trying various expedients to raise funds, was forced to consent to the summoning of another English Parliament,—the Long Parliament, spoken of in the next Chapter.]

CHAPTER XXVIII

THE LONG PARLIAMENT

[1640]

On Tuesday the Third of November, 1640, there sat down a Parliament which, as begins now to be more and more apparent, was the flower of all Parliaments, what we may call the acme where they attained their maximum, became notable and in due time imitable by all Nations, as we see them in

CHAP. XXVIII.] THE LONG PARLIAMENT 337

these days; wherefrom again they are gradually dwindling down towards their minimum whatever that may be. This was called the Long Parliament, for indeed it sat some thirteen years, had strange fortunes, and took preternatural-looking spectres by the beard, was extolled to heaven and deprecated to Tophet; but it might also be called the Great Parliament, the Father of Parliaments. Had the French Constituent Assembly, the French Convention, been foremost in time, they doubtless might have vied with it or surpassed it in singularity; but they were only children of it; if we will regard them well, they sprang from it as emanations, imitations in many ways; it was the grand original: that makes the peculiarity of it. For this Long Parliament did, after being duly extolled to heaven and deprecated to Tartarus, contrive to accomplish its task in this world; the task, in a rude shape, lay done and ineffaceable; no Charles-Second's Parliaments could erase 'from the Journals,' no man, not even a god, could erase the Fact this Long Parliament had performed among the sons of men. The gods themselves cannot alter the action that is done. Its task lay rude but accomplished; went on completing, perfecting, itself, the everlasting powers of Nature co-operating with it. And so in 1688, in a milder Second Edition, it came out presentable in polite drawing-rooms, as a 'glorious revolution of '88,' to the satisfaction of all parties whatsoever; celebrated with infinite bonfires, expenditure of ale and constitutional eloquence, from end to end of English land. And remains now as a Fact, presentable, patent, soliciting observation from all mortals. So that, in 1774 an American Declaration of Rights, an American Congress we may say, as the eldest son of it, could take effect. And then, and therefrom, in 1789, a French Constituent and Revolutionary Convention,—which properly therefore is the second in descent from it—its eldest grandson. The notablest grandson it ever had; a grandson set on a hill, a flaming mount, far-blazing with intolerable radiance, at one time like to have burned up the whole civilised world. Truly the notablest of all grandsons that had been or will be. But so conspicuous, at any rate, that now all peoples and kindreds are bent on having their Parliament as the one thing needful,—and evidently will and must have it, so that the great and other grandsons of this same Long Parliament are like to be many, as many in fact as there are civilised nations in the Earth. For even kings do now everywhere begin to see that this Parliament, freedom of debate, ballot, taxing, and such like, will go the round of the world, and cannot by earthly art be hindered from working itself out to a consummation, that all mortals may see clearly what it is,—whether the one thing needful or only one of the things needful. From the English Long Parliament and its works and King-killing, all this, as the Historical genealogist can see, takes its pedigree.

For man is such an imitative creature—very observable even in the genus Simia;[1] left in the deserts, and night coming on, the poor creature gazes nigh desperately to see if there be no human vestige; the print of human feet is in every sense as a guidance to him, as hope to his heart and light to his eyes. His imitative virtue: take that away from a man, you have taken all from him. You have stript him not of his clothes and shirt only, but almost of his very skin. He has no Tradition or continuance of Past into Future; the career of human development, the history of civilisation, extends to a maximum of three score and ten years. The man cannot speak; it is thousands of ages and their dumb struggle to express themselves that have taught men to speak. If, as Richter says, one new metaphor between the two Leipzig Bookfairs be a fair average, what length of time must the building of a Greek Language have cost? Stript of imitation the poor man cannot speak, he cannot even think, except extempore. What his wild eyes can discern as they flash out from him in wonder, in want, in thousandfold eagerness, that is his thought; not a stock of thought at all, but a scantling of insight from hand to mouth! When I think what man derives from imita-

---

[1] The Monkey tribes.

tion, his whole life-furniture, what he believes, knows, possesses, his dwelling-houses, his bookprintings, his very tastes, wishes and religions,—can I wonder that the Past seems worshipful, seems divine? Puseyisms, etc. and ('we will believe as our forefathers believed') cease to be wonderful to me.

Spiritual pedigrees are worth taking note of in a slight way; if much run upon they do not yield much,—and belong more properly to the province of Dryasdust and Co. To whom at present let us leave them.

Looking through the rubbish-continent and Rushworthian chaos, one discerns dimly afar off, two hundred years off, an Old London,—very curious, very dim, which one would like to see so clearly! Good Heavens, is it not certain as if we saw it face to face (having flown thither with the Time-hat[1] on our head), that they had all awoke out of sleep that morning in variety of humours, eaten breakfast, and set to their trades and tasks, such as were then going. Some five hundred thousand (?) human individuals as I learn or guess under the fog canopy. Reader, I will ask thee to do me the favour of asking thyself not in word only but in thought, whither that Day with the works, faces, persons, etc., that were in it has gone? The said Day in short where is *it*? Not nowhither, for I still see it. Thou standest mute. Thou hast no answer. Thy inability to answer is in proportion to the intellect thou hast! Grant me accordingly this other practical favour, To cease altogether talking about preternatural machinery and Epic Hero-biographies that cannot go on without visible descent of gods and such like. If all Olympus with Valhalla in the rear of it were to descend visibly some morning, and vanish again, so that one might take affidavit of it, what new wonder were there for any except children and minors? London city of 3rd November, 1640, *was* it not, and now in 1843 *is* it?

[1] 'Had we but the Time-annihilating Hat, to put on for once only, we should see ourselves in a World of Miracles, wherein all fabled or authentic Thaumaturgy, and feats of Magic, were outdone.'—*Sartor Resartus*, p. 254.

Gazing with inexpressible trembling curiosity into these old magic tombs of our Fathers, into that far vanished 3rd of November, 1640, I can see a city in considerable commotion, a character of excitation, expectation superadded to the common physiognomy of the place. The King it is true does not ride the city to-day, as the wont is, but comes almost privately by water. He rode the city three days ago with endless pomp, returning from the Scotch army and the treaty of Ripon,—a certain slender young man, of pale intelligent look not without an air of dandyism, by name John Evelyn,[1] saw him. The King does not come to ride again; but comes in gilt barge, only bargemen and a river population getting leave to look. His gilt barge and beefeaters, somewhat like his worship the present Lord Mayor's, I suppose, are a matter wonderfully indifferent to me,—by no means the thing I was in quest of.

People I do see there, whom I would give something to see clearly! That double-chinned elderly man, for instance, with the brisk smiling eyes though the face does not smile, but is heavy with long toil, imprisonment, the learned Mr. John Pym of Brymore. Or Mr. Hampden, Member for Bucks. Cheers from a stout population with doffed cap whenever he is discovered, I think I can discern for that man. A man of firm close-shut mouth, firm-set figure, and eyes beaming with intelligence and energy close-shut; the whole figure of him expressing delicacy almost female, reluctant to offend; beautifully veiling, tempering, in mildest habitudes, courtesies, principles, a fierce enough manly fire; what we call a thoroughly bred man of the English stamp: great delicacy, great firmness; and indeed as the centre of all, a very great pride, if thou wilt call it by such a name. Why should not such a man be prideful, himself equal to the highest men? A most proud but most cultivated, thoroughly well-bred man, Hampden of the Ship-money.

Antiquarianism goes for little with me: Good Heavens, do we not know that we too shall one day be antiquities? Never-

---

[1] The celebrated Virtuoso, Diarist, etc. (1620-1706).

theless, it would gratify me to understand in what manner Edward Hyde was dressed that day. And the little Lord Falkland, with his screeching voice but extreme gentility and intellectuality—in a clean shirt, he, I cannot doubt. Did Mr. Hampden ride up to Town attended by grooms?

Let the dead bury their dead. Why should any man re-enter upon the Laudian (Canterburian) controversy whether Altars should be built into the East wall, or on the long settled Divine Right of Kings? It is two hundred years ago, and much has come and gone since then. . . .

So that in these Long Parliament matters it is to be owned that the most part of the business has fairly escheated some time since to the Antiquarian Societies and Picturesque History Writers; in whose hands may it have a blessing. With the unconsumable in that business have we to do. If there be no unconsumable? But there is!

OLIVER CROMWELL—JAMES HEATH AS BIOGRAPHER.

Till Oliver's seventeenth year all records of him fail, except the sham records of Carrion Heath and others, not worthy of repeating any more. The Destinies have said, Be this man's youth and boyhood forever unknown to me. Let him emerge from the obscure, a full-grown man; with an athletic figure, to fix the world's eye, to make the world ask, Whence came these thews and sinews? but to ask without any especial response at all. Let the world try how it will respond; trace out significantly its own wisdom and folly by its manner of responding! Such being the arrangement of Destiny itself, clearly enough all æsthetic regulations, and historical wishes and regrets, have nothing to do but repress themselves and go cheerfully to work in conformity.

Smelfungus calls poor James Heath, who was son of the King's cutler and a royalist inhabitant of Grubstreet at that early epoch, generally by no other name than Carrion Heath, being to the heart indignant with him. Poor Heath, he had to write Pamphlets, compilations and saleable rhapsodic matter for a living, at frightfully exiguous rates per sheet, we are afraid; and with a world all got into amazing alterations since he quitted Oxford, and fancied he understood it all! This poor inhabitant of the Literary republic, was his fate a gentle one?—'I will ask thee,' says Smelfungus, 'what kind 'of blasphemy there is which can equal this of defacing the 'image of the Highest when such is beneficently sent among 'us, as at rare intervals it happens to go about in our Earth 'under the shape of a heroic man? Mark him who plies in the 'puddles to cover *it* with mud! He who thinks it worthy of 'such treatment, what kind of thinking apparatus, of soul as 'we say, must there be in him? It fills me with a certain 'sacred horror. Is Heroism common as road pebbles, then, in 'this country? Must industrious individuals get out of bed to 'obliterate the exuberance of it by long-continued discharges 'of mud? What can I call such a man but carrion? There 'was never any soul in him, or he would have taken to another 'trade; he would have died ten times rather than live by such 'a trade. He had no soul, I say, or his thought would not 'have been such a misthought, the summary of all conceivable 'misthoughts. He was a living carrion even while he digested 'and made a pretence to be thinking in Grub Street; he is 'become a dead carrion, and all men know him for what he is!' —O Smelfungus, my dark friend, why this severity? Heath and his like are a kind of Devil's Advocates, not without their uses in the world. Unsafe to canonise anybody without having heard the *Advocatus Diaboli* also to an end. Advocates claim a kind of privilege even to lie; much more may Devil's Advocates, Living Carrion, my dark friend.

But Smelfungus has his own notions about Carrion. This is what I find on a leaf concerning Toleration: 'Mahomet 'was quite right to say to men, Believe in Allah, or it 'shall go worse with you, ye scandalous individuals in the 'form of humanity. God is great and these appetites and 'breechespockets of yours are small. Awaken from your grease- 'element, or it will be merciful to extinguish you in it. What

CHAP. XXVIII.] THE LONG PARLIAMENT 343

'good can you ever do, what good ever experience? Darkness
'is in you. Darkness will alone come out of you. The living
'carrion that says there is no God, I will mercifully slay him,
'make him authentic carrion at least.' Heard ever mortal the
like? What hope is there of the Abolition of Capital Punishment, and any general condolence with criminal persons, if
men of genius, secretaries of Dryasdust societies speak such
things! We shall have wars again, perhaps civil wars, men
rising up in the general putrescence of social things, and saying, 'O general putrescence, behold, we are totally weary of
' thee, behold, we will not live beside thee, we are in duel with
' thee, and thou shalt die or we!' Was there nothing worse
yet heard of than death? Woe to the mortal sons of men
when in their benevolences, gluttonies, pruriencies and bottomless pocketocracies, they take to twaddling to one another
extensively in that dialect! Their day is not distant then.
An awakening is at hand, or else the eternal sleep.

The thing that thou actually lovest, choose that, even as
thou art minded; it is the voice of thy whole being that
speaks then. Paint that, sing it, celebrate it, work towards
doing it and possessing it, deaf to all else. It is rich with
blessedness for thee; every feature and figure of it emblematic
of good to thee: it is thy counterpart, that.

This man Oliver Cromwell, from Ely, more than any other
of these Members of the Long Parliament, vibrates my mind
towards him, excites all my curiosity. With what interest do I
see him ambling up at a firm journey-pace to Town for the discharge of Parliamentary duties, in rude country habiliments,
well wrapped against the cold,—with rugged weather-beaten
countenance! Did he ride alone, or came he up perhaps
with Mr. Hampden, his Cousin? At which Inn did he lie,
what manner of horse rode he? All this I would dispute with
Antiquarian Societies; but, alas, neither of us knows aught of
it. Consider the dim weather, the muddy ways, the portentous aspect of the time, long heavy darkness, uncertain
gleam of deliverance peering through it. Mr. Cromwell,

doubt it not, has cloaks, rough country wrappages of rather antiquarian style and cut, the cut of which can now be of no use to any tailor, or other; and rides with an infinitude of thoughts, spoken thoughts, or mostly unspoken. The infinite element of Thought, stern, solitary, sad and great, like the primeval sea with firmaments not yet divided, encompasses him always, bodies itself from time to time into Thoughts,—or does not so body itself, but lies silent as in obstruction as of death, which is but an obstruction of travail and of birth, equally painful, though a little profitabler! I have marked Mr. Cromwell as a choleric man; indeed his face speaks it. Look at that mouth, at those wild deep grey eyes, at that wart on the brow, at that massive nose; not beautiful, nor yet, in spite of calumnies, ugly: meseems in that peaceable flattish feature there lies a capacity, like that of Chimera's, of breathing fire! A troublous dark face, full of sorrow, full of confused energy and nobleness. I regret much that it is not of a Grecian ideal structure, the facial angle is not that of Mars or the Phidian Thunderer: what a pity not! It is the wearing work-day face of an Englishman, not the holiday exhibition of a Greek or other Jupiter. (A mixture of the lion and the mastiff, say physiognomists.) Mr. Cromwell, it must be added, is given to weeping: incredible as it may seem. I have seen that stern grim face dissolved in very tears like a girl's. For this is withal a most loving man: who knows what tremulous thrillings, wild pangs of fear and sorrow, burstings of woe and pity, dwell in such a soul! Hope is there, high as the Heaven; Fear also, deep as the Bottomless.—Let us look at Mr. Cromwell as he plods along from Ely City, out of the marsh country towards London and a Parliament which will be called Long.—O, Mr. Cromwell, did thinking being ever find himself in a more miraculous scene than this same? The sun and blue heavens overhead, the green earth underfoot, and these deep fog-continents that swim there. And this ugly mud-element of November will brighten into May and summer: it is enough to strike a man dumb. And I, how came I here? That is the miracle of miracles. Awakened out of still Eternity, I live, and for a kingdom and inheritance all this Immensity has been given me. Me I say; for though I draw not the rents or sign the lease-contracts of much or of any of it, yet according to my capabilities,—as I can look or hear, listen or understand,— from beyond the Dogstar to the Cambridge turnpike here, from the Fall of Adam, through the Four Monarchies,[1] down to the Long Parliament of Charles Stuart and present dull month of November, is it not mine, to look upon, to listen to, to understand, to sympathise with,—in a word to live in and possess, so as no mere rent-drawer can? Immensity is my Inheritance, and also the Eternity that is to come. Yes, Mr. Cromwell, that is the amazement.

To depicture the thoughts of Mr. Cromwell as he plods along on muddy highways towards London, at that epoch of scientific and literary history, with such theories of the universe and of Mr. Cromwell as a man could then have in the head and heart of him, were a wonderful task; which only a few readers, of the intensest kind, could be expected to take interest in. This man is of the sort we now call original men, men of genius or such like; the first peculiarity of which is that they in some measure converse with this universe at first-hand, and not under the employment of any scientific theory or in the nakedness of none,—these have ever, deny it as we will, a kind of divine worth for us.

Yes, had any James Boswell, riding cautiously alongside of these two, with ass-skin and black-lead, with understanding heart and ear, jotted down the dialogue of Mr. Hampden and Cousin Oliver! What fraction of the Bodleian Library, of all manner of Libraries, wouldst thou have been disposed to give in exchange for it? All Divinity Logics, Controversies of the Altar, Episcopacy, etc.? But so it is, O reader. Men have no eye for the gods; and Boswells I think are rarer than even Johnsons. In Idolatrous ages it is nothing but empty shambling clothes-screens and other Idols that they give us,

---

[1] Babylonian, Persian, Grecian, and Roman.

and it would almost seem as if there had been no gods there. The seven hundred and fifty-three still extant portraits of Charles I., what intrinsically are they worth to thee? Was it much nourishment that thy soul derived from looking never so deep into that man, or was it little or almost none? A bad world, my masters.

One fancies Mr. Cromwell riding Townwards in company with Hampden and others. A man not beautiful to look upon, grim, other than comely. O, ye Daughters of England, happily he is not bound to be beautiful; can without penalty suffer himself to continue ugly.—Ugly, and yet that is not the word. Look in those strange, deep, troubled eyes of his, with their look of never-resting, wearied thought-struggle, with their wild, murky sorrow and depth;—on the whole wild face of him; a kind of murky chaos: almost a fright to weak nerves; at which nevertheless, you look a second time, and sundry other times, and find it to be a thing in the highest degree worth looking at. For the chaos is indeed deep and black, yet with morning beams of beautifullest new creation peering through it. I confess I have an interest in this Mr. Cromwell; and indeed, if truth must be said, in him alone. The rest are historical, dead to me; but he is epic, still living. Hail to thee, thou strong one; hail, across the long-drawn funeral aisle and night of Time! Two dead centuries, with all that they have born and buried, part us; and it is far to speak together: how diverse are our centuries, most diverse, yet our Eternity is the same: and a kinship unites us which is much deeper than Death and Time. Hail to thee, thou strong one, for thou art ours, and I, at least, mean to call thee so.

FINIS

INDEX

ABBOT, GEORGE, Archbishop of Canterbury (1611-33), 85, 93, 94, 95, 98; refuses to take part in Lady Essex' Divorce Suit; of Puritan tendencies; first recommended by the Earl of Dunbar, 117; disapproves of the 'Book of Sports,' 139 n.; advises that England should aid the Elector, 164 n.
Adolphus, Gustavus, Lion of the North, 2, 263, 325.
Alum, manufacture of, 83.
Alured, Francis, 207, 208.
America, intercourse with, 86-89.
Anne (Queen of James I.), 48 n., 75, 78, 96, 98, 129, 130.
'Appello Cæsarem.' See Montague, Richard.
Arabella, Lady. See Stuart.
Archer, John, 332 n.
Aristocracy, Religious, 232.
Armada, Spanish, 149.
Armstrong, Archie, Court-fool, 245 n.
Arundel, Earl of, 141, 156, 254, 264, 265, 266.
Athole, Earl of, 3 n.
Azraël, Bridge of, 169, 169 n.

Bacon, Sir Francis (Lord Verulam, Viscount St. Albans), 33, 44, 56, 74, 93, 111; becomes Lord-keeper, 130; discovered the new way of discovering truth; not a great soul, which he seemed so near being; a beautiful kind of man, but of the earth, earthy, 131; ruined by ambition, secularity, insincerity, bribery, 132; played amazing tricks in the king's absence, 133; Arthur Wilson on, 133 n.; overhauled by Parliament, told to 'Go,' and goes the sorrowfullest of mortals, 170.
Balfour, Sir William, 199, 210.
Balmerino, Lord (Elphinstone), forges the king's signature to a letter to the Pope, 71, 71 n.
Bancroft, Richard, Bishop of London,

takes part in Hampton-Court Conference, 24, 24 n.; begs that 'schismatics be not heard against their Bishops,' 30; heart of, 'melteth for joy that Almighty God had given us such a king as since Christ's time hath not been,' 31.
Banks, Sir John, Attorney-General, 251.
Barlow, Bishop, Narrative of Hampton-Court Conference by, 29.
Bastwick, Burton, and Prynne, 271-4; speakers for the rights of Englishmen; fixed in pillories for two hours, mutilated and branded with red-hot iron, amid a silence which had become 'pale,' 272-3.
Bellarmine, 53.
Berwick, 254; Pacification of, 324-327, 328.
Best, Captain Thomas, truculent sea-bear, son of the Norse Sea-kings, demolishes the Portuguese Fleet, 'nigh Surat in the Road of Swally,' 90, 91.
Bible, New Translation of, asked for by the Puritans, 30; the Translation appears (in 1611), 85, 'barbarous enough to rouse, tender enough to assuage,' of a sincerity like very death, 85.
Bilson, Thomas, Bishop of Winchester, at Hampton-Court Conference, 24, 24 n.
Bohemia, and the Bohemians, 159-165.
Borroughes, Sir John, 196.
Bourchier, Elizabeth, marriage of, to Oliver Cromwell, 144.
Bourchier, Sir James, 144.
Breadalbane Castle, 2.
Brown, Mrs. John, the carrier's wife, 273 n.
Bruce, Edward (second Lord Kinloss), 73, 99-103.
Buckingham, Duke of (George Villiers), 47, 47 n.; description of, by D'Ewes, 143; goes with Prince Charles to Madrid, 152; impeached by the Com-

347

348　　HISTORICAL SKETCHES

mons, 191; discomfiture of, at Rhé, 195-196; named by the Commons as the bitter root of all these sorrows, 208; will try to play on the war-fiddle a second time, 216; assassinated by Felton at Portsmouth, 217.
Bull and Farnham, the Colchester Prophets, 288-96.
Burlamachi, 198, 199, 210.

Canute, King, visits Ely, 59.
Car, Robert. See Somerset.
Catherine, Queen of Henry VIII., at St. Neot's, 13.
Cecil, Sir Edward, sails to attack Cadiz, 196, 197.
Cecil, Sir Robert, Earl of Salisbury, 47, 54, 71 n., 111, 113.
Cervantes, Don Miguel de, a celestial Light-bringer; last ride of, 104-5; 'you are that brave Miguel,' 105; death of, 106; the Voice of the Spanish Nation, 106; worth all the Philips and one to boot, 107.
Chadderton, Lawrence, 24, 24 n., 29, 85, 123.
Chambers, Richard, refuses to pay Tonnage and Poundage, 222, 223, 226.
Charles I., has thoughts of being Archbishop of Canterbury, 78; 96, 97; goes to Madrid with Buckingham and Richard Graham, 152, 182; characterised, 181; Speeches and Letters of, 182; 'Eikon Basilike,' 182 n.; marries Henrietta Maria, 183; expels the Queen's French priests and attendants, 184; First Parliament of, 188; lends eight ships to the French to fight against Protestant Rochelle, 188; dissolves the Parliament of 1625, after two short Sessions, 189; dissolves his Second Parliament in a rage, 191; changes his hand, tries to conciliate the Commons, 209; has no sympathy with the heart-tendency of England, 221; thinks Tonnage and Poundage his, without grant from the Commons, 221; levies the same without a Bill, 222; dissolves his Third Parliament, calls the Commons 'vipers,' 232; Coronation of, at Edinburgh, 252-268; described and characterised; wholly the great man except the soul of him, 262; genealogy of, 263; at Birks, near Berwick, 325; accepts the Scotch Petition and agrees to a peace, 326; orders the Scottish Declaration to be publicly burnt by the hands of the hangman, 327; dissolves the Short Parliament, 330; in the North, with a straggling mutinous army to chastise the 'rebel Scots,' 335; consents to the summoning of another Parliament, 336; comes privately, by water, to open the Long Parliament, 340.
Chillingworth, 296, 318.
Chronicle, Parian, 265 n.
Clark, Archibald, Lord Provost of Edinburgh, 255; has a Speech to make, and multiplex ceremonies to do, 256; waits in painful expectancy, his breathing fluttered into a series of sighs; presents the keys of the City in a silver bason, 261.
Church, defined, 275; the *true* and the *seeming*, 275; grown to be an enormous magic-tree with little or no root, 276, 277; the Scottish, under a fatal cloud, 301.
Coke, Sir Edward (' Coke-upon-Lyttleton'), 111, 120, 124; uplifts the Litany, 168; the cause of liberty indebted to; never wanting with his sharp jest and witty turn; a master of precedents, 176; works the Petition of Right on the Potter's-wheel of a debating House of Commons, 200; thanks forever to, 200, 201; cannot speak for weeping, 206; his voice firmer now, 208.
Colchester Prophets, 288-296.
Conway (second Viscount), 333, 335.
Cook, Sir John, Secretary, 201.
Cornwallis, Sir Charles, cited, 77 n.
Cotton, Sir Robert, 197.
'Counterblast to Tobacco,' citation from, 54 n.
Court Precincts, 141-145.
Crew, Sir Thomas, 168.
Cromwell, Oliver, probably sees King James at Hinchinbrook, 11; little Oliver in the hand of his nursemaid, 11 n., 16; Nollykin all one wide-eyed wonderment, 16; 60; member of a New Company for draining the Fens, 63 n.; 66; marriage of, to Elizabeth Bourchier, 144; a sketch of, 145; in Charles's Third Parliament, 197, 203; 212; first Speech of, 224, 224 n.; 229, 230, 299, 314, 341; depicted riding up to Town to attend the Long Parliament, 343, 344; is epic, still living; hail to thee, thou strong one; hail across the long-drawn funeral aisle and night of Time, 346.
Cromwell, Richard, 'my Darling, not my Dick,' 13.
Cromwell, Robert, 12, 16, 61, 62.
Cromwell, Sir Oliver, son of the 'Golden Knight,' 9, 16, 19, 62.
Cromwell, Thomas, 13.

INDEX 349

Dalbier, John, 198, 199, 210.
David, Scotch King, 12.
Davila, 296, 296 n., 318.
Declaration of the Commons to Charles I., 203, 209.
Declaration, Scottish, burned at Cheapside, 327.
Denbigh, the young Earl of (Basil Fielding, Buckingham's nephew), offers to change clothes with Buckingham (at Plymouth), 196.
Denbigh, Earl of (William Fielding), goes in command of a Fleet for the relief of Rochelle, 196.
Denbigh, Lady (Buckingham's sister), 216.
Devereux, Robert. See Earl of Essex.
Devorgilla, Lady, 137.
D'Ewes, Sir Simonds, 141, 142; cited, 143-144, 155-157; 164.
Digges, Dudley, 191.
Discourse, King James's, in the Star-Chamber, 125-127.
'Dovetail,' sees an effigy of Guy Faux in the New Cut, 66; describes the same, making reflections and drawing deductions, 67.
Drummond, William, of Hawthornden, 259; cited, 259 n., 260, 260 n.
Drury-Lane Theatre, burning of, 127-130.
Dryasdust, 4 n.; loves only his own dreary jottings, 23; why summon spectres from the vasty deep of, 110; can't be sued in any Court of law, 304.
Duel, Sackville and Bruce, 99-103.
Duels, 78 n.
Dumfries, King James at, 137.

Edinburgh, Old, described, 253, 258, 304, 305.
Egerton, Chancellor. See Ellesmere.
Elder-Dramatists, 76; affair of, reaches its culmination, 85.
Eliot, Sir John, carries impeachment of Buckingham to House of Lords; sent to the Tower, and emitted again, 191; speaking like pistol-bullets, his very silence eloquent, 202; 227, 229; lies dead and cold, 298.
Elizabeth, Princess, the flower of the Court, 77; marriage of, to the Palsgrave, 97; a Queen of Hearts, if not otherwise a Queen, 98; 158, 164.
Elizabeth, Queen, Funeral of, 19-21; bemoaned with true tears, 20; a brave and great-souled woman, 21; 35.
Ellesmere, Lord (Thomas Egerton), 29, 31; acts as Lord High-Steward at the Overbury Murder Trials, 124.

Elphinstone, Sir James. See Balmerino.
Elwes, Sir Jervis, appointed Lieutenant of the Tower, 119 n.; is tried, condemned, and hanged for connivance in the poisoning of Overbury, 122; speech of, from the gibbet, 123.
Essex, Earl of (Robert Devereux), strikes Prince Henry for calling him 'son of a traitor,' 112; 114; marries Lady Frances Howard; goes abroad, 114; returns to England, and is divorced by Lady Frances; goes abroad again to learn the art of war, 116; 165; commands the Parliamentary army at the beginning of the Civil War, 114 n.
Evelyn, John, 340.

Falkland, Lord, 341.
Faux, Guy, and the Gunpowder Plot, 66-71; 219, 233.
Felton, John, buys a knife, 215; rides into Portsmouth, assassinates Buckingham, 217; in prison, 219; executed at Tyburn, 220.
Fen Country, unpicturesque, but interesting; the Islands in, 58; King Cnut visits, 59, 59 n.; Guthlac settles at Crowland in the, 60; draining of the, 61, 62, 63, 63 n.
Ferdinand, King of Romans, 160.
Ferrar, Nicholas, 234-241; at Little Gidding, 235; interviewed by Mr. Lenton, 238-240.
Finch, Sir John (the Speaker), 152, 201; brings a message from the king, 205; 206, 208; dare not put the question, 227; is held down in his chair, 229; becomes Lord Chief-Justice, 251.
Fortesque, *De Laudibus*, 296.
Frankenthal, Siege of, 165.
Franklin, the apothecary, concerned in Overbury's murder, 118; peaches and is hanged, 121.
Friedrich, the 'Winter-king,' chosen king of Bohemia, 161; sudden flight of, to Holland, 162.
Fryer, Sir Thomas, 217 n.

'Gaberlunzie' Song, 3.
Galloway, Mr., Minister of Perth, 29.
Gates, General, 86.
Geddes, Jenny, dimly seen in deep Closes, scouring, sweeping, as a poor servant; will one day send the king a message of a kind, 257; there remains but the shadow of her name, 307; belief of, 308; in St. Giles's Cathedral, smites a hired 'clacker,' exclaiming, 'Thou false thief, wilt thou sing a mass at my lug?' 309; hurls her stool

at the Bishop's head; is a Deborah in Israel, 310.
Gibb, John, brings a reprieve for Raleigh, 112, 140; unjustly assaulted and abused by King James, who is filled with remorse therefor, 146, 147.
'Gidding Parva.' See Little Gidding.
Godmanchester, 12.
Graham, Richard, 152.
Graham, Sir Robert, 3 n.
Gunpowder Plot, 66; Guido Faux and Co. in Whinniard's cellar, with thirty-six barrels of gunpowder, 69; failure of, 69; the conspirators (Warwickshire Hunt) all killed or hanged and beheaded, 70.
Guthlac, 60.

Hamilton, Duchess of, 308.
Hamilton, Marquis of, 143, 254, 263, 263 n., 264.
Hamilton, Sir Alexander, 333, 335.
Hampden, John, in Charles's Third Parliament, 202, 206, 229; Manor-house, Church and Mansion of, 317; occupation and character of, 318, 318 n.; impatience of, with Vatican Popes and Lambeth Pontiffs, 319; the noble speaker, has a talent of silence, too, 319; 340, 345, 346.
Hampton Court, Conference at, 23-43.
Hay, James ('Sardanapalus'), Earl of Carlisle, 50; made a Knight of the Bath, 73.
Hearne, Thomas, 236; extract from, 238-241.
Heath, James, 'Carrion Heath,' 341; Smelfungus on, 342.
Heath, Sir Robert, Lord Chief-Justice, removed from the Common-pleas, 251.
Henrietta Maria (Queen of England), 183, 184; beautiful and sprightly, but unfortunate in her religion; accompanied by a retinue of Jesuits and tonsured priests with pyxes and Popery equipments, the root of infinite sorrows to her; set to do penance; is driven quite beyond the vaporific point, 184.
Henry VIII., 13; dissolution of monasteries by, 25.
Henry IV. (of France), assassination of, 92; 95, 95 n., 183.
Henry, Prince, knighting of, 72-78; description of, by Sir C. Cornwallis, 77 n.; death of, 94-96, 96 n.; calls Robert Devereux 'son of a traitor,' 112, 114.
Henry II. 12.
Hereditary Principle, 1, 2.

Hinchinbrook, King James at, 9-19; once a Nunnery, 11; all in gala, 11; ambrosial sumptuosities at, 14; has become one of the houses of the Zodiac, 14.
Hobart, Sir Miles, locks the door of the House of Commons, 230, 232.
Holiday, Sir Leonard, with Nicholas Leate, drains Moorfields, 79, 80.
Holland, Earl of, 254; at Berwick, 326.
Holles, Denzil, 202; holds down the Speaker, 229; puts three Resolutions, 231.
Holles, Sir John (Lord Houghton, 1616; Earl of Clare, 1624), 73, 78 n., 141, 202 n.
Honours, sale of, 49.
Hopton, Sir Ralph, 203.
Hotham, Sir John 'ear-marked 'the Devil his,' 202.
Howard, Lady Frances, daughter of the Earl of Suffolk, 113; married to the Earl of Essex, 114; turns her ambitious thoughts on the Earl of Somerset, 114; gets a divorce from Essex, 117; is married to Somerset, 120; tried for the murder of Overbury, pleads guilty, and is sentenced to be hanged, 124; pardoned, and released from the Tower, 125, 125 n.
Howard, Thomas. See Arundel, Earl of.
Howell, James, Letters of, 153, 153 n.
Huntingdon, 9, 11, 12, 13; Oliver Cromwell Burgess for, 203.
Hyde, Edward (Earl of Clarendon, 1661), 264; meets Oliver St. John, 329-333.

India, intercourse with, 90-91.
Infanta (Princess Maria), sister of Philip IV., King of Spain, 147 n., 183.
Ireland, the bloody gashes of, closed for the first time in recorded History, 81, 82.
Isle of Devils, the, 88, 89 n.

James I. (King of Great Britain, 1603-1625), 3, 3 n.; at Hinchinbrook, 9; hangs a cutpurse at Newark, without trial, 10; enters London, 18; presides over Hampton Court Conference, 27; gives small countenance to Reynolds and Co.; 'No Bishop no King,' 30, 31; declares that the Puritans must conform or leave the country, 32; has quitted hold of the real heart of England, 42; of clear vision, if it were deep enough, 43; a semi-impostor within; wonderfully gifted, says Bacon; quick of speech and of ready wit, 44, 44 n.; of large, but flaccid heart, 45; government of, bad and

INDEX 351

unsuccessful; speciosities alone beautiful, realities unintelligible to, 46; favourites of, 46, 47, 54; a 'Second Solomon,' we vow, 48; progresses, huntings, and drinking-bouts of, 48; selling honours, giving honour to whom honour is *not* due, a contribution to the great Bank of Social Falsehood, 50; in continual want of cash, 50; hunger and hope, the inspiring genii of, 50; pronounced divine Discourses in the Starchamber; an immense Brood-fowl set over England ('cluck-cluck, ye unfortunate English'), 53; in trouble with his Parliaments, 54; discovers in Lord Monteagle's Letter a hint of the Gunpowder Plot, 69; wants a Scotch Cardinal; negotiates with the Pope, 71, 71 n.; a Sham-king only, and the Chief Chimera of England, 110; summons all the Judges to the Overbury Murder Trial, 120; a Rhadamanthus, but in theory only, 125; pardons fatal Frances and her husband, 125; Discourse of, in the Star-chamber, 125; a most vigilant, vehement, royal clucker, an 'old and experienced King,' 126; assumes the part of a real king, 127; Journey of, to Scotland, 134-138; loyal Addresses to, 135, 135 n.; business of, in Scotland, 135, 135 n.; desires to strengthen and extend Episcopacy in Scotland, 'No Bishop no King,' 136; returns by Dumfries, gives the burghers a 'Silver Gun,' 137; promulgates his 'Book of Sports,' 138, 139; abuses John Gibb, and is filled with remorse, 146, 147; desire for the Spanish Match, the whole Foreign Policy of, 148; not wise enough to discern the true grandtendency, 149; opens his Third Parliament, 155; Deputation of the Commons received by, 157; is forced to go voluntarily to the aid of Bohemia, 164; description of, at a stag-hunt, 267; falls into the New River, 267 n.; thanks God that the Prince can manage a dispute in Theology with the learnedest clerk, 297; death of, 188.

Jesuits, come to grief in arguing with James Ussher, Primate of Ireland, 232.

Jonson, Ben, 72; a true singer-heart; melodious as the voice of wood-doves, fitfully thrilling as the note of nightingales, 74; writes the Masque 'Prince Henry's Barriers,' 74 n.; the 'Satyr,' 75 n.; in wit-combat with Shakspeare, 76; 'honoured Shakspeare, on this side idolatry, as much as any man,' 76; 144, 166.

Jourdan, Silas, 86.

Kepler, Johann, Almanack-maker to Kaiser Matthias, 107; discovers the laws of planetary motions, 108; 132, 160.

Kimbolton, Queen Catherine at, 13.

'Kingis Quair,' 3 n.

Kings, Twelve chairs for the twelve, 35, 157, 157 n.

Kirton, Edward, 'hopes we have hearts and hands and swords, too, for a stroke with our enemies,' 207; words of, justified by the Commons, 209, 214.

Knewstubs, John, 24, 24 n., 57, 123.

Lamb, Dr., murder of, 210, 211, 212.

Laud, old Mr. William, the clothier at Reading, 83.

Laud, William (Archbishop of Canterbury), 83, 136, 137, 190, 214, 219; a disturber of the Church of England, 225, 230; has a three days' wrestle with Fisher, the Jesuit, 233; goes with King Charles to Edinburgh, 253; becomes Archbishop of Canterbury, 253 n.; promotion of, 268; Life of, by Heylin, 274-280; perplexing character of, 277; a clean-brushed, cultivated man; will prove it for thee by neverending logic, 278; at once persecutor and martyr, 279; turns his attention to the spiritual state of England, 282; has pricked a man or two that has handled him, 283; thinks the Churchdevotion has fallen into an imperfect condition, 284; will reform this: 'All ye that labour and are heavy-laden, come unto me and I will—order you to buy Canonical cloaks,' 285-286; is asked to say 'where Jonah found his Prayer-book when sunk in the whale's belly,' 287; finds 'no religion' in Scotland, 287; is playing a heavier game than he wots of, 300; decides that the Prayer-book and Liturgy shall be impressed into all churches in Scotland, 302; barricades his Lambeth Palace against a mob, and becomes a Chief Priest eclipsed or Archbishop girt-withtrembling, 332; impeached by the Commons, sent to the Tower and beheaded on Tower Hill, 279 n.

Leighton, Dr., seeks lodgings in London, 242; practises medicine, 243; in Holland, preaching, 244 n.; publishes 'An Appeal to Parliament,' 244; in |the Star-chamber, 245; in the Fleet Prison; makes his escape, 247; the 'Hue and Cry' after; branding and mutilation of, 248; Keeper of Lambeth House, 248 n.

Lenton, Mr., visits the Ferrars at Little Gidding, 236 n.

Leslie, Alexander, 325, 326, 334, 335.
L'Estrange, Hammond, 182.
Lindsey, Bog of, 23, 45, 58-66, 123.
Little Gidding, Nunnery of, 234-241, 254.
Liverpool, 84.
London, improvement of, 78-81; no new houses to be built in, 81.
Long, Walter, 228, 230.

Mansfeld, Count Ernest, 34, 197.
Manwaring, Dr. Roger, Sermons of, 194; a priest-flunky, 195; had his quietus yesterday, 199; promoted by the King, 213, 214.
Martinitz, Javeslav von, 160; thrown out of window, 161.
Masques, Ben Jonson's, 74-76; Beaumont's, at Princess Elizabeth's Marriage, 98.
Match, Spanish, 45, 147-153; closely related to James's Parliaments, 150; rejoicings at the failure of, 152.
May, Sir Humphrey, 201.
Men and Women, English, in the time of Puritanism, 268-271; in an evening party of; figures, looks, dress, temper and conversation of, 269-271.
Michell, Sir F., 128; how dealt with by a Puritan House of Commons, 171-173.
Milton, John, the scrivener's son, 81, 133; cited, 178 n., 274.
Mobs, Spanish, 149.
Mompesson, Sir Giles, a monopolist, 170; sharp eyes and beaks upon, 171.
Monopolies, 50, 154, 155, 250, 251.
Montague, Lord, founds an endowment of £40 to commemorate the Gunpowder Plot, 67, 70.
Montague, Richard (Bishop of Chichester), writes 'New Gag for an Old Goose,' 192; 'Appello Cæsarem,' 193; sentenced by Parliament to be fined and incapacitated, 193; keeps all his places, and becomes Bishop of Chichester, 214, 224.
Monteagle, Lord, Letter to, 43, 69.
Montgomery, Earl of (Philip Herbert), 143.
Montrose, Earl of, 266, 267, 334.
Morgan, Sir Charles, leads a force to assist the King of Denmark, 197.
Morton, Bishop, 61.
Morton, James, Earl of, 254.
Muir, Elizabeth, mother or grandmother of the Stuart line, 3, 181, 186, 263.
Mulberry-trees planted in England, 82.
Murder, the Overbury, 112-127.

Neile, Richard (Bishop of Winchester, Archbishop of York), 214, 218, 225.
Newburn, engagement at, 335-336.

'New Gag for an Old Goose.' See Montague, Richard.
Newport, Captain, 86, 87, 88.
New River, the, led into London by Sheriff Myddleton, 81.
Northampton, Earl of (Henry Howard), 97, 118, 119, 120.
Northumberland, Earl of, 93, 254.
Noy, William, 98; hesitates to become Attorney-General, then accepts, 249; the hatefullest of all men to us, 249; proposes the Ship-money Writ, 250; 'post-mortem' examination of, 251; Will of, 251.

Oath, the Ex-Officio, 31; the 'Etcetera,' 331, 331 n.
O'Neill, Shane, 82; Kennet on, 82 n.
Ophiuchus, 178, 178 n.
Osborne, Francis, 92: 'Historical Memoirs' by, 92 n.
Ouse, the River, held up in Bedford Levels, 12, 13, 62.
Overal (Dean, Bishop), 28.
Overbury, Thomas, becomes intimate with Car (Earl of Somerset), 113; is practically Under-Secretary of State, 113; vehemently opposes Somerset's marrying Lady Essex, 115; is sent to the Tower, 116; threatens mischief, if he be not attended to, 117; intemperate of tongue, 118; dies by poison, and is buried in the Tower, 120.

Palatinate, 48, 94; is on fire, 155; 158, 162.
Parliaments, in the olden time, 185-186; divided into Lords and Commons, 186.
Parliaments, James's, 150-165.
Parliament of 1604-1611, 153.
Parliament, the 'Undertaker,' 154, 155.
Parliament of 1620-1621, 155-165; makes a clearance of Monopolists, 173; gets into contradiction with the 'Dread Sovereign,' 173; strikes work, 174; sends a Deputation to the King at Newmarket, 175; is dissolved, 175.
Parliament of 1625, 188; takes to Petitioning on Religion, and is slow about Supply; is dissolved after two short Sessions, 189.
Parliament of 1625-1626, 190; takes to censuring, impeachment and Remonstrance; grants no Supply, and is dissolved as with a flash of fire, 191.
Parliament, Charles's Third,—*First Session*, 197-213; investigates the Burlamachi affair, Dalbier, Trailbaston, 198; the Petition of Right, the Palladium of our liberties, 199-200; glimpses of the leading Members of, 201-202; De-

INDEX

claration to the King, 203; message from the King to, 205; the Members of, burst not into parliamentary eloquence but into a passion of tears, 205-207; names the Duke of Buckingham and proceeds with the Declaration, 208; is prorogued, 212.

Parliament, Charles's Third, — *Second Session*, 221-232; considers the state of Religion before passing the Tonnage and Poundage Bill, 223; Oliver Cromwell's first recorded Speech in, 224; a happy issue to, as good as impossible, 226; Speaker of, dares not put the question, 227; royal proclamation for dissolution of, already drawn, 228; Mr. Speaker held down in his chair, 229; passes three Resolutions, 231; vanishes into infinite night, 232.

Parliament, the Long, the flower of all Parliaments, 336; might be called the Great Parliament, the Father of Parliaments, 337; glimpses of some of the Members of, 340-346.

Parliament, the Short, 330.

Pashur (Laud), girt-with-trembling, 295, 295 n.

Patience and Hope, 298-299.

Paul's Aisle, and Paul's Cross, 92-93.

'Peblis to the Play,' 3 n.

Pembroke, Earl of, 254.

Perth Monastery, James I. (of Scotland) slain in, 3.

Petition, Millenary, 14, 24.

Petition of Right, 199, 200.

Philips, Sir Robert, 169, 206, 225.

Platicr, Fabricius, committed to a fall of sixty feet, 161.

Portuguese of Goa, and Captain Best, 90.

Powhattan, King, the pipe-clayed, shell-girdled majesty, 89.

Prague Projectiles, 157-163.

Precedents, English love of, 176-177.

Progress, material, in England, 78-85; Spiritual, 85-86.

Purbeck, Viscountess, 111.

Puritan Riot, 127-130, 149.

Puritanism, first official appearance of, 24; will not go to Hades without doing a bit of work in this world, 33; will be the parent of many Shakspeares, 34; goes away abashed, but will come again with sword drawn for sheer battle, with headsman's axe for regicide, 36; a part of the indestructible, perennial sum of human things, 36; persuades to *practical* heroism, 57; 212.

Puritans, receive no countenance from Majesty at Hampton-Court Conference, 30; are ordered to conform or leave the country, 32; are forbidden to emigrate to New England, 298.

Pym, John, 166, 192, 201, 298, 340.

Raleigh, Sir Walter, 56; writing 'History of the World,' 93, 112; execution of, 140-141; death-speech, and life of, inarticulate tragedy, 141; the greatest sacrifice the Spaniards have yet had, 141.

Reynolds, Dr. John, born and brought-up a Papist; converts his brother and is converted by him; the leading Puritan at Hampton-Court Conference; the 'very treasury of erudition,' 28; 32, 36, 85.

Rochelle, 188, 188 n.; beleaguered, 215; surrenders to King Louis, 218, 219.

Rochester, Viscount. See Somerset.

Rolf, Mr., marries King Powhattan's daughter, 89.

Rolle, John, an Hon. Member, refuses to pay Tonnage and Poundage, 222, 226, 229.

Rowallan, Elizabeth Muir of, 3, 181, 263.

Rudd, Anthony, Bishop of St. David's, at Hampton-Court Conference, 24, 24 n.

Rudyard, Sir Benjamin, 166, 201.

Rushworth, John, citation from 'Historical Collections' of, 211; 335 n.

Rymer, Thomas, 106, 106 n., 142.

Sackville, Edward (fourth Earl of Dorset), kills Edward Bruce in Duel, 99-103; 162, 167, 168, 168 n., 202.

Sackville, Thomas, 100, 100 n.

St. John, Oliver, 329, 330.

Savile, Sir John, 322, 322 n., 323.

Scotch Coronation, 252-268.

Scotch folk, speech of, full of picturesqueness, humour, sly, deep meaning; what they are, and what they have done, 305, 306.

Scots, the, at Dunse Law, 324-327.

Scottish Declaration, Burning of, 327 n.

Sea-Venture, the ship, sails for Virginia, 86; in a 'most sharpe and cruell' storm, 86-87; wrecked on Bermudas, 88.

Selden, John, writes 'History of Tithes,' 192; speech of, cited from, 227; 265.

Shakspeare, beautifullest soul in all England, 21; makes Past, Present, and Future brighter for us, 22; a right royal, archiepiscopal one, 22; Plays of, 34; in wit-combat with Ben Jonson, 76; retires to Stratford-on-Avon, into a silence which no Dryasdust or other obscene creature will ever penetrate,

z

76; death of, 103; brightest creature known to me, adieu, 104.
Shirley, Sir Robert, ambassador from Persia, 90.
Slavata, Wilhelm von, one of the Prague Projectiles, 160.
Smelfungus, on Revolutions, 25; his striking 'modern Puritan Sermon,' 37-43; on speech and the Bog of Lindsey, 63-66; on an 'indiscreet Biographer,' 341, 342; on Toleration, 342, 343.
Smithfield, drained and paved, 80.
Somers, Sir George, 86, 88, 89.
Somerset, Earl of (Robert Car), Viscount Rochester, 46, 110, 111; royal favourite; Overbury his working Secretary, 113; responds to Lady Essex's advances, 115; marries the divorced Lady Essex, 120; is tried for murder of Overbury, 123; pleads not guilty, 125; is condemned to be hanged; pardoned by the King, and emitted from the Tower, 125; death of, 125 n.
Soubise, M. de, 188 n., 217.
Southampton, Earl of, 15; kindness of, to Shakspeare, 22, 23; 254.
Spenser, his frosty Allegories and Faery Queens, 57; 296.
Steward, Sir Thomas, Knight of Stuntney, 16.
Stewart, Sir Robert, 3 n.
St. Neot's, Town and Church of, 13.
Stuarts, a dash of Gypsy tragic in; their character and destiny, 3; kings of talent, but not of talent enough, 5.
Stuart, Mary, Queen of Scots, 4.
Stuart, James I. (of Scotland), the Poet-King, a right brave man, 3; assassinated at Perth, 3 n.
Stuart, James IV., a royal-looking man, with face beautiful and stern, 2.
Stuart, James V., character of, 3.
Stuart, James I. (of England). See James I.
Stuart, Lady Arabella, 93, 111.

Thomlinson, Mr., and the Thurloe Papers, 310, 311, 312.
Thurloe Papers, the, 310.
Tobacco, 'Counterblast to,' 53, 54; cited, 54 n.
Tonnage and Poundage, 154, 154 n.; the sheet-anchor of royal finance, 221;

Chambers and Rolle refuse to pay, 222; not to be levied without consent of Parliament, 231.
Tournaments, 141-145.
Trade's-Increase, the ship, 90.
Tradition, 314-317.
Trailbaston, 198, 199, 210.
Turner, Mrs., tried for murder of Overbury; condemned to be hanged; appears at Tyburn in yellow ruffs got up *à la mode*, 122.

Vane, Sir Henry (the elder), 329.
Vasa, the last, of Sweden, only the *case* of a true king, 2.
Vere, Henry (Earl of Oxford), 156, 165.
Vere, Horatio (Lord Vere of Tilbury), 47.
Villiers, George. See Buckingham.
Virginia, settlement of, 89.

Wade, Sir William, removed from the Lieutenancy of the Tower, 119 n.
War, the Thirty Years', 162.
Weldon, cited, 44 n.
Wentworth, Sir Thomas (Earl of Strafford), 167, 201, 202, 321; Tyranny's strong right-hand man, 321; gone over to the Four Surplices, to Whitehall and the gilt-formulas; an honourable soul seduced, 322; sees a new shorter course open to him, 323; a stern, downlooking man, full of thoughts, energies, —of tender affections gone mostly to the shape of pride and sorrow; noble enough, beautiful and tragical, at all events terrible enough, 324; accompanies King Charles to York, in the Second Bishops' War, 333.
Weston, Richard, Overbury's keeper in the Tower, 120, 121.
Weston, Sir Richard (Treasurer), walks in the Duke's footsteps, 230.
Whitgift, Archbishop, in dread of a 'Scotch-mist,' 15; at Hampton-Court Conference, 24: his last words, 'Pro Ecclesia Domini,' 32.
Widdrington, Sir Thomas, 255.
Williams, John (Bishop of Lincoln, Archbishop of York, 1641), Lord-Keeper, comes to high words with Buckingham, 190; a questionable maxim of, 190 n.
Wotton, Sir Henry, gone 'to lie abroad'; sees Kepler, 107.

Printed by T. and A. CONSTABLE, Printers to Her Majesty
at the Edinburgh University Press

www.ingramcontent.com/pod-product-compliance
Lightning Source LLC
Chambersburg PA
CBHW020227240426
43672CB00006B/446